Managing Services

The rapid increase in global services during the last few decades is without doubt one of the most challenging social, cultural, political and, especially, economic forces of our time. Services have supplanted agriculture, manufacturing and resources as the primary source of international competitive advantage in many countries, providing wealth, employment and almost unlimited future opportunities for growth, whether in traditional or more innovative forms. The complex nature, stakeholders and interrelationships of the global services sector have provided a broad range of opportunities and challenges for its strategic management, including conceptual, definitional, contextual and implementation issues.

This book explores the strategic management of services through an Integrated Services Management Model which links operational, marketing, financial and human resource management functions within a broad and diverse collection of international, regional and local service contexts. It contains numerous case examples, student projects and exercises, designed to illustrate common problems and innovative approaches, with a particular focus on the Asia–Pacific and Australasian regions.

Managing Services

Edited by
Alan Nankervis
School of Management,
Curtin University of Technology

CAMBRIDGE
UNIVERSITY PRESS

CAMBRIDGE UNIVERSITY PRESS
Cambridge, New York, Melbourne, Madrid, Cape Town, Singapore, São Paulo

Cambridge University Press
477 Williamstown Road, Port Melbourne, VIC 3207, Australia

Published in the United States of America by Cambridge University Press, New York

www.cambridge.org
Information on this title: www.cambridge.org/9780521606516

© Alan Nankervis and Cambridge University Press 2005

First published 2005

Printed in China through Everbest

A catalogue record for this book is available from the British Library

National Library of Australia Cataloguing in Publication data

Managing services.
ISBN-13 978-0-521-60651-6 paperback
ISBN-10 0-521-60651-9 paperback
Includes index.
ISBN 0 521 60651 9.
ISBN 9 78052160 6516.
1. Management science – Australia.   I. Nankervis, Alan R.
658.00994

ISBN-13 978-0-521-60651-6 paperback
ISBN-10 0-521-60651-9 paperback

Contents

Figures and tables   page vi
Contributors   ix
Preface   xi
Acknowledgements   xii

1   Services and their management   1
2   The services environment   35
3   Stakeholders and their influence on services   69
4   Managing strategy in services   108
5   Marketing management in services   155
6   Strategic operations management in services   203
7   Financial management in services   252
8   Human resource management in services   299
9   From managing 'service' to integrated services management   347

Index   353

Figures and tables

Figures

1.1	Growth in services since 1997	4
1.2	The goods–services continuum	7
1.3	Goods and services categories	9
1.4	Customer contact matrix	18
1.5	Service management matrix	19
1.6	Models of service quality	22
1.7	The integrated services management (ISM) model	26
1.8	The functional services management (FSM) matrix	27
2.1	The integrated services management (ISM) model	41
3.1	The integrated services management (ISM) model	72
3.2	An open system of an organisation and its environment	75
3.3	The diversity of stakeholders in a cinema complex	87
4.1	The integrated services management (ISM) model	110
4.2	Strategic management framework	142
5.1	The integrated services management (ISM) model	158
5.2	The functional services management (FSM) matrix	158
5.3	Total quality management	167
5.4	Cross-function 'process teams'	169
5.5	A continuum of transactional and relational exchange	180
5.6	Strategic management of customer value through customisation	183
5.7	Strategic business management and value innovation	187
5.8	The declining role of the marketing department in the marketing function (functional to integrated marketing)	192
6.1	The integrated services management (ISM) model	204
6.2	The functional services management (FSM) matrix	212
6.3	Strategy formulation	216
6.4	An integrated HR planning, staffing and scheduling framework	234
6.5	The three levels of scheduling	235
6.6	Service activities for a jet during a 60-minute layover	237
6.7	A process-orientation to innovation management	239
6.8	Changing challenges and trends for operations management	241
6.9	Rottnest Island Authority organisation structure	244
7.1	The integrated services management (ISM) model	254
7.2	Direct (disintermediated) financial flows	258

7.3	Indirect (intermediated) financial flows	258
7.4	The cash-flow cycle	269
7.5	Unit cost determination	272
7.6	Conventional hedging financing strategy	277
7.7	Financial risk management – types of risk	283
8.1	The integrated services management (ISM) model	300
8.2	The functional services management (FSM) matrix	301
8.3	A strategic human resource management model	303
8.4	Weak link	306
8.5	Schmenner's service process matrix 1986	317
8.6	Human resources planning model	322
8.7	Emotional labour	327
8.8	Employee development in the customer satisfaction wheel	330
8.9	Programs for employees at the Marriott	338
9.1	Mindset orientations for services	348

Tables

1.1	Country statistics: GDP (US$ million) and services value-added, 1997–2001 (% of GDP)	page 3
1.2	Fastest-growing job sectors, 1986–2001	5
1.3	Services classification models	17
2.1	Services as a percentage of GDP, 1999	36
2.2	World import and export of commercial services by region, 2002	36
2.3	Trade involvement of individual countries, 1999	37
2.4	Services exports and needs in LDCs, 2002	38
2.5	Stages of globalisation	44
2.6	Environmental drivers	46
5.1	Transitions of core business philosophies	162
5.2	Mass marketing versus one-to-one marketing	182
5.3	Schools of thought and their influence on marketing theory and practice	190
6.1	Operations management from stakeholder perspectives	206
6.2	Attributes of services and goods	208
6.3	Classification of the economic offerings of the four business sectors	209
6.4	Significant events in operations management	211
6.5	Four industry examples of the systems approach to operations	214
6.6	Organisational focus shift in location planning decision making	223
6.7	Factors influencing the general area location planning decisions of a range of service firms	224
6.8	Factors influencing particular site location planning decisions of a range of service firms	225
6.9	Activities and development permitted in the Rottnest Island terrestrial zones	248
7.1	Financial institutions in developed economies	259
7.2	A four-step hospital cost accounting process	274
7.3	Cost drivers in a hospital setting	275

7.4	Types of business risks with implications for the financial manager	284
8.1	Pattern of labour use strategies	312
8.2	Labour flexibility techniques	313
8.3	A sample job description	325
8.4	Hotel room attendant job description	326
8.5	The contingencies of empowerment	329
8.6	The benefits of SMWTs	331
8.7	Teams and work groups: It pays to know the difference	332
9.1	Sources of competitive advantage of global service organisations	350

This book is the outcome of the collegial activities of many academics in the School of Management at Curtin University of Technology in Perth, Western Australia. From its conception to eventual publication, school colleagues have enthusiastically and tirelessly worked to produce an innovative and high-quality text for both students and industry professionals. The following contributors deserve special recognition:

Associate Professor Alan Nankervis is the Research Director of the School of Management, Curtin University of Technology. He is the co-author of several books on human resource management and Asian management, and has worked in both the public and private sectors, in telecommunications, health and education (Chapters 1 and 8).

Werner Soontiens holds a PhD in international economics and is Program Director in International Business at Curtin University of Technology. He has extensive teaching and research experience in internationalisation in Southern Africa, East Asia and Australia (Chapter 2).

Cecil Pearson is the Senior Research Fellow in the School of Management within Curtin Business School, Curtin University of Technology. He has both academic and industrial experience, and consequently has published in both domains (Chapter 3).

John Milton-Smith is a Professor of Management at Curtin University of Technology. He has held senior management positions at RMIT and Curtin universities, most recently as the Deputy Vice-Chancellor, Curtin International. His special research interests are in business strategy, corporate culture, innovation and leadership (Chapter 4).

Dr Tadayuki Miyamoto is currently a Postdoctoral Research Fellow at the School of Management, Curtin University of Technology. Building on his early research career in marketing, he is leading research projects on holistic strategic management at one of Curtin Business School's areas of research focus – management of services organisations in the Asia–Pacific: development and sustainability (Chapter 5).

Ruth Taylor is the Academic Area Head of Services and Tourism Management in the School of Management, Curtin University of Technology. She has been involved in both research and teaching in the areas of services management and tourism management (Chapter 6).

Subramaniam Ananthram is a Research Associate at the School of Management at Curtin University of Technology. He has a double master's degree with majors in accounting/auditing and economics/finance, and has worked with various accounting and auditing firms. His research interests include global strategy, global mindset development and cross-cultural issues impacting management in services (Chapter 7).

Associate Professor Richard Grainger is currently Head, School of Management and CBS Associate Dean Human Resources, Curtin University of Technology. His teaching and research interests are international management, comparative management and Asian management systems. His industry and professional experience includes several years with Mitsubishi Corporation as an international (import/export) commodity trader, and more than ten years with the Australian Customs Service in the commercial investigation and commodity import/export areas (Chapter 9).

Samir Ranjan Chatterjee is a Professor of International Management at Curtin University of Technology. He has worked in management education and consultancy around the world over the past three decades. His current consultancies include working for the Asian Development Bank, the United Nations Development Program and AusAID (Chapter 9).

In addition, Dr Helen Singleton deserves our deep appreciation for her patient, but rigorous, editing of draft chapters; as does Glen Sheldon of Cambridge University Press for his support of the project.

The rapid rise of global services during the last few decades is without doubt one of the most challenging social, cultural, political and, especially, economic forces in almost all countries in the world. It has been the outcome of the combined influences of the decline of the more traditional agricultural and manufacturing sectors; the development of new technologies including telecommunications, information technology, nano-technology, and biotechnology; and changes in the expectations of consumers.

While in countries such as Australia, New Zealand, Malaysia, China and India services are a major economic and social influence, other regional nations are (to varying degrees) dependent on them for their very survival. In Singapore, for example, the absence of physical resources and disproportionately high education levels has ensured the economic dominance of services, and Thailand's tourism sector has long exceeded rice production as an export income earner.

The multifaceted nature of services has spawned a broad range of opportunities and challenges for their strategic management, including the delineation of their parameters; analyses of their broad global contexts; determination of their 'stakeholders'; the definition and quantification of 'service' dimensions, qualities and measures; and the applications of all of these issues to their integrated management functions, including marketing, operations, financial and human resource management.

Management issues discussed in the book include the difficulty of defining 'services', given their varied and diverse nature; their inherent 'vulnerability', and opportunities for greater sustainability; the management of multiple stakeholders; 'service quality' management; and the development of an integrated service management (ISM) model, which provides the framework for the book. The book's distinct difference from competitive texts lies in its strategic management (rather than marketing) perspective, and its Asia–Pacific regional (rather than northern hemispheric) focus.

The book addresses all of these issues through comprehensive theoretical and applied frameworks, accompanied by a very broad range of regional industry examples, case studies and student exercises. It also reflects the views and experiences of an esoteric collection of academic colleagues from the School of Management at Curtin University of Technology.

We hope that the book will enthuse students and professionals in their management of services, and stimulate their further development of the numerous opportunities and challenges.

Alan R. Nankervis
March 2005

Acknowledgements

Our appreciation is expressed to the authors and publishers for permission to reprint the following illustrative excerpts:

Chapter 1

p. 10: Ellis, E. 2002, 'Air Asia: No-frills seeker', *The Australian*, 24 September, pp. 21–2.

pp. 13–14: Mills, K. 2004, 'E-loans cut bank paper trail', *The Australian*, 27 March, p. 25.

pp. 14–15: *WA Business News*, 2003, 'Future industries: Outsourcing personal service-new offer!', 1 January, p. 8.

Chapter 2

pp. 38–9: Kripalani, M. 2002, 'Silicone Valley revisited', *Australian Financial Review*, 11 November, p. 81.

pp. 42–3: Beckett, P., and Portanger, E. 2003, 'US banks retreat from EU', *Australian Financial Review*, 21 May, p. 24.

pp. 50–1: Davis, M. 2002, 'Pact lowers hurdles, keeps safeguards', *Australian Financial Review*, 4 November, p. 6.

pp. 51–2: Hill, C. W. L. 2002, *Global Business*, 2nd ed., McGraw-Hill Irwin, Boston, pp. 224–6.

pp. 52–3: Boyle, J. 2003, 'BA flies into stiff headwind', *Australian Financial Review*, 20 May, p. 16.

p. 56: Buffini, F., Hepworth, A., and Priest, M. 2003, 'Business hits back over HIH reforms', *Australian Financial Review*, 22 April, pp, 1, 4.

p. 59: Webb, S., and Saywell, T. 2002, 'Untangling Temasek', *Far Eastern Economic Review*, vol. 165, no. 44, 7 November, p. 42. (Reprinted from the *Far Eastern Economic Review*, copyright 2005 Review Publishing Company Limited. All rights reserved.)

pp. 59–60: Hookway, J. 2002, 'Texting the tube', *Far Eastern Economic Review*, vol. 165, no. 44, 7 November, p. 37. (Reprinted from the *Far Eastern Economic Review*, copyright 2005 Review Publishing Company Limited. All rights reserved.)

p. 60: Holland, T. 2002, 'The perils of privatisation', *Far Eastern Economic Review*, vol. 165, no. 45, 14 November, p. 55. (Reprinted from the *Far Eastern Economic Review*, copyright 2005 Review Publishing Company Limited. All rights reserved.)

Chapter 4

pp. 131–2: Taylor, M., and Raja, K. D. 2004, 'Redefining customer service', *The Asian Banker*, issue 44, pp. 42–4.

pp. 148–9: Editorial, 2003, 'Tourism here "hurt by poor service"', *Straits Times*, Singapore, 13 November. (Article by courtesy of SPH–*The Straits Times*.)

Chapter 5

pp. 164–5: Heracleous, L., Wirtz, J., and Johnson, R. 2004, 'Cost-effective service excellence: Lessons from Singapore Airlines', *Business Strategy Review*, vol. 15, no. 1, pp. 34–5.

pp. 165–6: Kotler, P., and Fahey, L. 1982, 'The world's champion marketers: The Japanese', *Journal of Business Strategy*, vol. 3, no. 1, pp. 3–13. (Reprinted with permission, Emerald Group Publishing Limited.)

pp. 170–1: Lings, I. N. 1999, 'Managing service quality with inherent market schematics', *Long Range Planning*, vol. 32, no. 4, pp. 452–63. (Reprinted with permission from Elsevier.)

pp. 174–5: Gery, G. 2001, 'Service with a smile', *Knowledge Management*, vol. 4, no. 7, July.

pp. 178–9: Hanis, M. E. 1998, 'Reaching maturity', *Independent Banker*, vol. 48, no. 1, p. 80.

pp. 187–9: Gustafsson, A., Ekdahl, F., and Edvardsson, B. 1999, 'Customer focused service development in practice – A case study at Scandinavian Airlines Systems (SAS)', *International Journal of Service Industry Management*, vol. 10, no. 4, pp. 344–58. (Reprinted with permission, Emerald Group Publishing Limited.)

pp. 193–5: Reinmoeller, P. 2002, 'Dynamic contexts for innovation strategy: Utilising customer knowledge', *Design Management Journal*, vol 2, pp. 41–4.

p. 197: Muhamed, M. 2001, 'India: Customer management made easy', *Businessline*, vol. 16, August, p. 1.

Chapter 6

p. 219: Harcourt, T. 2004, 'Airlines check out DIY check-ins to reduce costs', *The Weekend Australian*, 12–14 June, p. 11.

p. 228: Cartwright, R. 2004, 'Aviation, QANTAS: The Australian Way', *Inflight Magazine*, July, p. 32.

pp. 240–1: Bisignani, G. 2004, Excerpts from address to IATA, Singapore, 'Industry News, QANTAS: The Australian Way', *Inflight Magazine*, July, p. 24.

pp. 243–9: Rottnest Island Authority, 2003, *Rottnest Island Management Plan 2003–2008*, Fremantle: RIA.

Chapter 7

pp. 291–4: Gurowka, J. 2000, 'Sun Life Insurance – A case study: Activity based costing implementation', *Focus Magazine for the Performance Management Professional*, *The Economic Times*, New Delhi.

pp. 294–7: Cagan, P. 2001, 'HIH Insurance: A case study', E-Risk Publication, November. Retrieved from <www.erisk.com/Learning'CaseStudies/HIHCaseStudy.pdf>.

Chapter 8

pp. 305, 306: McKinnon, M. 2004, 'Problem? Pass it on to someone else', *The Australian*, 14 February, p. 2.

pp. 319–20: Raghunathan, V. 2003, 'They have to speak the lingo', *The Straits Times*, 6 December, p. 6.

Services and their management

Learning objectives

After studying this chapter, readers will be able to:
- discuss the overall global significance of services
- explain the concept, nature and structure of services
- understand management concepts and theories
- discuss the main issues associated with the strategic management of services.

Introduction

There are many texts that focus on the strategies, plans and operational functions associated with the management of particular industries and organisations. Others explore the application of management concepts in industry sectors such as agriculture and manufacturing, or analyse services from operational or marketing perspectives. However, few books have attempted to examine global services from a strategic management perspective, which combines all management functions within an integrated approach. The reasons for this neglect reflect the complex nature of services, their unclear boundaries and shifting structures, their 'intangible' outputs, the perceived social and economic significance of services, and their inherent resistance to the direct transfer of manufacturing models of management.

However, services can no longer be ignored, nor their proper management responsibilities be abrogated, due to their primacy in the economies of all developed, and most developing, countries in the world. It is apparent that there is a need for the development of a strategic management approach for this important sector of the global economy. Services have now supplanted both the *primary* (agriculture, mining) and the *secondary* (manufacturing) economic sectors, as a predominant *tertiary* sector. As a clear example of the significance of services, 11 of the 16 Australian Bureau of Statistics (ABS) standard industry classifications are directly services-related, namely:
- public service departments and utilities;
- transportation and storage;
- tourism and hospitality;

- communication services;
- property and business services;
- cultural and recreational services;
- education;
- retailing;
- finance/insurance;
- health and community services; and
- personal and other services.

Global significance of services

The main reasons for the remarkable rise in the global significance of services over the last decade or so are associated with dynamic changes in the world economy, customer expectations and demands, and the opportunities offered by new technologies. The collapse of former centrally planned economies and/or their replacement with market-based economies (for example, the former Soviet Union and the People's Republic of China), and the development of new labour markets, including highly educated middle-class consumers, stimulated the growing demand for both more traditional (hospitality, retail) and more innovative (virtual retailing, telephony) services. Both the primary and secondary industry sectors (that is, agriculture/mining and manufacturing) have been transformed due to labour costs and production process issues, with the aggregation or conglomeration of global agricultural and mining corporations (for example, the Vestey pastoral company, the merger of BHP Billiton, Western Mining Corporation), and the transfer of many manufacturing operations to less developed countries with reduced labour costs (for example, Country Road, Nike, automobiles and white goods). Apart from these broad labour market issues and global business perspectives, which view the world (rather than particular countries or regions) as their marketplace, many primary and secondary sector organisations have realised that new technologies, such as automated production and electronic distribution, demand the reduction of workforces and the replacement of employees with technical processes.

In addition, the combined influences of new consumers (for example, Generation X and Generation Y, and an increasing global middle class) have both broadened and deepened customer expectations of the quantity and quality of services provided by service organisations, including innovative and value-added qualities, and the challenge of competitive advantage (Porter, 1999) through enhanced service quality. These expectations include immediate and personalised attention, corporate rather than product branding, and value-adding activities integrated with more traditional functions.

Some sources suggest that up to 88 per cent of the workforce in the United States is employed in services (Verma and Boyer, 2000, p. 5), compared with around 73–75 per cent in Australia (Matthews, 2004). Singapore's international trade in services was US$26.4 billion in 2001 (Aggarwal, 2003); Thailand's economic survival is heavily dependent upon the success of the tourism segment of its services sector; and, as Table 1.1 shows, similar imperatives underpin the economic policies of such diverse countries as Indonesia, Hong Kong and Korea. Some observers have even attributed Japan's slow economic recovery recently to the lack of growth in its services sector.

Table 1.1 Country statistics: GDP (US$ million) and services value-added, 1997–2001 (% of GDP)

Country	1997	1998	1999	2000	2001
Australia	419.1 (69.9)	374.0 (70.8)	407.6 (70.7)	390.1 (N/A)	368.6 (N/A)
China	898.2 (30.9)	946.3 (32.1)	991.4 (33.0)	1,079.9 (33.2)	1,159.0 (32.9)
Hong Kong, China	171.0 (85.2)	162.6 (85.0)	158.3 (85.5)	162.6 (N/A)	N/A
India	409.7 (44.9)	414.1 (45.8)	445.2 (47.8)	457.0 (48.2)	477.6 (48.4)
Indonesia	215.7 (39.6)	95.4 (36.7)	140.0 (37.0)	152.2 (35.9)	145.3 (37.1)
Japan	4 313.2 (64.8)	3 940.5 (65.8)	4 499.6 (66.4)	4 841.6 (N/A)	4 245.2 (N/A)
Korea, Rep.	476.5 (51.6)	317.1 (51.2)	406.1 (52.4)	461.5 (52.9)	422.2 (54.1)
Macao, China	7.0 (71.7)	6.5 (71.2)	6.1 (71.0)	6.2 (N/A)	N/A
Malaysia	100.2 (44.3)	72.2 (42.8)	79.0 (42.7)	89.7 (39.7)	87.5 (41.9)
Singapore	94.6 (65.1)	82.8 (64.5)	83.8 (65.2)	92.3 (65.6)	N/A
Thailand	151.1 (50.2)	111.9 (49.5)	122.5 (49.7)	122.3 (49.5)	114.8 (49.8)
Vietnam	26.8 (42.2)	27.2 (41.7)	28.7 (40.1)	31.3 (39.1)	32.9 (N/A)
World	29 795.7 (62.4)	29 604.5 (63.0)	30 664.1 (63.7)	31 498.1 (N/A)	31 283.8 (N/A)

Note: GDP (gross domestic product) is expressed in current US dollars.

Source: World Bank, *World Development Indicators 2002*, www.worldbank.org/data/dataquery.html.

In support of the growing social and economic importance of the services sector, the Singapore government has recently formed a Coalition of Services Industries in order to coordinate, streamline and promote its service sector, and to 'help to synergise business opportunities' (Aggarwal, 2003, p. A29). While Singapore is somewhat unique in the Asian region due to its significant lack of natural resources, comparatively higher levels of education, proportionately higher incomes, and acceptance of government intervention in its economy, the coalition is focused on managerial, technical and professional services, and provides a useful example for neighbouring countries, including Australia and New Zealand.

According to a recent ABS report, services provide 'the largest component of the Australian economy in terms of number of businesses, employment and gross value added' (ABS, 2002). Specifically, services embraced 65.5 per cent of all businesses and more than 73 per cent of total employment (ABS, 2002). The major employers include retail trade

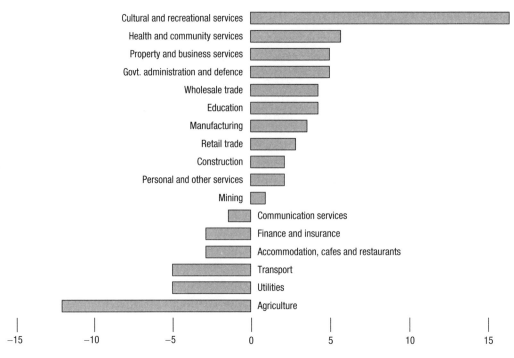

Figure 1.1 Growth in services since 1997

Source: Australian Financial Review, 8 October 2002

(15 per cent), property and business services (11 per cent), health and community services (9.5 per cent), and education (7 per cent). Growth sectors included property and business services, personal and other services, and health and community services, with a small decline in the government administration and defence sector (ABS, 2002).

However, as Figure 1.1 shows, the growth in some sectors in the last five years (notably cultural and recreational services, health and community services, property and business services, government administration and defence, and education) has been considerably greater than in others (for example, finance and insurance, accommodation and restaurants, and transport). The relative decline in sectors such as communications, transport, and accommodation, cafes and restaurants can be attributed to the dot.com 'bust' in the late 1990s; the vagaries of regional tourism in the era of terrorism and regional epidemics such as Sudden Acute Respiratory Syndrome (SARS) and bird 'flu'; and the use of new technology and new employment conditions (for example, casual, contract and part-time employees) in the transport, utilities and agricultural sectors. Conversely, the growth in cultural and recreational, health and community, government administration, and property and business services reflects both the ageing of the population and community demands for greater flexibility, especially work/life balances (for example, more leisure, hospital and real estate investment options); while increases in defence services directly address regional terrorism concerns, and education and trade services have grown to meet identified domestic and global markets.

Table 1.2 Fastest-growing job sectors, 1986–2001

Occupation	Growth in employment (number)	Employment in 2001	Growth in employment (%)
Special care workers	59,571	45,600	325
Child-care workers	71,076	53,700	309
Project and program administrators	92,131	68,200	285
Computing professionals	128,850	88,200	216
Marketing and advertising professionals	41,665	26,900	181
Business analysts	42,228	26,700	172
HR professionals	49,001	30,600	166
Financial dealers and brokers	39,789	24,700	163
Sales and marketing managers	101,290	61,000	151
Education aides	47,571	28,600	151
Waiters	83,662	47,100	128
Accountants	109,522	50,700	86

Source: National Institute of Labour Studies, *W.A. Business News*, 30 January 2003, p. 12.

Table 1.2 shows the kinds of service positions that have grown the most in Australia between 1986 and 2001. As the table illustrates, growth has been greatest in occupations such as special care and child-care workers, project administrators, information technology (IT) professionals, marketing and advertising specialists, business analysts, human resource (HR) professionals, financial dealers and brokers, accountants, and hospitality employees. As mentioned above, since 2001 the demand for IT professionals has declined significantly, but demand for carers (for both older people and children) is on the increase, due to the needs of ageing populations and dual working parents, business professionals responding to opportunities created by globalisation, and more competitive and personalised customer requirements.

These statistics highlight both the economic and social importance of services, as well as their diversity, comprised as they often are of multiple and apparently disconnected suppliers and disparate services. Given the unique nature, structure and outcomes of services, which are discussed later in this chapter and in more detail in the following chapters, it is challenging to construct a holistic model for the strategic management of this *tertiary* sector of the global economy. It is, however, both possible and necessary to appreciate the similarities as well as the differences between its constituent sectors, and therefore to develop principles, strategies, policies and practices that reflect and guide both strategists and operational managers within all service sectors.

This book strives to achieve these objectives by:

• analysing representative service sectors in terms of their structures, systems, functions and outcomes;

• comparing and contrasting management styles with those used in more traditional primary and secondary sectors; and

- proposing a conceptual framework for the application of strategic management principles within this complex and fragmented sector.

An integrated services management model, which forms the backbone of all the subsequent chapters, is presented and explained later in this chapter.

Although Bureau of Statistics categories conveniently divide all organisations into goods- or services-based businesses, and assist us to identify the major components of services, they fail to specifically delineate the multiple meanings of the term 'services', or to explain the similarities and the differences between services and goods.

The concept, nature and structure of services

Unlike manufactured goods, which are characterised by their amenability to measurement and quantification, services are often based upon a combination of intangibility, dynamic management, customer perceptions and expectations, and outcomes that are customised and variable, rather than uniform. Thus, shoes and automobiles are usually manufactured for mass consumer markets, according to rigid specifications, using standardised production processes and routine job functions. However, financial and tourism services may be highly personalised client interactions, or 'service encounters', within specialist markets (for example, 'high roller' gambling rooms and 'boutique' hotels) that involve sophisticated and varied service provider skills.

Some goods are highly customised for niche markets (for example, Ferrari vehicles, Rolex watches and Louis Vuitton travel goods), while other services (for example, McDonald's, supermarket scanners and automatic teller machines, or ATMs) are standardised and routinised for mass consumer markets. These observations suggest that there are both similarities and differences between goods and services for diverse consumer markets, and that the major defining feature of services is the more active involvement of customers and employees in their service delivery processes. This issue is discussed further in this chapter, and throughout the book.

Several authors (for example, Chase, 1991; Mersha, 1991; Cook et al., 1999) suggest that, rather than defining the specific differences between services and goods, it may be more useful to perceive them along a goods–services continuum (see Figure 1.2). These range from 'pure' goods to 'pure' services, with many organisations involved in a combination of both kinds of activities. The diverse perspectives presented in the following definitions give support for a more complex approach.

Concepts of 'services' and 'service'

There are many definitions of the term 'services'. The American Management Association, for example, in 1960 defined 'services' as:

> Activities, benefits, or satisfactions which are offered for sale, or are provided in connection with the sale of goods. Examples are amusements, hotel service, electrical service, transportation, the services of barber shops and beauty shops, repair and maintenance service, the work of credit rating bureaus. . . . (Cook et al., 1999, p. 319)

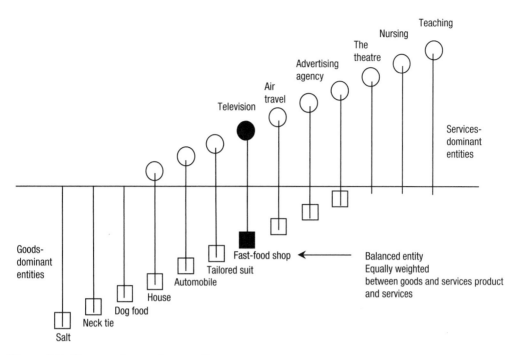

Figure 1.2 The goods–services continuum

Source: Adapted from G. Shostack, 'Service positioning through structural change', *Journal of Marketing*, vol. 51, no. 1, 1987, p. 41

The US government's definition (1972) is similar:

> . . . a wide variety of services for individuals, business and government establishments, and other organisations: Hotels and other lodging places; establishments providing business, repair and amusement services; health, legal, engineering, and other professional services; educational institutions; membership organisations, and other miscellaneous services. (Cook et al., 1999, p. 319)

Other authors describe the term 'service' variously as: 'personal performance' (Levitt, 1972); 'a product which is a process' (Henkoff, 1994; Shostack, 1987); 'processes involving customer contact' (Chase, 1978); or 'a deed, an act, or a performance' (Berry, 1980).

Quinn et al.'s definition is more analytical:

> All economic activities whose output is *not* a physical product or construction, is generally consumed at the time it is produced, and provides added value in forms (such as convenience, amusement, timeliness, comfort or health) that are essentially intangible concerns of its first purchaser. (1990, p. 60)

The definitions use a variety of terms to capture the essence of 'services' (and their differences from goods), including activities, benefits, satisfaction, amusement, performance, process, deeds and acts, all of which imply that services are the result of dynamic interactions between service providers and customers, and vary according to the expectations and perspectives of both.

Other authors provide definitions focusing on differentiations that include:

- distinctions between 'rented goods services', 'owned goods services' and 'non goods services' (Rathmell, 1966, p. 33);
- differences between 'tangible' and 'intangible' services (Zeithaml et al., 1990); and
- distinctions between tangible actions directed at people's bodies or physical possessions, and intangible actions directed at people's minds or assets (Lovelock, 1996, p. 11).

Berry (1980, p. 25) simply delineates goods as 'an object, a device, a thing', in contrast to services, which he defines as 'a deed, a performance, an effort'. Mersha (1991, p. 391) summarises the above characteristics with the observation that services are 'a bundle of tangible goods and intangible benefits provided in a particular environment'. Nie and Kellogg (1999, p. 339) assert that 'products are possessed and services are rendered, participated in, and experienced', and Grönroos (2000, p. 45) concludes that 'goods and services merge – *but on the conditions of services*' (our italics).

The implications that may be drawn from these definitions are that: services are different from goods in both their nature and systems of delivery; they rely more heavily than goods on customer, or client, perceptions and expectations; and, consequently, their outputs are more difficult to quantify than are manufactured goods. The following sections explore in more detail the similarities and differences between goods and services.

Distinguishing features of services

Many authors have attempted to discern the differences between services and goods, and there is general agreement that the fundamental differences lie in the roles of both the service providers and the service consumers or clients. Figure 1.3 illustrates the types of organisations included within services, in contrast to those in the 'physical goods' category. It also suggests that we may be moving into an era where goods and services are becoming merged, as part of a transformed 'quaternary' sector. Thus, biotechnology, medical devices and transaction processing contain elements of service (for example, research and development, and administrative functions) as well as tangible goods, such as hearing aids, heart monitors and databases.

The distinguishing features of services have usually been viewed from a marketing perspective, which focuses on customer perceptions, rather than on management decisions about their specification. While this is valuable, the *strategic management of services* requires organisational managers to clearly delineate the nature of the services they provide through the development of measurable criteria and associated service operations, and by means of financial and HR management systems which ensure consistency and cost-effectiveness. This is the primary theme of this text.

Many authors (for example, Zeithaml et al., 1990; Heskett et al., 1990; Grönroos, 2000; Verma and Boyer, 2000) have suggested that the defining characteristics of services revolve around four main qualities: their intangibility, inseparability, variability and perishability. These qualities are discussed in the following sections.

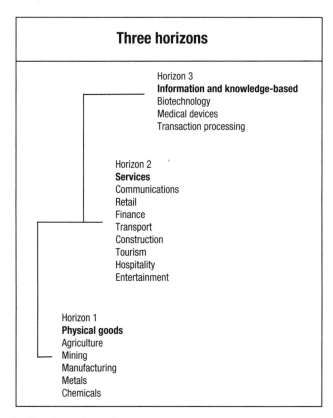

Three horizons

Horizon 3
Information and knowledge-based
Biotechnology
Medical devices
Transaction processing

Horizon 2
Services
Communications
Retail
Finance
Transport
Construction
Tourism
Hospitality
Entertainment

Horizon 1
Physical goods
Agriculture
Mining
Manufacturing
Metals
Chemicals

POSITIVE OUTLOOK: Port Jackson Partners has defined Australia's growth into three horizons: physical goods, services, and information and knowledge-based.

Figure 1.3 Goods and services categories

Source: Business News, 30 January 2003, p. 12

Services are intangible

Perhaps the most fundamental feature that distinguishes goods from services is the former's tangibility and the latter's intangibility. For, while most goods can be seen, touched or felt, services are seldom so palpable. We can readily touch or hold such everyday goods as hamburgers, automobiles, medicines, clothing and furniture. However, services such as legal advice, airline flights, a restaurant's ambience, medical or management consultations, educational experiences, or electronic funds transfer systems are not able to be touched or held. There is, nevertheless, a broad spectrum of types of services, ranging from those that combine the tangible and the intangible (for example, tailors, house builders, food vending machines), to others (for example, teaching, nursing, the theatre) that have considerably fewer tangible components (see Figure 1.2).

While services such as the preparation of legal wills and real estate conveyancing, and fast-food restaurants such as McDonald's or KFC, approach tangibility, some others (for example, ATMs, and theatre and car-park ticketing machines) have consciously reduced their personal (intangible) component to a minimum as part of their corporate business strategy. The following Air Asia example (Box 1.1) demonstrates how cost-minimisation corporate strategies, combined with targeted marketing plans, can provide a competitive industry position. In other words, it illustrates a strategic approach to the management of services organisations.

Box 1.1   The minimisation of service 'Air Asia: No-frills seeker'

With its red and white livery, it looks like Virgin; with its supermarket specials and marketing style, it feels like Virgin; and with A$18 one-way fares for the hour's flight from Kuala Lumpur to Penang, Asia's newest airline, Air Asia, wants to do a Richard Branson and 'release the travelling public from the airline tyranny'. It's not Branson's Virgin Blue that CEO Tony Fernandes wants to emulate, however; but, rather, the godfather of discount flying, Ireland's Ryanair, one of the world's best share market and profit performers in recent years. But Fernandes and his consultant, Connor McCarthy, have a job ahead of them. In an Asian market where discounted air travel is as rare as the one-sky policy that has seen discount flyers proliferate in Europe and North America, Air Asia is pioneering no-frills air travel from the seat of its principals' pants.

Air Asia is the latest of a lengthening line of Ryanair imitators in Asia, where travellers have long endured some of the highest fares on airlines with the poorest safety records. Japan has seen a spate of cheapie carriers – Skymark, Skyjet, and the now defunct Air Do – while in the Philippines, John Gokongwei's Cebu Pacific is taking on Philippine Airlines. Air Asia has considerably fewer cabin crew than traditional carriers, does not provide passengers with food, beverages or in-flight entertainment, and the pilots and flight attendants double as cabin cleaners or departure lounge staff. Air Asia is, however, required to abide by all the usual airline safety standards. While Air Asia cannot match Malaysian Airlines or Singapore Airlines on service, it seems ready to test them on price, setting up a hub in Johor Bahru and with plans to run cut-price flights on their stable routes to Jakarta, Bangkok, Surabaya and Bali. Even cheekier is an Air Asia plan to bus prospective passengers from downtown Singapore to Johor's under-trafficked Senai airport, a 30–45-minute journey on vacant freeways as against the 20–25-minute ride to Singapore's busy Changi. The extra 20 minutes might be compensated by fares 50 per cent under, say, the A$700 it costs for the two-hour Singapore to Bali return fare.

(*Source:* Adapted from E. Ellis, 'Air Asia: No-frills seeker', *The Australian*, 24 September 2002, pp. 21–22)

While Air Asia, Ryanair and Virgin have actively pruned the services component of their businesses as the main thrust of their corporate management strategy, some goods-based companies have chosen the opposite business direction. As an example, Nike, best known for its popular range of sports shoes, has developed its own 'theme' stores, known as Nike Town. In these stores, 'freedom, entertainment, colour, fantasy, technical shoe performance information, videos and music are part of the goods and services attributes, which are bundled with the core good – shoes'. This has been described as a 'design-your-own service encounter activity sequence' (Collier and Meyer, 1998, p. 1228). Pine and Gilmore (1998), citing

Disney World, Club Med, interactive games, Internet chat rooms, Planet Hollywood and the Hard Rock Café, suggest that we may even be entering a new era, in which 'experiences' are supplanting services, involving 'services as the stage and goods as props, to engage individual customers in a way that creates a memorable *event*' (p. 98).

Further diverse examples include the Harrods department store in London, whose core business is the retailing of exclusive goods, but which has also consciously created a tourist 'experience' for its many curious visitors. This experience has recently been enhanced by the establishment of an in-store 'shrine' to the late Princess Diana. The Pacific Coffee Company in Hong Kong claims to 'sell sanctuary' to its customers by providing 'high-speed wireless Internet connections that allow execs to instant-message their colleagues, update their PDAs or videoconference with clients as they linger over lattes' (Foroshar, 2003, p. 38). Given these scenarios, the management of services organisations, and the sector as a whole, requires proactive and integrated approaches to the careful specification of services, the organisation of efficient and effective delivery systems, and the application of appropriate marketing, financial and HR management strategies, within their particular internal and external environments.

Services are inseparable and co-productive

As the second differentiating characteristic of services, 'inseparability' and 'co-productivity' refer to the inherent link between the 'production' and the 'consumption' of services. Hence, both the service provider and the service customer are actively involved in the delivery process, and the input and the output of the service 'encounter' (Carlzon, 1987; Grönroos, 2000) usually occur simultaneously. The importance of a clear customer focus in this relationship (or transaction) is reflected in both marketing and operational management, and is discussed further in Chapters 5 and 6.

As examples of the inseparability component of services: dental and medical treatment can seldom occur without the simultaneous presence and actions of both the professional and the customer (except perhaps for the preparation of dental or medical prostheses); teachers and students usually participate together in educational experiences (whether face to face, or in 'virtual classrooms'); and travel of any kind (including 'virtual tourism') usually involves active interaction between service providers and customers, as do retailing, banking and call centre services.

However, arguably there are degrees of inseparability in all services. Hotel room attendants, restaurant dishwashing assistants, car mechanics, ophthalmologists, researchers, computer systems analysts and aircraft ground crew, for example, may have little or no direct contact with paying customers, although their services are crucial to the overall service delivery system. In these cases, they have a support role and provide the infrastructure for service delivery; their customers are internal (fellow employees), rather than external. In all cases, the quality of the services provided will inevitably be determined by the expectations, skills and past experiences of both the service providers and their customers. As an example, a recent Singaporean study suggests that 'Singaporeans want value for their money, so they will put cost and quality before good service. . . Service becomes something that can be forfeited' (Li, 2003, p. 4). This represents an unspoken, but apparently shared, understanding about the (lack of) service quality between service providers and their customers. The study further suggests that this understanding may be dependent on the nature of the services provided (for example, airlines and hotels versus taxis and fast-food outlets), the economy, and the degree of competition. 'With the bad times, people are more concerned about costs. But as the economy recovers, and as products and pricing become more generic, service will be the distinguishing factor' (Li, 2003, p. 4).

Hence, management of the 'inseparability' aspect of services focuses on establishing and maintaining the entire service delivery system by involving and managing both internal and external stakeholders (see Chapters 2 and 3).

Services are variable (or heterogeneous)

While the primary characteristic of mass-produced goods, especially those manufactured within factory systems or on production lines (for example, automobiles, clothing, food, furniture and pharmaceuticals), lies in their standardisation and conformity to rigidly pre-scribed specifications (*homogeneity*), services are inherently more diverse and customised (*heterogeneous*). Chase and Schmenner (cited in Mersha, 1991, p. 393) have developed a Customer Contact Approach which classifies all services into either 'pure' services, 'mixed' services or 'quasi-manufacturing' services, depending on the degree of customer or client contact involved in the service experience, and accordingly involving either more or less customisation and differentiation of the services provided. Their framework is similar to the goods–services continuum discussed earlier in this chapter. In their model, 'pure' service providers include entertainment centres, health agencies, hotels, public transport, restaurants and schools; 'mixed' services include banks and post offices; while fast-food outlets and supermarkets are regarded as 'quasi-manufacturing'. The purer the service provider, the more individualised and variable are its services, and the more complex its management challenge.

At the top end of the market, premium services provided by five-star hotels, Queen's counsel, up-market jewellery stores, elite clubs and professional associations provide highly personal services. At the lower end, supermarkets 'represent the industrialisation of an ancient retail service, much as the assembly line represents the industrialisation of ancient craftsmanship . . . tremendous economies, great efficiencies and much better products' (Levitt, 1972, p. 65). The diversity of possible services may in some cases be greater than any one provider can offer, and may therefore necessitate complex strategic industry alliances in order to meet customer or client demands, as Quinn et al. (1990) illustrate:

> The biotechnology industry is becoming a loosely structured network of service enterprises built around specialised core competencies and joined together (often temporarily) for one undertaking, while remaining suppliers, competitors, and customers in others. (p. 66)

Services managers need to clearly identify the nature of their services and their specific customer markets along this 'high contact–low contact' continuum. This has critical implications for the design and maintenance of appropriate service delivery systems; for hiring and developing suitably skilled direct and indirect service providers; and for ensuring that marketing, financial, operations, and HR management systems effectively support the desired levels of customisation in the services offered. These aspects are discussed in Chapters 4 to 7.

Services are perishable

The final characteristic of services that distinguishes them from primary and secondary sectors is in the 'perishability' of their outcomes. While tangible goods such as food, clothing, refrigerators, furniture, books and plants can, to varying degrees, be stored, warehoused, shipped or transported to different locations, the intangibility, inseparability and variability of services, together with the centrality of customer perceptions in the service delivery process, prevents either their storage or their reuse. As experiences or encounters, dreams (and sometimes nightmares), services merely occur as actions or events, and cannot be easily replicated. While it is true that efficient high-contact and low-contact services may be repeated daily, their heterogeneity ensures that each such experience will be, at least marginally, different.

In addition, unused airline seats, cancelled restaurant bookings, and patients' failure to attend a medical appointment or the choice of another supplier due to prior bad experiences have direct and often adverse effects on service organisations, sometimes in both the short term and long term. Some of these adverse effects can be redressed through: targeted marketing campaigns; improvements in the efficiency and effectiveness of operations, including booking and reservations systems and customer follow-up strategies; better recruitment, training and performance management programs for employees; and enhanced financial management techniques. Chapters 4 to 7 consider these aspects in more practical detail.

Examples of some practical ways in which services organisations can address their inherent difficulties consistently include 'service blueprinting', 'services flowcharting' and planned 'service recovery' strategies, discussed further in Chapter 6. They represent management strategies designed to systematically analyse, provide and then evaluate the effectiveness of service delivery processes, and to 'recover' from any identified deficiencies. The following illustration describes how one financial institution has endeavoured to use new technology to deal more efficiently with customer requests.

Box 1.2 'E-loans cut bank paper trail'

A bank based in southeast Queensland has achieved what many major banks are still struggling to do: it has eliminated the paper trail. Heritage Building Society reengineered workflow and IT systems so that mortgage loan applications could be sent electronically from 44 branches to its processing centre. 'The paper trail and document transport has gone away and a workflow to allow processing to be done in an ordered fashion means the work is split up and done more efficiently,' says Heritage CEO John Minz. Initially implemented to process mortgage loan applications, the system also has been used more recently to process some personal loan and credit card applications. As a part of the project, which cost slightly less than $1 million, branches around the state were fitted out with fax machines for sending images of loan documents to the central image server. High-speed scanners were also installed at central locations. With the loan processing system, workflow technology is partitioned into a range of processes and the applications flow through the steps. The bank has set up data links with mortgage insurers, credit reference authorities and land title searches, which are all handled automatically. According to Minz: 'We implemented new workflow queues that improved response times and image delivery time. That all cuts down the time frame to process a loan.' Since the FileNet-based system was deployed, he says, about 62 per cent more loans are processed per staff member. Heritage has achieved a 50 per cent drop in the cost of processing, and return on investment for the project was achieved within 12 months.

(*Source*: K. Mills, 'E-loans cut bank paper trail', *The Australian*, 27 March 2004, p. 25)

This section has explained some of the ways in which the outcomes and processes of services differ from their more traditional counterparts, such as manufacturing and agriculture. Perhaps the most important differentiating component is the unique nature of the relationship between the service provider and its customers. The effective management of this relationship involves a 'services paradigm', which comprehensively attends to the nature of the services offered, market demands and stakeholder relationship management, as well as operations, marketing, financial and HR management strategies and practices. Gummesson (1993, p. 78) suggests that this services paradigm needs to ensure 'a balance between human input and technology, between cost and revenue, and between customer perceived quality and productivity'. The following illustration indicates how one Australian entrepreneur is attempting to provide an innovative, personalised and cost-effective series of services that have evolved over time according to customer demands.

Box 1.3   Future industries: Outsourcing personal services – new opportunities

Consider It Done Personal Concierge Service – the name of this Subiaco business says it all. It is one of a growing number of businesses aiming to profit from the trend towards outsourcing of home and personal services. Whether it's walking the dog, buying gifts or groceries, or running errands, there are businesses in Perth that can do it for you. Lea Simons, a co-founder of Consider It Done, said her clients included busy professionals, interstate executives needing assistance while they are in Perth, and people wanting their homes looked after while they are on holidays.

The potential of this market has been highlighted by the success of the Jim's Mowing franchise. While lawn mowing has been outsourced for many years, Jim's has diversified into more than 20 other services, including house cleaning, dog washing, tree lopping, car cleaning, blind cleaning and bookkeeping. It now has 2,100 franchises around the world and generated operating revenue of $4.3 million in 2001/02. The parent company, Jim's Corp, issued a prospectus in January 2003 to raise $1 million from investors. Another successful franchise is Hire A Hubby, which describes itself as the complete home maintenance and repair service.

A relative veteran in the field is Stephen Greville, who has been running Home and Away for five years. His core services are pet care and home maintenance. 'This can mean having a pet looked after at 5 am or having the lawn watered at 9 pm if that is what the client has asked for,' Mr Greville said. Some clients hire Home and Away for a one-off holiday, while others have come to rely on the service. 'In one case a client had moved overseas. We arranged the packaging and freight of his furniture to the UK, sold his car, and found new owners for his dog, cat and rabbit,' Mr Greville added: 'All the new owners were vetted to ensure [the animals] were going to the best of homes.'

The Perth market had been more challenging than Sydney and Melbourne, where he worked previously, Mr Greville said. 'In Sydney and Melbourne, time is money. People are prepared to pay a reasonable rate.' However, many people in Perth still rely on friends or neighbours to help out while they are on holiday, he explained, only to discover on their return that gardens had not been watered and pets had not been fed. Mr Greville faces competition from 'cash only' operators, but said clients were recognising the importance of insurance cover and tax compliance.

Home and Away has $10 million of public liability insurance and is a registered business, GST compliant and accredited with the Tourism Council of Western Australia. It also has an agreement signed for each period of home or pet care, which details everything from the client's contact numbers to specific pet requirements. Mr Greville said that, apart from the convenience, there were some hard-nosed reasons for hiring a professional helper, especially during extended holidays. It meant that clients' homes had a lived-in look and were more secure. Some insurance policies are made invalid if a home is unoccupied and untended for 60 days or more. Mr Greville said the service may be tax deductible if Home and Away performed services such as retrieving emails and checking faxes for a client on a business trip.

(*Note:* 'Hire a Hubby' is a slang expression referring to the traditional husband's – or 'hubby's' – role in household repairs and maintenance.) (*Source:* Adapted from *W.A. Business News*, 30 January 2003, p. 8)

Classification of services

Within the umbrella of services, apparently dissimilar sectors such as banking and finance, tourism and hospitality, culture and recreation, health, education, property and business services, transportation, communication, retailing, and the various functions offered by government service providers, coexist, compete and collaborate within loosely coupled and dynamic structures and alliances. To complicate things further, government departments and authorities mingle with privately owned businesses, in partnership and competitively; and small, medium-sized and large organisations operate simultaneously. In addition, many business conglomerates and single organisations may provide multiple services, or a blend of goods *and* services, as discussed earlier.

Pharmacies, for example, routinely dispense medications (health services) together with toys, sweets and flowers (goods), as well as housing postal agencies or Internet cafes (communication services), and banking functions (financial services). Agencies such as the Australian National Roads and Motorists Association (NRMA), and the Royal Automobile Association, which were originally established to provide roadside services for motorists, now also sell insurance (financial services), and tour and accommodation bookings (tourism services). Motor vehicle retailers add on such related services as insurance and coffee shops. Other retailers, such as Myer, David Jones, Marks and Spencer, Sarinah (Jakarta) and Ngee Ann City

(Singapore), provide restaurants and Internet cafes alongside their more traditional clothing, furniture or plant products. Many of these retailers offer convenient 'home shopping' and delivery services, either by mail order or Internet catalogues. Some of these organisations clearly separate their goods and services functions within discrete profit centres or branches, but many do not. Of course, some examples may merely reflect the addition of 'non-core' activities to the 'core' functions of the organisation, as a result of mergers or planned diversification; in other cases, they represent the refocusing of traditional perspectives of the 'core' business.

The above examples illustrate both the increased blurring of the boundaries between organisations that provide goods and those that deliver services, and the difficulty of precisely defining the component parts of their services. The next section presents several models to assist in classifying services into their quintessential components.

As already suggested, the immense size, fragmentation and amorphous nature of services, and the dynamic relationships between service providers, defy simplistic definitions of their boundaries or components. Service organisations themselves display both similarities and considerable differences in their operations, processes and outcomes. Illustrating some of these similarities and differences, services have been divided into four dimensions:

- those that act on people's *minds* (for example, education, entertainment, psychology);
- those that act on people's *bodies* (for example, transport, lodging, funeral services);
- those that act on people's *belongings* (for example, landscaping, dry cleaning, repairs); and
- those that act on people's *information* (for example, insurance, investments, legal advice).
  (Lovelock, 1983, 1996)

However, in order to better understand these issues, it is useful to examine some of the other conceptual models developed to classify all kinds of services within the wider services sector. These are summarised in Table 1.3. It is helpful to take a closer look at some of the main models and their applications in different services. By so doing, important themes and issues are raised that are discussed in the subsequent chapters.

The table shows that classifications have been developed on the bases of numerous variables, including:

- the types of services provided;
- the kinds of service providers and their customers or clients;
- individual versus collective services;
- the comparative degree of customer contact involved in the service transaction;
- equipment versus people-based services;
- service specifications;
- tangibility or intangibility;
- the relative degrees of labour intensity and service complexity; and/or
- the nature of service provision systems.

Most of the above models cluster services and/or the organisations that provide them, according to:

- the *nature of the services* themselves (for example, rented/owned or non-goods services, their degree of tangibility or intangibility, service benefits);
- the *extent of customer contact*, or involvement, in the service experience; or
- the *characteristics of the service process* (for example, labour intensity, service delivery systems and structures).

Table 1.3 Services classification models

Author	Classification model	Summary
Judd (1964)	Rented goods services Owned goods services Non-goods services	A broad category that ignores banking/insurance and legal advice/accounting
Shostack (1977)	Type of seller/buyer Buying motives/practice	No specific application to services – applies also to products
Hu (1977)	Services affecting persons versus goods – Permanent/temporary reversibility versus non-reversibility	Individual versus collective benefits
Chase (1978)	Extent of customer contact in service delivery (high/low)	Product variability harder in high-contact services
Thomas (1978)	Equipment versus people-based services	Understanding of product attributes
Lovelock (1980)	Service content and benefits Service delivery procedures	Defining object served is crucial
Maister and Lovelock (1982)	Extent of customer contact Extent of customisation	Classification of facilitator services (that is, businesses of facilitating market transactions)
Schmenner (1986)	Degree of labour intensity Degree of service customisation	Improvement on the customer contact model
Shostack (1987)	Complexity and divergence – service process matrix	Analysis of service process
Larsson and Bowen (1989)	Customer disposition to participate; diversity of demand	Interaction between input uncertainty (that is, customer participation) and service process design
Mersha (1991)	Customer contact matrix	Accommodative and interactive services systems
Silvestro et al. (1992)	Professional service, service shop, mass service	Empirically derived model based on volume of daily activity
Kotler and Armstrong (1994)	Type of service firm: intangibility, inseparability, variability, perishability	Based on organisational purpose
Kellogg and Nie (1995)	Service process Service package	Analysis of a strategic linkage between marketing and operations in service management
Collier and Meyer (1998)	The nature of customer's service encounter activity sequence The number of pathways (routes) built into the service system designed by management	Service positioning matrix

Source: Adapted from D. Cook, C-H. Goh and C. Chung, 'Service typologies: A state of the art survey', *Production and Operations Management*, vol. 8, no. 3, 1999, pp. 332–5.

		Passive contact	
		Low	High
Active contact	High	• Health centres • Psychiatric services • Dental services	• Hospital inpatient care • Restaurants • Schools
	Low	• Data processing services • Catalogue merchandising services • Home offices of banks and insurance companies, etc.	• Hotels/motels • Public transportation • Resorts

Figure 1.4 Customer contact matrix

Source: T. Mersha, 'Enhancing the customer contact model', *Journal of Operations Management*, vol. 9, no. 3, 1991, p. 396

The first of these characteristics – the nature of services – has already been discussed and will be further explored in the following section on service quality. The other two characteristics deserve more attention.

Customer contact

In Table 1.3, Chase (1978), Thomas (1978) and Mersha (1991), among others, suggest that services may be classified according to the extent of the customer's involvement in the service encounter or experience. They argue that there is a continuum of possible 'active' or 'passive' contact from very high to very low. The degree of their involvement will distinguish between services, and will have different implications for the management of different services organisations, especially in relation to labour and capital intensity, the development of appropriate service delivery systems, and the utilisation of technology. As Figure 1.4 shows, organisations such as data processing services and merchandising services (for example, bank/insurance billing sections, hotel accounts departments and e-commerce distribution centres) are likely to encourage little active or passive customer contact, while health agencies necessarily require high levels of active patient involvement, but only minimal passive contact. Conversely, restaurants and schools usually demand high levels of both active and passive contact from their clients, although this may vary according to the types of services provided (for example, online learning and self-service food outlets). Other agencies (for example, public transport and resorts) provide the infrastructure for their clients, and rely essentially on the passive involvement of their travellers and guests.

The service process

Other classifications of services have built upon the customer contact matrix to include the operational systems that enable organisations to provide their services to their identified customers or clients. Schmenner's 'service process matrix' (retitled the 'service management matrix'), illustrated in Figure 1.5, represents many similar models. The central part divides all services into service factory, service shop, mass service and a professional service provider classification, based on the active or passive involvement of their customers, and then suggests

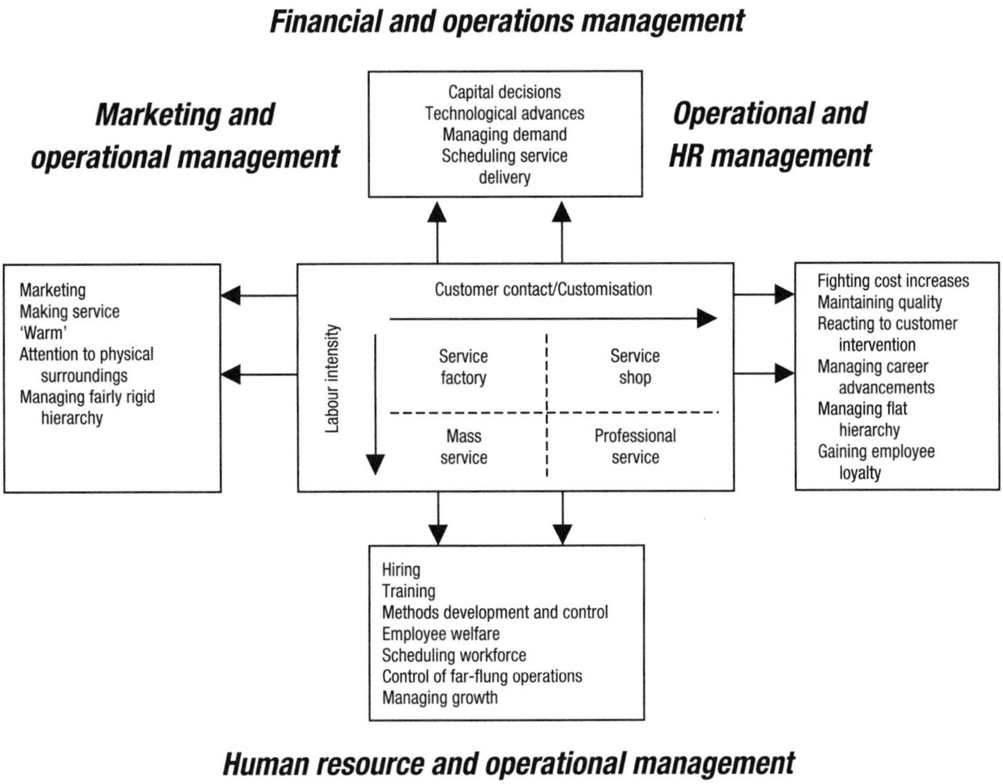

Financial and operations management

Marketing and
operational management

Operational and
HR management

Capital decisions
Technological advances
Managing demand
Scheduling service
delivery

Marketing
Making service
'Warm'
Attention to physical
surroundings
Managing fairly rigid
hierarchy

Labour intensity

Customer contact/Customisation

	Service		Service
factory		shop
Mass		Professional
service		service

Fighting cost increases
Maintaining quality
Reacting to customer
intervention
Managing career
advancements
Managing flat
hierarchy
Gaining employee
loyalty

Hiring
Training
Methods development and control
Employee welfare
Scheduling workforce
Control of far-flung operations
Managing growth

Human resource and operational management

Figure 1.5   Service management matrix

Source: Adapted from R. Schmenner, 'How can service businesses survive and prosper?', *Sloan Management Review*, vol. 27, no. 3, 1986 in R. Verma and K. Boyer, 'Service classifications and management challenges', *Journal of Business Strategies*, vol. 17, no. 1, 2000, p. 9

the management implications, whether in operational, marketing, HR management or financial management terms. It also illustrates the necessary integration of all of these latter functional management activities with each other, and with the corporate management strategies. As a whole, the model provides a template for the managers of services organisations to use in deciding on their desired types of services and their likely target customer markets, and consequently, in making strategic choices with respect to their service delivery systems and processes.

Verma and Boyer (2000, p. 10) cite Amazon.com, the US book and other products e-retailer, as an example of a services organisation that has consciously based its business strategy on a passive customer involvement model, as it has adopted a 'mass service' classification, with low customer contact and little customisation, together with high initial capital costs, but relatively low labour costs. Other passive examples might include call centres and employee records sections, which have changed from 'service shops', with high levels of customer contact and labour intensity, to 'service factories' or even 'mass services', through the replacement of human services by electronic systems, such as telephone screening and referral systems or online employee 'kiosks'. Chase (1991) suggests a number of techniques that organisations can use to simultaneously maintain customer perceptions of service, while reducing the associated costs and increasing their likely profitability. These include: handling all routine enquiries or requests by telephone or the Internet (for example, employee 'kiosks', Internet banking, customer booking systems); using appointments-only systems (for example, law firms, medical clinics); providing services at the client's home or office (for example, mobile car detailing, Tupperware, life insurance); extending the use of 'drop-off' facilities (for example, boxes in banks and post offices for paying bills, express check-out systems in hotels); and 'drive-through' options (for example, McDonald's, KFC).

Chase (1991, p. 66) divides these examples of the 'industrialisation' of services into *hard*, *soft* and *hybrid* technologies. Examples of the application of hard technology into services include airport X-ray equipment, automatic car washes, and 'never needs ironing' clothing; soft technology includes Internet travel planning, and DIY wills and furniture (for example, IKEA). Parcel tracking systems, automatic toll booths (with human collectors present), automated electricity meter reading, and remote IT help and repair services are examples of hybrid systems that involve both technological and human resources.

All of the discussed classification systems have advantages and disadvantages, but few are able to comprehensively, or precisely, divide services into comprehensive and integrated functional and corporate management sections. However, they help in understanding the complexity of services, and may assist managers to make difficult decisions about the kinds of services offered, their target customer markets, and the strategic choices they must make in relation to operations, marketing, financial and HR management issues. The next section explores the associated management dilemma of what constitutes *service quality* in different organisational settings, and how it can be measured and delivered.

Service quality

As previously discussed, services are by their very nature intangible, variable and perishable, and the service delivery process is inseparable from its outcomes. Given these characteristics, and the importance of customer or client perceptions and expectations in the assessment of the service, the development of service criteria in order to meet, or exceed, such expectations is a significant challenge. In fact, some managers avoid the task, and instead focus their measurement of service quality on infrastructural issues.

As an example, hotels are routinely classified on 'star' or 'diamond' classifications, provided by motoring organisations such as the NRMA or European Michelin classification systems. These systems grade organisations on a scale of 1–5 stars or diamonds. This is based on comprehensive and precise evaluations of their physical (or tangible) facilities (for example, rooms, restaurants, gyms, car-parking facilities, and so on), but with little or no consideration of the intangible qualities (for example, check in/check out service, food and beverage services, room service) by which hotels claim to differentiate themselves, and on which they base their operational and marketing strategies. From a management perspective, this then may lead to the crucial intangible elements of service being disregarded, the likely employment of unsuitable employees, and a failure to effectively manage their service performance to guest expectations, resulting in adverse effects on the image and profitability of the organisation.

However, while avoidance of the issue of service quality is perhaps an understandable response, given the difficulty of achieving and measuring it in services, it is no longer possible or acceptable. Managers need to recognise that their role is: to clearly and precisely define the criteria for their particular levels of service quality; to set and market appropriate standards; to regularly assess the achievement of these standards; and to ensure that service delivery systems reflect and reinforce these standards, with feedback from their internal and external stakeholders (see Chapter 3).

Brady and Cronin (2000, p. 34) suggest that 'although it is apparent that perceptions of service quality are based on multiple dimensions, there is no general agreement as to the nature or content of these dimensions'. They offer several anecdotal illustrations of the difficulties faced by managers of services organisations in their quest to define and measure service quality, and to ensure that expectations of service quality are met, if not exceeded:

Negative aspects of service quality
- 'The receptionist seemed very snotty. The nurse and the doctor were nice, but the attitude of the receptionist ruined my visit.'
- 'The doctor's office was clean, but people were sitting too close to each other. Germs were spread whenever someone sneezed or coughed. But the examination rooms were spread out and private, so I felt comfortable talking to the doctor.'
- 'It wasn't a pleasant experience, since everyone there was pretty unhygienic.'
- 'Overall I didn't like the outcome, because it took the doctor only three minutes to check me and I had to wait three hours just to see him.'

Positive aspects of service quality
- 'The attitude and personality of the service personnel definitely influenced my opinion. They were very friendly and warm.'
- 'The photo shop was decorated with bright lights and lots of colour. This caught my eye and evoked warm, comfortable feelings.'
- 'The operation was a success. There were no scars.'
- 'The one incident that stands out in my mind was when some money had fallen out of my pocket. The workers ran me down to give me my money back.'

(Adapted from Brady and Cronin, 2000, pp. 34–36)

These examples show that each customer is unique and it is a challenge to please all. However, services managers need to differentiate between the factors in the service delivery system that are manageable, and those that are not. Thus, while the size and cleanliness of medical offices, and the behaviours of service staff, are the proper responsibility of management, the 'hygiene' of fellow patients, or the healing of scars, is not. Many companies have addressed this issue in the form of 'service contracts', which specify the parameters of their service delivery systems. As a contemporary example, the Immigration Department at Beijing International Airport provides incoming passengers with a visible reminder of its service guarantees (timeliness, officer behaviours, procedures) by means of a series of large neon signs. Other organisations, such as banks and airlines, attempt to develop similar contracts or customer 'pledges' in the form of expected waiting or departure times, or 'money back

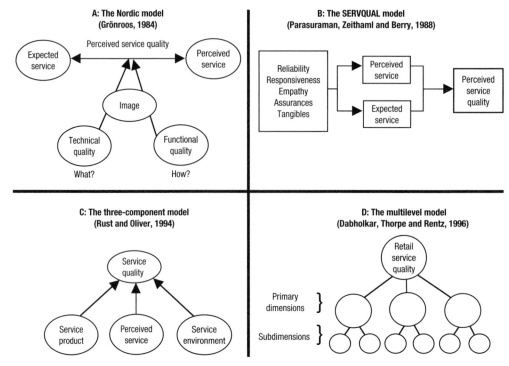

Figure 1.6 Models of service quality

Source: M. Brady and J. Cronin, 'Some new thoughts on conceptualizing perceived service quality: A hierarchical approach', *Journal of Marketing*, vol. 65, 2001, p. 35

guarantees', but these have not always been as successful as desired. As examples, a major Australian bank and a pioneering Indonesian airline both offered customers financial benefits for their failure to deliver timely services, but both were forced to withdraw their offers due to the associated costs.

Over recent years, several models have been developed in an attempt to define and evaluate the quality of service, in all its diverse forms. Figure 1.6 summarises these. While the models will be discussed in more detail later, it is sufficient at this point to observe that they contain both similar and disparate elements. Thus, while they all involve the expectations and subsequent perceptions of customers and clients, and divide services into several levels, the SERVQUAL (Zeithaml et al., 1990) model is arguably more inclusive of both customer (external) and service provider (internal) perspectives. However, most of these models have been developed from research in the marketing discipline, rather than from more holistic management frameworks; consequently, they provide only part of the picture in relation to the overall management of services. These aspects of management models are addressed in the following section, together with a brief overview of the significant management theories and concepts that have influenced all industries over the past century.

Management concepts and theories

The management discipline is relatively recent, having developed over the past century; hence, it historically reflects the needs and demands of the manufacturing sector rather than services. It has developed from early 20th-century classical management and organisational theories, and through quantitative and behavioural schools, towards systems and contingency theories, 'excellence' and total quality management. All of these theories have elements that can be applied in services, either wholly or in part, but some may appear to have more direct relevance to the 'pure' service component of the goods–services continuum than others, or to different sectors.

Classical management and organisation theory

These theories represent the origins of modern management thinking, and form the bases of many subsequent models. The main theories were developed by Frederick Taylor (1856–1915), Henri Fayol (1841–1925) and Max Weber (1864–1920). Taylor's theory of scientific management, for example, asserts that jobs can be scientifically analysed; employees can then be scientifically selected and trained to ensure job 'fit', within a friendly, cooperative and productive employment relationship. His work has been applied in 'time and motion' techniques, job design, production schedules, productivity bonus systems, and management planning and control systems, and was used by Henry Ford in his mass automobile manufacturing factories. It is also applicable to service organisations that involve routine service delivery systems and mechanistic jobs (for example, McDonald's, airline baggage handling, hotel room cleaning, hospital laundries), or in countries where hierarchical management systems are culturally acceptable. These approaches, sometimes referred to as 'McDonaldisation' (Ritzer, 1996; Smart, 1999), reflect the highly organised and efficient delivery system used in many McDonald's fast-food outlets.

Scientific management principles are difficult to utilise in high customer contact services, however, and the narrow assumptions about benevolent management–employee relationships are unrealistic in services organisations with strong union influences or confrontational industrial relations histories (for example, the maritime sector, government agencies). Fayol's main contribution to management and organisation theory was to identify the functions of managers as those of *planning, organising, commanding, coordinating* and *controlling* (later refined as *planning, organising, leading* and *controlling*). Weber, on the other hand, classified organisations as *charismatic, traditional* or *rational–legal*, the latter representing classical bureaucratic authority structures such as large public- and private-sector agencies. Again, these perspectives apply, to greater or lesser degrees, to services as well as to manufacturing organisations.

Sociology and industrial psychology

Sociological theorists, such as Mary Parker Follett (1868–1933) and Lyndall Urwick (1891–1983), emphasise the importance of social factors at work, including work teams, leadership styles and 'informal' systems, while industrial psychologists such as Hugo Munsterberg (1863–1916), Elton Mayo (1880–1949), Abraham Maslow and Frederick Herzberg (the

Behavioural School) focus on the needs of individual employees. Both of these influences on management thought have had enduring legacies, in the forms of semi-autonomous work teams, leadership models, 'personality' tests and profiling, motivation theory and Quality of Work Life programs, in both manufacturing and services (see Chapter 8).

Systems, contingency and 'excellence' theories

Systems theory conceptualises organisations as unified 'systems' with specific inputs and out-puts, linked through the interaction of jobs, technology, internal and external environments, and control mechanisms. As such, it is particularly useful in the design of service delivery systems that combine direct and indirect service providers, including multiple 'stakeholders' (see Chapter 3). *Contingency theory* (Tom Burns, Henry Mintzberg, Hershey and Blanchard) contends that every organisation and every environment is different, and therefore requires a 'contingent' approach. *Excellence theory* (Tom Peters and Robert Waterman) argues that productivity and profitability are the direct result of 'excellent' employee management approaches. Given the complex nature of service organisations and their service delivery systems, the close relationships between service providers and customers, and the crucial importance of meeting or exceeding their expectations, all of the above theories resonate with the prime goals of services management.

Total quality management

Total quality management (TQM) theory, proposed by W. Edwards Deming and implemented in Japan, the United States, Europe, and later in Australia and Asia, represents the marriage of traditional and more modern management ideas. It advocates the careful analysis of all organisational systems and processes with a view to their modification and improvement, using both quantitative and qualitative methods. Service organisations often apply TQM principles and techniques to both enhance their operations and achieve International Standards Organisation (ISO) accreditation (see Chapter 3). Thus, hospitals, educational institutions, hotels, airlines, universities and motor vehicle service agencies all apply TQM practices in their operations, and many of them seek ISO accreditation as either a global recognition of the quality of their services or a marketing device, or both.

Gummeson (1993) categorises management theories into three associated perspectives: the manufacturing paradigm; the bureaucratic–legal paradigm; and the service paradigm. Each of these categories originally reflected the contemporary significance of particular industries, but they are parallel rather than chronological frameworks. Thus, the manufacturing paradigm was developed according to the needs of mass production (classical management theory); the bureaucratic (rational–legal) paradigm reflects large public- and private-sector organisations (Weber and Fayol); and the service paradigm combines these and the other theories in the management of the relationships between internal and external 'stake-holders', towards a 'balance between human input and technology, between cost and revenue, and between customer perceived quality and productivity' (Gummeson, 1993, p. 78). Chapter 3 expands on the notion of 'stakeholder theory' in services. The following section presents the practical components of services management, which together build the framework that underlies the following chapters.

Strategic management of services

The above management theories variously contribute to the development of *strategic management*, which has become increasingly important with the growth in international, regional and local competition as a result of the globalisation of business. Strategic management theory suggests that all organisations need to be aware of the dynamic economic, political and social environments in which they operate (see Chapter 2); constantly assess their competitive position with respect to their services, their markets and their multiple stakeholders (see Chapter 3); adopt long-term perspectives on any necessary future changes in their organisational strategies and structures (see Chapter 4); and ensure that all management components (operations, marketing, finances and human resources – Chapters 5 to 8) are effectively integrated to best position the organisation to adapt rapidly to anticipated and actual environmental developments. Heskett (1987, p. 119) provides a useful guide to the elements of strategic management systems in the services industry – namely, the:

- identification of a *target market segment*;
- development of a *service concept*;
- codification of an *operating strategy* to support the service concept; and
- design of the *service delivery system*.

These components translate into overall business management strategies, supported by internal operational, marketing, financial, and HR management plans and functions. It can be argued validly that the strategic management of services involves similar generic management theories, approaches and techniques to those used in agriculture, manufacturing and mining. Nevertheless, the diverse nature of services, the complexities associated with their delivery (often involving a 'value chain' of disparate suppliers or providers), their frequently multiple stakeholders and the dynamism of their interrelationships, and the increasingly broad range of services provided – from highly standardised to highly customised – also requires different, more innovative and complex managerial solutions. The organisational cases, examples and illustrations discussed throughout this book present opportunities to consider these management similarities and differences within the dynamic context of local and global services, and the specific approaches appropriate for each organisational challenge. To aid understanding of the strategic management of services, the following model, the integrated services management (ISM) model, has been developed for the analysis of services management (Figure 1.7) and is briefly explained now. It will be applied in detail in the subsequent chapters. The model forms the overarching diagnostic and strategic framework for understanding the management of services.

The ISM model depicts any service organisation as comprising two interdependent, but discrete, domains of management – that is, the *corporate* (or *strategic*) domain, and the *functional* (or *operational*) domain. Both need to be managed effectively for organisational performance and survival. Strategic management is especially crucial in services, given their

Figure 1.7 The integrated services management (ISM) model

special vulnerability to external pressures and influences, such as political, economic, social and technological change, but the management of the service delivery process (a significant component of the service 'product') is equally important.

The model's two outer circles highlight the 'external' forces that continuously challenge the existence of many services and component organisations, and their multiple 'stakeholders'. These are the influences that need to be addressed by the strategies and plans of *all* senior managers (see Chapters 2 and 3). The inner core of the model (labelled 'Strategic business management') represents the senior management, their strategies and plans, and suggests that their role is also to coordinate the functional management outcomes of their middle and line managers in order to achieve their necessary broader organisational goals and outcomes. These dual, but interrelated macro- and micro-level roles are the essence of an integrated approach to the management of services.

The accompanying matrix of the model (Figure 1.8) encompasses the principal components of functional management – namely, the management of an organisation's *finances, marketing, operations and human resources*. As the matrix indicates, each management area is focused on a particular series of organisational aims and outcomes at the macro level (for example, 'finances' aim for overall profitability; 'operations' for efficiency; 'marketing' for effectiveness; and 'human resources' for productivity), as well as on attention to the micro level of service delivery issues. In addition, each management area must link with the

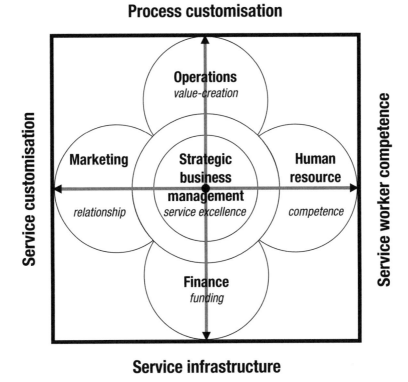

Figure 1.8 The functional services management (FSM) matrix

others, in order to ensure service efficacy and efficiency, and with the overall strategic business management of the organisation.

Structure of the book

The ISM model provides a diagnostic and evaluative tool, and a guiding strategic framework for the management of all levels of services, and will assist readers to analyse and discuss the complex issues and dilemmas faced in the strategic management of contemporary and future services. The following chapters address the various elements of strategic management:

- **Chapter 2** explores the broad economic, social and political factors that constitute the external environment for services.
- **Chapter 3** details the multiple external and internal 'stakeholders' who influence the nature of services, their modes of delivery and management strategies.
- **Chapter 4** discusses the broad elements of the strategic management of services, using a diverse range of case examples.
- **Chapters 5–8** then apply earlier discussions specifically to the management of marketing, operations, finance and human resources within services.
- **Chapter 9** completes the book, by summarising its overall themes and presenting some ideas on the likely future of services management.

Conclusion

This chapter provides a broad overview of the unique nature and characteristics of services, as an introduction to their overall management within a dynamic global context. It highlights their economic and social significance, complex structure, and what distinguishes services from goods. It further provides a series of industry classifications that have been used to distinguish services from manufacturing organisations. Finally, the chapter explores the meanings and definitions of service quality, and includes a brief history of management theories, before explaining the ISM model that underpins the text.

Exercises

Key questions

1 Discuss the economic and social importance of a chosen services sector, or a particular services organisation, in your local area. Identify some threats and opportunities that managers will need to take into account in their planning.
2 List four distinctive goods and four clear services, and compare the criteria for each (for example, McDonald's burgers, VisaCard, mobile telephones, furniture, clothing, motor vehicle sales and repairs).
3 Choose a services organisation (for example, a hotel, automobile association, hospital, university) and discuss its management issues. What are the crucial operational, marketing, financial and HR management issues?

Web exercise 1.1

Students should choose a service organisation and access the relevant website. Using the information provided, analyse the likely threats and opportunities posed to the organisation in the future, and highlight the crucial functional issues associated with this strategy. Using the ISM model (Figure 1.7), divide the latter into financial, marketing, operational and HR management factors.

Case study 1.1 La Montagne Guesthouse and Restaurant

The region

La Montagne Guesthouse and Restaurant was established five years ago in the centre of a scenic mountain resort region about 100 kilometres from a large Australian capital city. It is approximately 90 minutes by car from the seaport, or two hours by train. Both road and rail routes wind their way through attractive mountain scenery and a host of small, neat, old-fashioned towns, strung like a row of beads, to the summit. The region was very fashionable for honeymooners, wealthy families and weekend visitors in the 1920s and the 1950s, and has recently experienced a rebirth in tourism due partly to improved infrastructure (for example, upgraded rail lines, substantial road improvements), and partly to the initiatives of entrepreneurial tourism/hospitality operators. The latter have enthusiastically upgraded accommodation facilities, mounted expensive and effective marketing campaigns, and developed a broad range of tourist 'niche' attractions (for example, 'Christmas in July' events, guided walking tours, 'Winter Magic' carnivals, antiques markets and art displays).

These initiatives, largely unsupported by a conservative and at times obstructive local government authority, have over the last six years or so been successful in increasing the tourism numbers from approximately 1 million annually (1998) to around 2.5 million in 2004. Local businesses, buoyed by the increase in these numbers, have benefited immensely and have responded by upgrading or refurbishing their premises, expanding their product ranges, and adding new facilities aimed specifically at the tourist market (for example, new coffee shops, more modern and more diverse menus, advertising in different languages, extensive off-street parking, and tourist information).

Tourism marketing campaigns have aimed to broaden the range of markets (for example, internal Australian and inbound overseas tourists; young as well as more mature tourists; couples, singles and group tours; weekend and week-day visits; leisure and business conference guests; and both backpacker and expensive five-star accommodation), as well as expanding tourist seasons from a mainly winter focus to an all-year-round schedule. This latter aspect has been difficult, as traditionally this mountain region appealed mainly to those wishing to seek respite from city living by making a quick trip to the mountains in winter, lured by the misty mountain scenery and the prospect of warm log fires, comfortable beds, and 'old-fashioned', quaint and friendly (if discreet) service. Usually, summer tourism has been restricted to the city's beaches and cultural activities.

The region has attempted to maintain its 'olde-worlde' charm, while catering for the needs of sophisticated modern tourists, by offering special winter activities and upgrading tourist access to its many physical attractions, and by providing a very wide range of accommodation establishments (for example, backpacker hostels, 'bed-and-breakfast' facilities, motels, motor inns, guesthouses, lodges, four- and five-star hotels and resorts). The local government authority, anxious for licensing income, has been keen to support an increase in tourist accommodation without exercising any restraint on the numbers and quality of such establishments. As a result, individual hotels/motels/guesthouses experience varying levels of occupancy, from 30 per cent to 100 per cent, depending on seasonality, location and market segmentation. The local authority has given little support to tourism development in the form of easy access to scenic sights, reduced entry fees, additional tourist parking or upgraded information facilities. In some cases, there has been deliberate obstruction, with limited coach parking, inappropriate one-way streets and confusing (or inadequate) street signage.

La Montagne Guesthouse and Restaurant

This three-star establishment was purpose-built five years ago to benefit from the impressive growth in tourism, both national and international, over the last decade. Its two Japanese owners felt that the business could compete effectively and profitably in two separate 'niche' markets in the region – that is, the growing middle-class leisure market in Australia, and popular Japanese group package tours. They designed an 18-room, European-style guesthouse, decorated with English/European furniture and fabrics, with full ensuite facilities, and supported by a small coffee shop, cosy bar, sauna and intimate reading room. It was felt the guesthouse would attract the middle-class Australian leisure market. There was also some provision for small business conferences.

The restaurant, capable of serving 70 guests, was designed based on a Japanese 'watergarden' theme, complete with cook-at-the-table facilities, and Japanese watercolour prints and decorations. Originally, it employed one Japanese chef and two apprentice chefs, and two waitresses who were required to wear kimonos. The menu was entirely Japanese, the first in the region, and the food and service were of a high quality. The main focus of the restaurant was the Japanese group package tour lunch market, with good contracts negotiated with the largest Japanese tour operators in Australia. In the evenings, the restaurant sought to entice guesthouse patrons and, if possible, locals. It was felt that its unique cuisine would attract a substantial number of patrons from a diverse market.

Competitors to La Montagne in the neighbouring region were many, ranging from one five-star resort and one four-star boutique hotel, through to several motels, a 'quaint' guesthouse and B&B establishments, to a couple of older one-star hotels and a backpacker hostel. La Montagne's competitive strategy was to focus on the middle-range tourist market, and to supplement it with a 'captive' Japanese group package market. A small business conference market could also provide extra profitability. Thus, the establishment began with optimism and high expectations about the future.

Staffing

In the beginning, the staff establishment of La Montagne comprised an Australian male manager, a Japanese chef, two apprentices and two full-time waitresses. The Japanese owners visited frequently and telephoned, or faxed, the manager daily with policy decisions, menu suggestions, financial information and reservations enquiries. Over the last five years, the manager has changed three times, but all the other staff have been there from the start. The current manager, Judy, has been at La Montagne for 18 months, and was previously a part-time waitress there. She brought six years' experience of working in two local five-star resort hotels. While she has quite broad experience of hotel operations, including housekeeping, food and beverage, and reservations, she doesn't have any relevant qualifications, or any direct supervisory or management experience. She was chosen from a small number of applicants for the job because she was highly enthusiastic, got along well with the Japanese owners, and, as a mother with two young children, appeared stable and responsible. During the selection interview, much emphasis was placed on her personal qualities and family situation, perhaps at the expense of her managerial abilities. Since her appointment, Judy has learned to 'do the books' quite effectively, seems to have the staff 'on side', and has produced some innovative marketing and operations plans (for example, local promotions, theme nights, a new restaurant menu, and a coffee lounge for day-trippers). However, given the current situation of La Montagne, her plans will be difficult to implement.

Management styles

The Japanese owners of La Montagne visit the establishment approximately once every two months, usually separately, and it seems that their ideas for developing the guesthouse and restaurant differ considerably. On a recent visit the male owner suggested that to entice local and Australian guests the restaurant should broaden its menu to include Western meals. Conversely, on an earlier visit the female owner emphasised the need to attract more Japanese visitors, both on coach tours and single travellers, by strengthening the Japanese theme of the restaurant (and guesthouse), with additional Japanese decorations (for example, dolls, scrolls, Japanese menus) and encouraging all staff to wear traditional Japanese clothing. There has already been some resistance to this latter suggestion by the Australian staff.

Day-to-day communication between the owners and Judy occurs by way of faxed directives from Osaka, usually several times daily and expressing concern about rising goods and services costs. Judy is the nominal manager of the guesthouse, and can hire or fire staff within established limits (that is, no more than the present levels of staff), and is responsible for the ordering of supplies and overall daily operations. However, she has been specifically told that she can do no promotions without the direct authorisation of both owners, and that she should on no account expand the current advertising budget – limited largely to local regional advertisements. In addition, she has no overall control of the guesthouse's finances, except with the owners' approval.

This latter restriction has recently caused Judy considerable concern, as she has little flexibility to raise staff wages above the award wage in order to keep her (generally) cooperative and efficient employees, who are tempted to leave by the higher wages and better working conditions offered by regional competitors. Despite pleas to the owners on this issue, they seem either unaware of, or uninterested in, employee wages, conditions, or associated government regulations. There is even a sense that employees at La Montagne should be proud to work there, and that loyalty is the owners' expectation of employees. As a consequence, several of the staff have expressed their intention to look for better opportunities, and the Japanese chef is disturbed about the apparent indecision concerning the future direction of La Montagne. He is also aware of the higher available salaries for Japanese chefs in the capital city, although the owners' offer of a four-wheel-drive vehicle as part of his package has satisfied him for the moment. This will assist him to make more frequent visits to his family, who live in the capital city.

Financial management issues

As indicated, La Montagne's finances are almost entirely in the owners' hands, even down to the payment of suppliers and staff, and Judy can make few decisions without their direct approval. Since its establishment, and due largely to the capital expense of its construction, La Montagne has so far failed to make an annual operational profit. Consequently, the owners have adopted a cost reduction management strategy, reducing guest items (for example, shampoos/conditioners, tea/coffee) in the rooms, choosing cheaper suppliers, cutting down on proposed capital city promotional campaigns, and even reducing the menu options in the restaurant. Over the years, housekeeping staff has been cut from one full-time and one casual/part-time employee to only the full-time Australian employee; the kitchen staff have been replaced by the owners with two Japanese 'helpers' on minimal pay rates; and part-time waitresses in the restaurant have been substituted by on-call casuals.

Accompanying this reduction strategy has been a significant decline in the Japanese coach tour lunch trade, due to the loss of contracts with Japanese travel operators. The attraction of the unique Japanese cuisine to locals seems to have waned, as the restaurant is often only 30 per cent full in the evening. Even the guesthouse is suffering a decline of 20 per cent in patronage, although seasonality may be contributing to this. Against Judy's advice the owners have decided to raise the room rates by 15 per cent, to compensate for anticipated future losses. Already, La Montagne's room rates are comparable to those of four- and five-star properties in the region. A further rise would appear to make them uncompetitive.

Student projects
1 Analyse the strengths and weaknesses of La Montagne's management strategy. Consider, in particular, the operational, financial, marketing and HR management issues.
2 As a consultant group, prepare an innovative and practical recovery strategy. You may include the following features in your strategy:
   - service issues/'product' qualities;
   - financial management strategies;
   - accountability and responsibility issues;
   - HR management issues; and
   - operations management issues.

References and further reading

Aggarwal, N. 2003, 'Services industries team up for growth', *Straits Times*, 5 December, p. A29.

Berry, L. 1980, 'Services market is different', *Business*, vol. 30, no. 3, May–June, pp. 24–29.

Brady, M. and Cronin, J. 2000, 'Some new thoughts on conceptualizing perceived service quality: A hierarchical approach', *Journal of Marketing*, vol. 65, pp. 34–49.

Brown, S., Fisk, R. and Bitner, M. 1994, 'The development and emergence of services management thought', *International Journal of Services Industry Management*, vol. 5, no. 1, pp. 21–48.

Carlzon, J. 1987, *Moments of Truth*, Harper & Row, New York.

Chase, R. 1978, 'Where does the customer fit in a service operation?', *Harvard Business Review*, vol. 56, no. 6, pp. 137–42.

Chase, R. 1991, 'The customer contact approach to services: Theoretical bases and practical extensions', *Operations Research*, pp. 698–706.

Collier, D. and Meyer, S. 1998, 'A service positioning matrix', *International Journal of Operations & Production Management*, vol. 18, no. 12, pp. 1223–37.

Cook, D., Goh, C-H. and Chung, C. 1999, 'Service typologies: A state of the art survey', *Production and Operations Management*, vol. 8, no. 3, pp. 318–38.

Ellis, E. 2002, 'Air Asia: No-frills seeker', *The Australian*, 24 September, pp. 21–22.

Fisher, G. A. 1935, *The Clash of Progress and Security*, Macmillan, London.

Foroshar, R. 2003, 'Ready for takeoff?', *Newsweek*, 22 December.

Grönroos, C. 1991, 'Scandinavian management and the Nordic School of Services – Contributions to services management and quality', *International Journal of Services Industry Management*, vol. 2, no. 3, pp. 17–25.

Grönroos, C. 2000. *Services Management and Marketing: A customer relationship management approach*, 2nd ed., John Wiley & Sons, Chichester, UK.

Gummesson, E. 1993, 'Services management: An evaluation and the future', *International Journal of Services Industry Management*, vol. 5, no. 1, pp. 77–96.

Haynes, R. and Thies, E. 1992, 'Management of technology in service firms', *Journal of Operations Management*, vol. 10, no. 3, pp. 388–97.

Henkoff, R. 1994, 'Service is everybody's business', *Fortune*, vol. 129, no. 13, p. 48.

Heskett, J. 1987, 'Lessons in the service sector', *Harvard Business Review*, March–April.

Heskett, J., Sasser, W. and Hart, C. 1990, *Service Breakthroughs: Changing the rules of the game*, Free Press, New York.

Hu, L. T. P. 1977, 'On goods and services', *Review of Income and Wealth*, vol. 23, no. 4, pp. 315–38.

Johnston, R. 1994, 'Operations: From factory to service management', *International Journal of Services Industry Management*, vol. 5, no. 1, pp. 49–63.

Judd, R. C. 1964, 'The case for redefining services', *Journal of Marketing*, vol. 28, no. 1, pp. 58–59.

Kellogg, D. and Nie, W. 1995, 'A framework for strategic service management', *Journal of Operations Management*, vol. 13, no. 4, pp. 323–37.

Kotler, P. and Armstrong, G. 1994, *Principles of Marketing*, 6th ed., Prentice Hall, Englewood Cliffs, NJ.

Larsson, R. and Bowen, D. 1989, 'Organisations and customers: Managing design and coordination', *Academy of Management Review*, vol. 14, no. 2, pp. 213–23.

Levitt, T. 1972, 'Production line approach to services', *Harvard Business Review*, p. 43.

Levitt, T. 1976, 'The industrialization of service', *Harvard Business Review*, September–October, pp. 63–75.

Li, X. 2003, 'Bad service: Do we deserve it?', *Straits Times*, 7 December, p. 4.

Li, X. and Perry, M. 2003, 'Who gets served first?', *Straits Times*, 7 December, p. 3.

Lovelock, C. H. 1980, 'Towards a classification of services', in C. W. Lamb and P. M. Dunne (eds), *Theoretical Development in Marketing*, American Marketing Association, Chicago.

Lovelock, C. 1983, 'Classifying services to gain strategic marketing insights', *Journal of Marketing*, vol. 47, pp. 9–20.

Lovelock, C. 1996, *Services Marketing*, 3rd ed., Prentice Hall, Englewood Cliffs, NJ.

Maister, D. and Lovelock, C. 1982, 'Managing facilitation services', *Sloan Management Review*, vol. 23, no. 3, pp. 19–31.

Matthews, J. 2004, 'Innovation in services', paper presented to ANZIBA Conference, Canberra, 5–6 November.

Mersha, T. 1991, 'Enhancing the customer contact model', *Journal of Operations Management*, vol. 9, no. 3, pp. 391–405.

Mills, K. 2004, 'E-loans cut bank paper trail', *The Australian*, 27 March, p. 25.

Mudie, P. and Cottam, A. 1999, *The Marketing and Management of Services*, 2nd ed., Butterworth-Heinemann, Oxford.

Nankervis, A., Compton, R. and Baird, M. 2005, *Human Resource Management: Strategies and processes*, 5th ed., Thomson, Melbourne.

National Institute of Labour Studies. 2003, *W.A. Business News*, 30 January, p. 12.

Nie, W. and Kellogg, D. 1999, 'How professors of operational management view service operations', *Production and Operations Management*, vol. 8, no. 3, pp. 339–55.

Pine, J. and Gilmore, J. 1998, 'Welcome to the experience economy', *Harvard Business Review*, July–August, pp. 97–105.

Porter, M. 1990, *Competitive Strategy: Techniques for analyzing industries and competitors*, Free Press, New York.

Quinn, J., Doorley, T. and Paquette, P. 1990, 'Beyond products: Services-based strategy', *Harvard Business Review*, March–April, pp. 58–68.

Raghunathan, V. 2003, 'India call centres say hello to new challenges', *Straits Times*, 6 December, p. 9.

Rathmell, J. 1966, 'What is meant by services?', *Journal of Marketing*, vol. 30, pp. 32–36.

Ritzer, G. 1996, *The McDonaldization of Society: An investigation into the changing character of contemporary life*, Pine Forge Press, Newbury Park, CA.

Schmenner, R. W. 1986, 'How can service businesses survive and prosper?', *Sloan Management Review*, vol. 27, no. 3, pp. 21–32.

Shostack, G. L. 1977, 'Breaking free from product marketing', *Journal of Marketing*, vol. 41, no. 2, pp. 73–80.

Shostack, G. 1987, 'Service positioning through structural change', *Journal of Marketing*, vol. 51, no. 1, pp. 34–43.

Silvestro, R., Fitzgerald, L., Johnston, R. and Voss, C. 1992, 'Towards a classification of service processes', *International Journal of Service Industry Management*, vol. 3, no. 3, pp. 62–75.

Smart, B. (ed.). 1999, *Resisting McDonaldization*, Thousand Oaks, CA.

Thomas, D. R. E. 1978, 'Strategy is different in service businesses', *Harvard Business Review*, vol. 56, no. 4, pp. 158–65.

Verma, R. and Boyer, K. 2000, 'Service classifications and management challenges', *Journal of Business Strategies*, vol. 17, no. 1, pp. 5–24.

World Bank, *World Development Indicators 2002,* www.worldbank.org/data/dataquery.html.

www.abs.gov.au/ausstats/abs, retrieved 27 September 2002.

www.ryanair.com, retrieved 26 September 2002.

Zeithaml, V. 2000, 'Service quality, profitability, and the economic worth of customers: What we know and what we need to know', *Journal of the Academy of Marketing Science*, vol. 28, no. 1, pp. 67–85.

Zeithaml, A., Parasuraman, A. and Berry, L. 1990, *Delivering Quality Service: Balancing customer perceptions and expectations*, Free Press, New York.

The services environment

Learning objectives

After studying this chapter, readers will be able to:
- understand the composition of global trade in services and its impact on developing countries and trade regulations
- appreciate the meaning of globalisation for services, its drivers and future trends
- explain the impact of regionalism on services
- analyse the impact of issues in the national environment for service providers.

Introduction

The previous chapter discussed the significance and characteristics of services, and the need for an integrated services management model that incorporates a holistic approach in addressing its management complexities. This chapter discusses the diverse ways in which the macro and micro context, or environmental context, impacts on the dynamics and characteristics of service activities. In a sense, there is no significant difference between the environments in which services are delivered, and goods are manufactured and marketed. At the same time, the different nature of services justifies the argument that the services environment *is* considerably different. This chapter discusses how the environment contributes to the macro and micro challenges and opportunities that service providers now face. At the macro environmental level of trade in services, the impact of globalisation is discussed, together with the impact and realities of regionalisation. At the micro environmental level, the influences and impacts of national and country issues for services are also presented. Key aspects of the national environment considered include the political, economic, legal, technological, competitive and societal spheres, and how these various aspects contribute to the risk environment.

The global trade in services

Share of services in world trade

The share of services in world trade has been increasing over the past 15 years. The global market for business services is estimated to be US$3 trillion for 2001, accounting for

Table 2.1 Services as a percentage of GDP, 1999

Area	% of GDP	Country	% of GDP
World	61	France	72
Low-income countries	38	Belgium	72
Middle-income countries	56	United States	71
High-income countries	65	United Kingdom	67

Source: Adapted from World Bank, *World Development Report*, World Bank, Washington, 1999/2000.

Table 2.2 World import and export of commercial services by region, 2002

Export			Import		
Region	US$bn	%	Region	US$bn	%
North America	309	21.4	North America	248	17.0
Latin America	56	4.0	Latin America	65	4.8
Western Europe	763	46.3	Western Europe	716	43.9
Rest of Europe	60	3.4	Rest of Europe	65	3.4
Africa	31	2.0	Africa	40	2.7
Middle East	29	2.2	Middle East	45	3.3
Asia	322	20.6	Asia	367	24.9

Source: Adapted from World Trade Organization, 'International Trade Statistics, www.wto.org/english/res_e/statis_e/statis_e.htm, retrieved 7 April 2003.

approximately 10 per cent of global GDP. Exports of business services alone for 2001 are estimated to be US$734 billion, or 24 per cent of total global production (World Bank, 2002). Services are dominated by the developed world, as reflected in the composition of the GDP of their economies. In 1998, the US economy employed more than 73 per cent of its workforce in services.

Table 2.1 indicates that services have become increasingly more dominant as countries develop their GDP income. The champions in individual terms are Belgium, France, the United States and the United Kingdom. The dominant position in the service industries of the developed world, including Asia (with Japan, Singapore, Hong Kong and Taiwan as major players), is further illustrated by the concentration of export and import of commercial services.

Table 2.2 summarises commercial services trade data in 2002 and shows that the trade in services is dominated by Asia, Western Europe and North America. This trend affirms the concentration of world economic activities in these three regions. A more in-depth picture of trade in services can be obtained by considering the trade data of individual countries, as represented in Table 2.3.

There is a significant overlap between the value of exporting and importing commercial services of these countries. From a financial perspective, there are six countries that represent both the largest exporters and the largest importers of services. The same phenomenon is valid

Table 2.3 Trade involvement of individual countries, 1999

	Export				Import		
No.	Country	US$bn	Share	No.	Country	US$bn	Share
1	United States	240	18.2	1	United States	166	12.7
2	United Kingdom	101	7.6	2	Germany	125	9.6
3	France	85	6.4	3	Japan	111	8.4
4	Germany	79	6.0	4	United Kingdom	79	6.0
5	Italy	67	5.1	5	France	65	5.0
6	Japan	62	4.7	6	Italy	63	4.8
7	Netherlands	52	3.9	7	Netherlands	47	3.6
8	Spain	49	3.7	8	Canada	35	2.7
9	Belgium-Luxembourg	35	2.7	9	Belgium-Luxembourg	34	5.6
10	Hong Kong	34	2.6	10	Austria	30	2.3
11	Austria	32	2.5	11	China	29	2.2
12	Canada	30	2.3	12	Spain	28	2.1
13	Switzerland	27	2.1	13	Korea Republic	24	1.8
14	China	24	1.8	14	Taiwan	23	1.8
15	Korea Republic	24	1.8	15	Hong Kong	23	1.7
16	Turkey	23	1.8	16	Sweden	22	1.7
17	Singapore	18	1.4	17	Ireland	20	1.5
18	Sweden	18	1.4	18	Brazil	19	1.4
19	Taiwan	17	1.3	19	Singapore	18	1.4
20	Australia	16	1.2	20	Australia	17	1.3
21	Denmark	15	1.1	21	Russia	16	1.2
22	Norway	14	1.1	22	Switzerland	16	1.2
23	Thailand	13	1.0	23	Denmark	15	1.1
24	Russia	13	1.0	24	Norway	15	1.1
25	Mexico	12	0.9	25	India	14	1.1
26	India	11	0.8	26	Mexico	13	1.0
27	Malaysia	11	0.8	27	Malaysia	12	1.0
28	Greece	10	0.7	28	Thailand	12	0.9
29	Israel	9	0.7	29	Indonesia	12	0.9
30	Poland	9	0.7	30	Philippines	10	0.8

Source: Adapted from World Bank, *World Development Report*, World Bank, Washington, 1999/2000.

for the top 15 countries, with the exception that Switzerland, as an exporter, is replaced by Taiwan as an importer. In the top 30 exporters and importers, there are only four countries that do not simultaneously appear in both lists. Turkey, Greece, Israel and Poland, as exporters, are replaced by Ireland, Brazil, Indonesia and the Philippines as importers. Asian involvement in service industries includes eight countries in the top 30 exporters and 10 countries in the top 30 importers. Additionally, all eight countries in the exporters list (Hong Kong, China, Korea, Singapore, Taiwan, Australia, Thailand and Malaysia) are present in the importers list. The Asian region is well involved in trading commercial services in the international arena. This reflects not only the importance of services as a trade instrument in the Asian environment, but also the world-class level of infrastructure and quality associated with services in Asia.

Table 2.4 Services exports and needs in LDCs, 2002

Service	Exporting LDC	Potential importing LDC
Business support	Djibouti, Ethiopia, Madagascar, Mozambique, Nepal	All other LDCs
Energy	Bhutan, Cambodia, Uganda, Zambia, Mauritania, Tanzania	Benin, Burkina Faso, Guinea, Madagascar, Mozambique
Free trade areas	Djibouti, Vanuatu, Bangladesh	Gambia, Mozambique, Malawi
Health care	Tanzania, Uganda	Burkina Faso, Bangladesh, Ethiopia, Malawi
Back office	Bangladesh, Madagascar, Uganda	Djibouti, Mauritania, Mozambique, Nepal, Tanzania

Source: Adapted from International Trade Centre, 'Japan: New outreach, at home and abroad', *International Trade Forum*, issue 3, 2002, p. 16.

Services trade and developing countries

While developed economies and regions dominate services, developing countries are becoming more significant in their involvement in services. This is particularly evidenced in specialised aspects of services, such as 'back-office' operations. Since 1990, the growth in the export of services from developing economies has been 50 per cent higher than that from developed market economies, an annual growth of 10.5 per cent compared to 6.9 per cent. Developing countries account for approximately one quarter of global exports of services, and their share is expected to continue to grow (International Trade Centre, 2002a). The level of service exports is probably higher than official statistics record, because of the difficulties of collecting accurate data and the lack of prominence given to services exports by trade reporting bodies and governments alike.

A number of developing countries have achieved success in exporting services. Nepal, Haiti, Madagascar and Bangladesh have considerable back-office operations services for foreign clients. Consulting firms in developing countries are also working successfully for donor agencies – for example, a Vietnamese law firm assisting the implementation of an Australian aid project in Hanoi. The International Trade Centre indicates that there are significant complementarities between services exported by less developed countries (LDCs) and services needed by other LDCs. This suggests that there is a significant scope for increased trade in services among LDCs. Table 2.4 summarises these complementarities.

The following illustrative case from Bangalore, India, presents a vivid example of the role that developing or emerging economies are playing in services.

Box 2.1   Silicon Valley revisited

Bangalore is part of the impetus for research and development (R&D) in the technology boom. Intel's new US$25 million complex, aimed at designing new computer chips and employing 950 engineers on 24-hour shifts, is competing with Sun Microsystems' development of a centre for servers expected to employ 400 engineers.

At the same time, Texas Instruments, Cadence, Analog Devices and Cisco are rapidly expanding design centres for telecom products. In the software side of business, SAP has developed new applications for notebook PCs at its 500-engineer facility, and Oracle's 2,400-strong centre is generating products such as the Oracle Student System. In total, Bangalore is approaching the scale of many US centres. Since the beginning of 2001, 230 multinationals have set up shop in the city's industrial parks, employing about 25,000 engineers. Initially, back in the 1980s, multinationals took advantage of India's pool of low-cost, well-trained, English-speaking technicians to set up software code-writing operations. In the 1990s this developed into back-office centres for handling everything from billing queries to credit card applications. Now, Bangalore is turning into a strategic base for genuine R&D.

(*Source:* Adapted from M. Kripalani, 'Silicon Valley revisited', *Australian Financial Review*, 8 November 2002, p. 81)

As discussed in Chapter 1, most services are by their nature intangible and thus, technically, non-tradable. For a service transaction to take place, there needs to be an interaction between the supplier (producer) and the client (consumer). Cross-border services would only be an option where the required level of supplier–client interaction exists. A Malaysian transport company delivering goods from Kuala Lumpur to Bangkok, for example, will require insurance cover on its vehicle while it is in Thailand. The Malaysian insurance company will provide its service in Thailand, because of its existing local policy with the transport company.

An assumed need for proximity underscores a preference for the local supply of services over the export or import of services. In general, someone needing medical treatment would visit the local doctor, or hospital, rather than consult a doctor for hospital treatment in another country. However, in the case of specialist medical treatment, patients might consider options for treatment in other countries (for example, specialist medical clinics in Singapore and Australia). A particular case in point is the treatment of victims of the Bali bombing in 2002 in Australian hospitals. Emphasising another macro global/local service provision dimension, the Interflora service is based on the order being placed at a local florist in one country, while a local florist in another country delivers the flowers.

Regulation of services trade

Existing trade barriers in various forms are generally more focused on goods than on services. Local content requirements, transport and packaging preferences, and health regulations are aimed at goods, but could easily exclude service providers from doing business in the specific country. An American physiotherapist proposing to set up a practice in Singapore would need to have his or her qualifications and expertise assessed, and be registered with the local medical board, before starting to practise and treat patients. Notwithstanding the impact of this regulatory environment, many and varied forms of cross-border trade in services now operate successfully. The use of insurance policies for travel, trade, investment and tourism across borders is one example of the diversity of services covered by one industry in an international arena. Similarly, the export of education on a worldwide scale has turned into a financially attractive industry, and it is possible for variously located prospective students to choose to enrol in courses at, for example, the London School of Economics, the Australian Curtin University of Technology or the Open University of Hong Kong.

The regulation and deregulation in trade of services received prominence when services were included in the negotiations of the Uruguay Round of the General Agreement on Tariffs and Trade (GATT), concluded in 1995. The subsequent establishment of the World Trade Organisation (WTO) covers the General Agreement on Trade in Services (GATS), which regulates trade in services (WTO, 2002).

In an attempt to accommodate the large diversity of trade and the modes in which they are exported, GATS groups international interaction between suppliers and clients in four groups:

1 **Cross-border supply** covers the flow of services from one country to another (for example, banking or architectural services transmitted via telecommunication systems).
2 **Consumption abroad** refers to situations where a client moves to another country to obtain the service (for example, tourism, ship repair or aircraft maintenance).
3 **Commercial presence** implies that a service supplier of one country establishes a presence in another country (for example, car rental).
4 **Presence of natural persons**, where service providers move between countries (for example, teachers, accountants or doctors). (WTO, n.d.)

GATS is based on the most favoured nation (MFN) principle, market access and national treatment. GATS schedules cover 12 sectors (WTO, n.d.):

- business services;
- communication services;
- construction and engineering services;
- distribution services;
- education services;
- environmental services;
- financial services;
- health services;
- tourism and travel services;
- recreational, cultural and sporting services;
- transport services; and
- other services not included elsewhere.

There are 155 sub-sectors, and the commitment to GATS is country-specific. This implies that the extent and conditions under which GATS principles apply to a country will differ from country to country, and from sector to sector. The library sector is one example of a sector newly added to the GATS discussions. Although most countries' libraries do not operate as service businesses, and interest in further developing a trading business approach is limited, Japan and the United States have put forward a request to export library services in the future. In pursuing a trading services model, Japanese and American libraries will be exposed to higher levels of trade and, hence, be subject to the GATS regulations more than countries that are not opening up their library services to trade (Ericson, 2003).

Figure 2.1 The integrated services management (ISM) model

Globalisation and services

Figure 2.1 presents the ISM model, which underpins the ideas presented throughout this book. As the model indicates, the powerful and dynamic processes of globalisation variously shape the macro context in which services now operate. Hence, the reality of globalisation presents important issues that service managers must address. There are many different interpretations of the term 'globalisation'. For the marketer (see Chapter 5), globalisation may mean the promotion of a single product range, while in the communications industry it indicates the opportunity to communicate across national and language boundaries; in the tourism environment it means that tourists have access to more international destinations, while the investment banker has easier access to any stock exchange in the world. The implication of these industry perspectives is that the processes of globalisation contribute to an increasing volume of flow and counter-flow of people, finance, ideas and products. While there is much debate about the political and socio-cultural implications of globalisation, there is widespread consensus about the economic reality of globalisation, understood to involve the worldwide integration of global economic activities. In particular, the global economy is concentrated in the business activities of approximately 63,000 multinationals operating all over the world, and represented by about 700,000 foreign affiliates (Hill, 2002). Since globalisation means different things to different people, it is important to take into consideration the diverse academic and community interpretations of the phenomenon.

The powerful economic dimension of globalisation essentially derives from significant private-sector business activity in pursuit of competitive advantage based on economies of scale, lower production costs and larger market shares. Irrespective of the diverse nature of interpretations of the phenomenon of globalisation, its dynamic and complex influences cannot be ignored. There are many definitions of globalisation that variously emphasise different economic, political and socio-cultural aspects. However, Held et al. (1999, p. 16) offer a definition of globalisation that has important implications for the services activities of international organisations:

> A process, or set of processes, which embodies a transformation in the spatial organisation of social relations and transactions . . . generating transcontinental or interregional flows and networks of activity, interaction and the exercise of power.

This definition is useful for its emphasis on the *dynamic processes* associated with social relations, transactions, interaction, networks and the exercise of power. These represent crucial factors for services management to understand – for example, an airline servicing international routes cannot afford to fly without global alliances, or partners, or to ignore the practice of code-sharing that allows economies of scale among the partners. Similarly, in the overall tourism sector there is a strong drive for partnerships and associations that promote client loyalty by allocating membership points to the use of associated hotel, travel and car hire bookings. Membership of the Intercontinental Hotel chain's priority regular guest program allows customers to earn frequent flyer points on their preferred 'One World' airline carrier. A night in Singapore could, for example, translate in Qantas frequent flyer points. Another sector severely affected by the characteristic emphasis on the dynamic nature of relationships, transactions and networks in the context of the globalisation of the services environment is the banking sector, as demonstrated in Box 2.2.

Box 2.2   US banks retreat from Europe

The New York Stock Exchange-listed CIT finance group completed the biggest initial public offering (IPO) of stock in the United States in 2002 and collected fees of about US$180 million, or 4 per cent of the total raised. A similar exercise in France resulted in the banks netting only 1.5 per cent of the raised money. The difference between what the intermediaries were paid in the United States and in Europe is a disparity that is mirrored across many investment banking products, and is partly to blame for the US securities firms' retreat from Europe. The lower fee environment in Europe signals that a recovery there in the financial business sector could be slower and weaker than in the United States. A few years ago, US banks foresaw a different climate. Back then, the population and economic size of Europe was roughly the same as in the United States. Citigroup, Merrill Lynch, Goldman Sachs and others ventured into Europe in anticipation that the traditionally lower European fees would come in line with those in the United States, or that the volume of business they would generate would compensate for the lower rates. 'Everyone expanded into Europe believing that it was the place to be,' says Wilco Jiskoot, an ABN Amro banker. 'Now, the US banks are withdrawing capacity the fastest.' Unlike in the United States, where the industry is dominated by a few big banks, in Europe far more banks are chasing deals, and most of them are willing to accept lower fees. In addition, European banks such as Paribas and Dresdner have age-old connections and shareholdings in domestic companies that give them an edge over their US rivals.

(*Source:* Adapted from P. Beckett and E. Portanger, 'US banks retreat from EU', *Australian Financial Review*, 21 May 2003, p. 24)

Interpretations of globalisation

Given the importance of social relations, transactions, interaction, networks and the exercise of power in understanding the dynamic nature of globalisation, there are also different responses to its nature and impacts. Kirkbride (2001) offers four different responsive approaches: globalist, scepticist, transformationalist and anti-globalist.

Globalist approach: Globalisation is here to stay

This approach acknowledges the existence of globalisation and supports the idea that it will have a significant future impact. This view also argues that different stages related to the evolving nature of the global activities of business are identifiable. The dynamic nature and characteristics of these evolving stages are explained in Table 2.5.

Scepticist approach: Globalisation doesn't exist

This approach basically argues that globalisation cannot be defined, or articulated, in terms of its nature and, thus, is a myth. Scepticists use a range of historical, economic and political arguments to support this interpretation. The following ideas are included in this approach:

- Globalisation took place previously in the 1860s during the era of early development of modern industrial technology.
- The concentration of global investment and trade in services is predominantly in the developed world, and there is a limited involvement of the developing world. The driving economic forces are still states and markets.
- The power of developed nation governments is reinforced.
- Globalisation is no different from regionalisation or internationalisation, and the future could well hold a clash of regional blocs.

In other words, the globalisation trend is not something new, it does not occur all over the world, and it is potentially damaging.

Transformationalist approach: Globalisation does exist, but is more complex

This approach argues as follows:

- Globalisation represents an unprecedented level of global interconnectedness.
- Government powers are reconstituted.
- Globalisation leads to a 'new world order', in that it transforms political communities.
- The outcome will lead to simultaneous global integration and fragmentation.

Table 2.5 Stages of globalisation

	Stage 1	Stage 2	Stage 3	Stage 4
Industry evolution	Early globalisers believe in first mover advantages	Industry favours global players; lead players increase global presence; other players consider globalising	Industry consolidates in global, regional and niche players; global strategies increase in importance	Industry dominated by 4–10 players; intangibles competition, increased importance of non-market forces
Example	Legal services, real estate agents	Financial services	Airline industry	Consultancy firms
Actions	Visionaries lead	Alliances and acquisitions	Integrate acquired companies in global organisation	Develop a learning organisation
Issues	Regulatory, political hurdles; competitive reaction; building global skills and resources; timing the global strategy launch	Identify globalisation logic, market similarities; develop brand and positioning strategy; identify strategic partners and develop relevant processes	Increase global efficiencies; develop a global organisation	Attract, develop and retain global talent; develop processes to manage non-market factors

Source: Adapted from P. Kirkbride (ed.), *Globalisation: The external pressures*, Ashridge, Chichester, UK, 2001.

The transformationalist approach emphasises the diverse and dynamic ways in which the flow and counter-flow processes that derive from the increased movement of people, products and ideas result in complex global and local economic, political and societal transformation.

Anti-globalist approach: Globalisation exists and we don't like it

This approach considers globalisation to be a phenomenon with predominantly negative consequences. These consequences include:

- increased inequality between nations;
- key institutions (such as the International Monetary Fund (IMF), World Bank, WTO) and transnational corporations (TNCs) work only with the elite; and
- the free market policies promoted by the IMF and the World Bank are inappropriate and ineffective.

Criticisms of globalisation from this anti-globalist perspective include arguments that the poorest 50 countries in the world make up 10 per cent of the world population, but account for only 0.4 per cent of world trade, which is a decline of more than 40 per cent since 1980 (UNCTAD, 2001). In services it is argued that water privatisation, for example, has more negative than positive consequences. In addition, the privatisation of the water supply has meant more expensive and lower-quality water for some poorer communities. The following examples support this perspective: in Puerto Rico, water privatisation in 1995 led to water supplies being cut in poorer communities, while holiday resorts enjoyed a continuous supply; and in Argentina, the privatisation of water services was reversed after outrage over poorer quality and the doubling of prices (GATT, n.d.).

Irrespective of the approach one has towards globalisation, the reality is that service providers and their clients are affected by its presence. Hence, understanding the concept of globalisation, and the diverse responses to it, is critical for services managers. These various responses to globalisation have important implications for stakeholder management (see Chapter 3). In addition, key drivers or pressures/issues allow globalisation to play such an important role.

Drivers of globalisation

The overall presence and persistence of globalisation suggests that it is driven by some strong environmental and/or systemic issues. A term that is increasingly being used to refer to the interdependent characteristics of globalisation is 'the technology revolution', or 'technoglobalism'. Technoglobalism also refers to the role that technological advancement plays in building global interdependence. In most instances, it is difficult to identify whether globalisation drives technological innovation, or technological innovation drives globalisation. This makes the cause–result relationship very ambiguous. However, there is no doubt that modern telecommunications systems facilitate the establishment of subsidiaries, or the effective interaction between alliance business partners – for example, when mutual access to electronic booking details facilitates code-sharing between Qantas and British Airways. Telecommunications also lower the time and space barriers to interaction that previously made it very difficult to do business. The use of the Internet, for example, makes a message available the instant the sender sends it. Communication between a university lecturer and students in different countries has changed from having to allow for mailing time to instant contact. The delivery of educational material and the submission of assignments are now not hampered by differences in location and time zones. This reality allows people to communicate across vast distances, at a very low cost, and with dramatically reduced time cost. Similarly, Internet-facilitated services are available around the clock. Clients can book airline tickets, hotel rooms and rental cars at any time of the day or night, irrespective of their location.

Other drivers that facilitate globalisation are relevant to a specific environment in which a business functions. These drivers can be grouped as *market drivers, cost drivers, government and economic drivers* and *competitive drivers*. These environmental drivers are listed in Table 2.6.

From the examples presented in Table 2.6, it is apparent that globalisation presents numerous services business opportunities. These opportunities include increased demand for new and innovative service products, and business access to diverse global markets. Hence, the link can be made between the driving forces of globalisation and the dramatic growth of services. However, the global business environmental complexities present significant challenges for services managers. The rapid nature of changes instigated by globalisation creates

Table 2.6 Environmental drivers

Market drivers
- *Common customer needs*: Mobile telephone customers use identical services everywhere in the world.
- *Product awareness and preference*: Bali, Phuket and Langkawi are well-known tourist destinations.
- *Potential for parallel imports*: Mauritius provides a 'one-stop shop' back-office service for international investors (legal, finance, insurance).
- *Global customers*: Australian universities attract students from all over the world.
- *Global channels*: HSBC banking branches and services are available throughout the world.
- *Transferable promotion mix*: hotels promote individually, as part of packaged deals and frequent user packages.

Cost drivers
- *Global economies of scale*: Increasing numbers of broadband users of the Internet in Singapore push down individual cost.
- *Global sourcing efficiencies*: India has adopted a major role in providing IT back-office operations.
- *Low logistics costs*: Car owners have their cars serviced in local workshops.
- *Fast-changing technology*: Third-generation (3G) mobile phones push the boundaries of the wireless communication industry.

Government and economic drivers
- *Policies promoting services trade*: Joint research among nations to combat the SARS epidemic.
- *Integration of world capital markets*: Political leadership in Malaysia contributes to a significant flow of investment.
- *Compatible technical/environmental standards*: Ecotourism develops an environmental awareness on top of the tourism experience.
- *Deregulation*: Australian universities are allowed to enrol full fee-paying Australian students to achieve economies of scale.

Competitive drivers
- *Globalised competitors*: Airlines form joint ventures and use code-sharing as a competitive strategy.
- *Transferability of competitive advantage*: Tracking technology used for tracking vehicles for insurance purposes.

Source: Adapted from G. Yip, *Total Global Strategy: Managing for worldwide competitive advantage*, Prentice Hall, Englewood Cliffs, NJ, 1995.

environmental instabilities and uncertainties, the implications of which services managers must grapple with in order to be competitive, sustain advantages and manage risk.

The dynamic global services context has significant implications for stakeholder management (see Chapter 3), the strategic management of competitive advantage (Chapter 4), marketing (Chapter 5), operational management (Chapter 6), financial management (Chapter 7) and HR management (Chapter 8). Thus, managers of each of these areas must understand the implications of globalisation and account for these in their specific functional areas. Moreover, the integration of these understandings into a services management model is crucial for the operation of services in a global business context. While some organisations are still trying to come to terms with the dramatic changes of recent history, with the rapid nature of change under the influences of globalisation, successful services managers will need to understand and be able to predict future directions.

Future trends

A credo among successful players in the business world is: 'Either we take hold of the future, or the future will take hold of us.' Anticipated trends in future globalisation can be explained by the acronym FUTURE, which derives from the ideas associated with the following concepts: Fast, Urban, Tribal, Universal, Radical and Ethical (Dixon, 2000). Dixon argues that these concepts will have increasing impact on the environment within which service providers operate. These concepts can be summarised individually as follows.

Fast

The notion of 'fast' refers to the rapid acceleration of economic, political, technological and social changes. As experienced on 11 September 2001 and again on 12 October 2002, with the terrorist attacks on New York and Bali, the environment within which one operates can change profoundly within a short period of time. Hence, market research (see Chapter 5) cannot predict the future in a rapidly changing world – it just indicates what consumers think now. Business success requires a wider and longer vision. The impact of the digital society, networking, e-commerce, virtual reality and speech recognition technology also continues to change consumer behaviour. In the communications industry, the functions and attributes of mobile telephones render an instrument as technologically 'old' after six months. This rapid redundancy, in turn, impacts on pricing. The decision to purchase an instrument with specific functions at a specific price will inevitably be regretted a few months later when a newer version, with more functions, is available at a lower price. Similarly, communication via digital technology is adopted by some universities as a mode of keeping students and staff continuously informed. As a result, investment in university buildings beyond the reach of a diversely located, but digitally connected student body is less useful, and hence, may be classed as inefficient, or even obsolete, in the newly set tertiary education environment. The question for services is: *How will people adopt, adapt and survive accelerating change?*

Urban

Big demographic and social shifts affect every aspect of consumer behaviour with, for example, the increasing ageing and wealth of sectors of urban populations. The competition for talent, the increased numbers of women in the paid workforce, the growth of mega-cities, and a host of other factors, will have additional important effects on the dynamic nature of markets for services. Population decline and the lack of opportunities in rural and remote locations contribute to market decline. Services are often driven by economies of scale. Setting up hospital facilities, or specialised medical services, is dependent on the number of patients in need of these services. In a country like Australia, with a small population density in rural areas, the availability of specialist medical services is concentrated in larger cities, and so in response to low demand for services some smaller towns have visiting dentists and optometrists. These market-based societal characteristics are fundamental in determining the future shape of service delivery and availability. Decisions on the provision of service delivery sometimes have to be based on the reconciliation of often-competing public interest and profitability objectives. In rural areas, profitability may need to be subsidised, or reduced, while the large scale of the market in urban areas implies automatic returns.

Tribal

While an increasingly globalised world presents a homogeneous (shared) view of reality, tribalism presents heterogeneous (diverse) community views. Tribal communities may share collective values and behaviours based around ethnicity, religion, and other socio-cultural demographic factors, such as age, gender, occupation and interests, Tribalism is a powerful worldwide force. Tribalism underpins hundreds of conflicts and tensions across the world. The ongoing conflict between Catholics and Protestants in Northern Ireland, the language differences between English and French Canadians, and the ethnic differences between Chinese, Indian and *Bumiputera* (indigenous) Malaysians, are simple examples of the diverse community identity issues associated with tribalism.

For service providers, the specific marketing opportunities of tribalism can be a huge positive force. Niche branding and product/service loyalty strategies reflect the marketing opportunities tribalism presents (see Chapter 5). Every successful service creates a 'tribe', and every successful organisation thus becomes a 'tribe' on its own. For example, loyalty towards Holiday Inn hotels as a brand will inevitably be built on customer perceptions of sustained good service, which in turn ensures future bookings around the world (see Chapter 4). Knowledge of tribalism can be used to productively build strong teams, corporate identity, people movements and product lines. The key to successful mergers is to understand the role and impact of tribal culture and tribal leadership. In developing the tribal logic underpinning the corporate culture and leadership model of the Virgin brand, Richard Branson seeks to ensure that the staff have a positive attitude towards their employer and customers, and this sets Virgin apart from other service providers in the travel, communications and financial services.

Universal

The establishment of global super-brands creates pressures to manage global operations more effectively on a uniform logic by using new technologies and the emergence of virtual teams and companies. Daylight is the largest barrier to a universal 24-hours-a-day operation model for the global village. Globalisation alters the shape of all large corporations as competitors realign through rapid mergers, acquisitions, disposals or new partnerships. In this context, diverse reactions to globalisation in its current form need to be understood. Although traditionally multinationals are perceived to be producers of goods, services has increasingly also turned into a universal environment. After almost 50 years in business, Andersen Consulting changed its image to the global corporate image of Accenture. This image change is supported by a larger scope of services offered. Accenture is positioning itself as a 'one-stop shop' for multiple business services. Operating on a similar universal corporate basis, investment banking institutions now hold property interests around the world and act as landlords in the provision of office space and facilities.

The adoption of universal operation systems facilitated by new technologies creates convenience and opportunities, and builds business efficiencies. However, managers need to be aware of the cultural implications of applying universal systems in diverse operational contexts. For example, there is widespread acceptance of English as the language of international business. English may be accepted as the official global language, but in reality diverse forms of 'English' are used around the world. This pluralistic linguistic reality has significant implications for communications management, stakeholder management, competitive advantage, operations, marketing and HR management. The universal application of knowledge and information systems has similar intercultural management implications. Hence, it is critical for services managers to understand the cultural assumptions (predominantly Western) underpinning the universal business systems operations in order to be able to assess their efficiencies and effectiveness when applied in different locations.

Radical

The decreasing differentiation between left and right politics, and reduced government power, make corporations increasingly vulnerable to a growing number of radical single-issue groups. The rising number of radical and resistive single-issue groups has resulted in the cooperative development of powerful, but often disparate, community-based interest and non-government organisation (NGO) pressure groups. Their radical activities, also facilitated across time and space by digital communication technology, have significant implications for the management of services. Examples of radical interest groups include: genetic engineering and biotech foods, animal welfare and cosmetic product testing, child labour in the textiles industry, and unfair coffee trade with developing nations (pro-fair, not 'free' trade). In September 1999, more than 50 years after the end of the Second World War, the Simon Wiesenthal Center in Los Angeles announced a claim for Holocaust restitution. Under these claims, Swiss, Swedish, French and British banks and insurance companies were said to be responsible for illegally controlling financial assets forcibly turned over by Jews to the Gestapo. In response to this legal outcome, the Swiss Bankers Association (Swiss Bankers Association, n.d.) established a claims process in 2001 providing an opportunity to make claims to assets deposited in Swiss banks in the period before, and during, the Second World War.

The radical elements in the business environment must be addressed by services managers. These radical elements represent important stakeholder management issues (see Chapter 3), which have implications for risk management. Settlement of the 50-year-old case presented above indicates the longevity of risk implications for managers. However, knowledge of the radical elements in the global community can also present services with corporate marketing opportunities as being businesses that promote ethical, environmental, and sustainable products and services which, in turn, can create competitive advantage (see Chapters 4 and 5). Thus, it is important to remember that while in some instances radical community elements represent resistance to change, the activities of other radical groups may promote positive change and innovation that offer new value-adding business opportunities.

Ethical

Personal values, ethics, motivation and spirituality are all value issues that are becoming key concerns for large corporations. Retaining and motivating key executives needs more than money. The start of the 21st century has seen the collapse of a number of huge service institutions, such as Enron in the United States and HIH in Australia. The collapse of these service businesses has been attributed to the prevalence of unethical corporate behaviour. There are now calls for corporations to inspire, encourage and build a sense of family, even a better world. What is coming next? Where do corporate values come from, and what are global ethics? The key to success is to be able to show how your services contribute to a better kind of world, not only for individuals and their families, but also for the community-at-large and the whole of humanity. Thus, there is now increasing pressure on business to adopt the sustainability 'triple-bottom-line' (economic, social and environmental) corporate performance assessment approach. This reality has significant implications for stakeholder management in services (see Chapter 3).

Most businesses see the world as fast, urban and universal – but how many people in a nation need to be radical, ethical and tribal in order to change their world? Some financial advisory services are now specialising in 'ethical' investment portfolios. Organic food production and services represents an important growing sector. Industry partnerships are being established with indigenous Aboriginal communities in Australia, who are developing sustainable indigenous natural resource-based enterprises to serve an increasingly sophisticated international urban cuisine and cosmetic market. The telecommunications industry realises that economies of scale can only be derived from a healthy market segment, reliable and speedy service, and a global network. However, few have yet gone so far as to segment the market, worry about health and privacy concerns, and develop and promote voice transmission via the Internet. These examples highlight the importance of services managers being able to assess the positive and negative ways in which radical, ethical and tribal issues may impact on their particular services.

Regionalism and the services environment

The introduction of services in the WTO environment has led to an increased focus on services in regional trade agreements. Regionalism is sometimes referred to as regional integration, and it represents an agreement between countries in a particular region to reduce barriers to trade and services in order to allow the free flow of goods and services. The trend towards regionalism is popular, and regional arrangements are spread all over the world. Probably the best-known agreements are the EU, the North American Free Trade Agreement (NAFTA), the Association of South East Asian Nations (ASEAN) and the Asia Pacific Economic Cooperation (APEC), but there is a vast list of others. In general, it is anticipated that the benefits derived from the reduction of obstacles will exceed the potential disadvantages associated with the agreement by giving all participants improved trading conditions after the agreements are activated. The following illustrative cases discuss the background and implications of examples of Asian and European regional agreements.

Box 2.3 Singaporean–Australian Free Trade Area

An appropriate example of a free trade agreement with a services focus is the Singaporean–Australian Free Trade Area (SAFTA). Traditionally, regional trade agreements such as the EU and NAFTA focus on the reduction of barriers to trade in goods. Similarly, the SAFTA agreement, signed in late 2002, eliminates tariffs on all goods traded between Singapore and Australia. However, from an Australian perspective, the benefits of SAFTA are in the services area. Australian service suppliers and investors in sectors such as legal, financial and professional services, telecommunications, education and environmental services will be the main beneficiaries of the agreement. Changes in regulations at the Singaporean end of the agreement include the following:

- *Financial services:* An easing of restrictions on the number of wholesale banking licences granted to Australian institutions.
- *Legal services:* An easing on restrictions for practising law in Singapore.
- *Education:* Australian institutions will be subject to the same regulations as Singaporean institutions.
- *Professional services:* Residency requirements for Australians will be eased.
- *Telecommunications:* Changes to Singaporean competition regulations will make the Singaporean industry more accessible for Australian firms.

(*Source:* Adapted from M. Davis, 'Pact lowers hurdles, keeps safeguards', *Australian Financial Review*, 4 November 2002, p. 6)

Box 2.3 indicates the implications for services stakeholders in the Asian region of a free trade agreement between two nations. Box 2.4 describes the impact of regional agreements in Europe and their impact on stakeholders of services.

Box 2.4 The European Union

The most advanced area in terms of regional integration is the EU. The establishment of the single European market in 1993 set up a market of 430 million customers and facilitated the introduction of a single currency in 2002. The implications of this level of integration for services are multiple. Formerly protected and regulated markets were opened to an easily comparable competition. In addition, industries were simplified from 15 national markets to a single market, allowing economies of scale and cost efficiencies to materialise. The reality in Europe is, however, that significant cultural and ethnic differences still impact on market demands and service delivery and, thus, create the need for service diversification. The increased competition, however, also threatens profit margins and the market share of service providers, as was the case in the European insurance industry.

In mid-1994, the EU insurance industry was deregulated and liberalised. In 2002, the EU adopted a single currency, thereby facilitating the comparison of products across borders and service providers. Traditionally, the insurance markets were heavily regulated and there was a wide variation of competitive conditions and prices. A 10-year life policy in Portugal, for instance, was three times as expensive as the same policy in France. Insurance on a vehicle was twice as expensive in Ireland as in Italy, and four times as expensive compared to Britain. The single market concept for the first time allowed cross-border sales and marketing, and removed local approval for wording and pricing of insurance products. It took service providers in the insurance industry until about mid-1996 to realise the impact of the single market on their competitiveness and profit margins.

The reaction of the industry was an overwhelming trend to merge with similar companies in other countries. In 1996, two French companies, AXA and UAP, merged, resulting in a substantial control of the German market held by UAP. In 1997, the merger between the German insurer, Allianz, and the French insurer, AGF, was successful after Allianz maintained a French identity and management for its AGF branches. The Italian insurer, Generali, was involved in the Allianz–AGF merger by means of a takeover bid and withdrew only after the German and French companies agreed to sell a number of important subsidiaries, thus allowing Generali to become established in the German and French market. Since then, Allianz has strengthened its position by entering Belgium and Spain, and has established the largest pan-European insurance company.

(*Source*: Adapted from C. W. L. Hill, 'Postscript 2002', *Global Business*, 2nd ed., McGraw-Hill Irwin, Boston, 2002)

Most of the instability in the world in the late 1990s and early 21st century is regional in nature. The impact of events in the Southeast Asian region has been considerable. The Asian financial crisis impacted severely on the Southeast Asian economies, such as Thailand, Indonesia and Malaysia. The financial crisis emerged as a result of extensive borrowing by the banking sector in Thailand, but with the rapid flight of foreign investment, it quickly spread to the financial sector throughout neighbouring regional countries (Malaysia and Indonesia). Consequently, there was a significant regional economic slowdown as investors lost confidence in the former 'Asian Tiger' economies (Singapore, Hong Kong, South Korea and Taiwan) that had performed so well in the early 1990s. With the rapid flight of foreign investment, the banking sector in these economies came to a sudden standstill. Significant restructuring of these nations' banking sectors was then required to rebuild regional confidence.

The US and Bali terrorist attacks in 2001 and 2002, respectively, contributed to greater global and regional economic destabilisation, and the development of a significant military 'War on Terror' response by the Allied nations. The attack in Bali had particularly severe consequences for one of the best internationally known and high occupation-rate tourist destinations. Tourism in the region experienced a significant downturn. In addition, the SARS virus that engulfed southern China, Hong Kong and Singapore in 2003 hit the travel industry and health services hard. These traumatic events contributed to increased pressures on airline services, health-care and airport services, which have been forced to operate in a significantly different service delivery market and environment. Box 2.5 outlines a specific corporate airline industry response to the dramatically altered regional service delivery environment through the destabilising events such as terrorism and SARS.

Box 2.5   British Airways

British Airways joined a growing list of airlines that warned of a bleak outlook for the future after making a loss in the last quarter of 2002. Shareholders were not expected to be paid dividends for the 2003 fiscal year, despite a £72 million profit following a £142 million loss in the previous financial year. The BA chairman at the time claimed that the industry climate of a continuing global economic downturn, SARS and instability in the Middle East made forecasting revenue very difficult and 'visibility beyond the next quarter not clear'. BA's CEO, Rod Eddington, described the first three months of 2003 as like 'flying into a pretty stiff headwind'. To cope with the downturn, BA was expected to continue to slash costs. Its 'future size and shape' program was to slash 13,000 jobs by September 2003, and it was well on its way with 10,000 jobs already slashed. In addition, reducing capacity and ditching unprofitable routes contributed to £570 million of cost savings.

BA has had to retire its seven supersonic airplanes (Concordes) because insufficient passengers are willing to pay the higher fares needed to cover maintenance costs. Like many of its rivals, BA is slashing fares by as much as 60 per cent in an attempt to attract jittery passengers, resulting in a fall of their yield by 7.5 per cent. BA is one of many international airlines using lower prices and staff retrenchment to cope with the slump in travel that showed no signs of abating in mid-2003. Among these, Qantas has issued profit downgrades, Cathay Pacific has warned of the risk of running out of cash due to operating losses, and Singapore Airlines carried half the number of passengers in April 2003 that it had carried in April 2002.

(*Source:* Adapted from J. Boyle, 'BA flies into stiff headwind', *Australian Financial Review*, 20 May 2003, p. 16)

The national services environment

Traditionally, the most relevant environment within which any business has to function is the national environment, or, for a multinational organisation, the combination of multiple national environments. The national environment presents specific risks. For example, a change in health regulations will directly impact on the provision of services in that industry. The national environment comprises the specific political, economic, legal, technological, competitive and societal aspects of a country. Although it is useful to consider each aspect of the environment separately, in reality they are interdependent.

The political environment

Politics shape the interactions and functioning of any society. In practice, the political parties, ideologies, systems and structures by which a country is governed set the guiding parameters of the economy and society. From a commercial perspective, politics should be secondary to commercial interests, and too close a relationship between business and government is not considered to be an option. The stability of the government and its policies contributes to the risks associated with the political environment. For instance, the change of government in Ghana in 2000 led to a problem for the British bank HSBC. Earlier that year, the president of Ghana had authorised the finance minister to take out a loan to purchase a personal jet. HSBC treated the application as a commercial arrangement with the Ghanaian government and received the content of the Ghanaian UN accounts as security. When the new Kuofur government took office, it cancelled the repayments to HSBC and refused to use the jet. Due to the change in government, HSBC was forced to renegotiate the outstanding balance of about US$1 million (Pallister, 2003).

Additional dramatic political events that would increase the risk level are, for instance: a violent coup, a change in government with significant differences in ideology and thus policy implementation, the suppression of specific groups, and political groupings that reflect ethnic differences. Thus, cross-border service providers prefer a more stable political environment that ensures a status quo approach. In reality, new political leadership can present new opportunities and new threats. International players have to carefully assess the new environment, and devise plans to reduce the potential risks and tap into new opportunities resulting from that change.

As an example, the recent change in political leadership in Malaysia indicates the influence of a changing political environment. The strong performance of the newly elected prime minister of Malaysia, Abdullah Ahmad Badawi, has resulted in positive activity in the stock exchange due to a significant influx of foreign investment. His predecessor, Dr Mohammed Mahathir, was an outspoken statesman often characterised by extreme rhetoric and views in the international arena. On the local front, however, he failed to combat corruption and supported huge and expensive national projects. The handover to the more diplomatic and softly spoken Badawi was strengthened by a strong performance in the March 2004 election. This strong political mandate creates the kind of stability that is highly valued by foreign investors. With Malaysia being a moderate Islamic state practising liberal economic policies, foreign investment is encouraged further. In addition, the new prime minister's drive against corruption, demands for greater accountability and ethical governance, and cancellation of certain costly national projects, have all found the favour of foreign investors in services. Contrary to a previous poor performance by the Malaysian stock exchange in 2003, it reached a 46-month high in March 2004. This reflects a growth of 14 per cent in three months. Cheah Cheng Hye, chief investment officer of Hong Kong-based Value Partners Ltd, managing more than US$2 billion of investment in Malaysia, has indicated that Badawi's performance and attitude could address some pressing economic issues and propel the country and people to a higher level of prosperity (Moses, 2004).

The economic environment

Risks associated with the economic environment can invariably be linked to a government's political role and approach to managing the economy. The economic dimension of the national environment includes factors such as: the exchange rates, interest rates, unemployment, limitations to international trade, taxes and economic growth. All of these are directly, or indirectly, affected by government policy, or by regulations that frame specific goals and determine how these are to be achieved. In order to minimise the economic risk, service organisations will need to develop some form of assessment of the economic regulatory environment. In general, the stability of economic policy measures and indicators reflects the economic health of a country. The level of foreign investment essentially reflects the international level of confidence in an economy. Holt (2000) argues that there is a positive correlation between foreign investment and the economic growth rate of a country. These factors, in turn, lead to an increase in consumer expenditure and the establishment of a better tax base, which further stabilises the economy.

Another aspect of the economic environment is government involvement as a competitor in a specific industry. The involvement of governments in industries has reduced significantly over the past decade, and most governments have actively pursued the privatisation of government-owned industries. In some instances, however, the privatisation is limited to the business being registered as a private organisation, while the government retains control, or majority shares. One example of this in the telecommunications industry is Telstra in Australia, which is partly owned by the Australian government; another example is SingTel, which has the Singaporean government as its majority shareholder. The implication is that privately owned players in the telecommunications sector need to compete directly with government-owned players, who generally have a powerful network of contacts and potential influence in policy making. Another example is the Anglo-French train operator Govia, which signed a six-year franchise agreement to operate the English South Central commuter network. Part of the agreement is that Govia's profits are to be 'skimmed off' by the strategic rail authority once a certain level is achieved. At the same time, however, the company will receive £500 million of public subsidies over the six-year course of the deal (Clark, 2003).

The legal environment

In a similar vein to the economic environment, it is difficult to differentiate between the political and the legal environment. Although the legal system is separated from the political system to ensure an objective interpretation of legislation, the source of laws and regulations *is* the government itself. By introducing, altering, and abolishing laws and regulations, the government can directly affect the functioning of a commercial activity. The legal environment impacts far and wide on services. (For a more detailed discussion of the influence of the legal environment on HR management practices in services, see Chapter 8.)

The introduction of minimum wages, for instance, could render a profitable business venture unprofitable. Similarly, the introduction of new health regulations could close down, or limit, the activities of restaurants and fast-food outlets. Davidson and Griffin (2000) argue that there are three reasons why it is crucial to understand the legal/regulatory environment. First, the legal environment defines what an organisation can and cannot do. It establishes the limitations within which a service can be delivered and accepted. Second, government's sentiment towards the business sector is reflected in regulations. The price regulation of private health funds in Australia, for instance, reflects the government's belief that this sector should financially be tightly regulated. Third, intervention is not always an obvious and direct activity. It often builds through indirect and subtle regulations and controls that proliferate as a government becomes more bureaucratic. A complete ban on smoking in public places, for instance, could impact on the amount and frequency of patrons visiting their favourite restaurant. A lack of understanding of the legal environment holds the risk that commercial activities are disrupted in an attempt to comply with relevant regulations, or at worst, may be deemed illegal (see Box 2.6).

Box 2.6   HIH Royal Commission

A recent example of how the lack of regulations and subsequent re-establishment of rules impacts on an industry is the Royal Commission investigating the demise of HIH, the large Australian insurance company. The demise of HIH was partly attributed to unethical and/or illegal behaviour by its directors and executives. The role of the HIH Royal Commission was to identify shortcomings and propose renewed regulations to avoid similar occurrences in the future. The recommendations by the commission are multiple and stretch beyond the role of executives and directors. Interest groups have objected to some of the reforms, including:

- state Governments, who would lose their capacity to collect stamp duties from general insurance products;
- global reinsurers, who object to the changes and proposed stricter Australian accounting standards;
- lawyers, who fear the extended liability of corporate managers and senior personnel stretching to external advisers; and
- accountants, who criticise the proposed compulsory rotation of audit teams every five years.

The general criticism against the Royal Commission proposal is the notion that every service is expected to be itemised.

(*Source:* Adapted from F. Buffini, A. Hepworth and M. Priest, 'Business hits back over HIH reforms', *Australian Financial Review*, 22 April 2003, pp. 1, 4)

The technological environment

Technology significantly impacts on the ways in which services are delivered. Essentially, technology is the tool, or method, used to convert resources into products or services. In the 21st century, technology plays an increasingly important role, especially in services. For instance, banks actively promote online banking in order to allow economies of scale and reduce face-to-face, and thus more costly, interactions. The supermarket checkout reads bar codes to identify the actual product bought, add its cost to the shopping list, update the stock in the store, and eventually, activate reordering of new stock. The airline industry uses highly sophisticated computer-controlled cockpit-simulators to allow training to take place in as real an environment as possible, while eliminating any risks. Travel agents use interactive websites to gather data and make bookings, at the same time facilitating the special needs and requests of travellers. In general, the collection, dissemination and interpretation of information in electronic format allows for a more personalised and better-focused mode of service delivery. Service providers can ill afford to be behind in the use of technology, from operational, marketing and service delivery perspectives.

Despite its international status as a leader in the mobile phone industry, Nokia seems to be losing ground as a result of changes in the technology environment. By April 2003, there was no so-called 3G Nokia instruments on the market, while Motorola and NEC had a strong market presence in the 3G sector of the industry. The purpose of 3G mobile telephones is to extend the service of mobile communications beyond voice calls to include downloading video and music files. Although the 3G handsets only form a tiny part of the world mobile phone industry, Nokia needs to remain involved in new commercial launches since these provide experience and market credibility. Nokia's networks division is now outperformed by its competitors and, as a result, it made a 127 million euro loss, compared with Siemens' loss of 22 million euro. Although the loss stems partly from the continuing high costs related to the first-phase implementation of 3G technologies, the company's delayed market entry is detrimental for Nokia's image, reputation and profitability (Pringle et al., 2003).

The competitive environment
Under the dynamic influences of globalisation and regionalisation, as discussed previously in this chapter, business increasingly faces new and more intensive competition. The opening up of markets and technological advancements introduces new players in industries all the time. The competitive environment can be summarised by considering the following five forces (Porter, 1980):
1 *The threat of new entrants* reflects the ease with which a competitor can enter the market. The owner of a pizza shop may experience a threat from a new Japanese restaurant opening next door. In a similar vein, private hospitals may be threatened by increased funding for public hospitals.
2 *Competitive rivalry* reflects the relationship between dominant players in the industry. The domestic airfare battle between Qantas and Virgin Blue in Australia has led to unprecedented price competition on domestic airfares. Virgin Blue has cut its operating costs by not offering complementary meals and drinks on flights and allowing passengers to bring their own. More recently, Qantas has established a new domestic competitor – Jetstar – in order to regain market share.
3 *The threat of substitute products* or lack thereof, indicates the potential exposure, and need to adapt. Travel agents are aware that the introduction of the Internet and, subsequently, the establishment of 'virtual' travel agents, threaten their role as an intermediary. In spite of the assumption that virtual travel agents will be able to take over the physical travel agent's role, to date travel agents have not been badly affected by the new developments. This may reflect generational transfer issues.
4 *The power of buyers* reflects the dependency on clients by a service provider. If service provision is limited to a specific and limited target market, a dependence relationship is established. For example, the rail network operating in the mining region in the north of Western Australia is highly dependent on the mining companies that send their ore to the harbour. Apart from the mining companies, the rail network does not really have any clients.
5 *The power of suppliers* reflects the dependence of a service user on the service provider. The shortage of water in Singapore, for instance, leads to a dependency relationship with the supplier of water (Malaysia). In early 2003, there was a significant amount of tension between Singapore and Malaysia because of this dependency relationship, and hence, the power here remains with Malaysia.

The more accurate and detailed the assessment of the competitive environment, the fewer the uncertainties. Since technology is often a significant component of service delivery, it is imperative in services that participants continuously update their assessment of the competitive environment.

The societal environment

The societal environment reflects the cultural, ethnic and religious background of a country. The way in which a society acts and reacts is deeply embedded in the customs, morals, values, beliefs and demographics of the society. These factors determine the criteria for acceptable, or offensive, goods, services and standards of conduct. The use of appropriate social behaviour in specific contexts will ensure acceptance, and thus, business success. Serving and consuming alcohol, for instance, are socially acceptable in Australia, while it may be offensive in certain regions of Indonesia and Malaysia. Societal behaviour determines not only customer expectations and behaviour, but it also impacts on the appropriateness and nature of the actual service provided. Europeans, for instance, are used to a certain standard of hygiene and cleanliness in their physical environment. As tourists they often anticipate and expect the same level of hygiene in the facilities provided to them. Accommodation and hospitality-related services in other parts of the world are often criticised, because they do not live up to the benchmark back home. Similarly, some Europeans may feel uncomfortable doing business in an environment where unofficial payments need to be made to facilitate a transaction or an authorisation. The mere insinuation of involvement in a bribe, or corrupt activity, would be highly unacceptable to them. This behaviour may be more acceptable in other countries for a diverse range of reasons. The risks associated with the societal environment mean that misinterpretations of service delivery can easily occur when providing services to diverse cultural, religious and ethnic communities.

Undertaking public relations work in Singapore, for example, posed a significant obstacle for Tom West, who was transferred from a New York public relations firm to head the Singaporean branch. His job in Singapore was to raise positive media awareness of companies before they went public. He had little success before he learned that the Singaporean media environment is diverse. This knowledge meant that he then understood that to effectively reach all potential investors, Chinese, Malay and Indian, in Singapore it is necessary to use a variety of ethnic media, not simply the largest, or the English-speaking press (Hill, 2002).

The country risk environment

To differentiate between the political, economic, legal, technological, competitive and societal aspects of the environment is of limited value, because importantly, it is the degree of interdependence between these that ultimately determines their significance in a specific national environment. Davidson and Griffin (2000) use the term 'environmental turbulence' to describe the level of interdependence of the various environmental factors. The most common form of turbulence is a crisis of some sort, an unanticipated circumstance, or outcome or behaviour with the potential for severe damage. The origin of such a crisis could be any of the above environments, and it will most likely be a combination of factors. This turbulence is also summarised in the concept of 'country risk'. Country risk can be defined as the level of uncertainty associated with government continuity, regional politics, ineffective legal and regulatory systems, economic instability and uncertainty, and ethnic and cultural clashes. An appropriate country risk analysis assesses the multiple aspects of the national environment, and attempts to allow for the interdependence between the various elements of the national environment.

Following are brief descriptions of three different illustrative cases that describe the complexity of various national environments. Box 2.7 presents a picture of the complex economic and political issues associated with government involvement in diverse service provision areas.

Box 2.7   Temasek in Singapore

Temasek is a holding company of the Singaporean government with interests ranging from banks to telecom and logistics. Temasek, or at least the companies it holds, has not been performing as well as expected and there is pressure from the government to increase efficiencies. The interests of Temasek in Singapore are huge, in that the so-called government-linked companies (GLC) in its stable make up by weight more than 40 per cent of the Straits Times Index. At the same time, the GLCs make up about 33 per cent of the market capitalisation of the Singapore Stock Exchange. Since Temasek was formed in 1974, its holdings have penetrated every key segment of the economy, from ports, telecoms, stockbroking and shipping to power, food, the media, logistics, airlines, engineering, property, health care, education, and even zoos and aviaries. Temasek's portfolio has become a tangled web of often-competing companies. Temasek, for instance, has holdings, indirect or direct, in all three of the big telecom operators, SingTel, StarHub and MobileOne. Although Temasek recently developed a new charter under which it will function, it will retain control of companies deemed critical to the economy, such as airports, seaports and utilities. It is also argued that Temasek needs a controlling stake in companies that enable the government to achieve specific policy objectives by providing services for the public good. Such companies would include gaming, public broadcasting, subsidised services in health care, education, housing, and public amenities such as the Singapore Zoo and Bird Park.

(*Source:* Adapted from S. Webb and T. Saywell, 'Untangling Temasek', *Far Eastern Economic Review*, 7 November 2002)

It is apparent that the Singaporean environment is significantly influenced by the role that Temasek is playing on behalf of the Singaporean government. As a service provider, it is important to take note of the critical role that Temasek plays in the competitive, economic and political aspects of the Singaporean economy.

Box 2.8   Interactive TV in Manila

In the Philippines, interactive TV, although in a low-tech way, has developed into a profitable and attractive service. The Philippines' communication sector has tapped into broadcasters to form an alliance that allows the development of a new communications medium. Mobile phone users can send SMS messages that are displayed on a split-screen TV. In a country too poor to sustain widespread Internet access,

Filipinos swap information and create entertainment by fusing two low-tech, but widely used networks. This technology boosts revenues of both broadcasters and mobile phone companies. The GSM association estimates that of the 24 billion SMS messages sent each month across the world, 4 billion originate in the Philippines, a country with only 12 million mobile phones. The two dominant cellular networks, GlobeTelcom and Smart Communications, estimate that SMS accounts for between 26 and 40 per cent of their overall revenues. A hybrid of this technology is a Manila-based company called Wireless Services Asia, which provides ring-tone and icons to mobile phone users as far away as Venezuela, Finland and China, all sent by SMS.

(*Source*: Adapted from J. Hookway, 'Texting the tube', *Far Eastern Economic Review*, 7 November 2002)

This 'new' technology developed in the Philippines is an example of how appropriate use of technology can create the opportunity for a 'new' mode of communication, and influence developments in the technological environment. At the same time, it creates a local competitive advantage for the broadcasting and mobile phone industry, and presents the possibility to internationalise the unique technology.

The interdependent links between the regulatory environment, the economic environment and the competitive environment are indicated in Box 2.9. The result is that there is a clear perception of non-performance of the involved parties. In the case of the service provider in the China National Offshore Oil Corporation example, postponement of the IPO was interpreted in the local social environment as a breach of trust.

Box 2.9 Privatisation in China

Recent experiences with privatisation in China have impacted on the banking and foreign direct investment sectors. China Telecom was planned to be privatised in a public offering of US$3.68 billion. A lack of interest from foreign investors has resulted in a scaled-down offer of US$1.66 billion, an amount that investment bankers Morgan Stanley find hard to cover. The flotation of China Telecom was to be the biggest stock offering from Asia in 2002, and the third biggest in the world that year. The expectation for an oversubscription was based on the privatisation of China's Bank of China (US$2.6 billion) in July 2002. The Bank of China was a first opportunity to buy into China's large state-sector banks, while China Telecom follows the listing of China Mobile and China Unicom in 1997 and 2000, respectively. In addition, both listed telecommunication players have performed poorly and experienced price declines exceeding 70 per cent. An additional problem in the listing is the unwillingness of China to sell state assets below their book price (irrespective of the market price), and the concern that China Telecom announced it had regulatory permission to drastically hike tariffs on international calls (which, in some instances, translates into a price increase of 750 per cent). Both concerns underline the high corporate and regulatory risk in China. The damage of the lowered listing is not limited to China Telecom, but also impacts on the investment bank. In a similar

situation where the China National Offshore Oil Corporation was forced to postpone its IPO, the lead manager of the deal, Salomon Smith Barney, struggled to get
a foot in the door on subsequent privatisation deals.

(*Source*: Adapted from T. Holland, 'The perils of privatisation', *Far Eastern Economic Review*, 14 November 2002)

These illustrative cases show the complexity and interrelatedness of variables affecting the
services environment. They indicate why it is crucial to consider the different environmental
impacts of key players, or stakeholders. Each national environment will have political parties,
for example, that will variously influence policies and regulations in which service organisations must operate. As the environment differs for different services segments, so will the
stakeholder issues. The next chapter focuses on the issue of services stakeholders.

Conclusion

This chapter discusses the complex impact of the environment on services functions. The
most outstanding characteristics of the operational environment are its variety and the interdependence of environmental factors. Services organisations will invariably be regulated in
their national environment by a combination of political, economic, legal, technological,
competitive and societal factors. The dynamic nature of regional cooperation and globalisation trends contributes further to increased complexity in the interpretation of the actual
nature and scope of the business environment for services.

Exercises

Key questions
1 Discuss the increasing focus in international trade on services and service-related activities.
2 Discuss some of the views on the meaning of globalisation, and on future expectations of
   globalisation for services.
3 Explain how the worldwide trend towards regionalisation impacts on the services
   environment.
4 Explain the nature of the interdependence between different aspects of the national environment that together constitute the concept of 'country risk'.

Web exercise 2.1
Country risk assessment is an activity that has gained increased attention over the past few
years. Visit the public-sector website maintained by Duke University of the United States at
www.duke.edu/~charvey/Country_risk/couindex.htm and assess the scope, volume and rele-
vancy of information provided via the site. Visit the private-sector website of the PRS group
at www.prsgroup.com/icrg/icrg.html, and that of PNC at www.econ.pncbank.com/cra.htm, to
determine the differences and similarities of information provided. Assess the available information in respect of a specific activity in services, and indicate what other information is

necessary to develop a reliable picture of the actual environment. Go through the exercise to identify how much of this information is publicly available.

The following cases describe the national and international climate related to the impact of the environment on specific service industries. Both cases exemplify the notion that factors in the macro environment are indeed interdependent.

Case study 2.1 The new face of Indian IT

In tough times, India's top software firms are assuming multiple roles: code-cruncher, systems integrator and call centre. They are growing rapidly by taking on more business and larger competitors. In October 2002, two IT firms on opposite sides of the world announced their quarterly results. For Texas-based computer-services giant Electronic Data Systems (EDS), the news was bad: sales down by 3 per cent compared to the same quarter the previous year, new business down by more than 50 per cent, and job cuts for 5,000 employees. But for Indian software firm Infosys Technologies, the opposite was true: revenues were up 35 per cent, profits had increased 12 per cent, and new hires hit nearly 2,000. It's a telling comparison. As global IT giants struggle, India's top software firms are finding new ways to grow at a rapid pace, sometimes at the expense of companies many times their size. By going after larger jobs and expanding the kind of services they offer, they are notching revenue growth of 20–30 per cent per year even as technology budgets get squeezed. Their pitch of high-quality services at highly competitive prices is music to the ears of cost-conscious executives in the United States and Europe who don't see a worldwide economic recovery any time soon.

The story goes like this: India's top-tier software firms – Infosys, Wipro, Tata Consultancy Services, Satyam Computer Services and HCL Technologies, with more than US$2.5 billion in combined sales – are emerging from their cocoon of custom software development, on which they built their businesses. They are still the world's major code-crunchers, but now they are including systems integration and call centres among their services. They will even run part of your IT department for you, taking over staff or moving them to India. In addition, they are devising detailed contingency plans to reassure customers that their work is safe, even when the subcontinent is not.

These tactics also mean that increasingly they are going head-to-head with the big boys, such as EDS, Accenture and IBM, in a bid to win customers and spur growth in lean times. 'Indian IT companies are in the process of transforming themselves into very serious competitors,' says C. Srinivasan, managing director in India of A. T. Kearney, the consulting arm of EDS. 'They're beginning to tell a good story to clients, and clients are beginning to respond.'

The attempt to become a one-stop shop for cost-conscious multinationals is part of a major reorientation by the top Indian firms after a bruising two years that have slowed growth and shrunk profit margins. Before then, everyone was 'feeding at the trough', laughs Nandan Nilekani, CEO of Infosys. Since the Internet bubble burst in 2000, however, 'The trend among large corporations to rein in IT spending has never been stronger,' he says.

This means that pressure on profits will continue, though top firms say it is abating somewhat. While many of India's small and medium-sized tech firms are in trouble, the biggest players are poised to take advantage of the cost-cutting drives sweeping through boardrooms in the West. This time, however, the deals are not about sending hordes of bright young software engineers to developed countries on short-term contracts. Instead, for cost reasons, companies are more and more interested in 'offshoring' – doing work in India itself. Sales from such work jumped 64 per cent in the 12 months to March 2002, according to the National Association of Software and Service Companies (NASSCOM). Multinationals are also eager to consolidate their IT work with a few firms, rather than dealing with a dozen. 'Clients are saying: "Can you take total responsibility, and where you do it is your problem",' says S. Ramadorai, CEO of Tata Consultancy Services (TCS), India's largest software firm.

TCS is a good example of the trend. In 2000, it agreed with Japanese hardware giant NEC to collaborate in Asia and beyond. It also acquired an Indian firm with expertise in integrating software and hardware. 'The intent clearly is to bid for the big deals,' says Kiran Karnik, president of NASSCOM in New Delhi. Overall, says TCS's Ramadorai, big Indian firms are looking at larger, longer-term and more complex projects than in the past. In one such example, TCS recently announced a deal worth US$80–100 million over the next four to five years with GE Medical Systems that will involve implementing technology in several continents.

Vivek Paul, CEO of Wipro Technologies, says that companies no longer want to start with a small pilot project and ramp up, but would rather go the whole hog from the start. Paul says his firm is now working on several deals worth US$20 million or more per year, far higher than the industry's norm. All that adds up to a problem for US-based IT giants such as EDS and Accenture. 'Clearly, competition has increased in the last few months as they get further traction in the market, thanks to their references and credentials,' says Sanjay Jain, managing director of Accenture in India.

The Indian companies make no secret of the fact that they are eyeing the business model of the American IT giants, where services run the gamut from consulting to software code-crunching to the installation of hardware. Of course, they are nowhere near that size and scope. Moreover, when it comes to truly large IT deals that run into billions of dollars, Indian companies still would only qualify as subcontractors. Nevertheless, such IT giants 'are definitely taking note [of the Indian firms] and they are already losing some smallish deals' to Indian competitors, says Rita Terdiman, vice president at technology research firm Gartner. As a result, they are paying Indian firms the ultimate compliment: replicating their operations. EDS, Accenture, IBM and CSC have set up outsourcing centres in India to find ways to offer the same cost advantages Indian firms do. These two sets of competitors view each other with a healthy respect, but also with a dose of scepticism. IT majors don't believe that Indian firms can match their global reach or breadth of expertise any time soon. In turn, Indian firms don't believe that IT majors can duplicate their cost efficiencies.

Right now, it is Indian companies that are benefiting from the cost-cutting environment. Software industry executives say that investment firm Lehman Brothers is negotiating a large IT outsourcing deal in India, a first for the company, as is PepsiCo. The two companies didn't respond to requests for comment. They belong to a group of firms who are either looking at India for the first time, or greatly expanding the scope of the technology work they do here. Typically, customers have been concentrated in businesses such as banking and telecommunications, but today there is also interest from the automotive, energy and pharmaceutical industries, say executives.

Indian firms are not simply seen as a cheap alternative. For example, they continue to monopolise the most prestigious measure of software-code writing ability – SEI CMM Level 5 – developed by Carnegie Mellon University in the United States. While average CEOs might not appreciate that kind of 'geeky' honour, they can relate to something like Six Sigma productivity techniques, which aim to identify and eliminate errors in a company's internal processes. Firms such as Wipro have embraced Six Sigma with a vengeance.

In the meantime, Indian firms are tackling another challenge: the lingering impression that India is an unsafe place in which to base critical work. Ever since the war scare (with Pakistan) on the subcontinent in May and June 2002, the software firms have doubled their attention to contingency plans in case of disaster. Whereas customers previously only wanted back-up within the same city, they now want a plan to shift work elsewhere in India, and, if necessary, elsewhere in the world. Infosys announced that it would set up a centre on the island of Mauritius, in the Indian Ocean, for just that purpose. Preparing for the worst has shifted from being a secondary concern to a prime imperative. Privately, some software executives complain that those worries have become a growth industry for consultants, who will verify for clients that such plans are in place.

The top Indian companies are also pushing ahead with what they see as an important source of growth: providing back-office services for multinationals, whether answering customer calls and emails or processing a company's invoices and payroll. Such services grew 70 per cent in 2001. Wipro and Infosys have acquired or created businesses to address this need, and if possible, cross-sell them with their other services. Infosys, for example, is providing back-office services to GreenPoint Mortgage, a US home lender, along with its more traditional IT work. It is all part of leaving their narrower focus on software behind and growing into something much larger, says NASSCOM's Karnik: 'We're beginning to see visions at least of taking on the big boys.'

(*Source*: J. Slater, 'Indian IT's new faces', *Far Eastern Economic Review*, 14 November 2002)

Student projects
1 Indicate the impact of global trends and tendencies on the IT industry, specifically in India.
2 Identify aspects that are unique to the Indian environment, and explain their impact, and consequences, for the local IT industry.

Case study 2.2 Modifications and piracy in Hong Kong

Pirates in Hong Kong not only illegally copy computer games, but also modify consoles, so that they can play copied games, costing companies millions in lost profits. With flashing lights and blaring music, Microsoft held a media bash at Hong Kong's convention centre to announce that it would launch its game console – the Xbox – in East Asia at the end of November 2002. But just a five-minute walk away from the company's flashy press conference, in a computer mall called 188 Wan Chai Road, Xboxes have been on sale for more than a year. The mall, a warren of tiny stores packed with illegal copies of everything pirate-able – CDs, DVDs, software – is like many others in Hong Kong: all have shops displaying the black and green Xbox and stacks of its video games, such as 'Project Gotham' and 'Halo'.

Purchased from distributors in the United States, Europe and Japan, where Microsoft launched the product earlier, the Xboxes are illegally brought into the territory as parallel imports. But that isn't the key problem for Microsoft, or Sony, and Nintendo, which dominate the world's US$20 billion game-console industry. Their biggest headache is that most of these consoles are 'chipped' – installed with modified chips, called mod chips, that override the console's security system, allowing it to play illegally copied games and discs intended for both this and other parts of the world. 'Mod chips can definitely make quite a negative impact on the successful launch of a platform,' says Scott Warren, Microsoft's attorney, who oversees the company's anti-piracy efforts in the region.

When it finally launches Xbox officially in Hong Kong, Singapore, Taiwan and Korea, Microsoft will have to face off against two rivals, who have had a huge headstart: Sony, which unveiled its immensely popular PlayStation 2 in these four markets almost a year earlier; and the pirates who started selling Xboxes in Hong Kong as early as November 2001 when it was launched in the United States, and 'chipped' Xboxes only four months later. Dealing with the conventional competition offered by Sony may be easier for Microsoft than heading off the ever-savvy 'mod squads'.

Because they allow users to play illegally copied games, chipped consoles are a gaping gateway into software piracy, and thus, a direct threat to the profitability of console and games makers. Companies such as Microsoft and Sony sell their consoles at a loss, depending on the sale of games to reap their profits. Industry analysts estimate that Microsoft loses around US$200 on each Xbox it sells, but hopes to make up the difference by selling its game software at over US$50 a pop in the United States and HK$299 (US$38) in Hong Kong. At 188 Wan Chai Road, however, illegal copies of the Xbox title 'Halo' are already on sale for just HK$70. Sony's PS2 games, which are more plentiful and popular, cost just HK$40, in contrast to the official price of around HK$300 each. The entertainment-software industry estimates that it lost US$3 billion around the world in 2001, because of this type of piracy.

Asia is the worst offender: Datamonitor, a London-based research firm, estimates that up to 70 per cent of game software sold in the region is pirated. Hong Kong, thanks to its game-crazy population and open borders, is the best place in the world to find modified consoles and pirated computer games. 'Hong Kong has an infamous reputation for hosting some of the most active hackers,' says Frederic Diot, a game-industry analyst at Datamonitor. 'Cracked games and chipped consoles often emerge first in Hong Kong.' What's more, this illegal business is done in broad daylight. Hong Kong's pirates peddle their wares in brightly lit malls as police stroll by outside. Though the Hong Kong government has in recent years tried to crack down on software piracy, its efforts have focused mostly on business, not entertainment, software. Not surprisingly, some suspect the government's commitment to fighting piracy. 'The law is there. Hong Kong's laws are based on the Commonwealth law, so it's quite similar to the laws in Canada, Australia and the UK,' says Edward Adler, a partner at law firm Bird & Bird in Hong Kong. 'But does the Hong Kong government really have the resolve to enforce them fully? That's the question.'

Piracy is one reason Hong Kong and the rest of Asia outside Japan is almost always left for last by Sony, Microsoft and Nintendo when they launch their consoles. Sony only launched its PS2 in Hong Kong in December 2001, several years after the platform was made available in Japan. Even Microsoft, which is in a hurry to catch up with Sony, has taken more than a year to bring Xbox to the region. But with Asia expected to overtake the United

States as the largest market for game software by 2004, it's a region that is impossible to ignore. Datamonitor estimates that Asia's gamers will spend US$7.6 billion on software that year, compared to US$7.4 billion in the United States.

Unless governments crack down on piracy, much of that spending will be siphoned into illegally copied software that can be played on chipped consoles. The mod chips aren't really chips at all, but up to 30 different components and bits of wire that are soldered on to a console's main circuit board. They are available from underground distributors and Internet stores, but a buyer would have to take the console apart, dig into the heart of the machine to find the main circuit board, fuse on the bits and pieces, and then put it all back together again – something not many gamers know how to do. In Hong Kong, they don't need to know: almost all the Xboxes on sale have already been chipped. They sell for about HK$1,780 at 188 Wan Chai Road, and can be found for less in other neighbourhoods. Microsoft's recommended retail price for the console in Hong Kong is HK$1,599. 'Why wouldn't you get it chipped? It costs almost nothing more,' says Baxter Huang, a game enthusiast who bought a PS2 and Xbox, both chipped, in Hong Kong. 'It's actually hard to find a console in Hong Kong right now that *isn't* chipped or games that *aren't* copied.'

Launching the console officially in Hong Kong probably won't help Microsoft either, judging from Sony's experience. PS2 has been in the market for a year, but it hasn't been able to beat the pirates. In fact, more chipped PS2s are now on sale at 188 Wan Chai Road and other computer malls than before the platform's official launch last year, according to vendors. Even when gamers buy their consoles through legitimate distributors, many still bring them in to be chipped – for less than HK$200 at one shop at 188 Wan Chai Road. 'I think the natural result, unfortunately, is that the more product there is, the more the opportunity to pirate,' says Microsoft's Warren.

To combat the mod squads, Sony regularly alters the hardware specifications of its consoles, rendering the existing mod chips useless. But within a few weeks, the new system is cracked, and soon after the mod chips, tailor-made to override the new specifications, are out in Hong Kong. Microsoft announced in October 2002 that it had re-jigged its motherboards to lower the cost of manufacturing, and in the process neutralising the Xbox mod chips in the market. 'We didn't do it specifically for anti-piracy purposes, but it's a great side benefit,' says Alex Kotowitz, Xbox's senior director of worldwide sales. 'And we may do that more often in the future as well.'

Console makers are also starting to haul the mod squads to court. Though mod chips are illegal in jurisdictions such as Britain, Canada and the United States, an Australian court earlier this year ruled that they were legal, because the chips were simply modifying an item legitimately purchased from the console makers. The laws in Hong Kong are about to be put to the test. Microsoft, Sony and Nintendo are suing a Hong Kong company called Lik Sang, which sold mod chips through its website. 'It's one of the world's largest distributors of mod chips,' Warren says. 'And they made no bones about what their role was and what they were doing. This will be an important test case in the region.'

Yet shutting Lik Sang down would only be the beginning. 'If Lik Sang goes, there'll be hundreds of others in Hong Kong who will be more than willing and able to take their place,' says Gino Yu, head of the Multi-Media Innovation Centre at Hong Kong's Polytechnic University. 'It's an unending cycle.' And for every Xbox that's chipped, Microsoft will be another US$200 further away from ever turning a profit on its console business, which it spent billions of dollars to develop.

(*Source:* S. Yoon, 'The mod squad', *Far Eastern Economic Review*, 7 November 2002)

Student projects

1 Differentiate between aspects of the political, economic, legal, technological, competitive and societal environment that impact on the functioning and viability of the computer games industry.
2 What could the various players do to ensure improved protection of the intellectual property rights of games?
3 Explain how Microsoft could position itself to minimise the negative impact of the environment on its presence and operations in the region.

References and further reading

Beckett, P. and Portanger, E. 2003, 'US banks retreat from EU', *Australian Financial Review*, 21 May, p. 24.

Boyle, J., 2003, 'BA flies into stiff headwind', *Australian Financial Review*, 20 May, p. 16.

Buffini, F., Hepworth, A. and Priest, M. 2003, 'Business hits back over HIH reforms', *Australian Financial Review*, 22 April 2003, pp. 1, 4.

Clark, A. 2003, 'SRA caps profits on Govia's franchise', *The Guardian*, 13 May, www.guardian.co.uk/busines/story/0,3604,954618,00.html, retrieved 13 May 2003.

Davidson, P. and Griffin, R. W. 2000, *Management: Australia in a global context*, John Wiley & Sons, Brisbane.

Davis, M. 2002, 'Pact lowers hurdles, keeps safeguards', *Australian Financial Review*, 4 November, p. 6.

Dixon, M. 2000, Real success: Personal and corporate survival, http://www.globalchange.com/ppt/successplus/realsuccess11/sld004.htm, retrieved 07 April 2003.

Economist, The. 2004a, 'Asian airlines: Having fun and flying high', *The Economist*, 11 March, www.economist.com//business/displayStory.cfm?story_id=2502539, retrieved 17 March 2004.

Economist, The. 2004b, 'Low-fare airlines', *The Economist*, 11 March, www.economist.com/background/displayBackground.cfm?story_id=2502539, retrieved 17 March 2004.

Ericson, A. 2003, 'Free trade with library services? – No "all clear" regarding GATS', *Information for Social Change*, no. 17, www.libr.org/isc/articles/17-Ericson-Bakken.html, retrieved 26 March 2004.

European Commission. 2001, *Barriers to Trade in Business Services: Final report*, Centre for Strategy and Evaluation Services, Brussels.

GATT, n.d., 'Trade liberalisation statistics', www.gatt.org/transtat_e.shtml, retrieved 22 May 2003.

Held, D., McGrew, A., Goldblatt, D. and Perraton, J. 1999, *Global Transformations: Politics, economics and culture*, Polity Press, Cambridge.

Hill, C. W. L. 2002, 'Postscript 2002', *Global Business*, 2nd ed., McGraw-Hill Irwin, Boston.

Holland, T. 2002, 'The perils of privatisation', *Far Eastern Economic Review*, 14 November.

Hookway, J. 2002, 'Texting the tube', *Far Eastern Economic Review*, 7 November.

Holt, D. H. 2000. *International Management: Text and cases*, The Dryden Press, Fort Worth.

International Trade Centre. 2002a, 'Japan: New outreach, at home and abroad', *International Trade Forum*, no. 3, p. 16.

International Trade Centre. 2002b, 'Singapore: New mission, new name', *International Trade Forum*, no. 3, p. 26.

Kirkbride, P. (ed.). 2001, *Globalisation: The external pressures*, Ashridge, Chichester.

Kripalani, M. 2002, 'Silicon Valley revisited', *Australian Financial Review*, 8 November, p. 81.

Lague, D. 2002, 'The limits of laissez-faire', *Far Eastern Economic Review*, no. 21, November.

Mazrui, A. 2002, 'Globalisation and the future of Islamic civilisation', www.alhewar.com/ globalisation_and_the_future.htm, retrieved 4 November 2002.

Moses, R. 2004, 'Business community hopes for big BN win', *New Straits Times*, 19 March, www.nst.com.my/Current_News/NST/Saturday?Election?20040320073152/Article.htm, retrieved 25 March 2004.

OECS (Organisation of Eastern Caribbean States). n.d., The Eastern Caribbean ECIPS, www.caribisles.org/caribbean/count-19.htm, retrieved 10 June 2003.

Pallister, D. 2003, 'HSBC's jet deal turns sour in Ghana', *The Guardian*, 6 May.

Porter, M. E. 1980, *Competitive Strategy: Techniques for analyzing industries and competitors*, Free Press, New York.

Pringle, D., Latour, A. and Song, K. 2003, 'Nokia lags in rolling out 3G hardware, say executives', *Australian Financial Review*, 29 April, p. 41.

Slater, J. 2002, 'Indian IT's new faces', *Far Eastern Economic Review*, 14 November.

Swiss Bankers Association. n.d., 'Welcome to the dormant accounts website of the Swiss Bankers Association', www.dormantaccounts.ch, retrieved 13 June 2003.

UNCTAD (United Nations Conference on Trade and Development). 2001, Least Developed Countries Conference, www.gatt.org/transtat_e.html, retrieved 22 May 2003.

UNESCO (United Nations Educational, Scientific and Cultural Organization). 2000, '21st Century Talks Examine Future Forms of Cultural Globalization', www.unesco.org/bpi/ eng/unescopress/2000/00_132e.shtml, retrieved 4 November 2002.

Webb, S. and Saywell, T. 2002, 'Untangling Temasek', *Far Eastern Economic Review*, 7 November.

World Bank, 2000, *World Development Report*, World Bank, Washington.

World Bank, 2002, *World Development Report*, World Bank, Washington.

WTO (World Trade Organization). 2001, 'WTO services talks press ahead', *WTO Press Release*, 2 April.

WTO (World Trade Organization). 2002, 'International Trade Statistics', www.wto.org/english/ res_e/statis_e/statis_e.htm, retrieved 7 April 2003.

WTO (World Trade Organization). n.d., 'GATS: Facts and fiction, Structures of the GATS', www.wto.org/english/tratop_e/serv_e/gats_factfiction4_e.htm, retrieved 10 June 2003.

Yip, G. 1995, *Total Global Strategy: Managing for worldwide competitive advantage*, Prentice Hall, Englewood Cliffs, NJ.

Yoon, S. 2002, 'The mod squad', *Far Eastern Economic Review*, 7 November.

Stakeholders and their influence on services

Learning objectives

After studying this chapter, readers will be able to:
- explain the concept of 'stakeholder theory' and describe the range of possible stakeholders
- understand the applications of stakeholder theory to a variety of services
- appreciate the relationships between stakeholder theory and the quality movement in the management of services
- understand the roles of managers when servicing stakeholders
- appreciate the role of ethics and social responsibility when managing stakeholder interests.

Introduction

The notion that organisations have stakeholders is well established, and a great number of books and articles that address stakeholder concepts have become popular in the management literature. In spite of the availability of this material, considerable evidence demonstrates that the delineation, and treatment, of stakeholders is somewhat arbitrary (Post, 2003). This uncertainty stems from a lack of agreement on the meaning of the term 'stake', and subsequently, both broad and narrow definitions of the concept of 'stakeholder' have been offered (Donaldson and Preston, 1995). The lack of a consistent definition means that the classification of stakeholders, the interpretation of their relationships, and ideas about how an organisation might respond to the influence and interests of stakeholders becomes problematic (Hummels, 1998). The vagueness of concept and effect is highlighted in the way a bank's board of directors endeavours to address the varied, and sometimes contrary, interests of the bank's stakeholders. In fact, the way in which such boards prioritise the competing claims of shareholders, customer service levels, needs of the employees, and expectancies of the general public continually attract widespread community criticism. On the one hand, there is a high level of endorsement for the ideal that all interests are of equal importance. On the other hand, the competing interests of these groups are likely to result in their different treatment. Endeavours to understand variations in the way organisations deal with different stakeholders over time have contributed to the development of the concept of stakeholder management.

Ideas about stakeholder management have evolved over the last 20 years. This evolution has been in response to an increasing awareness of the complex, dynamic and diverse ways in which stakeholders affect and effect business performance, especially in the provision of services. Each day, local, national and international media report dramatic stories that present corporate and institutional examples of failures to adequately address and manage diverse stakeholder concerns. This chapter discusses some of the key ideas underpinning the evolving stakeholder literature in terms of shareholder/manager relationships, economic perspectives of ethical management, and the social responsibility of domestic and global corporations. Against the backdrop of these key ideas there is general agreement that stakeholder issues create diverse management challenges for organisations, but there is less agreement about the recommended strategies and mechanisms for managing these issues. Hence, this chapter discusses the key theoretical perspectives that underpin the contemporary ideas about, and approaches to, stakeholder management. Within the current wave of globalisation, the unprecedented technological advances, and the global spread of political and economic ideas, the variable and complex nature of stakeholder influences on business performance indicate that all functional managers need to have an understanding of how stakeholder issues impact on services – and on their organisations, in particular. This logic, which is developed throughout the book, further reinforces the value of an integrated services management model for business engagements.

Scholars have endeavoured to take these realities into account when drawing attention to the ways in which organisations are constituted and exist through relationships with several diverse constituencies (Bird, 2001; Kakabadse and Kakabadse, 2003; Guay et al., 2004). For example, Donaldson and Preston (1995) distinguish between the competing claims of stakeholders by using the terms 'normative', 'instrumental' and 'descriptive' to differentiate between managerial and organisational behavioural responses to stakeholder issues. Jones and Wicks (1999, p. 207) support the value of these three management and organisation behaviour categories when they write: 'These early formulations suggest (often simultaneously) that: (1) firms/managers should behave in certain ways (*normative*), (2) certain outcomes are more likely if firms/managers behave in certain ways (*instrumental*), and (3) firms/managers actually behave in certain ways (*descriptive*).'

These three approaches offer a framework for the reconciliation of business ethics and the differentiation of stakeholder categorisation. For instance, traditional economic theory asserts that the primary function of the corporation is to attain the highest possible economic benefit for a select few stakeholders (that is, the shareholders). However, a key principle of stakeholder theory is that managers should proactively address the needs and expectations of *all* stakeholders. The issue of how to do so sets a significant challenge for both managers and organisations, especially those responsible for organisational services, which ultimately impinges on all tasks. The Donaldson and Preston classification becomes useful with the addition of more precise stakeholder definitions, and greater coherence in the relationships between stakeholders (Berman et al., 1999). Indeed, the development of a finer identification and categorisation of stakeholders (for example, as primary and secondary groups) should enable managers to better consider various constituent interests, and hence, to determine which of the alternative approaches apply. Nevertheless, in spite of a large and evolving literature, there is often contradictory evidence and argument about the stakeholder concept.

The lack of consensus about how stakeholder theory adds to a better understanding of management processes exists for two primary reasons. First, historical developments in management theory that were concerned with interpretations of company survival, group dynamics, and strategic and ethical ideals, led to the identification of stakeholders. It is generally accepted that Freeman's (1984) book, *Strategic Management: A stakeholder approach*, launched the concept of stakeholders and provided the basis for the evolution of stakeholder theory. (Chapter 1 outlined a brief history of management theories.) Freeman's approach reflected the contemporary interest in behavioural approaches to management theory, which was an alternative to rational economic theory, and brought into focus a variety of disciplines that include sociology and industrial psychology. However, the powerful historical legacy of classical 'scientific' theory continued to dominate management and organisation theory. Consequently (as discussed in Chapter 1), although classical management and organisation theory could be employed to promote task effectiveness, and thus was valuable for manufacturing industries, these mechanisms were increasingly difficult to apply in the high customer contact services (or systems with complex stakeholder interests).

The second challenge for contemporary management thinking, in terms of stakeholder theory, is its association with a particular industrial era. In spite of the richness and innovativeness of Freeman's work, it was developed in a relatively stable period dominated by a large manufacturing base that influenced national economic development priorities and uniform notions about the ways in which people lived. Hence, interpretations of the ways of 'living' during this era were framed by the scientific logic of the manufacturing sector. The early stakeholder concepts preceded the theoretical management shifts associated with systems, contingency and quality theories, which were more analytical about production systems, the unique characteristics of a particular organisation, and the development of strategies to more successfully meet the diverse expectations of customers.

These theoretical developments were linked with the emergence of the notion of service. Freeman's early stakeholder ideas occurred before the development of the 'knowledge'-based society and the association of this post-industrial shift with the explosive growth of the communication and transportation systems, as well as other revolutionary technological advancements. These innovative developments have significant implications for a more complex conceptualisation of stakeholder theory. More recently, the global impact of dramatic events such as AIDS, SARS, 'bird flu' and terrorism demand further refinement of models for stakeholder management. More particularly, the very same revolutionary technological developments that facilitated the rapid development of the global economy also gave diverse stakeholders access to knowledge and information with which to critically scrutinise the activities of businesses and the quality of products.

These stakeholder issues link to the previous discussion in Chapter 2 on the complex and dynamic nature of the business environment and the interrelated impact of its political, economic, legal, competitive, societal and risk dimensions. The ISM model shown in Figure 3.1 represents these external environmental business factors in the outer-most circle. Stakeholders, another external force, are represented in the next circle. The following stakeholders are listed: suppliers, interest groups, employee unions, government bodies, shareholders, community, customers and competitors. This list indicates the diverse nature of external interests that will variously impact on the management of services. This stakeholder diversity

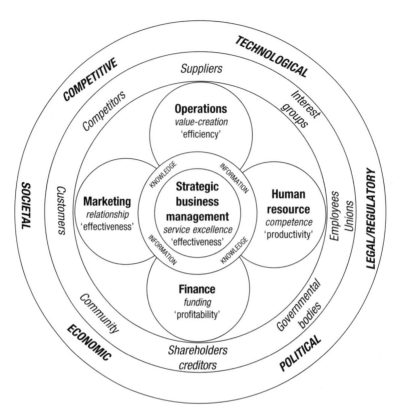

Figure 3.1 The integrated services management (ISM) model

underscores the complex nature of stakeholder management issues and the challenges associated with the development of practical management strategies. The ways in which managers of services respond to stakeholder issues is a critical factor in building and sustaining
a successful management strategy. Figure 3.1 indicates that stakeholder issues have implications for all internal functional business areas – marketing, finance, operations and human
resources. Hence, it is critical that the managers and employees in all these areas have a good
understanding of the ways in which stakeholder interests impact on the management of specific corporate functions. Thus, a successful service needs to adopt an integrated approach to
stakeholder management.

Who are the stakeholders?

The identification and management of stakeholders has recently attracted increasing attention (Reavill, 1998; Abzug and Webb, 1999; Key, 1999; Ogden and Watson, 1999). This
interest is reflected particularly in the North American and West European business literature (Mitchell et al., 1997; Rowley, 1997; Jones and Wicks, 1999; Jawahar and McLaughlin,
2001). The ideas that have been presented give some clarity and new direction to the
development and relevance of theoretical concepts, particularly 'in business and society and

business ethics' (Jones and Wicks, 1999, p. 206). For instance, recognition of the environmental impact of business activities has resulted in increased support for conservation. The critical concerns of diverse social movements for wide-ranging ecological and societal issues contributed to the development of an environmental ideology to underpin a new 'consensus between business interests, government officials, industry representatives and environmentalists about the need for sustainable development' (Harding, 1998, p. 35). A growing concern for societal and business ethics directly relates to greater accessibility to knowledge and information facilitated by the rapid spread of new communications technology. Thus, representatives of diverse stakeholder interests, though small in number in comparison to the majority of business stakeholders and mechanisms (also stakeholders), now have the opportunity to be actively involved in the decision making associated with specific industry, or government policies, and management practices through 'public participation' stakeholder consultation processes. The inclusion of *public participation* reflects stakeholder concern for greater transparency, and a more democratic approach to decision making, as at any time these stakeholder communities will vocally hold a range of often-competing value positions about environmental and societal issues associated with business. When these societal concerns question, for example, the appropriate and inappropriate environmental nature of particular development strategies, the issue of addressing the ethics of business cannot be avoided.

The study of business ethics has spawned vigorous debate in stakeholder theory. The *entrepreneurial* business approach promotes the merits of profitability, market penetration and wealth maximisation to enrich management and shareholders. In other words, the entrepreneurial business approach considers the achievement of traditional corporate wealth creation to be its highest ethical interest. Recent support for this entrepreneurial view is shown in the way that management emphasised selective favourable consideration to Frank Ciccuto, the CEO of the National Bank of Australia (NBA), and Paul Bachelor, the CEO of Australian Mutual Provident Society (AMP), at a time of significant decline in both organisations. Such actions ratify a belief that it is ethical behaviour to favour a chosen few stakeholders, and delineate the commitment of the firm to business ethics (Brigham, 1992). Nevertheless, there are alternative perspectives.

Ethicists and advocates of the stakeholder protection argument have championed efforts to reform the 'shareholder wealth maximisation' model (Dufrene and Wong, 1996). Supporters of this perspective argue that corporations, as social institutions, have responsibility beyond their accountability to shareholders (Carroll, 1979; Freeman, 1984). However, this view has also been fiercely contested, sending confusing and contradictory signals to organisations. In essence, the two sides of the debate stress either the value of economic capital performance, or sustainable 'triple-bottom line' (economic, social and environmental) performance criteria, but management and organisational strategies designed to address the complex challenges of sustainable development are only emerging. With little consensus, assessments of ethical behaviour are likely to have inconsistencies between stakeholder groups. Nevertheless, these issues are of crucial relevance to the management of services throughout organisations. Hence, the development of a comprehensive stakeholder theory is imperative to better understand and predict how corporations might respond to their environments, and in particular, the protection of their key stakeholder interests.

A call by Rowley (1997) for a typology of stakeholders (to categorise stakeholders) might be supported by the following example of an encounter with a service organisation. Suppose person A applies for a comprehensive car insurance policy with company X. As this is an inaugural application, person A does not have an insurance rating, and hence, company X is very likely to request a statement from the driver licensing authority for a report detailing person A's driving history, in terms of vehicle crashes, traffic regulation violations and driving infringements. In the framework of stakeholder theory, person A, company X and the driver licensing authority are all stakeholders, but what are the priorities of their stake in the final insurance agreement? Depending on the report from the driver licensing authority, an insurance policy may or may not be offered, with or without encumbrances. These impediments may not be directly related to the driving record of person A, but a function of social factors such as age, because statistical road trauma data suggests that there is a strong relationship between age and crash occurrences. The following questions might then be asked: are not the statisticians (those who obtained and collated the data), or the department that surveys driver habits and issues infringements, as well as members of the judiciary (who might be called upon to assess driving habits), in addition to a plethora of others associated with the administration of the transport domain, also stakeholders in this decision? How might the relative importance of these various constituents be assessed? From a broader corporate perspective, how should the points of view of the owners of the insurance company and the board of directors (or the shareholders, if it is a public company) be considered? The reality is that virtually any entity (singular or group) can, or may, affect the interactions between person A and company X. In the absence of a stakeholder identification and relationship framework, it becomes virtually impossible to consider how the competing stakeholder claims can be addressed.

For some time, the notion of multiple stakeholders has been used to broaden understanding of the relationships between a corporation and its external environment. This framework articulated a classic definition of the role of the stakeholder: 'A stakeholder in an organisation is any group or individual who can affect or is affected by the achievements of the organisation's objectives' (Freeman, 1984, p. 46). Earlier European stakeholder definitions did not use the term 'stakeholder', but linked the concept to constituent groups, stockholders and ownership, and perceived stakeholders as being central to corporate social responsibility (Jones, 1980). Alternatively, Preston and Sapienza (1990) traced the origins of the stakeholder approach, in the American context, to 1950 when the CEO of Sears, Robert E. Wood, listed the 'four parties to any business in the order of their importance as customers, employees, community and stockholders' (p. 362). Subsequently, numerous others have defined stakeholders in a variety of different ways (see Cornell and Shapiro, 1987; Alkhafaji, 1989; Hill and Jones, 1992; Langtry, 1994). These contributions, which suggest that many internal and external constituents, apart from stockholders, employees, suppliers and customers, can impact on organisational behaviours, have been conceptually illustrated.

Figure 3.2 is representative of the earliest stakeholder models. These frameworks present a 'transformation network' model in which the central cell (labelled 'Organisation') transforms inputs to outputs. In reality, the organisation can represent a company, a corporation or a social institution. The model outputs, such as accommodation at a hotel, a university lecture, an air flight, or a telephone conversation, are experienced by the customers, as shown by the right-hand cell. The suppliers, stockholders and employees provide inputs to the

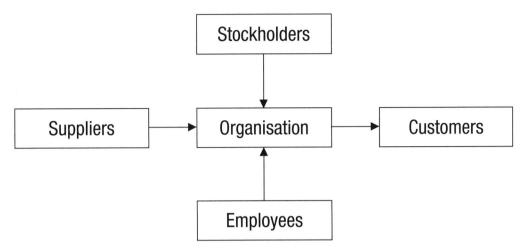

Figure 3.2 An open system of an organisation and its environment

organisation. Suppliers may provide the hotel structural layout and the various hotel services to be experienced; or, in the case of the lecture, the forum, visual and audio aids, as well as the presenter and associates. The stockholders can be the owners of the service provision firm, the financial share-owner representatives, or even the government, when the organisation is a national institution. Employees deliver the services. The personnel of the HR management department, and administrators and associates can be included within the employee category, as well as those who directly engage the customer. The constituents, nominated as suppliers, stockholders or employees, are but a select few of those peripheral to the organisation.

The arrowheaded lines within Figure 3.2 indicate the direction of flow of inputs and outputs to and from the organisation. Collectively, these four cells outside the organisation are referred to as the *primary stakeholders* of the organisation, as these entities have formal, official and contractual relationships with the corporation. These four cells contribute to the organisation's external environment. In this transformational network framework, these four external environment components are the general stakeholders of the organisation. Figure 3.2 is a relatively simple model that enables only limited explanations and predictions in very complex contemporary industrial societies. A measure of the extent (and a need for more comprehensive frameworks) of that complexity is demonstrated in the following Australian illustrative case, which outlines important stakeholder issues for the proposal to construct the Nathan Dam on the Dawson River in Queensland.

Box 3.1 The Nathan Dam development proposal

At the outset, the intention of the Australian federal government to fund the construction of an 880,000-megalitre dam near Taroom, Queensland, appeared to be in the public interest. For instance, when in operation, this dam would make controlled discharges of water for value-adding agricultural, industrial, urban and environmental uses. More specifically, once constructed, the dam would provide irrigation capacity that would allow a major expansion of the downstream cotton industry. Ultimately, the concept of building the dam had all the hallmarks of a decision that would positively impact regional economic sustainability. Yet, mindful of statutory regulations, the design phases were undertaken in close cooperation with the Queensland state government, which had conducted a number of environmental impact assessments for the project. Nevertheless, the Queensland Conservation Council and the World Wide Fund for Nature Australia appealed against the intent to construct the dam. This opposition to the project was based on grounds of possible chemical and nutrient environmental impact on the Great Barrier Reef World Heritage Area.

In spite of the potential to enhance employment opportunities from additional cotton ginning, food processing, as well as diversified cash crops, support for the plan was not universal. In particular, the expansion of the cotton cropping area would require additional use of aerially applied pesticides, which are toxic to a range of fauna, especially fish. Hence, arguments were advanced that if the pesticides were not effectively managed, the pollutant run-off would likely enter the Dawson River, which feeds the Fitzroy River and then flows into the waters of the Great Barrier Reef area. Thus, a legislative requirement to protect the heritage area was in direct conflict with the proposal to support irrigated agriculture, which was the justification for dam construction. Consequently, the federal minister for the environment and heritage was required by the Australian Federal Court to reconsider the relevant environmental impacts of the dam construction. Later, Chris McGrath, co-counsel for the two appealing environment groups that had challenged the ministers' decision to construct the dam, remarked that the court ruling would reverberate for decades in the Australian environmental legal system. This case indicates how complex political, economic, legal, competitive and societal stakeholder issues now impact on the business environment.

(*Source*: www.austlii.edu.au/au/cases/cth/federal_ct/2003/1463.html)

Origins and ethics of stakeholders

The Nathan case highlights the increasingly complex nature of the business environment, which in turn indicates the need to more accurately describe company behaviours. Prior to Freeman's (1984) concepts, earlier stakeholder notions were acknowledged in systems thinking, decision making and corporate planning (Barnard, 1938; March and Simon, 1958; Mason and Mitroff, 1981). It has been mooted that the installation of these organisational procedures were rooted in 'widespread public disillusionment and what was seen as a gross betrayal of public trust' (Wilson, 2004, p. 21) by corporations that had failed to sustain obligations to protect and improve the welfare of employees and society. In response to the unethical corporate practices, which were geared to enhance financial opportunity for a select few, doubt was cast in the community on the primacy of shareholder interests, or indeed, that corporations have a fiduciary obligation only to shareholders. Predictable reactions were litigation, calls for stricter regulations, and punitive legislation. Less inevitable was rethinking for corporate purposes, from which emerged the stakeholder approach, which has been used as an underlying rationale for the explanation of organisation and business imperatives (Carroll, 1989). These perspectives preceded a focus on the nature of accountability to different sectors of society through applying alternative management paradigms (Brenner and Cochran, 1991; Jones, 1995) to the promotion of a corporate social performance framework (Wood, 1991). Thus, recent management scholarship has variously contributed to agreement on the value of applying the stakeholder concept to models that describe and predict the operation of social institutions in specific contexts.

In particular, the incorporation of the understanding of stakeholder theory into productivity and quality-oriented service management models (see Chapter 1) has attracted extensive support. Initially, the interest in customer service as a basis for organisational renaissance was based around the structural idea of organisations as numerous cells, or departments, whose staff were engaged in ensuring customer satisfaction with clientele with high levels of disposable income (Walsh, 1995). Indeed, the more progressive organisations were endeavouring to capture larger customer bases, not only with a wider range of products, but also in the differentiation of their services. These marketing drivers, which were underpinned by perspectives of customers and markets having different service needs and expectations, drove the momentum for a generation of initiatives aimed to better fit production purposes to delight customers, and to meet performance guarantees. The intensification of this business approach was linked with the development of the social quality movement of the 1980s. This new approach was embraced by the progressive Western factories that, for example, manufactured cars, refrigerators, and a host of tangible goods in a competitive international environment, which included Japanese manufacturers.

During the 1980s the political development of economic rationalism, especially in the Anglo-based nations such as the United States (US) and the United Kingdom (UK), resulted in a strengthening of the private sector. Under economic rationalisation, reform transferred economic activity from national or local government-controlled agencies to non-government, profit-seeking institutions. This shift to private business activity was further strengthened during the 1990s following the collapse of the centrally planned Soviet Union economies. These newly independent nations proceeded to strategically reorient to market cultures (Chatterjee and Pearson, 1996; Pearson and Chatterjee, 1999). Similarly, supporting the economic rationalist direction, countries such as India engaged in free market reforms and liberalisation programs (Gopalan and Rivera, 1997) as a competitive economic strategy designed to create global business opportunities. Associated with this institutional political and economic restructuring were changes in management practice, industrial relations (see Chapter 8) and worksetting arrangements, steady increases in foreign investment, joint ventures, partnerships and direct ownership, and new legal statutes and regulatory regimes (Khalilzadeh-Shirazi and Zagha, 1994). These management practice changes were vital for services, such as education, health, social welfare, transport, financial services, and a variety of community infrastructures, which became key components of the new marketplace.

The removal of government revenue support meant that notions of accountability, efficiency, effectiveness and service quality penetrated the new economic management paradigms. The transfer from government to private ownership involves not only a shift in financial support from the public purse, but also significant changes in the composition and influence of stakeholders. A major concern for the wider community is how the varied and competing interests of the stakeholders should be balanced in terms of service quality, profit sharing, operational cost and transformation processes. Resolution of these complex issues, within the framework of stakeholder theory, requires the development of relatively robust and comprehensive models for management practice.

Stakeholder theory

This section tracks some of the key contemporary stakeholder theory debates. In spite of the core boundaries being outlined by numerous definitions, stakeholder theory still faces two main challenges. The first challenge is the lack of a clear and succinct, yet embracing, definition of the stakeholder concept. Despite it being fairly well established that the primary responsibility of a company is to serve the interests of the shareholders, a pivotal tenet of stakeholder theory is to ultimately serve all of those constituents identified as company stakeholders. Yet, for example, when Telstra announced that customers would be charged more for core services (that is, phone line access, new fees for paying bills by credit cards) shareholders benefited at the expense of stakeholders. In anticipation of greater profits Telstra's share-market value rose, which was favourable for investors (shareholders), but less acceptable for customers (stakeholders). In a competitive market environment, ignoring some stakeholder interests at the expense of others, as in the Telstra case, may result in a reduction in market share. Indeed, in November 2004, Telstra was able to buy back shares from 'small' shareholders at discounted rates (about $4.05 per share), which was considerably less than the price of $7.80 (per share) many had paid in the T2 sale of 1995 (West Australian, 2004a).

A second major challenge for stakeholder theory is how to classify stakeholders in order to understand the interrelationships between them. Although stakeholder theory has become important in the framework of organisational ethics, it is often quite difficult to precisely identify stakeholders and non-stakeholders. It has been experienced that terrorists may exist within the environment of an airline business; hence, within the paradigm of stakeholder theory, terrorists are organisational (airline) stakeholders (Phillips and Reichart, 2000). However, it is a dubious conclusion that terrorists (as stakeholders) are worthy of the same moral and legal considerations as other stakeholders (that is, employees, customers). While these two definitional and classification challenges prevail, it is most difficult for managers to comprehensively address all exigencies.

Central to the debate on the development of a stakeholder categorisation is the requirement to understand stakeholder influences and ideas about how organisations should, or might, or in fact do, respond to these influences. Moreover, a focus on stakeholder relationships highlights the importance of delineating between stakeholders because organisations tend to address 'multiple influences from the entire stakeholder set' (Rowley, 1997, p. 890). While some (Donaldson and Preston, 1995; Jones and Wicks, 1999) contend that Freeman (1984) created a rich stakeholder paradigm, others (Argandona, 1998; Key, 1999) argue that stakeholder theory is still incomplete and vague. Freeman's (1984) portrayal of the nature of organisational impact by 'surrounding' stakeholders has inspired the imagination of practitioners, social scientists and organisational behavioural scientists, who have specified either a broad (holistic) or a narrow (reductive) view of stakeholders. Freeman generally promoted the concept of stakeholders as 'actors' who influenced the achievements of an organisation. However, firms should identify if this influence is *direct* or *indirect*. In the pursuit of this advice, a variety of stakeholder categories that strategically influence the corporation have been developed. For instance, Carroll (1989), and later Wood (1993), have enriched the literature by identifying *primary* and *secondary* stakeholders, while Clarkson (1995) employs a narrow definition of *voluntary* and *involuntary* risk, depending on the extent of invested capital in the firm.

In spite of these endeavours to collectively improve understanding of stakeholder identification, consensus is yet to be realised. The position was succinctly expressed by Mitchell and colleagues (Mitchell et al., 1997, p. 853), who wrote that the concept of stakeholders is 'a maddening variety of signals on how questions of stakeholder identification might be answered'. Using Freeman's broad definition of a stakeholder, Mitchell et al. suggest the following three new classes of stakeholders:

- power to influence the firm;
- legitimacy of relationship; and
- urgency of the stakeholder's claim.

These three classes of *power*, *legitimacy* and *urgency* contribute to the notion that the extent of possession of these attributes by stakeholders is a function of their relative level of importance. This framework promotes more concise stakeholder identification and justifies claims about the legitimacy of particular managerial interactions. Nevertheless, when the CEOs of 80 large US firms (Agle et al., 1999) were questioned, only limited support for this argument could be demonstrated. Further attempts to develop a more precise stakeholder theory have found limited acceptance. Jones and Wicks (1999), for instance, explicitly argued for two divergent approaches to stakeholder theory, which they labelled as a 'social science' perspective and a 'normative ethics' (normative and instrumental) approach. Alternative views support a descriptive stakeholder theory (Jawahar and McLaughlin, 2001), or even an instrumental stakeholder theory (Heugens et al., 2002). Later, Kaler (2003) rejected the normative, descriptive and instrumental frameworks, claiming that these frameworks were primarily 'of content rather than use' (p. 74). (These three frameworks are discussed later in the chapter.) These and other examples highlight the central problem of stakeholder theory related to the application of frameworks to provide universal explanations and guidance for corporate behaviours in complex and dynamic business environments.

The enigma for stakeholder theory is that while a common thread of principle and context is reasonably well established, these primary features yield compromises. Thus, endorsement for the employment of the primary characteristics of stakeholder theory becomes expressed as 'contradistinctiveness' (Kaler, 2003, p. 71) between responsibilities towards stakeholders and shareholders, which is embedded in the diverse stakeholder orientation of the United States, and the UK shareholder nomenclature. This lack of consensus, interlinked with the issue of national context, introduces the idea of environment into a stakeholder theory. Moreover, despite stakeholder theory promoting a notion of egalitarianism for all organisational constituents, a movement towards greater equity becomes blurred as the interactions take place in different contextual settings. Thus, it is apparent that negotiated adjustments, modifications or concessions need to be employed to settle conflicting opinions. In practice, the credibility of a stakeholder theory is influenced by the environment of actors and contextual change. For instance, Internet booking now allows customers to arrange and pay for an aircraft flight without the previously required interactions with the sales staff of a tourist agency or at an airport counter. Indeed, banking and account payments on the Internet have become commonplace in many industrial societies. Moreover, at some universities prospective undergraduates can enrol for programs, pay for courses, purchase their texts (which are mailed to the student), and complete degrees without face-to-face contact with administrative or academic staff. Furthermore, there are now facilities for consumers to undertake self medical diagnosis on their home computers. In fact, there are now extensive e-service facilities available that have enormously changed the service interaction process in less than a decade. Consequently, the management of stakeholder issues will continue to change, as some stakeholder concerns become redundant while the emergence of new actors presents new management challenges. Thus, a major problem for managers is how to interpret the status of stakeholders.

Stakeholder legitimacy has consistently been a point of contention. A central management intention of the stakeholder approach was to broaden managerial roles and responsibilities to incorporate the wider interests and claims of non-stockholders, and to move beyond the narrow corporate economic goals of profit maximisation. Ideas such as that organisations have informal relationships (Barnard, 1938), and that institutions are 'accountable to many different sectors of society' (Eells, 1960, p. 55) provide the groundwork for the later development of stakeholder theory. Stakeholder theory endeavours to systematically describe and explain issues such as the primary nature of the stakeholders who deserve managerial attention, and what is at stake not only for defined groups of individuals (employees, customers), but also for complex communities, societies, institutions, and even the natural environment. These topics are important for managers, who are responsible for service, as these issues have economic, political and social implications for a host of institutional structures, international markets and, ultimately, the quality of social life.

The strategic importance of giving ethical primacy to servicing a diverse body of stakeholders was prominently demonstrated in the aftermath of the Southeast Asian financial crisis. Indeed, the collapse of the Thai baht in July 1997 triggered financial turmoil that has had lasting effects, not only in the Asia-Pacific region, but worldwide. These effects were exemplified as catastrophic declines in regional stock markets, continual volatility in national currencies, and failures of international financial institutions, including North American and Canadian institutions (Yoshikawa and Phan, 2001). In the wake of the financial crisis, poor enforcement of corporate laws and regulations was considered to be the main reason for the collapse of international business, domestic and global markets (Juzhong et al., 2000). These developments highlight the importance of the quality movement in corporate services, and the use of regulatory guidelines to attain quality of services is reflected in the contemporary ISO 14001, 18001 and 19001 accreditation series. Despite a growing acceptance that organisations have responsibilities, not only to their immediate shareholders, but increasingly to the wider community, these matters are still being vigorously debated and evolving in the stakeholder management guidelines and government regulatory statutes.

Stakeholders and the quality movement

The interweaving of community expectations, government regulations and managerial attention to stakeholder interests is reflected in the quality movement. Reforms aimed at developing a favourable quality culture are generally credited to Japanese manufacturing companies that pioneered total quality management and a number of other related initiatives, such as quality control, inventory control and the 'just-in-time' (JIT) approach during the late 1940s. These concepts, rooted in the ideas of the American consultant W. Edwards Deming, were developed to improve the quality of goods and services through statistical methods and employee involvement, and were particularly embraced by postwar Japan in order to build customer (stakeholder) numbers. The entry of Japanese goods into traditional Western-based markets invigorated concern for assessing 'best practices' in work processes within and between companies.

These quality issues are of particular importance in services, where competition is often based entirely on the customers' perceptions of comparative service quality (see Chapters 1, 4 and 5). Industry sectors such as education, financial services, health, hospitality and recreation, retail, and tourism and travel are becoming reliant on stakeholder perceptions of quality for their survival. Many service companies, such as financial institutions and banks, conduct a great deal of their customer interactions by telephone or email communications. Consequently, the company representatives are specifically trained for technology-based customer interactions, and the quality of the engagement and communication is often monitored and assessed. For instance, a standard for service performance used by the financial giant American Express is the speed with which lost or stolen American Express traveller's cheques are replaced. Leading airline companies have systems for replacing stolen or lost tickets, and consequently, there are institutional techniques for evaluating the promptness with which the corporation can provide passengers with new flight vouchers. Identifying these best practices has become known as 'benchmarking', and when these techniques are widely adopted in the international arena they are assessed by documentation now commonly referred to as the International Standards Organisation, ISO 9002 series.

The ISO 9000+ series quality standards were developed to identify the key elements of a quality system for manufactured products in domestic and international competition. They provide an overall framework to assess the quality of products, and the quality of the delivery system. The first criterion (that is, ISO 9001, 9002, 9003) emphasised the quality of results in terms of design and development, production and installation of processes, and final inspection and testing. These elements were designed for contractual situations, internal audits of work procedures and quality (product or good) assessment. The second criterion (ISO 9004–2) was a guideline for the development and implementation of quality management systems (TQM) more oriented to services. Nevertheless, while the intention was to achieve internal and external customer satisfaction (that is, quality of service), the processes were rooted in the standardisation of values for the manufacturing sector, and consequently, were not well suited for the diverse nature of services. Indeed, the components of the comprehension of quality are more complex. Today, a more educated society expects that, in addition to a reliable product, the production (process) will be in the interests of the sustainable 'health of society'. Questions such as whether the delivery was within the bounds of ethical conduct of the involved stakeholders, or whether the affairs of the stakeholders who delivered the service were within acceptable bounds of ecological sustainability, are now considered by consumers. Thus, the ISO 9000, while still employed, has been extended (that is, ISO 14001, 18001) to incorporate the newer social expectations of stakeholders.

Quality-enhancing initiatives to improve organisational effectiveness were extensively refined when global market networks exploded during the 1990s. In addition to financial, inventory and budgetary controls, as mainstays to increase the probability of meeting organisational goals and standards, task forces or quality teams were commonly used by organisations to intensely scrutinise work arrangements and practices. Cross-functional teams assessed, identified, diagnosed and made recommendations to address quality problems. These non-traditional organisational mechanisms had the effect of dismantling artificial barriers between departments and decentralised operating procedures. Additionally, analytical strategies were applied, which included statistical tools such as control charts, 'pareto' analysis and cost quality analysis. These new organisation-wide quality control approaches were dependent on expanding incumbent task autonomy and job knowledge, which began an emphasis on the re-skilling and re-education of employees. The overall aim was to ensure that corrective and preventive procedures would be quickly installed to minimise the perception of negative episodes, which included environmental consequences, or the impact on indigenous people's communities and ways of life. Paradoxically, this increased attention on better corporate governance, by businesses that were some of the most powerful in the world, had roots in a number of significant failures during the 1980s. A number of tragic and disastrous events verified the need for more rigorous and comprehensive assessments of corporate activity.

Notable examples of corporate malfeasance, unethical business practices, and excessive risk taking by leading corporations of the 1980s would include the following calamities:
- the *Exxon Valdez* oil spill on a pristine waterway in 1989;
- a chemical leak in Bhopal, India, in December 1985, which killed more than 2,000 people and blinded and injured over 200,000 more;
- the lacing of Johnson & Johnson Tylenol capsules with cyanide poisoned and killed customers on two occasions during the 1980s; and
- evidence that emerged during the 1980s showed that Dow Corning, as a major manufacture of silicone gel breast implants, had repeatedly ignored signs that the product was dangerous.

As a consequence of these catastrophes, organisations were recognised to have social responsibilities. Moreover, the common features of these events include their high remediation cost, their lasting negative impact on the reputation of specific corporations, and the need for their resolution by the emergent area of crisis management services.

This new stakeholder management stream goes beyond the limited early 20th-century ideas rooted in preclassical and classical manufacturing values. Despite growing international quality guideline accreditation (that is, ISO 9000 series), and stated company commitments to the protection and improvement of societal welfare, conveyed though vision or mission statements, policies and codes for ethical and moral integrity, and relevant audits, the frequency of dramatic accidents of the 1980s and beyond demonstrated the imperative for new environmental development guidelines. Hence, a new order of benchmarking, the ISO 14001 series, was developed to encourage and guide organisations to formulate internationally acceptable environmental management systems.

The second United Nations Conference on the Environment and Development, held in Rio de Janeiro in June 1992, strengthened the power of stakeholder influence. At this prestigious assembly the government heads of 170 countries were represented, and while governments and non-government agencies alike promoted international cooperation for

global agreements and partnerships 'in planning for environmental protection and social economic development' (Harding, 1998, p. 19), an integrated approach is yet to emerge. Nevertheless, stakeholder expectations for wider health and safety concerns continued to grow,
evidenced by changing legislative requirements, vibrant public campaigns, activist groups
and militant residential activity. Consequently, the ISO 18001 series, which identifies best
practice in internationally accepted management systems, was conceived. These documents
include a plethora of relevant information, as well as the underpinning for the development
of a quality industry that trains and determines corporate accreditation to these international
standards. This quality industry directly relates to more intense responses to wider stakeholder
concerns. However, attaining a more sustainable future requires profound changes in predominant value systems. For example, profit maximisation is important for retail business, but
stakeholders have been marginally influential in reforming the leading service organisations.
For instance, stakeholder concern to reduce household refuse levels and the high volume of
plastic bags in landfill waste has resulted in some recycling of plastic shopping bags and the
introduction of more sustainable alternatives. These actions demonstrate that stakeholders
can contribute towards protecting and preserving the wider global environment.

Companies with ISO 14001 accreditation are obliged to develop comprehensive
environmental management systems. The compliance with the legal requirements, administrative procedures and environmental management functions has four main effects:

1 Compliance with an international standards licence is an expensive operation. There are
significant expenditures to the agency or certification body, which has the authority to issue
licences and responsibility for the training and development of other stakeholders, including corporate staff, subcontractors, and suppliers, that are integrated in the compliance
procedures and processes. A fundamental premise of the founders of TQM (Juran, 1974;
Ishikawa, 1985; Deming, 1986) is that the cost of poor quality, realised through inspection
facilities and reworking defective goods, as well as in lost customers, can greatly exceed the
price of installing systems 'that produce high quality products and service' (Hackman and
Wageman, 1995, p. 310).

2 The endorsement of an environmental policy to encourage improvement in an organisation's environmental management system should improve environmental performance.
Institutions that minimise environmental impacts by, for instance, reducing emissions of
greenhouse gases and ozone-depleting substances, waste reductions, as well as efficient
resource use, are not only responding better to government (international, national and
local) guidelines for sustainability, but are, importantly, addressing the diverse stakeholder
perceptions on key social, economic and ecological concerns. Hence, this strategy can positively enhance corporate reputation.

3 Corporations that hold ISO 14001 accreditation have greater opportunities to engage in
global markets; in fact, a lack of accreditation can restrict, or even prevent, trading in international or regional markets. Indeed, a corporation that does not hold ISO 14001 certification cannot be a legitimate stakeholder of a company that does have a current licence.

4 A commitment to improve environmental issues and the prevention of pollution can
have a significant impact on company work procedures and interaction with interested
stakeholders. This point is elucidated in the following section, which outlines how adherence to the principles of ISO 14001 substantially affects the service domain of waste
management.

Environmental waste management

Institutions that embrace international standards for environmental waste management will gain the benefit of being identified as corporations that proactively address their stakeholder issues. Environmental waste management is a service system designed to minimise the potential and actual adverse environmental, health and safety impacts, the material losses, and the operational costs of using hazardous (for example, asbestos, oils, acids, synthetic fibres), and non-hazardous (for example, metals, timber dunnage, tyres) goods. These and other materials are consumed in large quantities, fully or partially, by the industrial sector, and this creates not only the potential for losses, poor utilisation and waste generation, but also opportunities to improve hazardous and non-hazardous waste-handling mechanisms.

Thus, environmental waste management services involve industrial-sector inventories and the analysis of business practices. These investigations into company policy and activity may be considered invasive in other sectors of the economy, and especially investigation into the conduct and functions of those corporations that are ISO 14001 registered. This reinvigoration of organisational design derives from the diverse stakeholder community pressures that have persuaded decision makers to assess more holistically how to maintain economic development while minimising social and environmental costs.

Today the idea of ecological sustainability has popular support. Hence, it has become a significant item on the political agenda. Corporate stakeholder pressure is driven by widespread community disillusionment with the historical approach of governments, their agencies and departments, and their limited efforts to redress problems such as degradation, restoration of natural habitats, reforestation, the proliferation of toxic wastes, and generally insufficient protection of ecosystems. These environmental 'nightmares' are becoming industrial 'dinosaurs' as the wider community of stakeholders critically participates in numerous forums such as taskforces, panels or commissions of inquiry, government and non-government entities, public hearings and advisory councils.

These 'public participation' strategies create a new opportunity for stakeholders to become involved in government decision making, as well as influencing changes in industry environmental policies and management practices. Adherence to the stringent conditions of ISO certification creates an important new role for a wide range of stakeholders who are responsible for implementing policy and administrative requirements. The range of activities and specialist work practices involved in the procedure is significant and includes the implementation of functions, such as monitoring and auditing compliance systems, the maintenance of regulatory procedures and records, and the key performance indicators (that is, total waste generated, energy consumption per unit of production, and the number of staff trained).

Stakeholders and service

Essentially, the functions of managerial decision making must now include stakeholder perspectives. In practice, managers address stakeholder expectations in variable ways; consequently, the decisions they make will have a range of outcomes (that is, satisfaction, loyalty, quality, commitment, and the development of institutional networks). For instance, several interrelated reactions followed the departure of the financial officers who instigated the 2004 Australian foreign exchange trading scandal. Notable outcomes include: the National Australia Bank acknowledged a loss of $360 million, the career of the CEO, Frank Cicutto was curtailed with a significant payment of cash and shares, several board members were replaced (Smith, 2004), and a new CEO was appointed as one of Australia's highest-paid bankers (Kennedy, 2004). Concomitantly, shareholders continued to sit on the 'sidelines' holding stock assets of relatively low value. Clearly, these reactions indicate that some stakeholders had greater influence than others. Hence, it is vital that powerful stakeholders are accurately identified in order to understand their potential influence on organisational decision making.

Figure 3.2 previously presented a simple framework for the identification of stakeholders. In addition to the four types of stakeholders shown (*stockholders, suppliers, employees* and *customers*), it is necessary to make distinctions between *primary* or *secondary* stakeholders, such as owners or non-owners, the levels of financial contribution, and their roles as contractors, claimants and outsourced resource providers. These additional stakeholder categories may be useful to differentiate between, for example, the legitimate customers (stakeholders) in a bank and balaclava-wearing bank robbers, who could falsely argue that they are also stakeholders undertaking banking 'transactions'. Thus, stakeholders can be identified by such attributes as *behavioural, institutional, resource dependence, power of influence, legitimacy* or *risk bearers*, while stakeholders who lack legitimacy may be *coercive*, possibly violent and even dangerous. A case example may include spectators at a football match who may claim stakeholder legitimacy because they engaged in a contract with the entertainment organisation by paying an entrance fee. However, when members of this group invade the playing surface, fight with other legitimate patrons, and later engage in antisocial behaviours causing damage to property, their claim for legitimacy becomes ludicrous. Social scientists now prioritise the development of a better definition of the concept of stakeholders so that managers can improve a service by better addressing the interests of legitimate stakeholders. For instance, three generic attributes of *power, legitimacy* and *urgency* have been used to delineate seven types of stakeholders, as well as a non-stakeholder category (Mitchell et al., 1997). Over time, new ways of characterising stakeholders emerge, as alternative approaches for the identification of stakeholders have been and are continuing to be devised in order to better understand and differentiate between the various types of stakeholder influences.

In Figure 3.2 there is an assumption of a dyadic relationship between shareholders. In the voluminous leadership literature, the relationship between the leader (stakeholder 1) and the subordinate (stakeholder 2) has been termed a dyad, which is often reported to be homogeneous despite observations that in contemporary workplaces stakeholders are not treated in the same way by other powerful stakeholders (that is leaders, managers). Moreover, seldom are stakeholders considered independently and in isolation of other stakeholders' interests. Indeed, 'firms do not simply respond to each stakeholder individually, rather they respond to the interaction of multiple influences from the entire stakeholder set' (Rowley, 1997, p. 890). A local council, for instance, not only endeavours to treat all matters that are likely to concern ratepayers, but simultaneously has wider interactions with employees, other local government bodies, business investors and developers, and a variety of individuals and entities. All are components of the service provision environment of the local council. It may appear that the local council has numerous direct relationships, but in reality a more complex pattern of associations operates. Coexisting with simple interactions will be other criss-crossing networks of interactions between wider stakeholder group representatives related to a business environment. For example, a ratepayer, who could be categorised as a shareholder or a customer might be interacting with the local government minister or the federal parliamentary representative, and both government officials, as well as their departments, might be seen as customers, suppliers or shareholders. In turn, these departments may engage with other environment issues, such as in a dog attack incident, which could involve the council ranger, the police service, the legal system, the ambulance association and the health department. This complexity highlights the urgency to resolve the second major challenge of categorising stakeholder influences. A contemporary model for conceptualising stakeholder relationships must include the multilateral and networked contacts between stakeholders, while acknowledging the unlikeliness of all stakeholders being simultaneously linked (Donaldson and Preston, 1995; Rowley, 1997; Gibson, 2000; Jawahar and McLaughlin, 2001).

Understanding how the interactions between various organisational resources affect the delivery of services (output) is invaluable in the increasingly competitive services domain. The importance of the relationships between personnel and material resources, which may be intangible (that is, services) in socially complex work settings, is well documented (Penrose, 1959; Wernerfelt, 1984; Barney, 1992; Teece et al., 1997). One service sector that is reliant on intangible resources, such as the knowledge-based assets, experience and skills embedded in human capital (Carpenter et al., 2001) is the entertainment sector, and more specifically, the cinema. Due to substantial investment over the past six decades, cinemas are now commonplace. The popularity of film has grown through improvements in customer service, along with significant and ongoing technological developments, making cinema complexes a valuable business niche in the entertainment sector. This is despite ongoing competition from home-based entertainment technology. Figure 3.3 illustrates the complex interrelationships involved between stakeholders in a cinema complex.

The central component of this cinema complex stakeholder framework is similar to the delineation of the primary stakeholder groups shown in Figure 3.2. However, Figure 3.3 is dissimilar in four main ways.
- A greater diversity of stakeholders is shown.
- The stakeholder set included is incomplete. For instance, stakeholders such as marketing and advertising or utilities (power, gas, telephone, Internet) and transport are not included because of space limitations. Moreover, all stakeholders are dependent on others for their survival, and consequently, their actual linkages are far too complex to be fully shown.
- The connections between the nominated stakeholders are shown as pairs of arrowheaded lines, as all stakeholders with legitimate interests should have an equal opportunity to participate in the network transactions. Thus, any stakeholder can initiate and influence an interaction, which can be unidirectional, bidirectional or multidirectional. As these transactions can virtually affect any stakeholder, the arrangement becomes 'a bewildering complex for management' (Mitchell et al., 1997, p. 856).

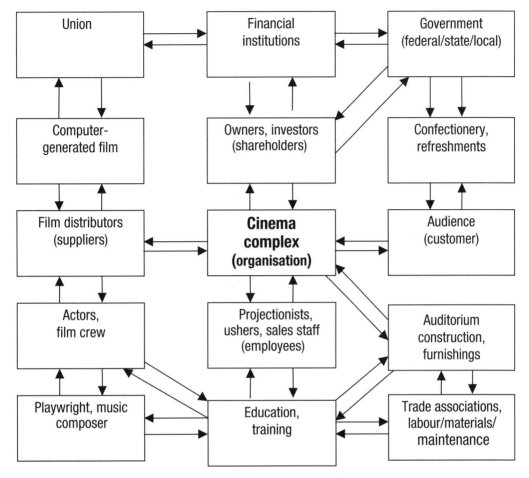

Figure 3.3 The diversity of stakeholders in a cinema complex

- To simplify the depiction of the stakeholder range, only some of the pairs of arrow-headed lines are shown in Figure 3.3. For example, the stakeholders classified as 'financial institutions' are only shown as transacting with the three adjacent stakeholders (union, shareholders and government), while it should be obvious that there are likely to be simultaneous transactions with any other stakeholder.

Clearly, networks such as those shown in Figure 3.3 abound in many cultural, institutional and competitive environments, and their ability to successfully cope will be contingent on a capacity to access managerial human capital. As relationships between stakeholders multiply, management qualities become increasingly critical for organisations and, indeed, all connected stakeholders. Those entities with greater ability to leverage their competitive strengths are more likely to exploit their interests. Hence, stakeholder relationships are always asymmetrical. The most powerful groups of stakeholders have the greatest opportunity for accessing resources, which in turn gives them more power to further influence other stakeholders, through bargaining power, and their ability to combine geographically dispersed resources and to create innovative forms of competitive advantage. Stakeholders who lack appropriate job experience, HRM skills, and complementary knowledge do not have the capacity to be able to adjust to their dynamic environments and, hence, are potential candidates for takeover, liquidation or decline. In spite of the powerful management role in stakeholder frameworks, there is considerable evidence that managers do not always acknowledge stakeholder influences equitably.

While stakeholder theory has enhanced the study of management and organisational practices, it has also attracted considerable criticism, such as:

- It promises much, but delivers little (Brenner and Cochran, 1991).
- It is lacking in complexity (Key, 1999).
- It is incomplete in model linkages (Rowley, 1997).
- It gives arguments that are contradictory and diverse (Donaldson and Preston, 1995).

Yet, despite these and other criticisms, stakeholder theory continues to evolve and to be pivotal in improving performance in organisational services. Hence, in spite of some of the difficulties associated with stakeholder management, stakeholder theory cannot be ignored.

Stakeholder theory and the issue of business ethics

Stakeholder theory has become an important framework for business ethics. A key assertion of stakeholder theory is the need for the company to consider the interests of all affected constituents. An example of this contention could include prison officers, who have the primary role of fulfilling a range of societal interests including punishment, rehabilitation and incarceration of prisoners in state correctional institutions whereas the inmates are very likely to have different interests. The notion that a 'business needs to consider the interest of groups affected by the firm' (Gibson, 2000, p. 245) is a departure from the assertion that the primary objective of an organisation is to maximise the interests of particular groups such as owners and shareholders as promoted by traditional theories. In this tradition, a distinction is made between *primary* and *secondary* stakeholders, where the former have official and *contractual relationships* with the company. However, this categorisation of stakeholders will not necessarily reduce uncertainty. In the case of the correctional institution, community argument exists that the prisoners and their guards are primary stakeholders, while other servicing stakeholders (for example, utilities, education and health) are considered to be secondary stakeholders. It might also be argued that although the prisoners are 'paying' in time, it is unlikely that they have a formal official or contractual relationship (conventional ways of distinguishing primary stakeholders) with the Department of Justice. This lack of a strong positive influence between prisoners and their penitentiary is indicated by the recidivist level of the inmates.

Moreover, this notion of stakeholder interests as being key strategic assets (or costs) to a company is demonstrated by the closure of a large hazardous waste plant at Brookdale (Media Statement, 2003a; 2003b), located within the Perth metropolitan area, after a prolonged campaign by local residents (secondary stakeholders). Such stakeholder groups critiqued the traditional maximisation of the wealth of the primary stakeholders. Indeed, the stakeholder groups did seek to reform traditional perspectives that subscribe to the maximisation of the wealth of the primary stakeholders. More contemporary views incorporate the notion that all stakeholders have intrinsic value. Hence, the aim is to ensure that no set of interests dominates, and that the commitment of business to a wider community-driven and consensus-based 'common good' ethic is a desirable expectation.

The notion that stakeholder interests influence the operations of a company in the interests of the common good provides a strong argument to distinguish between competing stakeholder claims. The aim to pursue a balance between the extremes, to obtain the greatest possible profit for shareholders, and an agenda to extend organisational responsibility to the interests of all entities with a stake, are the tenets of *social responsibility* (Argandona, 1998). This is an appealing position for ethicists despite the paradigm being neither entirely economic nor fully social yet, it does have a broad basis for the ethical point of view. However, it suffers from being relatively vague, and adoption of the philosophy attracts criticisms because specific strategic objectives can have negative consequences. For instance, an organisation may over-hire to reduce local unemployment, and to enhance societal welfare, thus exercising broader social responsibility. This action fails to fulfil its key financial profit-seeking obligations and so undermines the company (resulting in a loss to the shareholders), eventually leading to insolvency and closure, which will ultimately lead to a violation of contracts with all stakeholders.

Stakeholder frameworks

Distinctions about how organisations should consider stakeholder interests in order to adequately address the moral or ethical perspective have been made by Donaldson and Preston (1995). These authors identified four central tenets, which, they contend, need to exist in order to align the nature and extent of operational duties between the actors (stakeholders) affected by the firm. Their pivotal argument is that stakeholder theory is managerial, and consequently, they have endeavoured to address the confusion between the nature and purpose of stakeholder theory with four tenets that are mutually supportive, yet with critical differences:

- *Normative:* how companies should behave.
- *Instrumental:* likely outcomes from such actions.
- *Descriptive:* how companies do behave.
- *Managerial:* the implications for stakeholders.

These concepts, which provide some structure to stakeholder frameworks, could be applied to analyse conundrums such as the ethics of rainforest clearing to promote the economic development of Third World countries, while affluent people in First World countries seek to live in pristine natural environments. These four components are now discussed.

Normative approach

A central concern for stakeholder theory is to identify the primary function (the strategic objective) of the organisation (Gibson, 2000). The subjugation of the primary function can lead to unwanted events, as demonstrated when the Western Australian state government privatised (1) the Brookdale waste treatment plant, and (2) the administration of court security as well as prisoner transportation (from prison to court and back to prison). Both of these actions resulted in events that created considerable stakeholder grievances. The government perceived that it was in the interest of the community for hazardous materials (batteries, industrial salts and chemicals, oils) and biological wastes from grease traps and septic systems to be treated at a centralised waste management site; and for the community and environment to be protected from convicted criminals by a private business firm. In hindsight, these primary functions could not be reconciled with the best financial wealth-maximisation interest of the operators (their primary function), as the treatment plant failed to operate within the licence conditions, causing vocal community concerns, and hence, the waste treatment plant was forced to close. In addition, both the government and the Department of Justice have been considerably embarrassed by repeated incidents of prisoner escapes, which have been instrumental in the government reconsidering the procedures for transferring prisoners to and from the courts, as well as more rigorous incarceration practices to ensure community security. These two cases illustrate that a firm will have certain strategic objectives (the primary function), and managers are obliged to closely examine how various stakeholders are potential threats, or benefits, to achieving these aims. In other words, short-term financial cost savings to maximise wealth creation may result in high cost penalties if these strategies raise critical stakeholder concerns. This reality compels corporations to identify the philosophical and moral guidelines for company operations. A normative approach is appropriate, as it is claimed that many organisations are unlikely to comprehensively fulfil the responsibilities they have to all the stakeholder groups (Jawahar and McLaughlin, 2001).

An additional example is provided by the recent actions of AMP, which paid large severance payments to two successive retiring CEOs, who had been the corporate architects of a disastrous foray into the UK financial market. This executive action was considered to be irresponsible by the majority of stakeholders. (Many sold their shares and publicly voiced strong opposition.) Moreover, the company's financial position deteriorated when the value of AMP stock was slashed in the financial markets. This case, and the privatisation of waste treatment and prisoner security, which involved the Western Australian state government, demonstrate how organisations can lawfully, yet variously, deal with different stakeholders simultaneously. The more complex stakeholder environment indicates that organisations must apply sophisticated ethics and sustainability management frameworks and reconcile these with the pragmatic economic values that motivate business.

Although the primary objective of any organisation is survival, an ancillary, but related aim is to maintain stakeholder satisfaction. Recognition that customer satisfaction is critical for the survival of an organisation is one of the most controversial issues for managers. Managers, especially in services, need to understand the complex human dimensions of their workforce and productivity issues. Historically, the human relations movement of the 1960s championed job satisfaction as a prerequisite of performance. More contemporary approaches promote the more complex interrelationships between job satisfaction, commitment, turnover and productivity (see Chapter 8). However, the question arises as to whether it is unethical for organisations to design jobs, arguably to enhance job satisfaction, while compelling employees to undertake a narrower scope of work in the interests of achieving financial corporate benefits. This type of approach to HR management in the pursuit of profit maximisation is found in fast-food and retail outlets that require employees to perform simple and standardised tasks in repetitive cycles. Conversely, do employees have a moral obligation to engage in their work in adaptable, meaningful ways by exercising initiative and creativity in the pursuit of corporate efficacy?

These ethical questions that attract the attention of managerial relationships with employees 'are based on normative, moral commitments rather than on a desire to use those stakeholders solely to maximise profits' (Berman et al., 1999, p. 492). The fundamental principles that underpin these issues are that 'the economic and social purpose of the corporation is to create and distribute increased wealth and value to all its primary stakeholder groups, without favouring one group at the expense of others' (Clarkson, 1995, p. 112). This, however, becomes difficult for organisations to practise when claims of shareholders are based on fundamental moral principles that may be difficult to balance with other strategic imperatives. For instance, a timber company that claims to be acting ethically by providing economic benefits to all key stakeholders would experience production difficulties from stakeholders with high ecological interests who drive long steel nails into trees marked for felling. This scenario shows that business ethics and work production strategy do not always fit together well, with additional consequences for job satisfaction. The intrinsic value of stakeholder interests is more likely to be recognised when these interests are incorporated into the corporation's strategic decision-making processes.

Although the relative importance of the primary stakeholders has yet to be adequately addressed, a distinction has been attempted by Donaldson and Preston (1995). Their normative theory, as a basis for the operation of stakeholder theory, reverses traditional arguments in terms of stakeholder interest and the concept of stakeholder *intrinsic value*. The concept of 'intrinsic value' as applied to moral principles is identified in normative stakeholder orientations by examining corporate outcomes that appear to be moral, but are advantageous to the firm (for example, they create economic benefit or a good reputation). Two examples can be given of a moral principle that forms a normative foundation for *intrinsic* versus *strategic decision making*. The first, positive, example is the recommendation to use pilots for future oil tanker movements, rather than to use only double-hulled vessels in the pristine waterways of Alaska. The second, more negative, example is the reluctance by the Chinese government to notify world health authorities of the early outbreaks of SARS. These actions demonstrate how an organisation, or service provider, may design strategy around their moral obligations to stakeholders in recognition that this is fundamental to the standard of responsibility they have for stakeholders. Conventionally, organisations may have degrees of interest for stakeholders, as indicated by AMP's retiring executives being rewarded, at the expense of other primary stakeholders. Stakeholders can be defined as entities that have legitimate interests in procedural and substantive aspects of the organisation, despite the level of interest the organisation holds for those stakeholders. This view links together *interest* and *intrinsic value*. Hence, the interest of all stakeholders is of intrinsic value; therefore, all stakeholders merit consideration for their own sake.

This perspective of equity significantly departs from more common economic-based assumptions of neoclassical theory, to underpin the fundamental value that the organisation should be managed in the best interests of the shareholders. The contemporary argument supports the contention that the long-term sustainability of the firm will offer stakeholders greater benefit and protection, while addressing its social responsibility. This is a radical departure from the traditional company stakeholder interest in primary stakeholder (shareholder) relationships. Ultimately, the normative approach is identified by the fundamental moral underpinnings that guide alternative decision-making approaches to determine the treatment of stakeholders: (1) either with a concern for profit maximisation; or (2) to impact firm financial performance by treating stakeholders in a responsive way that more closely addresses their interests.

Instrumental approach

The instrumental approach to stakeholder theory is concerned with the impact of stakeholders on corporate effectiveness. This approach indicates growing acceptance that corporations exist to achieve success in the marketplace by strategically managing stakeholders. The instrumental approach concerns the *adoption of mechanisms* (not strategies) that are expected to lead to desirable outcomes. A recent example occurred during 2004 when Mitsubishi Australia considered closing some of its motor vehicle plants in South Australia, not because they were unprofitable, but because the firm had greater interests at home in Japan. Likewise, throughout the 1990s, many firms adopted outsourcing, downsizing and restructuring, or 'lean and mean' HR management strategies (see Chapter 8). There is considerable anecdotal evidence that these economically prudent actions seldom improved financial returns, that the actions were considered by the wider community as exercises in poor social responsibility, and that the organisation acquired less autonomy with, but a greater dependency on, stakeholders. These examples suggest that investment in high-quality stakeholder relationships contributes to higher levels of trust and commitment, which, in turn, are likely to result in a more favourable competitive advantage. Indeed, a successful instrumental approach is dependent on the firm having a deep and rich understanding of stakeholder relationships. This understanding requires a comprehensive mapping of the environment (actors and context) to effectively enhance communication networks and improve stakeholder relationship management.

Some commentators have argued that the instrumental approach may lack moral or ethical underpinnings (Goodpaster and Holloran, 1994). These authors contend that after undertaking a comprehensive analysis to assess what is in the organisation's best interest, ethics may well be eliminated in preference for organisational prudence. For example, it was a prudential decision by the manager of the electroplating company to instruct employees to flush hazardous wastes into the surface drainage system, rather than adopting the more expensive action of having the caustic and corrosive solutions sent to the waste treatment plant. However, this action was both unlawful and immoral, as the liquid solution was environmentally damaging. In short, organisations may act in the belief that chosen alternatives will have preferred outcomes, which later may not eventuate, and in fact result in unpredicted, but dysfunctional outcomes. That is, the predicted goals were based on amoral foundations. This concept is revealed in an organisation that uses participative goal setting on a recommendation that it will build corporate citizenship, greater organisational profitability, and improved client satisfaction, to claim pursuit of 'the common good'. However, when forced later to assess the impact of the participative job design, and facing financial uncertainty, a loss of market share from global monetary contraction, or other corporate dilemmas, this company is likely to tighten fiscal controls. It will, in fact, return to the application of traditional task control mechanisms based on hierarchical and authoritarian rules to keep the business profitable. Essentially, in adopting the instrumental approach, it matters less about the idea that a particular operational approach will have benefits for the company and the good of the society, and more about the idea that a particular action will reconcile self-interests and moral dilemmas.

Descriptive approach

Descriptive stakeholder theory identifies the reality of what is now going on in the business. Fundamentally, a stakeholder approach explains how strategic thinking is practised in business operations and work arrangements, and how these functions are linked to commercial success. Hence, 'stakeholder theory is arguably descriptive' (Donaldson and Preston, 1995, p. 66). In contrast to normative and instrumental stakeholder approaches, the descriptive stakeholder theory approach is based on the identification of stakeholders and analysis of specific stakeholder perspectives and issues by social science researchers and practitioners. These social scientists are able to elucidate about stakeholder values and interests, and the complex nature of their associations with the concerned organisation. Within this information the potential impact of stakeholder interests and actions on an organisation's performance can be taken into account. The value of this descriptive approach is to provide guidance for acceptable structural and operational arrangements.

The descriptive approach illustrates the interrelationships between stakeholder attributes, contextual factors and managerial behaviour. Ideally, the descriptive dimension can be used to describe, explain and specify how organisations interact with stakeholders. This descriptive approach is based on the analysis of descriptive information. This information is gathered through mapping the various relevant institutional and community aspects across the political/legal, economic, socio-cultural and environmental dimensions of a specific stakeholder and organisational environment. The challenge is to effectively and coherently integrate multicultural, multidisciplinary and diverse specialist functional perspectives. Thus, analysis of descriptive information can identify the basic rights of stakeholders, the impacts on ecological sustainability, community equity concerns such as the implications of business activities for the disadvantaged, minority groups, and other social issues, which are becoming the realm of protective legislation. This descriptive approach has, for instance, been used to describe how stakeholder interests can be taken into account in the strategic design of particular business ventures to better understand the way managers think about their role, and even how board members consider the interests of the corporate constituents. For example, an analysis of the electronic tapes that recorded the chaos and frenetic confusion of the events of 11 September 2001 in the United States demonstrates how air traffic controllers, air traffic managers and associated government officials were overwhelmed and confused by the dramatic events (Cock, 2004; West Australian, 2004b; 2004c). Some 10 minutes after the first plane crashed into the north tower of New York's World Trade Center at 788 kilometres per hour, the Federal Aviation Authority still had not contacted the military. After a further hour, debate was still continuing about how to protect New York. Consequently, fighter pilots were unsure of the nature of the threat, and were given insufficient interception information or authority to destroy the hijacked planes. Indeed, only after all four hijacked planes had crashed did Vice President Dick Cheney order fighter aircraft to shoot down the hostile planes. This is a disturbing description of how the catastrophe was played out in a stakeholder framework, and demonstrates how aviation officials and military personnel struggled to deal with an unimaginable, unprecedented crisis for which they were untrained and unprepared.

Managerial approach

Stakeholder theory obviously has important implications for management. Scholars of management, social sciences, business ethics and a variety of related fields now explore how to organise, evaluate and integrate these multidisciplinary frameworks into a more comprehensive management approach. In fact, the discussion on stakeholder theory in this chapter indicates the diverse ways in which stakeholder theory has been used to better understand how some service organisations are actually managed. Stakeholder theory is fundamental to understanding the pivotal place of managers in addressing these issues. While on the one hand, managers are themselves a specific type of stakeholder, on the other hand, they additionally have a central role in stakeholder–manager relations. The importance of managers in stakeholder theory is central to the notion of organisations as being coalitions of individuals. Within organisations, disparate demands arise, and it is the primary role of managers to reconcile the various dynamic claims of the stakeholders (Cyert and March, 1963). Extending the concept of organisations as coalitions of varying interests is the notion that managers have dependency on particular stakeholders, which they identified as resource allocators (Pfeffer and Salancik, 1978). It is the 'holders' of critical resources (finance, labour, material, information) who, as primary stakeholders, capture the attention of managers.

Managers are obliged to prioritise stakeholder relationships. These priorities need to be based on an understanding of the complex and dynamic ways in which local, national, regional and global economic, political, legal, competitive, societal and risk issues may impact on business performance (see Chapter 2). It is managers who have the central responsibility of addressing stakeholder claims through strategic decision making and the allocation of strategic resources. Managers may have a limited capacity to simultaneously address a number of demands, and hence, they need to prioritise demands and make decisions about an appropriate action agenda (see Chapter 4). This agenda could be determined through consideration of factors such as the legitimacy of the request, the power of the claimant, or the urgency of the matter.

Despite acknowledgment of the theoretical value of this type of approach, it is more likely that the nature of response will be determined by the manager's perception of the importance of the stakeholder (Mitchell et al., 1997). Those stakeholders who attract the highest level of attention may be considered most important by the manager. This issue links with stakeholder calls for greater transparency in and accountability for managerial decision-making processes. In addition, managers may need to raise their own critical awareness about how they prioritise and make decisions. However, while it is recognised that the manager's personal attributes impact on the decision-making process, the manager's role is central in reconciling the divergent interests of salient stakeholders in their professional environment. The issue of managing knowledge and communication becomes crucial to achieving successful business and stakeholder community outcomes. The following illustrative case demonstrates the complexity of managing the interests of a diverse range of stakeholders.

Box 3.2   The Trans Territory Pipeline (Blacktip to Nhulunbuy)

A conundrum for national governments, especially in regional locations, is how to progress economic and social capital without compromising indigenous and ecological sustainability. This paradoxical challenge, which involved an extensive number of diverse stakeholders, is presented in the case of the proposed development of the Trans Territory Pipeline from Blacktip to Nhulunbuy in the Northern Territory. Specifically, a project estimated to have a worth of A$2 billion that will expand the capacity of the largest alumina refinery in the Southern Hemisphere is being undertaken in one of the most remote and culturally sensitive regions within the Australian mainland. The central objective of the project is the conversion of the refinery powerhouse, which currently uses liquid fossil fuel oil, to operate on natural gas (Pearson, 2004). This natural gas will be supplied in an underground steel pipeline from the Blacktip gasfield in the southern part of the Joseph Bonaparte Gulf, to the refinery, which is on the edge of the town of Nhulunbuy, in Arnhem Land. The pipeline, some 1,000 kilometres in length, will require an easement on land that is owned by 27 indigenous Aboriginal clans. A service organisation has been generated to give due consideration to the legitimate interests of those entities that believe they have a stake in the project. The following section outlines how this is being practically addressed within the framework of normative, instrumental and descriptive approaches.

With a commitment to innovation, a consortium of refinery company representatives, along with the gasfield owners and the pipeline operators, drew on theoretical stakeholder management ideas to facilitate a public participation process concerning the impact of the pipeline route. A central organisation was established to proactively address stakeholder interests beyond the profit maximisation function, and determine the most suitable pipeline easement based on the incorporation of specific societal and environmental sustainability stakeholder expectations. In addition to the basic stakeholder consultation framework that included suppliers (gasfield and pipeline operators), shareholders (landowners), customers (the refinery) and employees (construction pipeline and expanded refinery staff), a multitude of other interested stakeholder groups were also included. These interested stakeholder groups included the governments (federal, state, local), their departments, advisers and counsellors, as well as numerous government regulatory regimes, and non-government organisations (Greenpeace, WWF Australia). While some of these groups have formal, official or contractual relationships with the proposal developers, other stakeholder groups are incorporated on the basis of the social responsibility framework. The primary role of the central organisation is to facilitate inputs and outputs from all the identified stakeholder groups so that their various perspectives are transparently included in a consultative and collaborative interaction process in order to obtain a memorandum of agreement for the Trans Territory Pipeline Route.

The *normative* approach to this case is that completion of the project ought to make a meaningful contribution to ecological sustainability. Conversion of the refinery power-house to natural gas will result in the emission of lower levels of carbon, and produce 24 per cent less greenhouse gas emissions than fuel oil for the same energy output. This means that the use of natural gas for domestic and industrial activity will have less impact on the natural environment, and hence, is considered to be more sustainable. The pipeline will be buried to minimise interference with the local fauna and flora, and its visual impact. In addi-tion, the development project will create 2,000 new onsite jobs for the construction of the pipeline and the building of the refinery extensions. Additional support positions are needed to make and transport the pipes; and subsequently, after construction, there will be ongoing maintenance, operational and infrastructural tasks. Upgrading the refinery to double its out-put from 2 million tonnes per year (mty) to 4 mty will create new career opportunities for skilled workers, which in turn will contribute to a more sustainable regional outlook as addi-tional health, education, transport and other service industries develop. Indeed, the gas supply has been anticipated to last for 20 years, and Nhulunbuy's population is expected to double from its current 4,000 people.

The *instrumental* stakeholder approach is concerned with the impact stakeholders may have for corporate effectiveness. A key outcome is that the conversion to gas will make a direct contribution to the Australian government's greenhouse challenge to advance the ideals of the Kyoto Protocol. An expanded refinery output is likely to result in lower per unit pro-duction costs through economies of scale, the generation of relatively less harmful emissions, wealth creation for a larger cohort of skilled employees, as well as an intensification of local auxiliary service groups (for example, medical, transport, education, retail traders). Moreover, not only will owners of the pipeline easement (land) acquire new wealth, but increased export sales will give better returns to the refinery shareholders, and increased government revenues from taxation will provide additional funding for expenditure on important environmental assets and services. These outcomes reflect the principle of fairness and appeal to the ethical view of the common good.

The *descriptive* approach explains how the stakeholder interests of the Trans Territory Pipeline project are being considered. Indeed, meetings, discussions and engagements are ongoing as exigencies arise daily. Although there is reasonable access to communication infrastructure such as telephone, facsimile and email to support the necessary flow of infor-mation between stakeholders, significant value is placed on 'face-to-face' dialogue. This is because the local and indigenous communities, over whose land the pipeline transects, speak three different languages – English, Yolgnu Matha and Creole. Few people can communi-cate in all three languages. Yolgnu Matha and Creole are both largely oral-based languages, although Yolgnu Matha has a written form. This linguistic complexity means that a high pri-ority needs to be given to face-to-face interaction in order to build shared understandings and trust between the diverse stakeholders.

In order to convey respect to the local indigenous community as the traditional landowners, the Australian government has decreed that the final agreement will be writ-ten in Yolgnu Matha. Thus, bilingual dictionaries have had to be prepared and translators (more than one) present at the meetings that include the indigenous peoples. As the issue of land rights underscores the Trans Territory Pipeline route agreement, land map details that accurately indicate local community territorial boundaries must be prepared. Thus, the land had to be surveyed, maps prepared and community land titles registered. In an extensive landscape that accommodates numerous small isolated communities, connected by roads that are mostly dirt and gravel and completely unserviceable in the 'wet season', most people have to be helicoptered to and from stakeholder meetings.

All of these complexities have been dealt with by the central consultant service organisation. Considerable progress in reaching stakeholder agreements is indicated by the agreements of most of the Aboriginal clans to the proposed pipeline easement, and in several areas pipe laying has commenced. A convincing case can be made that stakeholder concerns have been extensively and ethically addressed. However, it is apparent that the ongoing maintenance of social harmony – and, therefore, support for the development – will be dependent on the establishment of an institutional authority charged with the responsibility of ensuring that the common interest issues will continue to be addressed.

Stakeholders and service

There are at least three reasons for the incorporation of stakeholder theory into services management. First, a historical legacy provided an impetus to create new management paradigms in response to the need to develop more acceptable organisational practice. The following examples indicate historical shifts in acceptable practice. Records suggest that more than 700,000 Chinese workers were conscripted by Qin Shihuang in the third century BC to build his mausoleum and some 8,000 terracotta soldiers, charioteers and archers to protect his tomb (Irving, 2004). During the construction period of 36 years these artisans would have been provided with basic sustenance and accommodation. A hallmark of the Industrial Revolution was environmental degradation. Factories were instrumental in the degradation of large tracts of land, while consuming huge amounts of natural resources, and discharging vast quantities of sewage and toxic waste. This is evidenced by many countries having inherited the types of problems historically associated with the proliferation of pollutants and hazardous chemicals. Indeed, the Tigris River, one of the great waterways of the Middle East, since earliest times has been used as an open sewer for human and industrial waste, and hence, is now in urgent need of rehabilitation. Likewise, many national governments that previously failed to address environmental concerns, when facing community pressure, have established legislative policy strategies and government service agencies responsible for the assessment and implementation of remediation strategies such as reforestation, and the restoration of wetlands or mine sites. The reactive impetus for the development of comprehensive legislative and regulatory government strategies has come from numerous environmental disasters, such as major oil spills, nuclear reactor problems (for example, Chernobyl and Three Mile Island), explosions at liquid gas facilities, or spillages of large quantities of chemical solvents or sewage. In response to these environmental disasters, various stakeholder communities now demand greater participation and consultation roles in the development of more sustainable approaches to development.

Changing community expectations have led to the expansion of the service facilities. These arrangements are involved in the development of new legislation, the preparation of tougher industry regulations, the creation of development guidelines, advisory panels, specialised committees, and commissions of inquiry, task forces, the appointment of an ombudsman or a representative, as well as the opportunities for public submissions invited through the media. Thus, there is a myriad of mechanisms for public participation that are available to stakeholders engaged in the pursuit of facilitating more responsible organisations and managerial behaviours in contemporary institutions. The targets for these professional services are those corporations that produce goods, the oil and chemical industries, the construction and development field, and all those associated with natural resource consumption. The management is increasingly being challenged by an extensive range of global, national and local stakeholders 'to address environmental degradation and rehabilitation while maintaining the objective of economic growth' (Harding, 1989, p. 39).

Consequently, there is a range of public participation mechanisms available to stakeholders to engage in the promotion and development of more responsive and responsible organisational performance. As an example of innovative community consultation processes, in 2003 the Western Australian government's Ministry for Planning and Infrastructure held a 'Dialogue with the City' forum with 1,100 participants. The day-long event, the largest of its kind in the Southern Hemisphere, included residents, community groups, and representatives of industry and government who joined together to debate the direction for the future 25-year plan for the metropolitan region. This event was part of a wide range of consultative community strategies, such as: community surveys; an interactive website and chat rooms; features in the media; art and writing competitions for schools; a televised debate; forums with diverse community groups; and the ongoing engagement of over 100 people from the community, industry, and local and state government. The goal is to create more integrated guidelines, policies and a strategic plan for a more sustainable approach to the city's future development.

The service dimension to production management is a second reason to incorporate stakeholder theory. Production firms that employ traditional formal patterns of interaction and coordination to link individuals and tasks will have a service function, or in the case of larger firms, a service department. This is an additional area to other departments or sections, such as human resources, production, sales and marketing, and relevant groups of employees in their main functional (or specialised) area. These organisational arrangements are often presented as organisational charts to show the 'chain of command', the main clusters of titled job positions, as well as horizontal and vertical reporting relationships. In conventional organisations the service department has limited interaction with other departments, as the prime responsibility of the service department employees is to provide after-sales service. However, many stakeholders now consider that an organisation's responsibility does not cease at the end of the production cycle. In other words, stakeholders are now concerned with matters of customer service. There is now strong evidence to demonstrate that the quality of service delivery is built in through the activities of all relevant contributors (employees, suppliers of materials, and management system), and that a high level of quality service is unlikely to be achieved by only inspecting work at the end of the service delivery cycle. Consequently, services management is more comprehensively addressed not by traditional administrative, bureaucratic or economic management models but, more likely, by a more integrated systems approach guided by stakeholder theory.

A third reason why stakeholder theory is important for services management lies in the areas of customer decision making. During the 1970s the concept of a quality product or service was defined only in broad terms such as endurance, price and aesthetic appeal. Consequently, customers were treated uniformly, but by the 1990s consumers had greater expectations about quality. Additional features besides cost, attractiveness, strength and durability are now important to customers. These features include such dimensions as privacy, independence, personal service, and ethical, environmental and socio-cultural aspects of good and services. For instance, Body Shop International has gained a high level of international patronage for its cosmetic products by educating the potential customer (stakeholder) that the goods (that is, soaps, lotions, creams, shampoos) are manufactured from sustainable flora (and not fauna), and moreover, that the company strives to support sustainable local environmental and social development. The education of customer choice empowers stakeholders as 'makers of meaning' (Stamp, 1995, p. 3) to use their judgment to decide whether or not to undertake transactions with a company (Lawrence, 1998). Chapter 5 further discusses these marketing and consumer choice issues.

Organisations that fail to maintain high quality levels of stakeholder transactions may well find themselves without customers (Walsh, 1995). For too long, organisations have neglected stakeholder attitudes and aspirations, and continued to provide goods and services that they consider satisfactory for the purchasing public. Yet, over time, there have been fundamental global changes that have affected lifestyles and, consequently, individual consumer expectations. The industries that produce tangible goods might respond to this transformation challenge with a more inclusive strategy meaning that 'the process must start with people. The system must be made to fit the people, not the people to the system' (Walsh, 1995, p. 36). Thus, the more successful service providers are likely to be those that have visionary business practices that intertwine customers' personal values and purchasing behaviours. For example, McDonald's, one of the most widely established fast-food outlets, has been aggressively promoting 'less fat meals' and more nutritional food lines. Interestingly, these initiatives appear to be following increased community awareness of linkages between diet and health, the high incidence of obesity in Western societies, and relationships between these issues and the growth in fast-food outlets. The need to address such societal expectations and preferences will compel organisations to employ managerial systems that balance stakeholder values with commercial imperatives.

Services management

A hallmark of international competition is the diffusion and pervasiveness of services management. Engagement with the global marketplace has compelled organisations to heighten the quality of business practices at global, national and local levels. The result has been a profound transformation of competition across these levels, along with the shift from manufacturing to the expanding domain of services. The momentous reshaping of stakeholder interests has been marked by the entry of services into most aspects of our lifestyles. The 1970s was an era of economic expansion when the Western world was challenged by foreign competitors, and particularly, by the Japanese with their higher-quality cheaper products. Customer service relations departments, along with a host of other innovative business operations, were introduced into US manufacturing firms during the 1980s as competition strategies to mimic the core attributes of the Japanese management style. There was little alternative for the US automakers, whose dominant market position had declined and who, in the early 1980s, were experiencing losses of billions of dollars through decreased sales. These remarkable changes stimulated an enormous thirst for services during the 1990s. This accelerated impetus for growth in services was stimulated by the collapse of a number of centrally planned socialist systems and the emergence of a competitive market-based economy, new career opportunities created by technological developments and the pace of information transfer, changes in skill composition from mass education, and the increased participation of women in labour markets. Stemming from these changes were the proliferation of new labour markets and new demographic profile characteristics, such as two income earner households, more highly educated workers who are in better-paid jobs, with changes in skill composition and the increased role of women in paid work. As community affluence grew, so did stakeholder spending power, which in turn increased the demand for services (or the 'McDonaldisation' phenomenon) and the management of service.

Few people in developing and developed countries would not have been exposed to the McDonald's chain of fast-food outlets. Since Ray Kroc purchased the US franchise rights in 1955 the organisation has expanded enormously and now sells 'Big Macs' on every continent. At the heart of this enormous success is aggressive marketing, and the employment of standardised and routinised production processes. While these work arrangements are primarily designed to give the customer quality fast food, they also are the cornerstone of counter service. It is the personal experience between the customer and the McDonald's counter staff that will shape stakeholder opinions of how they felt about the services interaction, how they were spoken to and, overall, whether they were satisfied with the treatment received. It is well documented that customers hold a normative view about how they believe they should be treated. The gap between this and the service actually provided (the service 'gap'), in the framework of the 'met–unmet' expectations theory (Porter and Steers, 1973; Muchinsky and Tuttle, 1979; Bottger, 1990; Pearson, 1995), will determine the extent of customer satisfaction. Dissatisfied customers are likely to complain, to tell a wide audience of potential customers about their perception of poor service, and are unlikely to patronise the company again. In a climate of intense competition, such as between fast-food outlets and restaurants in the food retailing sector, many organisations have reinvented themselves in response to customer expectations.

In addition to organisations that provide a mixture of goods and service, there is also an increasing abundance of organisations that have purely service functions. These firms are collectively referred to as the services domain. Although service is an intangible activity (see Chapter 1), and is difficult to assess, this element is crucial for success. For instance, today's homes are reliant on garbage removal and other domestic services, such as water, gas and electricity, as well as the labour of different tradespeople to undertake such tasks as carpet cleaning, plumbing or other service repairs to household equipment, or even home renovating. Moreover, in the fulfilment of social equity and quality of life ideals, most individuals are beneficiaries of services that include transportation, hospitality, education, health, law or even welfare, and finally death.

All of these interactions require relationships between customers, companies and their social surroundings, and managers need to proactively address stakeholder interests to achieve improved efficiencies and ensure growth. An overriding need to ensure that proper account is taken of customer interests is the essence of the value of stakeholder theory. Traditional approaches assert that organisational survival was primarily achieved by the maximisation of return on shareholder investment. In contrast, stakeholder theory indicates that successful businesses will take into consideration the interests and expectations of a variety of stakeholder groups, including shareholders. It is the contention of this chapter that stakeholder theory has universal value for the production sector, for profit and non-profit organisations, for those firms such as retailers that have a goods and services component, as well as for 'pure' service organisations. Indeed, the very survival and continuing success of these businesses are highly dependent on an integrated stakeholder-based approach to services management.

Conclusion

Significant investment is being made in identifying and managing stakeholders. In particular, during the past two decades significant attention has been given to developing stakeholder theory as an alternative to the traditional economic and social structural models previously developed to predict organisational behaviour. To replace these dominant theories, scholars have focused on stakeholder theory, which underscores a more comprehensive management approach that aims to integrate social behavioural dimensions with economic expectations. The central objective of this framework is to describe how companies respond to the multiple and interdependent influences of stakeholders who exist in contemporary environments that are exceedingly complex.

The role of managers is a critical feature of the stakeholder framework. Ultimately, the benefits attained by particular stakeholders are determined by how managers prioritise competing claims. For instance, the community is frequently aggrieved by price 'hikes' in vehicle fuel, which is a commodity that affects the cost of almost every other good and service in an industrial world The dominant view is that the oil corporations are more driven by the profit-seeking demands of shareholders and less by the ethical priorities associated with wider social objectives. The resolution of such specific stakeholder interests may be represented by individuals, citizen groups, government or non-government bodies, as well as public entities, indigenous peoples, trade unions and minority groups. These stakeholders provide opportunities for discourse to reach mutually acceptable outcomes that impact on institutional strategies for global action on ecological sustainable development. And across these arrangements, managers have a vital role as they endeavour to address the competing claims of the various stakeholders within the three aspects of stakeholder theory: (1) normative, (2) instrumental, and (3) descriptive. The normative concern is how managers ought to deal with stakeholders, the instrumental approach provides consequences for the management treatment of stakeholders, and the descriptive approach is concerned with how managers actively deal with stakeholders. In practice, it is managerial activity that determines how others perceive corporate values, the way the organisation addresses its stakeholders, and its economic corporate performance.

Exercises

Media exercise 3.1

From leading newspapers, select a topic that has attracted widespread community attention – for example, the collapse of HIH, One.Tel or Ansett. Briefly outline the important features of the topic in a paragraph of about 150 words. Who are the stakeholders of the topic, and what dimensions of stakeholder theory are being employed by these groups?

Case study 3.1 Firestorm

It was late afternoon and Greg Thompson, a farm hand, was repairing the farm's northern gate. This gate kept sheep in the adjoining paddock out of the wheat crop, which was to be harvested in a few days' time. Today had been one of the worst in Greg's experience. Since early morning the wind had been blowing from the northeast, which was unusual for this time of the year, and at times had gusted to gale force. In fact, right now, topsoil and pieces of bush, together with bits of material violently torn from trees, were sweeping in copious streams across the open ground. Just one more piece of steel to cut, thought Greg, as he brushed grit from the corners of his eyes and wiped his sweaty brow. Cutting the steel was an easy job, and soon sparks were flying from the wheel of the motorised cutter that was fastened to the tray of his truck. The sparks were ripped away to mix with the flying dust, and soon Greg's sense of satisfaction with the job turned to shock when he saw that the ground cover was alight. Despite Greg's efforts to beat down the flames, they roared away into the wheat crop.

The siren's mournful wail drew volunteers to the fire station like moths to a flame. First to arrive was Bill Perger, the oldest crew member, who had been a fire-fighter as long as he cared to remember. Next was Mary Easter, a mother of three, who was now behind the wheel of the fire truck, gunning the motor ready for a quick getaway. Climbing into the rear seat of the cab was Alan Clancy, who had changed his mechanic's overalls for his fire-fighting kit. On the other side, ready to go, sat Jack Lee, the owner of the Lake Grace local store. Soon the fire truck was speeding down the main street into a wall of billowing red dust and rolling debris. With lights flashing and horn blaring, it headed for the billowing black scar on the horizon. 'This is going to be a bad one,' said Bill. 'All the local farmers have been alerted, and they are pooling equipment, but this wind is going to create tremendous problems.' 'Yeah,' said Alan. 'The weather guys say it's because of a cyclone that's tearing down the coast.' 'With some luck it will be gone tomorrow,' said Jack.

'The weather forecasters were right,' said Dr Chew, as he walked slowly down the narrow gravel road with the Lake Grace sergeant of police. It was a fine, still morning, the sky was blue, but all around there was an eerie silence and a pungent, acrid smell in the air. The landscape was testament to the severity of the fire, for everything had been consumed, except for the blackened protruding sticks that had once been bushes and shrubs. Elsewhere there were wisps of faint blue smoke that drifted from smouldering pieces of material that had been stumps or broken limbs of trees. As they rounded a bend in the track, which quickly dropped away to a dry, sandy creek bed, the horror of what had happened was all too apparent. The scarred fire truck, now only recognisable by some markings on the door, was sitting on blackened rims. Huddled together inside of what had been the cab were the bodies of the crew, who had sought refuge together as the wave of fire, at least 20 metres high, had roared up the valley. 'I don't envy your job here, Doctor,' said the police sergeant. 'But we can't remove the bodies until they are pronounced deceased by a medical practitioner. Also, you'll be required to give evidence at the impending coroner's inquiry.'

This account is representative of country Australia during the height of the summer season. Clearly, scenarios such as the one described here are a major crisis for a small community, but there are a great many more crises for individuals (in other places) who may have been involved with the main participants. Nevertheless, from these crises people move forward. Sometimes the path is through learning positive things from the crises.

Student projects

1 Examine the critical stakeholder elements of this case in terms of the organisational, human resources, political and cultural management dimensions.
2 In the above case, a number of stakeholders are identified. Nominate and categorise them. There are latent stakeholders who have legitimate interests in the events of the case. Delineate and categorise these stakeholders separately. Now, in a group with other class colleagues, discuss your results. What is a salient observation of this discussion?

References and further reading

Abzug, R. and Webb, N. J. 1999, 'Relationships between non-profit and for-profit organizations: A stakeholder perspective', *Nonprofit and Voluntary Sector Quarterly*, vol. 28, no. 4, pp. 416–31.

Agle, B. R., Mitchell, R. K. and Sonnenfeld, J. A. 1999, 'Who matters to CEOs? An investigation of stakeholder attributes and salience, corporate performance, and CEO values', *Academy of Management Journal*, vol. 42, no. 5, pp. 507–25.

Alkhafaji, A. F. 1989, *A Stakeholder Approach to Corporate Governance: Managing in a dynamic environment*, Quorum Books, Westport, CT.

Argandona, A. 1998, 'The stakeholder theory and the common good', *Journal of Business Ethics*, vol. 17, no. 9/10, pp. 1093–102.

Barnard, C. 1938, *The Functions of the Executive*, Harvard University Press, Cambridge, MA.

Barney, J. 1992, 'Integrating organizational behavior and strategy formulation research: A resource-based analysis', in P. Shrivastava, A. Huff and J. Dutton (eds), *Advances in Strategic Management*, vol. 8, pp. 39–61, JAI Press, Greenwich, CT.

Berman, S. L., Wicks, A. C., Kotha, S. and Jones, T. M. 1999, 'Does stakeholder orientation matter? The relationship between stakeholder management models and firm financial performance', *Academy of Management Journal*, vol. 42, no. 5, pp. 488–506.

Bird, F. 2001, 'Good governance: A philosophical discussion of the responsibilities and practices of organizational governors', *Canadian Journal of Administrative Sciences*, vol. 18, no. 4, pp. 298–312.

Bottger, P. C. 1990, 'Voluntary turnover: An empirical test of the met expectations hypotheses', *Asia Pacific Human Resource Management*, vol. 28, no. 3, pp. 18–27.

Brenner, S. N. and Cochran, P. H. 1991, 'The stakeholder model of the firm: Implications for business and society research', in J. F. Mahon (ed.), *Proceedings of the Second Annual Meeting of the International Association for Business and Society*, pp. 449–67, Sundance, UT.

Brigham, E. 1992, *Fundamentals of Financial Management*, 6th ed., Dryden Press, New York.

Carpenter, M. A., Sanders, W. G. and Gregersen, H. B. 2001, 'Bundling human capital with organizational context: The impact of international assignment experience on multinational firm performance and CEO pay', *Academy of Management Journal*, vol. 44, no. 3, pp. 493–511.

Carroll, A. B. 1979, 'A three-dimensional conceptual model of corporate social performance', *Academy of Management Review*, vol. 4, no. 4, pp. 497–506.

Carroll, A. B. 1989, *Business and Society: Ethics and stakeholder management*, South-Western, Cincinnati, OH.

Chatterjee, S. R. and Pearson, C. A. L. 1996, 'Implementing human resources in a transitional society: An empirical study in Mongolia', *MSM Research Papers*, vol. xvi, no. 1, pp. 21–28.

Checkland, P. B. 1981, *Systems Thinking, Systems Practice*, John Wiley, Chichester.

Clarkson, M. B. E. 1995, 'A stakeholder framework for analysing and evaluating corporate social performance', *Academy of Management Review*, vol. 20, no. 1, pp. 92–117.

Cock, A. 2004, 'The series of bungles that cost 3000 lives', *Sunday Times*, 20 June, p. 55.

Commonwealth of Australia, 1990, 'Ecologically Sustainable Development', *A Commonwealth Discussion Paper*, Australian Government Publishing Service, Canberra.

Cornell, B. and Shapiro, A. C. 1987, 'Corporate stakeholders and corporate finance', *Financial Management*, vol. 16, no. 1, pp. 5–14.

Cyert, R. M. and March, J. G. 1963, *The Behavioral Theory of the Firm*, Prentice Hall, Englewood Cliffs, NJ.

Deal, T. E. and Kennedy, A. A. 1982, *Corporate Culture: The rites and rituals of corporate life*, Addison-Wesley, Reading, MA.

Deming, W. E. 1986, *Out of Crisis*, MIT Center for Advanced Engineering Study, Cambridge, MA.

Donaldson, T. 1999, 'Making stakeholder theory whole', *Academy of Management Review*, vol. 24, no. 2, pp. 237–41.

Donaldson, T. and Preston, L. E. 1995, 'The stakeholder theory of the corporation: Concepts, evidence and implications', *Academy of Management Review*, vol. 20, no. 1, pp. 65–91.

Dufrene, U. and Wong, A. 1996, 'Stakeholders versus stockholders and financial ethics: Ethics to whom?', *Management Finance*, vol. 22, no. 4, pp. 1–10.

Eells, R. 1960, *The Meaning of Modern Business*, Columbia University Press, New York.

Freeman, R. E. 1984, *Strategic Management: A stakeholder approach*, Pitman, Boston.

Freeman, R. E. 1999, 'Divergent stakeholder theory', *Academy of Management Review*, vol. 24, no. 2, pp. 233–6.

Freeman, R. E. and Evan, W. M. 1990, 'Corporate governance: A stakeholder interpretation', *Journal of Behavioral Economics*, vol. 19, no. 4, pp. 337–59.

Gibson, K. 2000, 'The moral basis of stakeholder theory', *Journal of Business Ethics*, vol. 26, no. 3, pp. 245–57.

Gioia, D. A. 1999, 'Practicability, paradigms, and problems in stakeholder theorizing', *Academy of Management Review*, vol. 24, no. 2, pp. 228–32.

Goodpaster, K. and Holloran, T. 1994, 'In defence of paradox', *Business Ethics Quarterly*, vol. 4, no. 4, pp. 423–9.

Gopalan, S. and Rivera, J. B. 1997, 'Gaining a perspective on Indian value orientations: Implications for expatriate managers', *International Journal of Organizational Analysis*, vol. 5, no. 2, pp. 156–79.

Guay, T., Doh, J. P. and Sinclair, G. 2004, 'Non-government organizations, shareholder activism, and socially responsible investments: Ethical, strategic, and governance implications', *Journal of Business Ethics*, vol. 52, no. 2, pp. 125–39.

Hackman, J. R. and Wageman, R. 1995, 'Total quality management: Empirical, conceptual and practical issues', *Administrative Science Quarterly*, vol. 40, no. 2, pp. 310–42.

Harding, R. (ed.). 1998, *Environmental Decision Making: The roles of scientists, engineers and the public*, The Federation Press, Sydney.

Heugens, P. P. A. R., Van Den Bosch, F. A. J. and Van Riel, C. B. M. 2002, 'Stakeholder integration: Building mutually enforcing relationships', *Business and Society*, vol. 41, no. 1, pp. 36–60.

Hill, C. W. L. and Jones, T. M. 1992, 'Stakeholder-ageing theory', *Journal of Management Studies*, vol. 29, no. 2, pp. 131–54.

Hummels, H. 1998, 'Organizing ethics: A stakeholder debate', *Journal of Business Ethics*, vol. 17, no. 13, pp. 1403–19.

Irving, M. 2004, 'Soldiering on in Shaanxi', *West Australian* (Today Supplement), 17 June, pp. 14–15.

Ishikawa, K. 1985, *What is Total Quality Control? The Japanese way*, Prentice Hall, Englewood Cliffs, NJ.

Jawahar, I. M. and McLaughlin, G. L. 2001, 'Towards a descriptive stakeholder theory: An organizational life cycle approach', *Academy of Management Review*, vol. 26, no. 3, pp. 397–414.

Jones, T. M. 1980, 'Corporate social responsibility, revisited', *California Management Review*, vol. 22, no. 3, pp. 59–67.

Jones, T. M. 1995, 'Instrumental stakeholder theory: A synthesis of ethics and economics', *Academy of Management Review*, vol. 20, no. 2, pp. 404–37.

Jones, T. M. and Wicks, A. C. 1999, 'Convergent stakeholder theory', *Academy of Management Review*, vol. 24, no. 2, pp. 206–21.

Juran, J. M. 1974, *The Quality Control Handbook*, 3rd ed., McGraw-Hill, New York.

Juzhong, Z., Edwards, D., Webb, D. and Capulong, M. V. 2000, *Corporate Governance and Finance in East Asia: A study of Indonesia, Republic of Korea, Malaysia, Philippines, and Thailand*, Asian Development Bank, Manila.

Kakabadse, N. K. and Kakabadse, A. 2003, 'Polylogue as a platform for governance: Integrating people, the planet, profit and posterity', *Corporate Governance*, vol. 3, no. 1, pp. 5–38.

Kaler, J. 2003, 'Differentiating stakeholder theories', *Journal of Business Ethics*, vol. 46, no. 1, pp. 71–83.

Kennedy, E. 2004, 'NAB's $21.4m man', *West Australian*, 28 May, p. 4.

Key, S. 1999, 'Toward a new theory of the firm: A critique of stakeholder "theory"', *Management Decision*, vol. 37, no. 4, pp. 317–28.

Khalilzadeh-Shirazi, J. and Zagha, R. 1994, 'Achievements and the agenda ahead', *Columbia Journal of World Business*, vol. 29, no. 1, pp. 24–31.

Langtry, B. 1994, 'Stakeholders and the moral responsibilities of business', *Business Ethics Quarterly*, vol. 4, no. 4, pp. 431–43.

Lawrence, R. P. R. 1998, 'Quality assessment, total quality management and the stakeholders in the UK higher education system', *Managing Service Quality*, vol. 8, no. 1, pp. 55–63.

Lewis, G. 1998, 'The vulture has landed', *Australian Financial Review*, 22 July, pp. 11–12.

March, J. G. and Simon, H. 1958, *Organizations*, Wiley, New York.

Mark-Ungericht, B. 2001, 'Business and newly emerging civil society actors: Between conflict and new forms of social dialogue', *Global Business Review*, vol. 2, no. 1, pp. 55–69.

Mason, R. O. and Mitroff, I. I. 1981, *Challenging Strategic Planning Assumptions*, Wiley, New York.

Media Statement. 2003a, 'State government outlines timeline for closure', Minister for Environment, Australia, 1 March.

Media Statement. 2003b, 'Brookdale waste treatment plant to close by December 31', Minister for Environment, Australia, 9 December.

Mitchell, R. K., Agle, B. R. and Wood, D. J. 1997, 'Toward a theory of stakeholder identification and salience: Defining the principle of who and what really counts', *Academy of Management Review*, vol. 22, no. 4, pp. 853–86.

Muchinsky, P. M. and Tuttle, M. L. 1979, 'Employee turnover: An empirical and methodological assessment', *Journal of Vocational Behavior*, vol. 14, pp. 43–77.

Nishikawa, J. 1998, 'A change of guard in Asia', *Straits Times*, 12 June, p. 17.

Ogden, S. and Watson, R. 1999, 'Corporate performance and stakeholder management: Balancing shareholder and customer interests in the U.K. privatized water industry', *Academy of Management Journal*, vol. 42, no. 5, pp. 526–38.

O'Toole, J. 1985, *Vanguard Management*, Doubleday, New York.

Pearson, C. A. L. 1995, 'The turnover process in organizations: An exploration of the role of met–unmet expectations', *Human Relations*, vol. 48, no. 40, pp. 405–20.

Pearson, C. A. L. 2004, 'Ecologically sustainable development delivered through stakeholder concepts: The Trans Territory Pipeline from Blacktip to Gove', in P. Sauer, A. Nankervis and S. Mensik, *Sustainability in Global Services: Selected essays*, pp. 51–65.

Pearson, C. A. L. and Chatterjee, S. R. 1999, 'Managerial work goals and organizational reform: A survey of senior Indian managers', *Asia Pacific Journal of Economics and Business*, vol. 3, no. 1, pp. 76–92.

Penrose, E. 1959, *The Theory of the Growth of the Firm*, Basil Blackwell, London.

Pfeffer, J. and Salancik, G. 1978, *The External Control of Organizations: A resource dependence perspective*, Harper & Row, New York.

Phillips, R. A. and Reichart, J. 2000, 'The environment as a stakeholder? A fairness-based approach', *Journal of Business Ethics*, vol. 23, no. 2, pp. 185–97.

Porter, L. W. and Steers, R. M. 1973, 'Organizational work and personal factors in employee turnover and absenteeism', *Psychological Bulletin*, vol. 80, pp. 151–76.

Post, F. R. 2003, 'A response to "The social responsibility of corporate management: A classical critique"', *American Journal of Business*, vol. 18, no. 1, pp. 25–35.

Preston, L. E. and Sapienza, H. J. 1990, 'Stakeholder management and corporate performance', *Journal of Behavioral Economics*, vol. 19, no. 4, pp. 361–75.

Reavill, L. R. P. 1998, 'Quality assessments, total quality management and stakeholders in the U.K. education system', *Managing Service Quality*, vol. 8, no. 1, pp. 55–63.

Rowley, T. J. 1997, 'Moving beyond dyadic ties: A network theory of stakeholder influences', *Academy of Management Review*, vol. 22, no. 4, pp. 887–910.

Smith, S. 2004, 'Moves to resolve impasse at NAB', *West Australian*, 3 May, p. 32.

Stamp, G. 1995, 'The dilemmas of empowerment', *Human Resource Management International Digest*, vol. 3, no. 2, pp. 2–3.

Teece, D., Pisano, G. and Shuen, A. 1997, 'Dynamic capabilities and strategic management', *Strategic Management Journal*, vol. 18, no. 7, pp. 509–33.

Trevino, L. K. and Weaver, G. R. 1999, 'The stakeholder research tradition: Converging theorists – not convergent theory', *Academy of Management Review*, vol. 24, no. 2, pp. 222–7.

Trice, H. M. and Beyer, J. M. 1993, *The Culture of Work Organizations*, Prentice Hall, Englewood Cliffs, NJ.

Wakabayashi, M., Kondo, M. and Chen, Z. 2001, 'Cross-cultural managerial skill practices: Filipino and Chinese managers under Japanese style management', *Global Business Review*, vol. 2, no. 1, pp. 15–35.

Walsh, J. 1995, 'Putting people in the process at BT', *Managing Service Quality*, vol. 5, no. 4, pp. 35–37.

Wernerfelt, B. 1984, 'A resource-based view of the firm', *Strategic Management Journal*, vol. 5, no. 2, pp. 171–80.

West Australian. 2004a, 'Telstra buys its shares back', *West Australian*, 16 November, p. 7.

West Australian. 2004b, 'How America's defence failed', *West Australian*, 19 June, p, 10.

West Australian. 2004c, 'Wake-up call shook a superpower's defenders', *West Australian*, 19 June, p. 10.

Wilson, I. 2004, 'The agenda for redefining corporate purpose: Five key executive actions', *Strategy and Leadership*, vol. 32, no. 1, pp. 21–26.

Wood, D. J. 1991, 'Corporate social performance', *Academy of Management Review*, no. 16, pp. 691–718.

Wood, D. J. 1993, *Business and Society*, Scott, Foresman, Glenview, IL.

WCED (World Commission on Environment and Development). 1987, *Our Common Future*, Oxford University Press, Reading, Berkshire.

Yoshikawa, T. and Phan, P. H. 2001, 'Alternative corporate governance systems in Japanese firms: Implications for a shift to stockholder-centred corporate governance', *Asia Pacific Journal of Management*, vol. 18, no. 2, pp. 183–205.

Managing strategy in services

Learning objectives

After studying this chapter, readers will be able to:

- distinguish between traditional approaches to strategy and more recent strategic management models
- appreciate the conceptual logic underpinning strategic management models
- grasp the relationship between an integrated strategic management perspective and the management of the practical operational, financial, marketing and human resource management aspects of service
- explore and explain the blurring of the traditional boundaries between goods and services
- understand why a more comprehensive and integrated approach to strategic management is now required in order to design and sustain competitive advantage towards service
- analyse a selection of specific service case examples from a strategic management perspective.

Introduction

The previous chapters explored the growing importance and distinctive characteristics of service and the various challenges involved in managing it. They analysed the global, regional, national and local environments within which service is provided, and discussed the complex and dynamic nature of stakeholder management issues that now impact upon organisations as they place greater emphasis upon service. This chapter focuses on the conceptual aspects and practical implementation implications of a strategic management approach to service. In doing so, it also discusses the critical importance of taking a strategic management perspective in applying the integrated services management model. The ideas presented in this chapter provide a foundation for the subsequent chapters, which in turn analyse the specific issues associated with the marketing, operational, financial, and HR management (HRM) dimensions of the ISM. The central tenet of this chapter, which highlights the greatly increased service focus for *all* organisations, combined with the unrelenting and ever-expanding service expectations of consumers, is the need for radically different and more innovative management approaches than those employed in the past.

The earlier chapters adopted deductive and prescriptive frameworks (that is, concepts and theories, illustrated with industry examples) to guide discussion. This chapter deliberately presents an inductive approach, drawing upon original research data and using a series of illustrative case examples to identify and discuss key management issues and the specific challenges of designing a strategic management framework to address the increasingly complex issues involved in the provision of effective service. The research undertaken includes an international survey and a number of focus group discussions. The value of this approach is that it should help to restore the relevance of strategic management as a conceptual tool for business strategists. The underlying assumption is that in order to achieve the benefits of a strategic management approach, such as foresight, learning, innovation and building customer value, a much stronger service perspective than has been the case hitherto is required. In addition, the development of these capabilities has organisation-wide performance implications; hence, the careful coordination of the basic management functions, including marketing, operations, finance, and HRM, is considered to be crucial in achieving and sustaining strategic performance objectives. Thus, this chapter aims to indicate how a range of strategic management decisions link together to form a more integrated and enduring basis for building a competitive strategy around business models that put heavier emphasis upon the quality of service performance. Through this discussion and case study examples, it will become apparent that there are many opportunities to improve service delivery performance and create new and innovative sources of competitive advantage.

Management and strategic management

The previous chapters discuss various theories and concepts of management that largely derive from primary and secondary industries, and then have been applied uncritically to services. As discussed in Chapter 1, the main principles of management theory centre around either the job or the task; the employees who perform these jobs and tasks; and/or the managers who are responsible for individual and organisational performance, and their contributions to overall organisational effectiveness, competitiveness and profitability. According to management theories, organisational success, or failure, hinges on two critical capabilities:

- their macro-ability to be 'strategic' and 'competitive' within their global, regional, national or local contexts; and
- their micro-ability to effectively and efficiently manage their operations, finances, marketing and human resources.

These various organisational aspects and their inter-linkages are illustrated in the ISM model in Figure 4.1. As the model indicates, strategic management is the central core that shapes the conceptual framework that underpins all other management functions and integrates the various internal and external contexts. However, it is the contention of this chapter that the deeper ramifications of this basic idea, and the critical role of strategic management in uniting strategic and functional objectives and activities, are still emerging in the

Figure 4.1 The integrated services management (ISM) model

services management field. There is significant learning and innovation required to develop practical strategies and mechanisms for achieving sustainable strategic advantages based on service. The various spheres in the model indicate the complexity of management issues that senior management must address in order to achieve consistent and enduring service excellence.

The next section discusses the evolving theoretical frameworks that inform and distinguish the concepts of competitive strategy and strategic management. Following this discussion, a number of illustrative cases are presented. These cases narrate diverse customer experiences, perceptions and interpretations derived from a range of service contexts and situations. The intention of this inductive approach is to make the reader aware of the pivotal role of strategic management and its practical implications for designing excellent service enterprises. It is vital for managers of every organisation to have a deeper understanding of the customer's centrality in creating and implementing effective business strategy, and of the role of service in establishing and sustaining competitive advantage. The chapter concludes with a discussion of the pertinent strategic and operational management issues to be explored in the subsequent chapters. Many of the ideas presented in this chapter directly overlap with those presented on management and marketing in Chapter 5.

Strategic management theoretical frameworks

In the decade from 1980 Michael Porter published a number of major works on business strategy that significantly elevated the subject. Nevertheless, he wrote in the tradition of scholars who defined strategy as the means for successfully positioning the organisation against its competitors. As an economist, Porter concentrated on techniques for analysing industry structure, placing competitors into strategic groupings and creating a basis for competitive advantage. In other words, business strategy was to be determined within identifiable groups of competitors. Following on from Porter's pioneering work, there was a growing interest in the dynamics of competitive strategy and the development of guidelines for strategic choice (Warren, 2002).

When Porter (1980) originally placed the concept of 'competitive strategy' and the five forces that determine industry profitability at the top of the management agenda, there was still a widely entrenched assumption that the competitive environment was relatively stable and predictable. Business strategy models were based upon assumptions drawn from manufacturing industry. Indeed, service and 'services', which were classified as a 'fragmented industry' by Porter, received very little attention. There was virtually no reference to the ways in which 'service' was already becoming a major source of differentiation and competitive advantage in all sectors of the economy. However, a chapter on services was included in *The Competitive Advantage of Nations* (Porter, 1990). The traditional distinction between goods and services was still made, but an important advance in Porter's thinking was his treatment of 'hybrid' industries as a special category in which goods and services are bundled together in a value chain. He argued that strategy should guide 'an entire value chain' and that a value chain could become much more than the sum of its parts. It was this break-through concept of the organisation as a value creating and delivering entity which subsequently served to undermine the convenient classification of goods and services as separate categories, pave the way for the reconceptualisation of business strategy, and provide the key to effective strategic management in the New Economy.

Porter's market-based model of strategy held sway throughout the 1980s; however, with the accelerating impact of globalisation, deregulation and information technology, its limitations became glaringly apparent. Whereas Porter's model assumed a certain level of industry stability, and that change would be *evolutionary*, it became apparent by the early 1990s that, especially in areas such as financial services and telecommunications, the changes were revolutionary. Some of the most dynamic new global players, such as Microsoft, Nokia and IKEA, were successful precisely because of their ability to straddle industries, ignore the existing rules of competition and construct a *unique* market space.

A dominant feature of the New Economy is the radical power shift from producer to customer and the need for a different approach to business strategy. As a consequence, the New Economy might well be conceived of as the Service Economy. In the Old Economy, strategy was largely based upon analysing industry structure, understanding the forces influencing profitability and then choosing the most appropriate markets to compete in. However, as customers have become more discriminating and demanding, strategists have been forced to focus much more upon creating unique sources of value and building stronger relationships with customers, just as Honda, Dell, GE, Federal Express and IKEA have done. With the empowerment of the customer, and the resulting emphasis on value innovation, has come a progressive blurring of traditional boundaries, including the boundaries between industry classifications, between products and services, between the various organisations in the supply (that is, 'value') chain and, most importantly, between the specialised functions of management. However, none of these boundaries are relevant to the customer. From a customer perspective, perceived value is what matters, and therefore the concepts of 'value' and 'service' are essentially interchangeable; the measure of service is its value to the customer, that is, the extent to which it satisfies a need or confers a benefit *from the customer's point of view.*

The new competitive challenge, according to the strategy gurus of the 1990s, Hamel and Prahalad, was getting to the future first. In their ground-breaking book, *Competing for the Future* (1994), they argued that the era of industry evolution was over. The new generation of leading firms had the capability to reinvent the product or service concept. Like the examples mentioned above, Wal-Mart, Canon and Starbucks radically reshaped their industries, changed the old rules of competition, and completely blurred the boundaries between products and services.

Dismissing the prevailing strategic planning approach to managing strategy as 'a pedantic planning ritual', which produced lots of plans but no *strategic intent*, Hamel and Prahalad also argued the case for a stronger management perspective on strategy. Whereas the analysis of industry structure and competitive advantage was useful up to a point, it failed to explain the reason *why* some companies seem able to continually create new forms of competitive advantage while others seem able only to copy and follow. The explanation given by Hamel and Prahalad lies in the ability of the successful firms to craft 'strategic architecture' based on *foresight* regarding the shape of future markets. The challenge of 'getting to the future first' requires, first, an ambitious and inspiring stretch goal and, second, the capability to identify, develop and leverage the distinctive core competencies necessary for attaining it. This approach to strategy places greater emphasis upon the organisation's resource capability for shaping the *future* market, as opposed to simply competing in the current one.

In shifting the focus of strategy making towards *value innovation*, Hamel and Prahalad opened the way for others to construct a more integrated strategic framework. Since the only significant arbiter of value is the customer, the strategic challenge for senior management is to build organisations that not only serve the customer of today, but also anticipate, and ideally invent, the customer of the already emerging future. The key to successfully meeting this challenge lies in the ability of senior managers to conceive a unique and compelling value proposition (from the customer's perspective) and then to put in place the core competencies needed to implement it. If the development and combination of these competencies is sufficiently unique, then, as with IKEA, there is an exceptional value proposition, or perceived bundle of benefits, combining products and services, which is attractive to customers all over the world. The IKEA value proposition is the end result of a brilliantly sequenced chain of value-adding activities, which require highly developed competencies, not only in global coordination, but also in specific areas such as design, sourcing of materials, low-cost production, packaging, logistics, merchandising, customer relations and branding.

So, the concept of the *value chain* has had a profound impact on both management and marketing (Moore, 1996, pp. 71–72). The effective implementation of a value chain requires not only an integrated strategic approach to management, but also a significantly different view of the role of marketing (see Chapter 5). The creation of a 'value chain process' inevitably involves reliance on cross-functional teams, the application of strategic core competencies with a strong external orientation, and a shared commitment to serving customers, as pioneers such as Wal-Mart, McDonald's and Toyota have demonstrated. These strategic ideas acknowledge increasing customer awareness of a more complex notion of 'value' underpinning their consumer decisions. Indeed, as consumers around the world have become increasingly concerned with lifestyle, and much more aware of ways to improve it, 'quality-embracing' ideas reflecting the multiple benefits of this approach have gradually replaced price as the main criterion for consumer choice.

Judgments about quality are highly subjective (Imparato and Harari, 1994, pp. 238–43). Like beauty, the notion of quality is in the eye of the beholder. Personal values, preferences, ideologies and even priorities at a particular time or occasion, not just price, will dictate whether a cosmetics customer opts for Chanel or The Body Shop, and whether an air traveller will opt for Qantas or Virgin Airlines. To be able to deliver quality products and services effectively and consistently requires a deep understanding of the customer and the multifaceted nature of the relationship between the customer and the business.

Reflecting the importance of the moment of service delivery, and running parallel to – but largely independent of – the strategy mainstream, was a growing volume of literature on 'service management'. In the 1990s, Karl Albrecht undertook extensive research and wrote a number of books that identified service as a major source of differentiation and competitive advantage. Although Albrecht's model was directed mainly to what he called the 'service economy', it had wider implications because it advocated a customer-centred organisation that makes the customer's needs and expectations the central focus of the business. Successful service provision requires a different management approach, which includes identifying 'moments of truth' and 'cycles of service' from the customer's perspective, and then putting systems and competencies in place in order to meet and often exceed the customer's expectations (Albrecht and Zemke, 1985; Albrecht and Bradford, 1990). The new service management movement argued that it was no longer adequate to rely solely on the marketing function to promote products. Instead, organisations needed to relate to their customers in a much more integrated way. 'Service management' was put forward as a 'transformational' concept that included a specific organisational philosophy, a new way of thinking, a new frame of values and a new set of skills. This movement was a stepping-stone towards a more integrated strategic management approach that paid more than lip-service to the distinctive *service* management challenges in serving customers effectively.

In moving beyond Porter's market positioning approach, Hamel and Prahalad's competency/resource-based view and Albrecht's customer-led philosophy, there is clearly a need to pay more careful attention to the leadership and management challenges confronting service strategists. An integrated approach emphasising value creation requires a multidimensional strategy model (Cusumano and Markides, 2001, pp. 18–24). If it is to be comprehensive and transformational, an integrated strategic management framework will need to address five related and equally important *leadership* and management challenges:

- designing and implementing an innovative business model;
- building a service culture;
- developing the necessary core competencies to successfully implement the business model's value chain;
- creating organisational learning capability; and
- establishing an enduring brand around the business model.

Despite an increasing flow of new business courses and textbooks in strategic management, only limited progress has been made in meeting these criteria. The most common approaches emphasise the various levels of strategy within an organisation and then highlight the context, content and processes of strategy (Viljoen and Dann, 2003, pp. 16–20; De Wit and Meyer, 2004). However, none of the proposed frameworks have really resonated with practitioners, or fully captured the special leadership and management challenges that confront strategists, as they seek to leverage service as a source of competitive advantage.

Development of a new, integrated strategic management approach

With customers becoming the main strategic priority for management, it is increasingly apparent that the next management challenge lies in determining the types of *processes*, *competencies* and *skills* that are needed to acquire and retain them. While a more limited notion of business strategy and service quality had already emerged by the mid-1990s, it soon became apparent that there was a need to develop an integrated management framework. It obviously had to capture the pivotal role of senior management in conceptualising and implementing a customer-centred business model. Unfortunately, in practice, many of the transformational concepts were interpreted by senior management as involving a hierarchical transmission approach, through which values and behaviour designed at the top are dispersed down through an organisation. Instead, managers need to pay more attention to issues of culture, with a view to building commitment and cooperation around the business model, and then to set in place strategies to empower and support employees to manage the critical interfaces with customers.

By the mid-1990s, it had become apparent that traditional strategies – such as the analysis of discrete industry profiles, the diversification of the business portfolio, the pursuit of vertical and horizontal integration, and attempts to achieve optimum economies of scale and scope – were by themselves insufficient to bring about a sustainable competitive advantage. The case for a new integrated model was underpinned by the conceptual logic that, unless both management and employees, and especially front-line staff, are intimately involved in all the quality development and delivery processes, there is a real danger that proposed changes may only contribute to confusion and indifference. This lack of clarity about role and purpose may, in turn, contribute further to the risk that employees feel manipulated, and hence only 'go through the motions' of demonstrating commitment to quality and service goals. This growing awareness made it obvious that the old strategy logic no longer applied.

Gradually the emphasis shifted away from establishing competitive advantage in particular industries towards the challenge of creating, and then branding, a unique market 'space' (Hamel and Prahalad, 1994; Moore, 1996). The spectacular success of companies such as Wal-Mart highlighted just how inadequate the old strategy concepts were. Indeed, Wal-Mart's success resulted in the following question being asked: 'What industry is Wal-Mart in? Is it retailing, wholesaling, information services, logistics, or is it in all four?' (See discussion in Moore, 1996, pp. 167–88). Recognition of the more complex nature of this type of business led to a further refinement of the new 'strategic management' paradigm. This complexity underlined the need to replace the increasingly anachronistic word 'industry' with the notion of a 'business ecosystem'. 'The term circumscribes the microeconomics of intense coevolution coalescing around innovative ideas. Business ecosystems span a variety of industries' (Moore, 1996, pp. 19–20). It is important to recognise that, although still widely used, the word 'industry' has become an extremely imprecise term. Sometimes it refers to business collectively (for example, 'a representative appointed from industry'); on other occasions it is applied to a particular sector of the economy (for example, 'manufacturing industry'); and then again it is used for more specialised areas of activity (for example, 'the automotive industry', 'the health-care industry').

The more complex, interdependent and dynamic principles that guide healthy ecological systems are useful for interpreting the 'organic' business ecosystem, which characterises the services 'industry'. The inner sphere on Figure 4.1 – which includes the following stakeholders: suppliers, interest groups, employee unions, government policy and regulatory bodies, shareholders, community, customers and competitors – indicates the heterogeneous and interactive nature of the diverse 'life forms' in the business ecosystem. A strategic concept closely related to the 'business ecosystem' is the 'opportunity environment' which, is described as the 'space of business possibility characterized by unmet customer needs, unharnessed technologies, potential regulatory openings, prominent investors, and many other untapped resources' (Moore, 1996, pp. 16, 32).

With the shift in the business focus away from a preoccupation with competitors towards creating and serving loyal customers, the field of strategic management has evolved as a concept to clearly express long-term commitment to the design and implementation of a business model specifically aimed at capturing a market opportunity. From an organisational leadership perspective, the challenge is to design the processes, build the competencies, and develop the relationships necessary for serving existing, emerging and imagined customers of the future. Acknowledgment of the value of an integrated framework moves the strategy debate beyond a short-term search for market niches and service product differentiation. Instead, the integrated approach emphasises the need for continuous innovation and the special nature of relationships, which underpin the characteristics and qualities of a successful corporate brand. Thus, during the late 1990s it became increasingly apparent that an organisation's most valuable asset was the way in which the corporate brand symbolically embodied and conveyed customer values.

In taking a more strategic approach to services management, no one element is more important than branding. As markets become more crowded, competitive and complex, the value of a strong, clear corporate brand increases. A powerful brand gives a company, product or service a personality of its own which transcends its components. If the brand is built upon a firm base of core values, which are carefully protected and projected, it can survive and flourish. The outstanding brands of the 1920s, such as Colgate and Kodak, are still the market leaders today. However, it is apparent that branding has been neglected by many traditional service providers. With services, the challenge is to brand the invisible elements and ensure that their tangible manifestations keep faith, as Shell, Disney, CNN, Infosys and McDonald's have tried to do.

Despite the success of these corporate examples, there appears to have been a long tradition among many services providers of relying almost totally on technical or professional expertise, assuming that a good reputation will result and ensure continuing success. Indeed, in some professional areas, elitist codes of conduct and conservative traditions prohibited advertising altogether and never came to grips with the role of brand management. The strategic management challenge of reconciling tangible and intangible branding elements has been evident in the widespread critical media attention faced by Shell over recent years. The company has struggled to reconcile its highly ambitious and publicly stated 'triple bottom line' sustainability and corporate responsibility objectives with the damaging exposure of unethical behaviour by top management, the poor handling of environmental issues, and serious failures in the management of business–government relations in a number of developing countries.

These ideas link to the dramatically changing nature of the business environment under the influences of globalisation, as discussed in Chapter 2. In particular, they highlight the numerous and diverse ways in which the impact of political, economic, legal, technological, competitive and societal changes impact upon and shape service strategy options. In addition, they highlight the importance of stakeholder management (see Chapter 3). Hence, it is apparent that a more integrated and complex strategic management approach, based around matching diverse customer expectations and quality service delivery, is now required.

Management's response to the challenges of the new services economy

The management discipline has clearly been very slow to reflect the growth, importance and distinctive challenges in designing and delivering service. There are four main reasons for this:

- Most management writers have taken manufacturing industries as their frame of reference. The management of manufacturing industries has been culturally dominated by the reductive and mechanistic scientific logic of classic hierarchical management systems. Accordingly, there has been a heavy bias towards a formal organisational perspective, concentrating on strategies, functions, roles and behaviours that influence overall corporate performance, rather than on the value chain, which serves the needs and expectations of customers and other key stakeholders.

- The intangible, invisible and difficult-to-define nature of the service element has meant that it has been easily taken for granted. The major growth of the so-called service economy has been relatively recent and reflects the rise in demand for personal and domestic services, the exponential spread of IT, the increasing power of consumers, and the increasing trend for companies to focus on their core business activities while outsourcing their non-core functions. The management discipline is still coming to terms with the wider implications of these complex HR and stakeholder management issues.

- Management is a relatively new academic discipline, compared with the 'learned professions' such as medicine, law, engineering and public administration. These high-status professional occupations have traditionally enjoyed a high level of self-regulation and autonomy and, as a result, adopted a superior and condescending view of those non-professionals engaged in commerce and trade. For example, it was considered to be inappropriate, indeed *unprofessional*, for a professional practice to overtly advertise its services or to 'tout' for clients, or to be 'managed' like a business. A clear distinction was drawn between the *clients* of a professional practice and the *customers* of a business. This long-standing elitism has culturally framed and inhibited discourse on services management.

• The non-professional services 'boom' of the past 40 years coincided with the rise of marketing as a separate business discipline. By definition, marketing is concerned with the creation and servicing of 'markets' (that is, customers) and marketing theorists were quick to identify the unique challenges in defining and communicating the intangible benefits associated with 'services'. Accordingly, it was not long before topics such as 'service marketing' and the 'marketing of services' became standard components of the marketing curriculum. Hence, the development of a marketing approach, as opposed to an integrated management approach, to many service activities became the norm, and thus the demarcation of functional boundaries was reinforced and the adoption of strategic management practices was further delayed.

The gradual emergence of a strategic management perspective for service activities can be traced through the evolution of integrating customer-centred concepts such as 'quality', 'customer value' and 'value chain', and the growing recognition of the importance of emphasising service dimensions in branding strategies.

From the marketing of services to the strategic management of the brand

The extraordinary success of Japanese companies in the world markets during the 1970s and 1980s put the issue of quality at the top of the management agenda throughout the Western world. Companies such as Toyota, Sony and Canon were seen to be successful largely as a result of 'total quality management'. However, when Western imitators adopted TQM, they applied it mainly to production processes. Although TQM was adopted eventually in the service area, its application was half-hearted and superficial. (See additional discussions of TQM in Chapters 1, 3 and 5.) Instead of reviewing strategies, structures and systems, and critically evaluating the value chain, the main focus was on fine-tuning the existing bureaucratic silos and on identifying, codifying and regulating the behaviour of front-line service delivery personnel. Thus, it can be concluded that the TQM approach to service quality was from a marketing perspective, rather than an integrated management perspective.

With widespread use of excessive service rhetoric and advertising 'hype', service increasingly became synonymous with superficial cosmetic, intrusive and manipulative behaviours, such as the inconsiderate, 'scatter-gun' telemarketing campaigns conducted by banks, telecommunications companies and credit card providers. Very few service-oriented companies have developed the capability of consistently providing service based on identifying customer needs *and* regularly exceeding their expectations. Instead of pursuing this customer-focused approach to quality services delivery, for many companies the concept of service excellence has become a platitude. Even today, service providers continue to equate service with the delivery of 'more' or, worse still, the *illusion* of 'more'. As the survey (Milton-Smith, 2003) results discussed later reveal, it is disappointing that, in an era where it has become conventional wisdom to regard service as the key to business success, very few consumers are able to nominate more than one or two organisations, if any, as being excellent service providers from their own experience.

In response to the pressure to be customer-focused, one currently popular approach is customer relationship marketing (CRM). (See Chapter 5 for a discussion on CRM strategy and tools.) In practice the emphasis has been more on targeted marketing than on relationship building and management. Moreover, when applied as a marketing strategy, this approach can easily be interpreted as the ultimate invasion of privacy, in that its ultimate aim is to achieve a sense of 'customer intimacy' (Peppers and Rogers, 1999, pp. 6–14). Justifying the value of CRM, a prominent financial planner recently stated that financial planning is now less about 'product' and more about 'intimacy'. He explained that customers want 'intimacy' as a result of the trusting personal relationship that comes with 'the enterprise culture of a local small business person' so that they can feel confident about the wider 'institutional support' for the financial services product (Cooper, 2004).

The notion of 'customer intimacy' can be a useful philosophy for building quality customer relationships, but in practice it is applied without sensitivity, sufficient background research, or a well-integrated approach to satisfying customers' needs. In other words, a poor services product superficially wrapped in a veneer of intimacy will not deliver lasting results. Aggressive telemarketing campaigns promoting additional credit cards or pre-approved credit card limit increases are obvious examples. It is apparent that there is a continuing gap between the assumptions of service providers and the expectations of their customers. With growing customer knowledge about quality products and services, more people know that they want – but feel frustrated that they do not receive – unobtrusive seamless-web services. Despite massive investment in CRM by retail banks around the world, there is strong evidence that cross-selling and profit per customer have not increased. Once again, the failure is largely due to poor management. In most banks, 'business units continued to be organised around specific products and customer segments hindering the integrated management of overall customer relationships' (Farrell, 2003, p. 112).

By contrast, some market leaders, such as Coca-Cola, Starbucks and IKEA, have already demonstrated that the key to winning and retaining customers is to build brands that reflect the needs, priorities, values and aspirations of their targeted market segments. This can only be achieved through the disciplined and integrated management of all the important relationships with the organisation's major stakeholders (see Chapter 3). As a consequence of this mindset, marketing comes to be seen as more of a whole-of-company philosophy, rather than as a specialised business function (Forsyth, 2003; J. Lee, 2004). Indeed, some marketing specialists argue that the more traditional notions of marketing have become redundant. (See an extensive discussion in Chapter 5.) Together, these new insights indicate that the time has come to reconceptualise the business model and to design it from the 'outside-in', rather than, as in the past, from the 'inside-out'. In other words, the new business model should be designed in response to specific consumer needs and environmental realities, rather than senior management's narrowly preconceived assumptions about customers and products. Such a model could more effectively identify and strategically respond to new business opportunities by developing a mutually interactive relationship with customers.

There are clear signs that, even in leading global companies, the marketing function is in crisis. The rapid shift from a product-push to a market-pull competitive environment requires a much more integrated strategic approach than most marketing practitioners have traditionally adopted. Dissatisfaction with marketing's performance is reflected in the high proportion of marketing departments that have recently been, or are currently being, reorganised. Nearly half of all *Fortune 500* companies have appointed chief marketing officers (CMOs) 'because they need someone who does more than what is expected of a conventional leader of marketing' (McGovern and Quelch, 2004). However, in most cases, and especially in markets where product or service innovations confer only short-term advantage, simply promoting executives imbued with the old marketing culture has proved futile. The churn rate for CMOs has been extremely high, which indicates that more fundamental organisational changes are required. Perhaps the most urgent change is to find a way of linking the senior marketing role with other key organisational functions so that, under the leadership of the CEO, there is a continuous shared strategic management perspective, focusing on the interrelated challenges of business concept innovation and of designing a constantly adapting value chain connecting the organisation with the customer (Hyde et al., 2004).

In this era of hyper-competition and ultra-selective consumers, perceived value from the customer's perspective is increasingly multidimensional and involves satisfying highly differentiated needs and preferences, as well as conferring special benefits that are individual, experiential and aspirational. Without a carefully calibrated business model, implemented through a sophisticated and customised value chain, it is impossible to meet such a demanding *pot-pourri* of expectations. In such a complex process, many of the traditional marketing functions have become issues for strategic management, rather than responsibilities for marketing operations.

Three key service leadership challenges

The three key service leadership challenges are to:

- stimulate business model innovation in service organisations;
- build a front-line service culture; and
- create a learning organisation.

Stimulating business model innovation in service organisations

The remarkable success of budget airlines such as Virgin and Ryanair, furnishing retailers such as IKEA, and fast-growing coffee shop chains such as Starbucks, reflects the triumph of leadership vision, foresight and creativity over traditional marketing push and persuasion. In each case, new mass markets were invented around clusters of customers who had been ignored or were poorly served by existing service providers (Burgelman, 2002). The French launch of Starbucks, in Paris early in 2004, underlines the point. Paris is a city with no shortage of cafes, bars and restaurants. Yet, even in a city which deeply resents the so-called invasion of American culture – the 'coca-colonisation' of the world, as some French critics have portrayed it – a city where the cafe is claimed to have been invented, the no-frills and casual Starbucks experience appeals to many young people much more than the traditional Parisian cafe with its formal waiters, slower service and higher prices (Kaminski, 2004). Like the budget airlines, Starbucks gives the customer choice and control, as well as an element of fun, and the opportunity to express individuality and personal preference. It is a phenomenon that powerfully demonstrates the advantage of business model innovation at a strategic level, as opposed to a tactical market positioning approach that accepts the 'taken-for-granted' limitations of the existing competitive environment.

One of the most significant examples of the shift to a more strategic, customer-focused management model is to be found in what has been traditionally described as 'the airline industry'. Increasingly, airlines are entering into partnerships to offer customers an extensive range of integrated value packages, including highly targeted and communicated campaigns, which incorporate a diverse range of travel, tourism and transportation experiences. In addition, they frequently provide exclusive opportunities to purchase merchandise, therapeutic services and privileged access to special events.

The rapid growth of the 'no-frills' airline segment highlights the shift from service marketing to serving the customer and giving the customer the freedom and flexibility to determine what represents 'value'. Here customers have the option of choosing minimal service. As competition in this segment intensifies, value innovation increases. For example, Ryanair, the European 'no-frills' market leader, has recently introduced a further round of even more extreme cost and price cuts. These measures even include dispensing with seat pockets, which will produce savings both in equipment and cleaning budgets. Other initiatives include the replacement of reclining seats and the removal of window blinds. The latest economy drive comes on top of an existing 'no-frills' format based upon the elimination of free food, drink and seat bookings, a requirement that passengers walk from air terminals to their aircraft, and landing at airports that are often remote from the passenger's final destination. Ryanair has even been criticised for not providing wheelchairs for disabled passengers (Taylor and Raja, 2004).

The simultaneous growth of budget airlines and business class travel is no contradiction. It demonstrates the modern consumer's demand for maximum options, flexibility, convenience and quality of life. On some occasions, a passenger will pay a large premium in order to experience the luxury and pampering of business class; on other occasions, the same passenger will surf the Internet for hours to locate the cheapest fare in order to attend a specific event such as a sporting fixture or family gathering (Mackintosh, 2004). In virtually all countries, and despite racial and cultural differences, a middle-class lifestyle involves many choices and tradeoffs in satisfying perceived needs, individual aspirations and the desire for personal wellbeing. As consumers become more affluent, highly educated and demanding, they place greater emphasis upon spiritual and emotional fulfilment, or, as Maslow (1968) put it, their 'higher order needs' and the desire 'to have it all'.

The ubiquity of terms like 'lifestyle', 'image', 'personal growth', 'self-expression', 'network' and 'quality time' underlines the desire by consumers all over the world to define, develop and project themselves and to connect with a variety of practitioners, products, providers and partners that help them to achieve this. The quest for personal meaning and identity is a journey with both internal and external dimensions, and these aspects are intertwined and inseparable. A person may choose, or not choose, a particular car because of how or where it is made, or because of its design, as opposed to functional criteria; in part, the decision may be shaped by strong personal values and preferences, but it may also be motivated by a desire to make a statement to others about social status or personal style.

It is becoming clear that the aura of a brand – whether it relates to a product, a service or, indeed, a country – has profound implications for a consumer's higher-order needs and for successful business model innovation. Brand values, over and above the functional merits of the product, have great significance for people who, for example, care deeply about ethical integrity, saving the environment or rectifying social injustice.

The old classification system of dividing the economy into two neat and separate categories, goods and services, while convenient for economists and government statisticians, bears little relationship to the economy of the new consumer and the lifestyle that middle classes and aspiring middle classes around the world are demanding. With the arrival of the 'new consumerism' and the narcissistic shopper, the reality of the marketplace has been transformed. Invisible appeal, invisible benefits and invisible added value have created a completely new economic dimension, management perspective and marketing challenge. When choices are strongly influenced by a need for self-expression, self-indulgence or self-fulfilment, or by a need to keep faith with one's own ethical beliefs, then clearly managers must reconceptualise the products and services they are offering as multifaceted value propositions. The consumer who is seeking simultaneously to satisfy both lower- and higher-order needs will almost certainly demand a package of benefits, a comprehensive 'solution' including both physical, emotional and aspirational aspects. Only in this way can the remarkable global success of brands such as Nokia, Rolex, Virgin, Haagen-Dazs, Harley-Davidson, Vespa and The Body Shop be fully understood.

The blurring of the boundaries between goods and services is highlighted by the spectacular expansion of new industries concerned with the enhancement of personal health, fitness and wellbeing. In the United States, for example, it is estimated that consumers spend in excess of US$19 billion annually on dietary supplements (Kerk, 2004). Similarly, there has been a rapid proliferation of weight-loss programs and diet plans in almost every developed country. Furthermore, in 2002 it was reported that the American market for manicures, waxing and steam treatments had tripled within three years. Indeed, in the past decade the spa phenomenon has swept the world. The concept of the spa is to provide a luxurious, full-service package of pampering and revitalisation, often including the expert guidance of doctors, nutritionists, physiotherapists and exercise physiologists (Keates, 2004). Apart from specialised 'wellness centres', many hotels provide variations on the spa theme as well. A further extension of this trend is the growing demand for personal development and team building and is reflected in so-called corporate survival courses, boot camps and adventure ranches. Invariably, these programs are integrated with a unique cosmetics range and a guru's formula for living a healthier, happier, more fulfilling life. Linked to, and increasingly the final destination of, the same market is the booming cosmetic surgery industry, which is the clearest possible confirmation of just how significant 'higher-order needs' have become in modern society (Economist, 2004).

Building a front-line service culture

In most organisations there is a huge distance between top management and the front line of service delivery. Those who actually deliver service and determine service reputation are usually a long way from the top. Traditional chain-of-command hierarchies send a clear message to both staff and customers. This top-down management approach invariably produces a culture in which those at the bottom of the pyramid have the least important jobs and the lowest status. Accordingly, reflecting this top-down culture, people on the front line are often poorly paid, have little influence on decision making and receive minimal training. (See Chapter 8 with particular regard to the casualisation of employment in services.) Despite brief flirtations with passing management fads such as quality circles, empowerment techniques and incentive schemes, the underlying corporate culture of the great majority of organisations continues to reinforce bureaucratic systems and compartmentalised responsibility.

With the significant economic and political power invested in hierarchical management systems, old management mindsets die hard and senior management is reluctant to relinquish its dominance and devolve power. This resistance to change is certainly apparent in organisations engaged in the provision of service. Despite the rapid growth of the so-called knowledge-based service economy, managers have been very slow to adapt their strategies, structures and competencies to meet the challenges of environmental change and increasing customer demands. Customers are increasingly well informed and discriminating and, given the intense competition in the marketplace, numerous consumer-based community groups wield unprecedented collective power. By contrast, the availability of well-trained, highly motivated service professionals has not kept pace with the growth of service-oriented organisations, or with the increasing demands and expectations of customers (Jacobs, 2004).

It is ironic, therefore, that, in most cases, customer service is delivered by people who feel undervalued by their employers. Too often, services staff strive to meet sales targets from positions that are insecure and at risk. Alternatively, staff are forced to perform tedious clerical duties that detract from their primary customer relations roles. Is it any wonder that front-line staff often feel exploited? They rarely see their jobs as a career, or even as a stepping stone. More often they see it as a temporary means-to-an-end or, worse still, as a painful necessity. As one focus group participant, a long-standing information officer at a large welfare agency, put it:

> I've been in this job nine years. I just hang on and hope that I don't get retrenched in the next round of down-sizing. They keep changing the policies and never tell me. So, when people ring up wanting details, I always transfer them upstairs. The most important thing is to put a smile in your voice and tell them to 'have a nice day'. That way they don't mind so much if you can't answer their questions. This job helps pay for the kids' school fees. I need to last out for another 18 months and then take long-service leave. I'll review the situation then.

In this workplace culture of fear, insecurity, disempowerment and boredom, it is not surprising that in surveys of consumer perceptions, such as those carried out in Perth, Singapore and Lyon, France, by John Milton-Smith and discussed later in this chapter, very few examples of service organisations with front-of-mind reputations for service excellence emerge. With poor internal relationships between senior management and front-line staff, inadequate flows of communication from the top, and low levels of trust, it is predictable that, in general, corporations will have limited capacity to build strong and trustworthy customer and wider stakeholder relationships. By contrast, when the organisation's main objective is to create value in the customer, the manager's role 'is redefined from institutionalising control to embedding trust, and from maintaining the status quo to leading change'. Instead of being concerned primarily with being the 'builders of systems', in the new culture managers are transformed into developers of people (Cusumano and Markides, 2001, p. 20).

Despite using catchphrases such as 'the customer is king' and 'people are our most important asset', very few organisations actually put real strategies and structures in place to realise the rhetoric (Straits Times, 2003). In most cases, marketing is used as a substitute for strategic management. A genuinely customer-driven organisation would not shrink from inverting the corporate pyramid so that senior management have a much greater involvement in the detail and delivery of service, and front-line staff have more influence on the design and implementation of the value chain. Nevertheless, there is no substitute for leadership. According to the most famous service 'gurus', Karl Albrecht and Ron Zemke, the starting point of a customer-centred organisation is the strategic decision by top management that 'the customer always comes first'. It is their responsibility to create 'cycles of service'. However, for a deep service culture to develop, top executives need to find strategic and practical ways to model and demonstrate service values. In all sorts of practical and visible ways, they must show that when there are competing priorities and pressures, the customer always does indeed take precedence (Albrecht and Zemke, 1985; Albrecht and Bradford, 1990).

Creating a learning organisation

Among the main implications of this change is the need for managers to create 'learning organisations' (Senge, 1992). A learning organisation is one that invests in the capacity to gather, interpret and act upon strategic information in order to create innovative new sources of customer value. Hence, the notion of learning for an integrated services management strategy involves all of the areas connected to the value chain. Infosys is an example of a successful company with a complex business ecosystem that has developed and branded a business model designed to take advantage of, and sustain, its limitless business possibilities. A Bangalore-based software designer and IT consultancy, Infosys has become a world leader by providing superior, cost-effective customer service. Its clients include 60 of the *Fortune 500* companies, including Citigroup, Cisco and Nordstrom. In the latter case, the client actually employs 90 Infosys programmers – 15 in Seattle and 75 in Bangalore. The company's particular capacity to build partnerships and to work intimately with its clients helps Infosys to differentiate itself and its service products from its competitors (Milton-Smith, 2003, p. 554).

At the other end of the value chain, senior Infosys management creates 'thought leadership groups', which provide the impetus for the innovation required to design, deliver and deploy specific solutions to particular clients. There is wide participation and multidisciplinary professional collaboration in these leadership groups, as managers, consultants and technical specialists all work together. In so doing, the group's teacher and learner roles tend to shift interchangeably, transferring ideas and incorporating new development frameworks, while, at the same time, liaising closely with alliance partners, supplier networks and partnerships. Hence, in a very practical sense, Infosys *is* a learning organisation. With this corporate emphasis on collaboration and learning, the main reason for the remarkable success of Infosys is the overarching way it manages its business model and service processes, rather than its core expertise in IT or marketing.

As the Infosys example demonstrates, successful service providers need to have the capacity to anticipate, identify and respond to emerging trends and changing demands. As learning organisations, they require extremely sensitive antennae. The only way to achieve this capability is to be extremely open to, and interactive with, the operating environment, working closely with all stakeholders and, especially, customers and suppliers. Clearly, this approach has major implications for organisational structure. The combination of cutting-edge knowledge, world-class resources and competencies, and the highest level of adaptability in serving customers requires an organisation that is both loose and tight, nuclear and networked, efficient and effective. The focal point of the learning organisation is its brain: 'Build the company around the software, and build the software around the customer' (Imparato and Harari, 1994, p. 75) Bureaucratic fortresses, like some of the advertising agencies, universities, banks and hospitals around the world – simply to cite some of the more obvious examples – have continued to survive only because of their monopoly position, the passivity of their customers or the perceived cost of switching. However, the remarkable success of, for example, the China-Europe International Business School (CEIBS) in Shanghai, China, is an ominous warning to complacent incumbents of the devastating impact that a new, strategically managed service provider can have.

Within a decade of its establishment, CEIBS has become China's top business school and one of the highest ranked business schools in the Asia-Pacific region. It is an excellent example of a strategically managed learning organisation. Unlike many other business schools that have shackled themselves to tenured second-rate staff, mediocre fee-paying students and an undifferentiated curriculum, CEIBS took the high road from the beginning. It has targeted the future business leaders of China, as well as foreign graduates who are likely to be doing business with them. Offering only a few highly branded flagship programs, CEIBS operates with a small nucleus of full-time staff and a distinguished network of visiting international professors. Heavy emphasis is placed upon strategic partnerships with leading multinational corporations (MNCs) and other world-class business schools. As a result, CEIBS enjoys a level of prestige that is totally disproportionate to its size, resources and length of operation. It is a highly successful business model.

In contrast with CEIBS, Saatchi and Saatchi, having become the world's largest advertising agency by the early 1990s, then tried to become even bigger through an ambitious strategy of rapid expansion (McDonald and Cavusgil, 1990, p. 16). The move was ill-judged, and Saatchi and Saatchi's performance suffered badly. The company misread the environment and the needs of its customers (Atlantic Media Company, 2003). It simply followed an old growth formula based on the principle that expansion is an end in itself. Although it made sense for advertising agencies to match the global strategies of their large MNC clients, other changes were taking place that militated against the effectiveness of huge, full-service providers and which were to lead instead to their disaggregation.

There is growing audience fragmentation and media proliferation. Just as consumers are increasingly prepared to pay for the media they want to access, so are they exercising more direct control over their exposure to advertising. From the advertisers' point of view, it is becoming much harder to reach consumers by traditional advertising methods. Thus, while media consumption is increasing, especially in areas such as the Internet and DVDs, it is generally in media not financed by advertising. A situation is emerging where advertising is at the consumer's discretion and control (Economist, 2004). Accordingly, advertisers are demanding much more active partnership with their agencies, and are becoming much less tolerant of client conflicts and overlaps. Large international agencies are resorting to network structures with the major groups now being made up of numerous small local firms, partnerships and alliances (Roberts, 1998, pp. 107–9).

Furthermore, clients are beginning to recognise the importance of branding as a long-term strategic objective, as opposed to relying simply on short-term advertising campaigns (Gregory, 2004, p. 36). They are learning that branding requires integrated strategic management and cannot just be outsourced to an agency. Branding is as much about management as marketing, and includes a wide variety of elements such as customer service, product/service delivery, staff development and knowledge management, quite apart from the more traditional marketing functions. Even in the marketing area itself, significant changes have been occurring that involve a move away from mass-marketing techniques towards micro-marketing initiatives designed to build a reciprocal relationship with customers and stake-holders, in order to respond in a more closely targeted, customised way to their needs and preferences. As a consequence, managers from client organisations are beginning to take much more direct responsibility for communicating with stakeholders and working with specialists in the various marketing and communications disciplines. These are largely tactical reactions to the pressures of hyper-competition and lack of strategic input from the corporate marketing function. What is really required is a commitment to the principles of the ISM (see Figure 4.1), so that there is a strong strategic focus on the customer and all functions, especially marketing, are held accountable for contributing to that strategy, for the effectiveness of the service value chain, and for the return on investment (McGovern et al., 2004, p. 72).

Box 4.1   Valuing customer loyalty

Mike Gleeson travels frequently around the Asia-Pacific region on business. He is a member of various airline and hotel loyalty programs. Initially, he was sceptical of using these programs and generally followed the advice of his company's travel officer and took the best deal available at the time. On the few occasions when he tried to redeem points for a free flight or hotel accommodation, he was told that the quota had already been filled. He was particularly annoyed when his preferred hotel informed him that extra points would be required as his visit would coincide with a major trade exposition. Mike complained to his wife, 'These so-called loyalty programs are all one-way.'

Some time after this disappointing experience, Mike received an invitation to become a 'Platinum Card Holder' of the Paradise Hotel Group, which included a very generous free gift. It seemed like a good deal, so he accepted almost immediately. Despite some minor conflict with his company's travel officer, Mike stayed in Barclay hotels exclusively for the next few years. He explained his perception of customer value in using this service facility to the travel officer: 'Although their rates are higher, I actually save money with Paradise because I can take one or two guests to their Elite Lounge for free breakfasts and cocktails when I'm discussing business.'

Upon arriving at the Shanghai Paradise Hotel, Mike was delighted to be upgraded to a suite and to find a box of chocolates in his room. Accompanying the chocolates was a card saying, 'This is our way of thanking you for staying with us 50 times over the past three years.' Later that night, Mike attended a small reception hosted by the hotel's manager for regular guests. He was quite flattered when the manager proposed a special toast to him in front of everyone present.

However, soon afterwards, the relationship began to turn sour. After arriving in Hanoi, following an early flight from Singapore, Mike was forced to sit in the hotel lobby for nearly three hours. A somewhat officious reservations clerk said bluntly, 'Check-in time is from two o'clock. But as you're a regular guest, we'll try to give you a room around one – possibly 12.30.' Then, a week later, after returning home to Sydney, Mike was browsing through a recent issue of an airline magazine for frequent fliers. He was astounded to find a special privilege offer, targeting the airline's frequent flier members, which gave almost immediate access to the Paradise Hotel Group's Diamond Card. Under this new alliance, 'Blue Ribbon' passengers became eligible for upgrading to the hotel's most exclusive membership status if they stayed at a Paradise hotel four times within the first three months of joining. Mike was furious. 'I've been a platinum member for years – a really loyal customer,' he said to his wife over breakfast next morning, 'and yet they're prepared to let a completely new member come in right over the top of me just to secure the support of an airline.'

The goods–services continuum as a value chain: Implications for the leadership agenda

From a long-term perspective, a consumer-based approach demands integrated strategic management, rather than marketing campaigns. For example, recognition of the growing importance of brand values and customer relationships has meant that business power has progressively flowed downstream to specialist retail channels, the points at which customers actually engage with brand choices and make purchasing decisions. One important conse-quence of this corporate power shift is a trend away from big-budget advertising campaigns and more emphasis on point-of-sale merchandising and relationship-building activities.

In response to a more customer-focused approach, it is now common practice for com-panies with a strong corporate brand identity to establish and service their own boutiques *inside* large department stores. Cosmetics, fashion and other luxury goods companies are leaders in this practice. These industries recognise the interwoven goods and services char-acteristics of their products, and the importance of building and sustaining direct service relationships with their customers. Hence, highly trained company consultants with both a deep product knowledge and understanding of the needs of their customer base will provide customers with personalised advice. Customers receive free demonstrations, invitations to fashion shows, exclusive previews of products, emailed or mailed brochure newsletters of new product releases, and bargain sale previews. In addition, to further fulfil 'lifestyle' consumer identity segments, companies sponsor charity fundraising events, community arts projects, and various competitive and community-based sporting events. The men's and women's fashion clothing and accessory company Country Road, outdoor sporting goods and fashion company Salomon, and cosmetics and fashion brand Chanel are examples of 'life-style brands focused on specific and very different consumer segments. The strategy is to build close and long-lasting customer relationships, not just based on the sale of quality products, but through the development of personal trust and brand loyalty, which results from a deep qualitative understanding of the consumer's needs. In summary, in businesses where products are intangible, complex or difficult to evaluate, such as healthcare, cosmetics and hotels, customers frequently look for evidence of corporate values and quality in the staff themselves and the way in which client–company relationships are managed' (Berry and Bendapudi, 2003, pp. 100–1).

From a strategic management point of view, the critical service success factors relate mainly to the management of the value chain, maintaining control over outsourced functions, and the motivation and empowerment of front-line staff who have face-to-face contact with customers, as opposed to the more remote nature of traditional marketing strategies and advertising campaigns. The main priorities for staff development include building competencies that relate to espousing brand values, interpersonal communication, and deep knowledge of product attributes and applications. Staff interactions with customers are based on a positive, personal experience and not just a mechanical transaction. Intrinsic and extrinsic service and product benefits are equally important. Typical benefits for a significant purchase of clothing or cosmetics, for example, might include perceived product quality, a unique or new product feature, personal advice and attention which creates a feeling of self-esteem, and a general sense of satisfaction from the purchasing experience.

Apart from establishing privilege clubs, alumni groups, loyalty programs and financial incentives, giving customers the opportunity to 'buy into' the business model can be an excellent strategy for building a long-term relationship based upon the solid foundation of shared values and a sense of mutual engagement. Whether it is mixing one's own fragrance at The Body Shop, exploring and matching furnishing options at IKEA, trying new products at Chanel or Estee Lauder, or discussing coffee preferences with the *baristas* at Starbucks, customers increasingly make service decisions that enhance their lifestyle and reflect their individuality. In designing the value chain, the ability to build a relationship based on deep understanding of the customer's individual needs and preferences requires a combination of organisational capabilities, especially in the areas of innovation, HRM, and front-line customer service competencies, with emphasis upon interpersonal communication and customer relations. Some of the key performance indicators of an effective service value chain give an indication of the capabilities and competencies that need to be developed in order to achieve it. These indicators include:

- A well-developed philosophy that if staff are not serving a customer directly, they should be serving (supporting) people who are. Unless the segmented thinking and priorities of the various functional departments of organisations are integrated, seamless service delivery is virtually impossible. This challenge is reflected in the complaint of a newly arrived overseas student in Perth: 'It took me days to enrol and pay my fees. After getting confusing and conflicting course information from various departments, I finally went to the library and found a handbook and sorted it out myself.' (Focus group participant)
- Customer needs determine the design of the organisation and the deployment of resources (see Chapter 6). Accordingly, the organisation is configured from the outside in, rather than, as is traditionally the case, from the inside out. IKEA and Amazon.com are excellent examples of this design principle.

- A collaborative, multidisciplinary approach to customer service is employed and facilitated by clear individual and collective accountability strategies for promoting overall quality service performance (see Chapters 5 and 6). This management approach entails service partnerships between line and support staff, especially involving R&D, production, marketing and service delivery personnel.
- The service directives and guidelines from senior management are reinforced by HRM policies and practices (see Chapter 8), which ensure that every individual employee is not just given accountability for customer service, but is also granted the necessary empowerment, training and essential resources to do the job.
- The organisation's front-line staff are motivated and empowered to identify and address the full range of customer concerns. Even if they cannot provide all the answers and solve all the problems, staff will take ownership of the customer's needs and avoid 'passing the buck'. This means the staff must have very good listening and response skills, along with the capacity to take initiatives to respond to customer needs and concerns.
- The organisation emphasises the critical importance of its corporate communications and interactions with customers. For example, the evolving marketing strategies of Coca-Cola are designed to respond to the changing lifestyle, trends and fashions of its target markets through the effective use of values-laden slogans. Whether it's 'Things Go Better With Coke', 'It's The Real Thing', 'Coke Is It', 'Can't Beat The Feeling' or 'Always Coca-Cola', the ability of the brand to communicate with its loyal customers goes far beyond conventional marketing practice and is based on deep qualitative-based research into changing consumer needs, values and lifestyles. (See Chapter 5 for an extensive discussion on the area of marketing research.)
- The organisation not only gives its customers what they ask for, but, far more importantly, it continually invents new sources of value to surprise and delight them, and often in ways that the customers themselves would probably never have thought of. Coca-Cola is the classic example of a timeless brand built around a simple product, which allows for only very limited product innovation. From time to time, new offerings such as 'Vanilla Coke' will emerge. However, the continuing appeal of Coca-Cola lies in the special relationship that successive generations feel that they have with the brand. This has been achieved by skilfully managing the communication and reinforcement of brand values.
- The organisation takes special care and shows sensitivity in the way that it connects with individual callers and customers, ensuring that they are made to feel welcome and special. Greeting is an important skill. Just as customers complain about being ignored, so they often dislike the overt familiarity practised by some telemarketers, car salespersons and check-out staff. A too familiar and chatty communication style that attempts to short-circuit longer and more measured approaches to consumer interaction may be interpreted as being presumptuous and/or intrusive, and may therefore give offence.
- The organisation ensures that the outsourcing of service functions (also discussed in Chapter 8) does not undermine brand values and is, therefore, not just dictated by cost considerations. Rather, outsourced functions are carefully integrated into a 'seamless web' of customer service competencies to avoid delays, 'buck passing' and double handling. Given that so many companies and customers are unhappy with the results of outsourcing, much more emphasis needs to be given to developing core competency in value chain coordination, with particular reference to HRM issues and system design.

The issue of outsourcing from a service quality perspective requires special attention because it has become so prevalent. The management challenges posed by outsourcing should not be underestimated (Kotabe, 1992, p. 98). As global markets continue to grow and global brands proliferate, so also does competition accelerate and cost pressure intensify, strengthening the logic for outsourcing, not only of production activities, but also increasingly of low-end service functions. Managing and standardising the quality of global production systems is difficult enough, but managing the complexities of outsourcing services around the world is even more formidable. The trend to locate call centres in lower-cost countries provides an excellent illustration of the outsourcing challenge, and the degree of difficulty is magnified by the need to work across different time zones. Every potential obstacle to effective communication comes into play.

Without the benefit of face-to-face contact, and in the absence of facial expressions and physical gestures, there is a great scope for misunderstanding and loss of goodwill. Language, speech patterns and cultural differences can inhibit the ability to transfer information and solve problems on the telephone. Apart from accent and pronunciation, tone of voice, use of idioms, and even the style of conversational banter can greatly influence a call centre operative's ability to satisfy a foreign customer. Accordingly, service providers in the Philippines or India, for example, need a high level of technical knowledge, diagnostic skill and contextual awareness, as well as the ability to communicate effectively with customers from a diverse range of cultural contexts and educational backgrounds. These requirements have major implications for HRM policy and practice, and especially for recruitment criteria, job design, training programs and career path development.

Service reputation survey

Despite the emphasis on customer service contained in many corporate mission statements, very few organisations have succeeded in establishing a reputation for it. Indeed, it would appear that there remains a huge opportunity to gain competitive advantage in this area. The survey conducted by Milton-Smith in Perth, Singapore and Lyon indicates that most consumers have difficulty nominating more than one excellent service provider, based on their own personal experience.

Between September 2002 and May 2004, Milton-Smith randomly surveyed 196 adults in Perth, 149 in Singapore and 86 in Lyon. Participants were invited to list examples of outstanding service without restriction, including home services, professional services, business services, public services, manufactured products, and so on. Milton-Smith also conducted a number of focus groups to explore views about service providers in greater depth. Of the survey respondents, 23 per cent in Singapore, 18 per cent in Perth and 15 per cent in Lyon failed to nominate any organisation in response to the question: 'Can you think of any organisations which, in your experience, have always given you excellent service?' Very few public-sector institutions were named. Fifty-six per cent of all respondents could nominate only one consistently excellent service provider over a minimum two- to three-year period. It was noteworthy that barely 5 per cent nominated four or more organisations. There would therefore appear to be significant room for organisations to develop competitive advantage around customer service in the future.

The majority of the service providers nominated in both surveys were relatively small, local organisations (58 per cent). They included retail shops, car dealers, hairdressers, dentists, mobile phone distributors, tax agents and freight forwarders. This pattern was particularly evident in the Lyon responses. The very wide cross-section of industries and firms nominated reinforces the view that service is a very personal experience, and that there can be a large gap between the provider's perception of the service delivered and the customer's perception of the service actually received.

The most frequently cited large organisations in Singapore were Singapore Airlines, the Ritz Carlton Hotel, Federal Express, Robinsons (a department store) and DBS Bank. In Perth the clear winners were Skippers (a local new and used car dealership mainly specialising in Mitsubishi, Hyundai and Volkswagen cars) and Singapore Airlines, followed by IKEA, the Hyatt Hotel and the RAC (road service club). The two most popular large service providers nominated in the French survey were Carrefour and IKEA. It is noteworthy that, according to some Singaporean respondents, the reason why Singapore Airlines was not nominated more frequently was due to a widespread local perception that ground staff and cabin crew discriminated *against* Asian passengers, and gave preferential treatment to 'Westerners'.

The findings of the focus group discussions in Australia, Singapore and France revealed that there is a major opportunity for organisations in most industries to build a competitive edge by better managing service delivery from the customer's perspective. Just as service providers often fail to deliver the service their customers expect, just as often they provide service their customers don't want. For example, a number of Perth participants critically commented on restaurants where the waiters are excessively solicitous. 'Why is it that, when you're in the middle of your first mouthful, a waiter will suddenly pounce and ask if everything is okay?' complained one regular restaurant patron. Similarly, almost all focus group participants noted the annoying propensity of banks, telecommunications companies, and charities to conduct their market research and telemarketing at dinnertime. There was a general view that additional attention, additional benefits, and additional or bonus products rarely translate into overall added value for the customer, and almost always result in increased costs and higher prices.

By contrast, other participants in the focus groups commented upon the remarkable success of companies such as Starbucks (Singapore), IKEA, Virgin (Perth), Officeworks (Perth), and Carrefour (Lyon). Each of these companies was praised for giving the customer a high degree of flexibility and choice in determining the required level of service. Observations suggested that not only is some so-called service excessive and unwanted, but frequently customers prefer to choose their own level of service. A basic flaw in the way CRM is practised is the apparent assumption that companies can and should control the relationship. This is clearly a mistake and flies in the face of mounting evidence that customers now expect a relationship where they are in control. As the success of Amazon.com, IKEA, Starbucks and Virgin has shown, customers want the freedom to customise the service they receive.

Despite the widespread belief that CRM is the key to developing and securing business success (Peppers and Rogers, 1999), this research suggested that in many cases customers do not necessarily want an intense relationship with their service providers. Furthermore, they do not want the inconsistencies of extreme bursts of effusive attention punctuated by periods of mediocre or inconsistent service provision. Depending upon the context, the notion that less service may actually represent more value to the customer provides an important clue in rethinking the service paradigm. The implication is that managers need to have a deeper understanding of the needs of their potential customers. An obvious problem with the application of CRM so far is that the providers attempt to control and dominate the relationship.

The sentiment emerging from the study focus groups is that the CRM approach is often resented by consumers. More particularly, they want a professional relationship, rather than an intimate relationship, with a services provider. Accordingly, the application of CRM to achieve more sustainable and long-term quality customer relationships requires an integrated management strategy, rather than just marketing. It aims to create a relationship based on a very delicate, but well-supported balance. Among the descriptors emerging from the group discussions that offer a useful guide to managers committed to service quality are 'efficiency', 'flexibility', 'responsiveness', 'being consistent', 'friendly', 'meeting expectations', 'recognising my loyalty', 'making it a pleasant experience', 'remembering my needs and preferences', and 'always providing good value for money'.

By looking at service from the perspective of the customer rather than the provider, it becomes apparent that the traditional economist's distinction between 'goods' and 'services' becomes somewhat artificial. From a customer's point of view, every commercial transaction involves a more or less attractive package of benefits with both tangible and intangible elements and which are subject to highly individual customer priorities and preferences. Thus, for example, the mobile phone is not just a telephone. It has other intangible elements associated with its use. It is designed, sold and used as an extremely flexible and convenient tool for maintaining relationships, communicating information, building networks and contributing to personal security in emergencies.

Superannuation is another hybrid. A superannuation scheme is frequently conceived as a 'product' tailored to the savings, retirement, estate planning and 'peace-of-mind' needs of particular clients. It is much more than an investment account. When a mobile phone or superannuation scheme fulfils its promise, along with the customer's wider service provision expectations, it is because the product and the service functions are working synergistically, and creating what the customer perceives as ongoing added value. A service only becomes a service at the point of delivery to the customer. It is a perception that is fragile, emotional and very personal, as the experience of bank customers frequently confirmed during the focus group discussions (see Box 4.2).

Box 4.2   Banks: Delivering service or serving the customer?

Standard Chartered is one of the world's best-known international banks. It is listed on both the London and Hong Kong stock exchanges, but it is also well-established in Asian, Middle Eastern and African growth markets. In recent years, Standard Chartered has embarked upon a massive program to improve its customer focus, including training and empowering staff to provide solutions, as opposed to performing routine transactions, and to transform branches into 'relationship centres'. According to the bank's head of consumer banking in Hong Kong, the program differs from traditional CRM strategies in that it is 'driven from the customer's viewpoint' and, having determined 'the sort of customer experience that customers want', the appropriate 'processes, technologies and capabilities' are then put in place.

It is clear that Standard Chartered's service philosophy is a recognition that service must now be seen as a relationship *jointly* managed by the provider and the customer, rather than one that is largely controlled by the provider. Bank customers want much greater flexibility and many more options than in the past. Sometimes they need access to a convenient, user-friendly self-service system; on other occasions they require professional advice, personal assistance, or even just the reassurance of face-to-face contact with front-line staff. This capability demands a strategic shift from 'delivering service' to 'serving the customer'. Whereas the former approach incurs the risk of excessive standardisation and marketing hype, the latter dictates that organisations will become much more adept at managing a mutually beneficial ongoing partnership.

(*Source:* M. Taylor and K. D. Raja, 'Redefining customer service', *The Asian Banker*, issue 44, 2004, pp. 42–44; Standard-Chartered.com, Overview, retrieved from www.standard-chartered.com/global/home/aboutus.html, 30 July 2004)

Apart from distorted priorities, including the dogged determination of some banks to make transactions as impersonal as possible, it would appear that banks (including Standard Chartered) have yet to overcome the problem of attracting, training and retaining enough quality front-line staff to keep pace with the rapid growth of services and the ever-increasing service expectations of their customers (see, for example, Mouthshut.com, 2004). However, this challenge is not made easier by the entrenched tradition of ensuring that front-line bank staff are usually the lowest-paid, most poorly trained and the most highly mobile employees in the organisation. To be truly world-class, banks must have both world-class technology *and* world-class staff, *including those at the front line*.

Perhaps the most important finding from this research project is that very few organisations have succeeded in building a 'front-of-mind' reputation for excellent service with their customers. The sort of feedback and the necessary insights for achieving this are generally masked by the tendency to conduct broad-brush customer surveys with a marketing motive in mind. They merely ask participants to nominate the best airlines or to rank insurance companies. So, the challenge remains, even though there is widespread business recognition that, in an environment where it is increasingly difficult to gain and sustain a competitive edge in technology-based innovation, superior service is the surest way to build enduring competitive advantage. In light of this understanding, it is remarkable that more organisations have not succeeded in establishing a customer service relationship that regularly exceeds expectations and is not just based on taken-for-granted standards.

Examples of service excellence

Four of the most frequently mentioned examples of service excellence in the previously discussed survey material were the Skippers Group (Perth), Singapore Airlines, Virgin Airlines and IKEA. Each company will now be discussed in greater detail with a view to exploring and comparing strategies, structures, management systems and other critical success factors (see boxes 4.3 to 4.6). In addition, a number of service failures will be examined in order to construct an integrated strategic management model for services.

Box 4.3   The Skippers Group

Skippers' CEO John Hughes's very high public profile and personal reputation were well established in the minds of the survey respondents. Focus group participants described him as 'a real leader', 'a straight shooter, who is fanatical about high standards', and 'the ultimate professional'. As a corporate leader, Hughes has promoted his strongly held personal values, philosophies and principles, which he applies in his business undertakings. His mission goals of fair dealing and courtesy are consistently applied and personally overseen by him. They have been translated into a pervasive culture that customers immediately sense and appreciate.

Hughes is both a man of vision and a very practical, highly visible, hands-on manager. His leadership strategy is based upon his belief in the power of strong customer-centred values and a determination to translate these values into a core competence. His success in achieving this is reflected in the quality of his salespeople, who exhibit high levels of dedication and loyalty, and whose quality service performance is acknowledged continuously in customer feedback. Adulatory testimonials from delighted customers play a significant part in Skippers' marketing strategy. Apart from word-of-mouth recommendations, Hughes regularly places full-page advertisements, containing up to 50 extracts from recent letters of appreciation, in local newspapers with the headline 'All car dealers are not the same' as a promotional strategy. These letters, which Hughes proudly files and stores in a cupboard behind his desk, clearly document the many reasons why so many people find dealing with Skippers to be such a positive experience. Numerous specific examples of unexpected service or attention to detail are cited, and many customers indicate their continuing loyalty to and trust in the company.

It is notable that what Skippers' customers really value is not a barrage of loyalty programs, free gifts, self-congratulatory newsletters and intrusive phone calls, but rather the knowledge that John Hughes and his colleagues are accessible and responsive at all times, and can be relied upon to provide honest, efficient, high-quality service. Skippers lets the customer drive the relationship and, in doing so, ensures that it is an experience most customers want to perpetuate.

Box 4.4   Singapore Airlines

If ever there was an ambitious corporate vision and stretch goal, Singapore Airlines has it. Based in a tiny Asian country with a small population and no domestic airline service underpinning it, Singapore Airlines became a world leader within a decade of its establishment. It is another example of a company widely regarded as a world-class service provider (Temporal, 2000, pp. 186, 149–52). Focus group participants offered numerous examples of service excellence from their own personal experience. Once again, these examples highlight the importance of integrating ambitious strategic goals with carefully dovetailed operational management; in other words, getting the small details right and consistently translating the promise into reality. At the same time, critical comments were directed at Singapore Airlines' HR selection strategy of appointing front-line service staff on the basis of stereotypical notions of beauty, rather than their quality customer service skills. Several participants felt that the corporate imagery of the 'Singapore Girl' signalled, and indeed reflected, an outdated, sexist HR strategy resulting in female cabin attendants being treated as 'deferential', 'servile' and 'mere objects of beauty'. However, these criticisms were balanced by positive comments about Singapore Airlines' innovative service initiatives and facilities. Examples where the airline had exceeded expectations were cited by several respondents. Nevertheless, while Singapore Airlines' service is still rated higher than that of its competitors, there was a widespread view that its quality and consistency has declined in recent years.

One long-standing member of Singapore Airlines' loyalty and rewards program, Krisflyer, drew attention to outsourcing problems based on first-hand knowledge of a chasm between the rhetoric and the reality of service provision. While acknowledging the generally high standard of the airline's overall service quality, personal experience indicates an inappropriately high level of organisational bureaucracy and unresponsiveness in dealing with premium 'PPS Club' passengers. For example, although 'PPS Club' passengers are given various privileges and gifts, there are often delays of more than an hour when trying to make telephone contact with Krisflyer. The airline cannot claim to provide a quality service in this case.

Another similar incident with significant implications for both customer satisfaction and company reputation derived from an experience that involved the unfair confiscation of frequent flyer points. An administrative error by Singapore Airlines resulted in two personal accounts being established for an individual member. After trying to report this problem on numerous occasions with a view to consolidating the accounts, suddenly, without notice, the second account was closed. The points disappeared with no advice or explanation given and all appeals were rejected. It is ironic that Krisflyer, which is designed as an elaborate loyalty program, could actually become a key trigger for disloyalty because of its poor service delivery. The fact that it is not managed directly by the airline itself highlights the risks involved in outsourcing part of the service value chain. Given the importance of premium passengers to a quality airline, there is a powerful argument for treating the management of the loyalty program as a core competence.

Box 4.5 Virgin Airlines

One of the most effective strategies for building and branding a successful service culture is for the CEO to become the organisation's major publicist and public face. Branding the invisible is never easy, and it is always difficult to communicate service values through traditional advertising. However, when the CEO becomes a credible 'brand champion' in the minds of the staff, customers and other stakeholders, priorities and expectations are much easier to manage. For example, Sir Richard Branson has become the symbol for everything that the Virgin Group represents. Virgin has grown into a major global corporation without a core business and with relatively little advertising. Its business model is an extension of Branson's own image and personality. A walking mission statement, Branson has portrayed himself as the cheeky challenger, opportunistic and fun-loving, always prepared to tackle corporate 'goliaths' and to go against conventional wisdom and established corporate power. A relentless publicity seeker, he is famous for his media pranks and practical jokes. No challenge is too daunting for Branson – British Airways, Qantas; no obstacle is too great – attempting to circumnavigate the globe in a balloon. The bizarre Virgin Empire has been, and remains, an eclectic conglomerate, including businesses as diverse as airlines, trains, condoms, cola, lotteries and music. Some of its businesses fail, others succeed, but the common theme of the Virgin Group is taking on the establishment, shaking the complacency of the market leaders, and giving 'the people' the option of an honest, 'no-frills' alternative at a much cheaper price (De Wit and Meyer, 2004, pp. 680–701).

Branson makes a practice of communicating with staff at all levels, and so diffuses the impression of hierarchy. He wears casual clothes, joins his employees at the pub and involves them in his numerous publicity stunts. A lack of formality, combined with skilled professionalism, is also the basis on which he operates Virgin Airlines. Cabin crew are efficient, but relaxed, and good fun at the same time. Frequent flyers are given special offers online, but they must be taken up almost immediately. In the same way, Virgin Music Group and Virgin Records have created a much greater choice and a much more customer-friendly shopping environment for music and entertainment consumers. In every case, Branson has attempted not only to challenge complacent market leaders in traditional businesses, but also to create new markets largely comprised of 'outsiders', who identify with the values and philosophies he espouses (Cusumano and Markides, 2001, p. 209). Virgin's customers are people who want the option of no service, or minimum service; they are people who like to break the rules, and to do things and express themselves differently. As one regular Virgin Airlines traveller commented during a focus group discussion:

I've always resented the class system on airlines. You are made to feel like cattle if you travel economy, like I do. Virgin is much more democratic. The crew aren't as stuffy – they're nice and friendly. And I like the way you get personal email offers. Some of the deals are incredible. It means I get to visit my friends and relatives; if I had to pay the normal fare I couldn't do that.

Branson declines to define and document a detailed business philosophy. He believes that it is dangerous to create the impression that there is a single model or 'recipe' for business success. However, having said that, he is quite forthcoming in describing his own approach. From the very beginning of his career, when he founded a magazine, his primary goals were to be creative and take risks, to do things that were original, to be proud of what he did, and to have fun. Two of his most obvious personal characteristics are performing practical jokes and standing out from the crowd, and these characteristics have strongly shaped the way he operates in business. Branson's preference is to create new businesses rather than to buy them. Apart from the satisfaction of building a viable business from 'scratch', Branson points to two other advantages that probably provide the clue to his remarkable achievements. The first is the ability to attract, challenge and fulfil the talents of bright, enterprising people; staff are proud to work for Virgin. The second is the ability to respond quickly and effectively to gaps in the market, and to serve customers better than they are being served by the 'big business' market leaders.

Given the importance that he attaches to having highly motivated staff and extremely loyal customers, Branson also thinks it is critical to keep his businesses relatively small in order to maintain a culture that is vital, flexible and efficient. He summarised his views in one of his most significant public speeches. Addressing the British Institute of Directors in 1993, he said:

Our priorities in managing the business do not appear in most management textbooks or most British companies. We give top priority to the interests of our staff; we give second priority to the interests of our customers; and third priority goes to the interests of our shareholders.

Despite his aversion to so-called management philosophies or prescriptions, it is clear that Branson has developed a brilliant model for delivering customer service excellence. Although he is often dismissed as a self-promoting opportunist with an uncanny flair for marketing and publicity, closer inspection of his companies makes it abundantly obvious that there is a consistent strategic management thread running through them. To focus on the 'froth and bubble' is to ignore the management skill that lies beneath. The management structures and processes of Virgin companies are unconventional and unsettling to some critics precisely because they are focused on the values of service, quality and innovation, and on converting them into core competencies. Again to quote Branson (www.virgin.com/uk/aboutvirgin):

There are three things which are particularly important in achieving and maintaining quality: we must get out of our offices and listen to, and motivate, our staff, for, if they are interested in, and responsive to, customers, you are more than halfway towards satisfying them; finally, we must keep our employees well informed.

With particular reference to service management, this profile demonstrates the importance of an imaginative, values-based leadership style and the ability to conceive a business model for serving customers better. Leading by example has a big impact on culture (Leavitt, 1986, pp. 188–90). While management traditionalists may not like Branson's style, the simple fact is that he stands as a role model for dynamic customer service leadership and expects his senior executives to do the same. Virgin has become Britain's leading brand name, and Branson has become Britain's most popular business leader, not just because of clever marketing, but because people value the services the company provides and the innovative contribution to the field of service management that Branson has made.

(*Source:* Adapted from Richard Branson, *The Autobiography*, Longman Cheshire, London, 1999; Richard Branson, *Losing My Virginity: How I survived, had fun, and made a fortune doing business my way*, Three Rivers Press, New York, 2002; www.virgin.com/uk/aboutvirgin)

Box 4.6   IKEA

One of the most striking examples of a new business model based upon value-adding relationships and processes is the Swedish home furnishing company IKEA. Like McDonald's before it, IKEA represents one of the most radical and successful business innovations of the modern era. It has transformed an extremely traditional, highly fragmented furniture and home furnishings industry by providing multiple sources of customer value that straddle numerous industry segments of the past, including design, manufacturing, retailing and direct marketing. In doing so, it has created a new service experience. IKEA has built and maintained a unique market space in a traditional industry by successfully leveraging global forces and creating a completely new set of core competencies unmatched by any of its competitors and making shopping for home furnishings a unique experience.

IKEA's central 'business idea' derives from its founder's philosophy of 'democratic business design'. It is elaborated in the company's vision statement as follows (www.ikea.com):

The vision is to create a better everyday life for many people; we make this possible by offering a wide range of well-designed functional home furnishing products at prices so low as many people as possible will be able to afford them.

Together, this egalitarian vision and quality product design and service delivery principles have changed the rules of the furniture and home furnishings business worldwide. It has not only transformed the taste of millions of homemakers, but it has also introduced a unique shopping experience whereby shoppers have virtually open access to the company's entire inventory. Today, IKEA's 'business idea' is reflected in its network of over 150 stores, 1,800 suppliers, 42 trading service offices and 25 regional distribution centres worldwide. It offers over 10,000 different products universally, which is clear evidence that it has a value proposition that crosses international boundaries, cultures and demography.

In every sense, IKEA is a learning organisation. It learns from its customers, whom it describes as 'partners'. The company uses its trading service centres in 33 countries as vital sources of local market intelligence. Most importantly, it draws on the ideas and input of its global workforce (described as 'co-workers'), each of whom contributes to the 'collective effort' through their involvement in the 'entire process' from market research, product development and production, right through to customer service and sales (Milton-Smith, 2003).

IKEA's egalitarian and participatory culture supports its business strategy very effectively. Through the application of democratic, highly decentralised and empowerment approaches to management and services, IKEA ensures that a service ethic permeates every area of the organisation. Front-line staff have excellent product knowledge that allows them to engage with customers and to act as consultants rather than mere salespersons (Temporal, 2000, p. 126).

The key descriptors for the IKEA management and production system are 'world-class design', 'global production and logistics', 'value-adding processes', 'total flexibility', 'employee empowerment', 'customer intimacy' and 'low price'. It is the total package – the integrated business model – that is the real innovation, rather than particular aspects of strategy, product design or service delivery. In the case of IKEA, the combination of good design, low costs and low prices are certainly important, but these advantages are achieved as a result of a philosophy, vision and value system that has completely redefined the furniture and home furnishing industry and, as a result, provided a revolutionary new value stream for customers (Miles, 2003). Many of IKEA's products are disassembled and, in most countries, there are no home deliveries. Thus, there are considerable savings on manufacturing, packaging and distribution costs. However, instructions for furniture assembly are clear and simple, and most customers welcome both the cost savings and the opportunity to play an active role in designing their home decor.

IKEA demonstrates the importance and power of designing the organisation around the customer. Instead of the traditional introverted hierarchy of management functions and reporting relationships, IKEA concentrates on the management of knowledge, relationships, processes and competencies in order to keep inventing new and better sources of value for its customers. This case highlights the critical interplay between the management and the creation of knowledge, on the one hand, and a corporate culture that encourages and supports learning on the other. This profile illustrates the effectiveness of a service organisation built upon clear and simple core competencies enshrined in a strategic vision, and supported by a customer-focused and empowering organisational culture.

Service failures

The banking sector

During the focus group discussions, the most frequently criticised service providers in the Perth, Singapore and Lyon surveys were the home maintenance suppliers, higher education institutions, banks and financial services firms. Comments made by the participants left little room for doubt that the hostility that people feel towards the major banks is without parallel among service providers. In light of the number, scale and drama associated with high-profile bank failures in the 1990s, this is not surprising. Mistrust of banks also highlights the complex nature of damage to reputation when organisations fail to deliver what they promise or what their customers expect. For example, deep resentment at branch closures underlines the widely held community assumption that banks have an additional social responsibility that goes beyond their financial commitment to shareholders. There is an obvious gap between the bank's and the community's view of stakeholders obligations. Despite the convenience of ATMs and Internet banking, customers also expect easy access to a higher level of face-to-face service when they need it.

One Australian Perth survey respondent described his difficulty in getting specialised information and a quick decision regarding the 'topping up' of an existing housing loan. 'In the old days, I used to drop in and have a chat with my local branch manager,' he said. 'Now I'm supposed to have someone called a customer relationship manager, but the person keeps changing and, in any case, I don't know how to contact them. They're not even listed in the phone book.' This clearly disgruntled customer finally got approval for the top-up loan three weeks after the initial request. The process included a frustrating 'run-around' of eight telephone calls, lost application forms and one branch visit. Summarising his over-all perception of the experience, the customer said: 'I was confronted with an impenetrable Chinese wall of generic phone numbers, call centres, recorded messages, long waits, repetitious "musak", and a faceless procession of incompetent junior clerks identified only as "Kylie", "Brad", "Craig" and "Amber".' Over a 15-day period, this customer of nearly 20 years' standing dealt with bank staff located in Perth, Adelaide and Brisbane for what had previously been nothing more than a routine transaction.

The tertiary education sector

Reference to universities generally triggered a chain reaction in the focus groups. Although complaints about universities were most common in the Australian focus groups, some of the most vocal critics were Singaporean students. At the same time, it was acknowledged that since universities were exposed to market forces in the 1980s, much of their elitist 'ivory-tower' arrogance and lack of accountability has been challenged and addressed and a process of institutional reform has taken place. However, although they are now less elitist and more open, much of the institutionalised administrative and financial inefficiency remains. For example, creditors, visitors, information seekers, enrolling students and potential partners regularly complain about long delays, serial 'buck passing', confusing directions, bureaucratic procedures, segmented structures and indifferent front-line personnel. Several incidents illustrating the frustrations experienced by some overseas fee-paying students were discussed. One overseas student, about to participate in a Summer School, claimed that, upon returning to Australia, he rang a particular university department through the central switchboard on 7 January, only to be greeted by an unfriendly recorded voice saying, 'We will be closed until 5 January; please do *not* try to leave a message.' Another postgraduate fee-paying student from France told of overcrowded classrooms and of being told by the lecturer, on several occasions, to bring her own chair or enrol in another subject.

Home maintenance and delivery services

Some of the most unsatisfactory service scenarios derived from the focus groups involved home maintenance and delivery services. While the most common complaints involved unreasonable charges, the following example highlights the problem of failing to give a reasonable indication of arrival times. A young couple claimed that, because of work pressures, they found it almost impossible to complete their home renovations. 'Both my husband and I are never at home during working hours,' the woman explained. 'Because of security concerns, we are unwilling to leave the door key in the letterbox or under the doormat,' she said. Recently, a plumber informed her that he would make a house call between 10 am and 2.30 pm, and that he could not be more specific. This forced the woman to take a day off work. At 2 pm the plumber telephoned to say he would be at least one another hour. Her frustration continued even after the plumber finally arrived at 3.30 pm. After locating the source of the problem, he told her in an off-hand manner that he had forgotten to replenish the stock of parts and components he normally carried in his van. He would need to visit the local hardware shop before he could complete the job. Forty minutes later he returned, completed the job, and then charged the client, who was by this time fuming, for the time he was away.

This experience, which was mirrored by many other respondents, suggests that there is a major opportunity for home maintenance and delivery firms to create new market space by more effectively meeting the convenience needs of their customers and making a greater effort to earn their trust. The key is to build long-term client relationships and a word-of-mouth reputation simply by applying basic management skills in developing a customer value chain. From the comments of focus group participants, this chain would complement technical competence, inventory control and time management with a commitment to personal values, including courtesy, fair dealing and consideration for others.

Consumer guidance: The issue of rating and ranking service performance

Given the scale and scope of the services sector, it is surprising that in many areas of the market there is very little consumer guidance. The experience of buying professional, business and personal services, to say nothing of home maintenance services, can be daunting, stressful and disappointing. Apart from word-of-mouth recommendations, there are relatively few readily available and reliable market signals such as ratings, rankings, other forms of performance evaluation or service quality indicators. Of course, most service suppliers in advanced countries promote themselves as members of specialist associations or accrediting agencies. However, this form of endorsement generally relates to technical skill, as opposed to actual service delivery. Although newspapers, magazines, travel guides and Internet websites frequently review service operators such as restaurants, airlines, hotels and investment managers, for example, most professions are protected from the blowtorch of close market scrutiny. Old habits die hard.

The tradition of showing deference to the established professions continues in many societies. It is difficult to find examples where professionals such as doctors, dentists, lawyers, accountants, architects and engineers are publicly rated on the basis of their service to previous clients. It is difficult to find a rational explanation for this gap, especially in view of legislative changes in many countries designed to deregulate markets, increase competition and protect consumers. It is all the more perplexing, given the extent of survey and anecdotal evidence from the focus groups indicating dissatisfaction with professional services, especially in the area of financial planning.

Although the rating and ranking of investment funds has become commonplace, it is difficult for investors to assess the track record of financial planners, despite the fact that, over the past decade or so, financial planning has been the newest and fastest-growing profession. It mirrors the ageing of the baby-boomer generation and their search for financial security in their retirement years. However, as with other professions, professional standards have not kept pace with market growth. Financial planning has been a haven for retrenched corporate executives and ambitious opportunists without proper qualifications or experience. Accordingly, the industry has been characterised by aggressive short-term marketing imperatives and loose ethical standards, rather than prudent long-term management strategies. As a result, a high level of suspicion, mistrust and stigma has enveloped the industry, with an increasing number of retirees publicising their bad experiences and heavy losses (Ruth, 2004). For example, a recent critical analysis of American Express Financial Advisors revealed just how flawed and mismanaged the business has become. From a client perspective, even an established brand name such as American Express provided no protection from devious and rapacious exploitation. As the analyst pointed out:

> Financial advisers use the planning process to draw clients in, but they depend on product sales for their livelihood, current and former advisers say, 'The financial plan is their big claim to fame. But if that's all you did, you'd starve to death,' says Judy Reed, an adviser who left American Express in early 2002 after more than a decade with the company. Other former AMEX advisers say that when they presented a financial plan, they dubbed it 'The Close', because of its usefulness in selling high-fee products, including proprietary funds and insurance that paid more to the salesmen – and to the firm. (Simon, 2000, p. M5)

In short, having created the impression that they are acting in the best interests of their clients, by providing objective, expert financial advice, many planners have actually engaged in a game of deceit, selling high-fee, in-house products, receiving secret kick-backs and commissions, while at all times carefully disguising their massive conflicts of interest. At the very least, there is a need to ensure a much higher level of transparency with respect to fees charged and commissions received.

The examples discussed above indicate that the time to take a more comprehensive and integrated customer-focused approach in business strategy is long overdue. The service perspective requires much greater emphasis than it has been given in the past. Management writers have generally been prepared to leave customers at the mercy of the marketers. These cases indicate the costs associated with financial and marketing decisions when they are not carefully integrated into a more holistic management strategy. They highlight the urgent need for a strategic management model that can be applied to services generally. Given that management writers have tended to focus on management issues from the organisational perspective, this tendency, coupled with the exponential growth and competition in services, has meant that there has been an overreliance on marketing strategies to manage customer relations and notions of service quality.

Towards a new strategic management model

What insights and conclusions can be drawn from the examples described above in services management? Perhaps the most obvious common characteristic of the successful enterprises is that they have done much more than rely on incremental growth. All started from humble beginnings and became market leaders – in some cases, global leaders – within a generation. This ability to leap-frog over the competition and quickly create large markets is best explained by the emphasis each company placed upon serving customers in a unique way. Another common feature was their capacity to serve an existing market *and* invent a

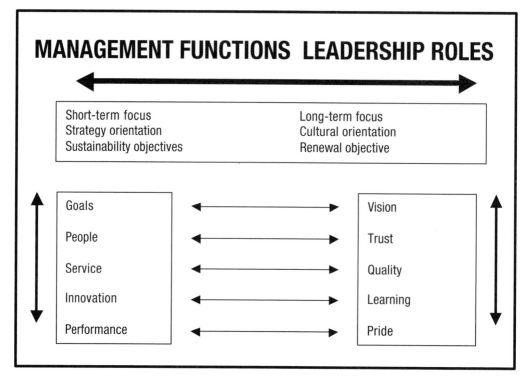

Figure 4.2 Strategic management framework

future market simultaneously. This combination of short-term efficiency and long-term vision appears to be the foundation stone for a successful strategic management approach. However, without ambition, focus and the necessary competencies, none of these companies could have grown as rapidly and as sustainably as they did. This extra dimension seems to derive from the shared passion, values and ethics which only inspiring leadership produces.

Based on this analysis, and upon previous research, a strategic management framework is offered as a general template for developing and reviewing the management of strategy in organisations, especially service organisations. This framework aims to incorporate all of the critical success factors identified in the successful examples discussed earlier.

Most definitions of strategic management are too vague, linear and one-dimensional. Instead, a new, integrated framework is proposed which highlights the importance and inter-relationship of management functions and leadership roles in building a successful and endur-ing organisation (see Figure 4.2) based upon the careful balancing of short-term and long-term performance targets and the systematic alignment of business strategy and corporate culture.

A number of key objectives and assumptions underpin the new strategic management framework developed in this chapter. The primary aim is to put forward a senior-level man-agement template designed to give the organisation stability and continuity, in so far as it is possible, while, at the same time, capitalising on opportunities that may derive from uncer-tainty and change. It addresses the ongoing challenge of balancing management functions and leadership roles. In essence, strategic management confers upon the CEO the ultimate respon-sibility for building an organisation that successfully facilitates long-term adaptation without compromising short-term efficiency. In practical terms, this entails conceiving, articulating and implementing an integrated business model based upon the critical elements of the ISM, so that the necessary resource infrastructure, staff competencies, operational processes, and marketing communications and relationships are in place for winning and retaining loyal customers through the creation of unique value-adding activities. Thus, whereas management functions centre on competitive strategy, organisation structure and business efficiency, leadership roles are about communications, relationships and culture building. The art of managerial leadership is to address sustainability and renewal objectives simultaneously and to create the capability for winning both the battle and the war. As the following illustrative case demonstrates, unless people's commitment, cooperation and contributions are effectively mobilised, the task of strategic management is incomplete.

Box 4.7 Centrelink

A public-sector organisation that has committed strongly to a strategic management approach is Centrelink, which is responsible for managing Australia's welfare. Centrelink's Customer Experience Strategy has been designed as 'an over-arching framework to put the customer at the centre of its business' and aims for ambitious improvements in customer satisfaction. With a customer base of 6.3 million and a widely dispersed network of offices and agencies, the change program aims to transform the customer experience. The model is highly integrated and attempts to achieve optimum fit between strategy, structure and culture in reaching this goal. Major targets include:
- streamlining business processes to achieve better coordination, less duplication and greater efficiency;
- having the capability to respond to a wide variety of customer expectations and preferences in accessing services; and
- addressing both the physical and emotional aspects of the customer's service experience, ensuring consistency in service standards across the system.

However, despite these ambitious aims, Centrelink has not always been as successful as desired (see Chapter 8).

The growth trajectories of companies such as Wal-Mart, IKEA, Starbucks and Virgin reflect the power of something more than an ambitious goal orientation. Each company was propelled forward by a founder with a compelling, infectious vision of what the business should and could become. There was no simple formula, but a shared characteristic was an emphasis on core values. In the case of Sam Walton, the founder of Wal-Mart, there was the home-spun philosophy of treating the customer as a guest, backed up with the appointment of 'people greeters' at the front door of every store. Both Sam Walton and Richard Branson believed strongly in the importance of injecting a spirit of fun into their communications and dealings with people. Indeed, Branson has made his own personal philosophies the mission for the Virgin Group as a whole, which includes an emphasis on adventure, learning from failure and having fun at work.

A capacity for self-ridicule, combined with the ability to earn respect, has contributed greatly to the culture-building contributions of leaders such as Walton and Branson. It has helped them to communicate to every level of their organisations, and to the wider community as well. By bringing themselves down to earth, by 'walking the talk', and by their own examples of humility, they have demonstrated that people matter and that no one is more important than the customer. The same demonstration of democratic values has helped to reinforce the primary business objectives of companies such as Wal-Mart, Virgin and IKEA, of providing quality goods and services to a mass market.

The democratic vision of IKEA's founder, Ingvar Kamprod, has permeated the company's culture. It radiates from the business mission to the front-line staff. There is minimal hierarchy, and everyone, from top to bottom, has the title 'co-worker'. The way people are treated at IKEA has engendered an impressive culture of trust, which is reflected in the empowerment and discretion given to all staff, as well as in the way products are described and displayed. The same connection between respect for people and trust in the business lies at the heart of the remarkable success of the Skippers Group in Western Australia. By putting the onus on his sales personnel to confirm that they have won the trust and respect of every customer, as measured by five core values, John Hughes has clearly demonstrated to his staff and his customers that his business goals are in fact his business values. As Robert Dilenschneider, the former CEO of one of the world's leading public relations firms, put it: 'When culture and vision are well matched, magic can happen' (Dilenschneider, 1992, p. 27).

At the most superficial level, every organisation has a concept of the service it provides and the customers it targets. Of course, some organisations achieve greater success than others because of their marketing capability. In Western Australia, for example, as in most cities, there are car dealerships that have flourished for many years due to their competence in managing basic business operations, especially sales and marketing, and their ability to retain distribution rights for a popular brand of vehicle. However, the Skippers Group has achieved a unique status and level of success due to its reputation for superior service quality. Similarly, in very different ways, both Singapore Airlines and Virgin have created a unique market space by providing a special and distinctive kind of service. Both Virgin and Standard Chartered target customers who seek both minimum service and maximum self-service options. Their success underlines the point that, in services, quality is defined by the ability to meet or exceed the customer's needs and expectations, rather than by indiscriminately pursuing a 'more is better' strategy.

There is a close connection between service quality and innovation. An obsession with providing customers with new, better and frequently unexpected sources of added value is the hallmark of outperforming companies. Singapore Airlines' success has been attributed to its commitment to 'set standards of service that others can only follow', the latest of which is the first regular, direct scheduled flight service from Singapore to Los Angeles. From his earliest vision of Italian coffee bar culture taken to every corner of the world, Howard Schultz of Starbucks has transformed what is basically a commodity product into a universal coffee-drinking experience by educating the market to appreciate quality coffee standards in a multitude of forms in a congenial social environment. Quality service can only be sustained by constant innovation, which, in turn, relies heavily upon a deeply ingrained learning culture. Just as Richard Branson has built a business empire upon the ability to learn from the mistakes of others, as well as his own, so Sam Walton before him instituted Wal-Mart's weekly 'Saturday Morning Meeting', which is attended by all regional field managers to compare notes and debate current issues. This meeting has become the centrepiece for collaborative strategic decision making which 'helps calibrate and adjust the vision in a constant cycle'.

All of the companies under discussion have maintained an impressive level of bottom-line performance over long periods. They have been ruthlessly goal-oriented; however, in each case, growth and profits have been secondary outcomes, rather than primary points of focus. Higher-order motivation has inspired exceptional levels of staff loyalty, performance and pride, which has had a positive impact upon customers, suppliers and other stakeholders. Howard Schultz frequently startles financial analysts by refusing to discuss 'commerce', and by insisting that Starbucks' priority is with 'making the human connection' based upon ethics and values. In an earlier era, Kamprod of IKEA devised his brilliantly successful business model around a philosophy of offering lower prices by cutting costs, but never cutting back on innovative ideas or quality. Inevitably, all companies are under pressure to pursue short-term advantage by ignoring the implications for long-term reputation. But, as even great companies such as Nestlé, Nike and Shell have found to their great cost, betrayal of ethical standards not only erodes the value of the company but also diminishes the self-respect and pride of major stakeholders, especially the employees.

Conclusion

As discussed in Chapter 1, the continuing classification of goods and services into two clearly separate categories is an increasingly artificial and misleading exercise. The previous two chapters emphasised the complex and dynamic impact of the business environment in which service providers operate. They highlighted the importance of stakeholder relationships and the many management challenges associated with building quality stakeholder networks and relationships, and the many management challenges involved in building and maintaining them. For managers today, instead of regarding goods and services as separate categories, it is more realistic to consider them as overlapping and interdependent.

As this chapter has demonstrated, from the customer's perspective it is important for managers to think in terms of a goods and services continuum. What matters most to customers is the perceived benefit of the total value position. It is of no consequence to the customer whether or not the offering is visible or invisible. As managers move towards a value chain mindset, goods and services increasingly become integrated and inseparable elements. The transition from a services marketing to a value chain mindset requires a new way of thinking about strategy. Instead of focusing narrowly upon market conditions and behaviour of competitors, managers need to concentrate much harder on their customers and on the customers they seek to create in the future. The design and delivery of an innovative and compelling value chain, and translating it into a viable business model, goes far beyond pushing an aggressive marketing plan on confused and bombarded consumers. Instead, it involves the careful creation of an integrated business model, which includes all of the elements that combine to satisfy and exceed customers' expectations, while taking account of the variables that could conspire to undermine it. As the ISM model (see Figure 4.1) clearly indicates, an innovative business model requires the creative input and performance accountability of all the management functions working as a team, generating new ideas and taking responsibility for corporate outcomes (Johansson, 2004, pp. 79–80; Kleiner, 2004, pp. 30–32).

Without the critical core competencies, continuous coordination and a corporate culture committed to serving the customer's needs and priorities, the business model is just a theory or a concept. Without the capability of learning from insights into past experience, knowledge about current trends, and foresight as to where the future is heading, managers will lack the essential ingredients for reviewing, refreshing and reinventing the value chain. Without the leverage and warrant of a powerful brand that captures and communicates the values and benefits that its stakeholders expect, an organisation will fail to fulfil its true potential.

It is important than managers fully appreciate the strategic significance of a consumer-based approach to branding, because it is the key to building a loyal, long-term customer base. A well-branded value chain is much more than the sum of its parts, because it creates the premium that customers are willing to pay for, including invisible attributes such as safety, reliability, prestige and elegance. Regardless of whether one is involved in managing professional, personal or domestic services, on the one hand, or service elements of consumer or industrial products, on the other, the strategic management challenge lies in creating, communicating and consistently delivering a unique value proposition to the customer.

An effective brand is the foundation for building and maintaining a long-term relationship with stakeholders, and its credibility is based upon the fulfilment of promises. A reputation for integrity and quality is an organisation's greatest asset and must be managed with consistency and care. What ultimately differentiates the financial adviser, or the car dealer, in the mind of the customer is not just the 'physical' products they sell – the investment funds and the motor vehicle – but, rather, the reputation values that the customer associates with their brands. Brand values can communicate very directly and deeply, and impact in an extremely personal and subjective way, but they are constantly being tested against the blowtorch of individual expectations and experience.

Finally, as a template for analysing cases and as a guide to practitioners, this chapter puts forward a strategic management framework (Figure 4.2) developed by the author. It provides a model that stresses the need for an integrated and balanced approach in managing strategy. It incorporates both short-term and long-term strategic imperatives, the equal importance of sustainability and renewal objectives, and the need to address simultaneously both the critical organisational functions of operational management and the leadership roles that are vital in translating business model priorities into the attitudes, norms and practices of a positive corporate culture.

Exercises

Web exercise 4.1

Select a few high-profile services industry corporations. Find their websites and vision statements. Analyse these to identify their corporate culture and discuss the implications of these for strategic management. Similarly, analyse the leadership profiles presented of CEOs and senior management, and discuss the implications of these for leadership style and, hence, the specific competitive strategic management organisational approach adopted.

Case study 4.1 A banking challenge

Loyola Brown has banked with Customer First Bank for over 15 years. Three years ago the bank was taken over by one of Australia's largest banks and Loyola noticed that the friendly personal service, for which Customer First was famous, began to decline. In fact, on one occasion, when Loyola tried to contact her local branch manager, she found there were not even any branch numbers listed in the telephone book. When she visited the bank and tried to make an appointment with the manager, she was told that he no longer worked there and that, furthermore, the position of branch manager had been abolished. The person at the bank's enquiry counter told Loyola, 'We now have regional customer relations consultants, but I'm not sure whether you've been allocated to one yet.' In response to Loyola's request for a consultant's contact number, she was told: 'We're still sorting out our corporate clients, but we should get around to you in a few days – just bear with us, because it's taking a while to organise our new system.

More recently, Loyola sold her business and arranged for the proceeds to be paid into her Customer First cheque account. She then intended to place most of the funds, about $275,000, in a fixed term deposit account for about three months while she took a holiday and looked around for another business. Just prior to the settlement, and because she didn't want to lose interest, Loyola made enquiries at her Customer First branch about transferring her money directly into a deposit account as soon as her cheque had cleared. 'Could you let me know when the cheque has cleared?' she asked. 'Sorry, we're very short-staffed and we're not really allowed to do that sort of thing,' the young bank officer replied.

Several days later, Loyola confirmed that her cheque had cleared. As she was not feeling well, she decided to take up the bank's suggestion to open a deposit account by telephone. When she consulted the telephone book, she saw there were various entries for Customer First Bank, but there was no specific entry for 'Term Deposit Accounts'. After some deliberation, Loyola concluded that she should try 'Customer Service', which the phone book indicated was available '24 hours, 7 days a week'. Upon ringing the number, she was confronted with a recorded message, which gave her five phone-button-based options. With considerable uncertainty, Loyola pressed '0' and was greeted with another set of recorded options. After selecting '0' again, she was advised by a staccato voice: 'All our lines are busy at present. Your call is important to us, so please wait.' Several renditions of 'Greensleeves' later, Loyola finally managed to speak to a human voice, but it was an anticlimax.

When she outlined her request, 'Wendy' informed Loyola that she couldn't discuss interest rates because 'I'm just a call centre operator. It sounds to me like you need to talk to a financial planner. Why don't I transfer you to one?' 'No, no,' Loyola responded quickly. 'All I want is a three-month term deposit.' Finally, Loyola was transferred to 'Brian', who operated what he described as the 'Customer First Interest Rate Hotline'. When Loyola started to outline her requirements yet again, she was interrupted mid-sentence by 'Brian', who pointed out that she was speaking to the wrong person. 'I'll transfer you to somebody in Brisbane. I can't process term deposits. I only tell the financial advisers what the appropriate interest rates are.' By now Loyola was feeling extremely frustrated and angry, especially as she was now running late for a doctor's appointment. Just as she was about to hang up, 'Stephen' came on the line. Loyola decided that she would try to finalise things, given that she had spent so long on the call already.

'Stephen' took down her details and then said that he would need to check on the appropriate interest rate. 'By the way,' he added. 'Are you a shareholder in the bank, or do you have any other investment accounts with us? Because, if so, we could give you a slightly higher rate as a preferred customer.' At this point, Loyola, who had been controlling her irritation, exploded: 'I've been a faithful, long-suffering customer of this stupid bank for 15 – actually, *more than* 15 – years. But if this is how you're treating me, I won't be for much longer. Are you telling me that somebody who bought 100 bank shares last month would get a better interest rate than me? I'm shocked!'

Loyola asked 'Stephen' to call her back within ten minutes with the interest rate details so that she could use her phone to cancel her doctor's appointment. She realised that, as a result of the delay, she could not possibly make it in time. As she confided to her husband later, she felt too upset to leave the house. More than 40 minutes had passed before 'Stephen' phoned again. 'I'm sorry about the delay,' he began, 'but I had trouble contacting the person I needed to speak to. Although we can't offer you a better rate this time, in future you'll qualify if you go ahead with this term deposit.' Loyola's response was terse: 'My husband has just contacted Global Bank, and they have offered me an extra 0.3 per cent interest if I transfer my business to them.' On hearing this, 'Stephen' said urgently: 'Please don't do that – you've had such a long relationship with us. Just give me a minute and I'll see if we can match them. . . .'

Student projects
1 What are the main service issues raised by this case?
2 Describe the service culture at Customer First Bank.
3 Do you think that bank shareholders should be given a preferential interest rate? Why?
4 Should Loyola switch to another bank? Give your reasons.

Case study 4.2 The bus driver from hell

Paradise Tours is a Singapore-based company that caters mainly for the local market. Apart from packaged tours, it also offers a basic bus service to various cities in Malaysia. One of its most popular packages is 'Paradise Pleasures', which is a three-day holiday in Malaysia's Genting Highlands.

Connie Lim had travelled with Paradise Tours previously. So, when she and some work colleagues felt they needed a break, Connie recommended that they should all go on a 'Paradise Pleasures' long weekend. The group decided to leave on a Friday morning and return on a Sunday night, so that they would only need to apply for one day's leave. This was granted, although the manager pointed out that, because of heavy pre-Chinese New Year orders, it was somewhat inconvenient to have five workers away at the same time.

The bus trip to the Genting Highlands was uneventful and on schedule. The bus driver told them that he was normally assigned to 'Paradise Pleasures' and had driven both ways on over 200 occasions. However, this time he was staying over in Malaysia to assist with a corporate golf day, he told Connie and her friends. Another driver based in Kuala Lumpur would be driving them back to Singapore.

Things started to go badly from the beginning of the return trip. Connie's party were packed and ready to leave their hotel half an hour before their scheduled departure, but the bus didn't collect them until after they had rung the bus company to find out where it was. The driver arrived nearly 90 minutes late. Then, although he was supposed to drive straight to Singapore, he stopped without any explanation at a roadside cafe for 20 minutes and proceeded to eat a snack. On returning to the bus, the driver casually mentioned to his surprised and angry passengers that he had been unable to have dinner at home due to the inconvenient pick-up time.

The passengers were even more annoyed when the bus made yet another unscheduled stop, this time making a detour down a narrow side road to collect one of the driver's relatives. 'My auntie hasn't seen her sister-in-law for over two years, so I'm taking her with me to Singapore,' he explained.

An hour later, just when most of the passengers were starting to doze off, the driver suddenly announced that he himself was sleepy and needed to take a short rest. 'My youngest son has fever and kept us awake most of last night. I'm very sorry, but I'm doing this for your safety.' The passengers were irate; they were already hours behind schedule, they pointed out. The driver offered no further apology, merely stating that the passengers should be more understanding and that he would be 'okay' after a short nap.

The nightmare continued. As the bus approached Singapore, the driver said that he would need directions in order to locate the Paradise Tours bus terminal. It soon became clear that he had only a hazy idea of Singapore's street layout, and it was well after midnight when the bus finally reached its destination.

The exhausted passengers told the driver that they intended to report him to the company's management. When they asked for his name, the driver refused to give it. He climbed back on to the bus, leaving the startled passengers on the pavement. Several of the passengers were met by relatives or friends; however, most had to wait for a taxi and then pay an after-midnight surcharge. Far from being refreshed and relaxed by their holiday, Connie and her colleagues arrived home feeling weary, tense and furious about the way they had been treated. Connie herself was unable to sleep for several hours and then, after falling into a very deep sleep, woke late and had to take a taxi in order to get to work on time.

During her lunch break, Connie telephoned Paradise Tours to lodge a complaint. She described in detail the events of the return journey. After listening to her complaint, the general manager, Mr Chua, said that the company could not accept responsibility, as it had only chartered the bus and didn't own it. 'I'm sorry. I understand the inconvenience you have suffered, but it was completely outside our control,' he added.

Connie wasn't deterred. 'You can't escape responsibility,' she said. 'And I believe that you should compensate us for the cost of our taxi surcharge last night, and for the taxi I had to take to work this morning.' Mr Chua merely laughed and said that he had to hurry away to a meeting.

(*Source:* Adapted from Editorial, 'Tourism here "hurt by poor service"', *Straits Times* (Singapore), 13 November 2003)

Student projects

1 What criteria would you use in evaluating the bus driver? How would you rate his performance? Is any follow-up action required?

2 Do you think Paradise Tours should pay compensation? If so, compensation for what and to whom?

3 Create a customer service 'value chain' for Paradise Tours, identifying the structures, policies and competencies needed to implement it.

Case study 4.3 Lifestyle Wealth Management

Lifestyle Wealth Management (LWM) was established in Sydney in 1985 by Bob Nelson, a successful former insurance salesperson. Bob recognised a major gap in the financial services industry: the lack of comprehensive financial planning and total wealth management facilities for middle-class professionals nearing retirement. His business model was to provide customised private banking to a wider market. During the past decades, he had noted the frustration of many of his friends and associates in trying to manage their own investments in real estate and equities. Similarly, he was increasingly aware that many managed funds superannuation schemes were underperforming and were unlikely to adequately provide for their members in retirement.

Bob was surprised how easy it was to become a qualified financial planner and to establish LWM. Within a few years, the company employed 12 advisers and managed five funds representing a total value of over $2 billion. With a strong marketing campaign based on the theme 'Leave your lifestyle to us', LWM became a major sponsor of cultural events and professional development activities. By 1995 its marketing budget was about $350,000. Promotional and sponsorship activities included a part-funded chair at a leading business school, regular public seminars in five-star hotels, CDs providing investment analysis, and expensive newsletters and glossy brochures. LWM's 'distinctive approach' was summed up in one of its brochures:

> We trust in the long-term performance of the equities market but we don't try to predict the future, pick winners or take unnecessary risks; instead, we build a model of the market and encourage our clients to maximize the diversification of their portfolios.

Ray and Janice McGuire signed up with LWM in 1999 when Ray turned 55. Both Ray and Janice held senior positions in the public sector and had five children, two of whom had serious disabilities and required continuous professional care. Despite their current high salaries, Ray and Janice's previous employment, family commitments and savings history meant they had not made adequate provision for their retirement. It was not surprising, therefore, that they were attracted by an LWM television advertisement, which promised: 'We will ensure that you can realise your financial goals; all you need is commitment, discipline and LWM.' After five meetings with their LWM adviser, Ray and Janice received and approved a financial plan.

Their adviser, Reg Underwood, encouraged them to sell most of their assets, apart from the family home and cars, to commit 20 per cent of their combined salaries for at least five years, and to place the proceeds in LWM's Rapid Growth Fund. At first Ray and Janice were quite happy with LWM's performance. Reg Underwood, whose previous career had also been in the public sector, sent them monthly statements. Twice a year, there was a brief portfolio review. Just before Christmas, a cocktail party was held at which Bob Nelson gave LWM clients an overview of the investment markets. The only area that raised slight concerns for Ray and Janice was their inability to get a clear statement of the various fees and expenses charged and withdrawn by LWM.

By 2002, things had changed. The fall in the equity markets had resulted in a 36 per cent drop in the value of their portfolio, and Ray and Janice were disturbed to find that, in response, LWM was embarking on even more aggressive marketing campaigns. The advertising tag-line now advocated patience: 'All you need is commitment, discipline, LWM and *a long-term investment perspective.*' It was becoming increasingly difficult to get through to Reg Underwood, due to staff reductions and the routine use of answering machines at LWM. The regular portfolio review sessions had become more perfunctory, and Reg spent most of his time defending LWM's investment strategy and emphasising the need to 'hang in'. Most irritating of all, Reg showed little interest in hearing about changes in their circumstances. Ray and Janice found they had to resort to sending him emails to explain that, after putting ageing parents into nursing homes and paying for full-time care for one of their children, there were now very serious cash flow problems, which had not been anticipated.

In one of his emails to Reg, Ray reminded him that 'When we paid $2,000 for an up-front financial plan, we were told that it would be automatically reviewed in the light of changing circumstances.' Six days after sending this email, a message was left on their answering machine from Michelle, in Reg's office, advising them: 'Reg is out of town at a conference and will be in touch when he returns. Meanwhile, we're sending you our new brochure.' A few days later, a glossy brochure from LWM arrived, inviting Ray and Janice to attend a new monthly series of seminars on 'investment strategy'. It also announced a new 'multi-factor' investment philosophy and the development of new software for designing client portfolios.

Ten days later, Ray and Janice received an email from Reg stating that he had 'looked at your situation but unfortunately, because of the state of the equity markets around the world, there seems little scope for changing our strategy or encouraging you to withdraw funds. Please be patient.'

By coincidence, on the same day that they received Reg's email, Ray and Janice received another message on their answering machine. 'Hi, Ray and Janice. This is Troy from Reg Underwood's office. You might have noticed that LWM has been named one of the Australia's 10 fastest-growing companies. We are taking three tables at the awards night dinner and, because you are long-standing clients, Reg would like you to attend as our guests and share in our success. It's on 5 October. Let us know if you can come and we'll send you the details.' When they heard the message, Ray turned to Janice: 'Bloody hell! I'll tell them what they can do with their invitation. . . .'

Student projects

1 If you were appointed as a consultant to review LWM's strategies, structure and management, what recommendations would you make? Include some comments on:
   a) the management of customer communications and relations; and
   b) appropriate strategies for business development.

2 Propose an appropriate advertising tag-line for LMW which, in your view, would be both an attractive and ethical way of communicating with prospective clients.

Case study 4.4 States of frustration

When Jacinta Adamson's mother bought herself a new car, she gave her old one to Jacinta. However, the car was not actually registered in Jacinta's name. Indeed, for more than two years, Mrs Adamson continued to pay most of the expenses apart from petrol. Then, without much notice, Jacinta was given a significant promotion by her employer and transferred from the local Bearbrass office to a new branch interstate. She enthusiastically packed her belongings and arranged to have the car transported.

Soon after her arrival, Jacinta had the car registered in Centralia and received new registration plates. With the car now transferred into her name, she looked forward to exploring her new home state. Several months passed and everything was going smoothly when, late one evening, she received an anxious phone call from her mother. A letter had arrived from the Transport Department in Bearbrass demanding the return of the old number plate. 'What have you done with the plates? We need to return them immediately,' Mrs Adamson said to Jacinta. 'Please sort it out quickly or I will be fined. I could even lose my own licence.' Jacinta was perplexed. She had assumed that the plates would be sent back to Bearbrass by the Centralian Department of Transport once the new plates were issued. 'Surely this is something the state transport authorities do every day? We live in such a mobile society now, it's hard to imagine why moving interstate should be a problem,' Jacinta replied. She advised her mother to ring the state Transport Department in Bearbrass and get them to contact the Centralian office.

After negotiating a series of recorded messages and prompts, and then being kept on hold for what seemed like an eternity, Mrs Adamson was shocked by the officer's abrupt and unsympathetic manner. 'The fact that the plates are in Centralia is your problem,' she was told. 'We have no contact with them.' When her mother told her about the call, Jacinta decided to take the initiative. She contacted the Centralian office again and was assured that the number plates would be on their way to Bearbrass very soon, although it was clear that the officer was uncertain about which department in Bearbrass they should be sent to. 'You can relax now,' Jacinta told her mother. 'It's all under control. You don't have to do a thing. The plates will be returned in a day or so, I'm sure.' However, the reality was that Jacinta could not drive her car, because the Centralian office still held her old plates and could not issue the new ones because the car was not in Jacinta's name.

Three weeks later, Mrs Adamson received another letter instructing her to return the number plates urgently or pay $110. Failure to do so by the new deadline would result in court action and the possible loss of her licence to drive in her own state, she was warned. Mrs Adamson was now extremely stressed, and rather annoyed that her daughter had left her in this predicament. 'It's very unfair,' she told Jacinta. 'I gave you a car – that should be enough. The least you can do is sort out the paperwork and spare me all this pressure.' Jacinta replied: 'It's very unfair of you to say that, Mum. It's not my fault. I'm finding all this very stressful, too. While all these bureaucratic hassles are going on, I'm also trying to settle into a new flat *and* cope with a new job.'

Over the next two days, Jacinta rang the Centralian Transport Department several times. She spoke with a different officer each time, and was again assured that everything was all right. However, on the third day she discovered that the plates were still in Centralia and that the transport officers could not hand them over until the necessary paperwork was completed transferring the car into Jacinta's name.

Student projects

1 Identify the management deficiencies that are causing Jacinta's 'bureaucratic hassles'.
2 Design a customer-friendly process for dealing with interstate transfers of this kind.
3 Have you ever experienced problems similar to Jacinta's when dealing with government agencies? If so, what management initiative would be required to prevent such problems occurring in the future?

References and further reading

Albrecht, K. and Bradford, L. 1990, *The Service Advantage*, Dow Jones-Irwin, Homewood, IL.

Albrecht, K. and Zemke, R. 1985, *Service America: Doing business in the New Economy*, Dow Jones-Irwin, Homewood, IL.

Atlantic Media Company. 2003, *AAF Survey of Industry Leaders on Advertising Trends*, American Advertising Federation, Washington.

Berry, L. and Bendapudi, N. 2003, 'Clueing in customers', *Harvard Business Review*, February.

Branson, R. 1999, *The Autobiography*, Longman Cheshire, London.

Branson, R. 2002, *Losing My Virginity: How I survived, had fun, and made a fortune doing business my way*, Three Rivers Press, New York.

Burgelman, R. 2002, *Strategy is Destiny*, The Free Press, New York.

Cooper, C. 2004, '[It's all about the] service', *Management Today*, February, pp. 12–18.

Cusumano, M. and Markides, C. 2001, *Strategic Thinking for the Next Economy*, Jossey-Bass, San Francisco.

De Wit B. and Meyer, R. 2004, *Strategy: Process, Content, Context*, 3rd ed., Thomson Learning, London.

Dilenschneider, R. 1992, *A Briefing for Leaders*, Harper Collins, New York.

Economist, The. 2004, Editorial, 'Snake oil', *Economist*, 7 February, p. 59.

Farrell, D. 2003, 'The real new economy', *Harvard Business Review*, October.

Forsyth, R. 2003, 'Why marketing isn't working any more – a definitive answer', crm-forum, www.crm-forum.com, retrieved 13 June.

Gregory, K. 2004, *The Best Branding*, McGraw-Hill, New York.

Hamel, G. and Prahalad, C. 1994, *Competing for the Future*, Harvard Business School Press, Boston.

Hyde, P., Landry, E. and Tipping, A. 2004, 'Making the perfect marketer', *Strategy and Business*, winter, pp. 37–43.

Imparato, N. and Harari, O. 1994, *Jumping the Curve*, Jossey-Bass, San Francisco.

Jacobs, R. 2004, 'The empire strikes back', *Financial Times*, 19–20 June, p. W3.

Johansson, F. 2004, *The Medici Effect: Breakthrough insights at the intersection of ideas, concepts and cultures*, Harvard Business School Press, Boston.

Kaminski, M. 2004, 'Starbucks in Paris', *Asian Wall Street Journal*, 30 January – 1 February, p. 11.

Keates, N. 2004, 'Spas get niche treatment', *Asian Wall Street Journal*, 13–15 February, p. 8.

Kerk, C. 2004, 'Spa speak', *Weekend Business Times* (Singapore), 14–15 February, p. 16.

Kleiner, A. 2004, 'Recombinant innovation', *Strategy and Business*, winter, pp. 30–34.

Kotabe, M. 1992, *Global Sourcing Strategy*, Quorum Books, New York.

Leavitt, H. 1986, *Corporate Pathfinders*, Dow Jones-Irwin, Homewood, IL.

Lee, A. 2004, 'Ryanair to give new meaning to "no-frills experience"', *Straits Times* (Singapore), 16 February, p. 6.

Lee, J. 2004, 'Getting the customer to love brands', *Sydney Morning Herald*, 6 May, p. 25.

McDonald, M. and Cavusgil, T. (eds). 1990, *The International Marketing Digest*.

McGovern, G., Court, D., Quelch, J. and Crawford, B. 2004, 'Bringing customers into the boardroom', *Harvard Business Review*, November, pp. 70–80.

McGovern, G. and Quelch, J. A. 2004, 'The fall and rise of the CMO', *Strategy and Business*, winter, pp. 45–51.

Mackintosh, J. 2004, 'Carry your own bags, but sit in a leather seat', *Financial Times*, 16 February, p. 17.

Maslow, A. H. 1968, *Toward a Psychology of Being*, 2nd ed., Van Nostrand, Princeton, NJ.

Miles, I. 2003, 'Services innovation: Coming of age in the knowledge-based economy', in B. Dankbaar (ed.), *Innovation Management in the Knowledge Economy*, Imperial College Press, London, pp. 59–81.

Milton-Smith, J. 2003, 'From knowledge management to learning culture', *International Journal of Knowledge, Culture and Change Management*, vol. 3, pp. 551–67.

Moore, J. 1996, *Death of Competition: Leadership and strategy in the age of business ecosystems*, Diane Pub. Co., New York.

Mouthshut.com. 2004, 'Personal finance' www.mouthshut.com/readreview/3038-1.html.

Peppers, D. and Rogers, M. 1999, *The One to One Manager, Real-World Lessons in Customer Relationship Management*, Random House, New York.

Porter, M. 1980, *Competitive Strategy: Techniques for analysing industries and competitors*, The Free Press, New York.

Porter, M. 1985, *Competitive Advantage: Creating and sustaining superior performance*, The Free Press, New York.

Porter, M. 1990, *The Competitive Advantage of Nations*, The Free Press, New York.

Roberts, J. 1998, *Multinational Business Service Firms*, Ashgate Publishing, Aldershot, UK.

Senge, P. 1992, *The Fifth Discipline: The art and practice of the learning organisation*, Random House, Sydney.

Simon, R. 2004, 'Investors feel deceived by financial plans', *Asian Wall Street Journal*, 10 February, p. M5.

Simons, C. 2004, 'One-stop shop', *Far Eastern Economic Review*, July, pp. 64–66.

Standard-Chartered.com. 2004, 'Overview', www.standardchartered.com/global/home/aboutus.html, retrieved 30 July 2004.

Straits Times, The. 2003, Editorial, 'Tourism here "hurt by poor service"', *Straits Times* (Singapore), 13 November.

Taylor, M. and Raja, K. D. 2004, 'Redefining customer service', *Asian Banker*, issue 44, pp. 42–44.

Temporal, P. 2000, *Branding in Asia*, John Wiley, Singapore.

Temporal, P. 2002, *Advanced Brand Management*, John Wiley, Singapore.

Viljoen, K. and Dann, S. 2003, *Strategic Management*, 4th ed., Pearson Education, Sydney.

Warren, K. 2002, *Competitive Strategy Dynamics*, John Wiley, Chichester, UK.

5
Marketing management in services

Learning objectives

After studying this chapter, readers will be able to:
- discuss the different interpretations of marketing in relation to the evolution of management and marketing discourse, and the relationship between a holistic strategic business management philosophy and an integrated conceptualisation of marketing
- appreciate the role of cross-function management and employees' systemic strategic thinking as critical management tools with which to successfully institutionalise a process-oriented organisational perspective and enable the holistic implementation of the marketing concept
- explain the relationship between integrated marketing and total quality management
- describe the contextual background behind the emergence of services marketing and management, and discuss the new relationship marketing paradigm and its associated challenges
- understand different contributions of total quality management and business process reengineering to strategic business management thinking and practice
- define the new role for the marketing department
- discuss the criticality of effective management of customer and market information and knowledge for the successful implementation of the marketing concept and strategic business management.

Introduction

The previous chapter highlighted some of the key strategic management challenges now faced by many organisations in the context of the growing importance of marketing services, or the *servitisation* of businesses (see Vandermerwe and Rada, 1988). The extensive illustrative case-based discussion underscored how business success in services is determined by the quality of a range of strategic management decisions and actions made in relation to both the external and internal organisational environment. Strategic management, at both a corporate and business unit level, has significant management implications for the operations of business functions (for example, marketing, operations, finance and human resources). In essence, strategies formulated at the higher levels of an organisation provide critical inputs to the development of operational strategies at a lower level of the organisation.

As discussed in the previous chapters, an organisation is a complex system comprised of various subsystems that interact with the external environment. The sustainability of an organisation depends on the competence of management in transforming inputs obtained from outside, based on a unique coordination and integration of its subsystems, into valuable outputs to the external environment. In this regard, an organisation needs to be viewed as consisting of a set of interdependent *processes*, which transform inputs to outputs based on the internal resources and capabilities. Traditionally, processes were understood as sequences of tasks and activities. In recent years, however, a more elaborate view has emerged, which argues that processes are explicitly and implicitly programmed patterns of interaction, communication, coordination and decision making (see Garvin, 1998; Christensen, 2000). Unfortunately, despite this theoretical development, strategic decisions are still made at many organisations based on the traditional overly specialist, functional view of work along the conventional function-based organisational structure – that is, strategic management, marketing, operations, finance and human resources management.

In an ever-intensifying service-driven market, organisations and managers can no longer afford to assume that the optimisation of each subsystem would inevitably lead to optimum performance at a system level (that is, a strategic business unit or an organisation). The management literature has long argued that the pursuit of the isolated optimisation of subsystems often fails to manifest itself as an overall optimisation of the organisation's performance. Such functionalistic management thinking is confined by the logic of functional organisational architecture (that is, a bounded and reductive notion of skill, resource requirements, tasks, and a confined domain of decision making and accountability). Too often, it promotes 'turf battles' over control and power over the allocation of scarce organisational resources and creates a gulf between subsystems. This myopic function-based approach to strategic management does not allow both managers and employees to realise and respond to opportunities and challenges associated with the coordination, integration and innovation of business processes beyond their functional boundaries. To retain its relevance and enhance competitiveness in the context of ever-intensifying service-based competition, fuelled by the need for value innovation, an organisation needs to embrace a strategic business management philosophy based on the strategic systemic thinking of both managers and employees. If an organisation fails to institutionalise this holistic integrated management and employee approach, the pursuit of business excellence will be in jeopardy.

As previously argued through the inductive case-based discussion in Chapter 4 on the strategic management of services, strategic systemic management thinking is instrumental to business success. Nonetheless, many organisations and managers still find the task of strategic business management and the promotion of systemic strategic thinking among employees a real challenge. This chapter addresses the need for, and benefits of, a holistic strategic business management approach to be applied to strategic functional management, while identifying the shortcomings of conventional compartmentalised strategic thinking and behaviour. Each of the operational management chapters presents theoretical and practical management issues unique to their respective management areas. However, for the purposes of integration, some key services management issues reappear across the various chapters. Initially this might appear to be repetitive; nevertheless, it is the most effective way to represent the interdependent nature of an organisation's subsystems and, hence, to appreciate the value of strategic business management.

This chapter now opens discussions on the management of four operational functions (that is, marketing, operations, finance and human resources). It addresses the criticality of a strategic business management perspective in the light of the development of contemporary marketing thinking and practice from a historical perspective. Thus, this approach differs markedly from standard marketing textbook approaches, which build on rich descriptions of marketing tools, techniques and theories, but are less concerned with the important philosophical issues that underpin the integrated marketing concept and marketing function as a precursor to a successful implementation of strategic business management. The assumption underlying this approach is that readers will more deeply understand why and how, despite being embedded in the earliest 'concept of marketing', the fundamental, yet critical business philosophy underpinning a business management ideal failed to be translated into practice and, hence, to mobilise a new and integrationist role for the function of marketing.

Catalyst for an integrated marketing and strategic business management paradigm

Figures 5.1 and 5.2 present the now-familiar integrated services management model and functional service management matrix, which was introduced in Chapter 1. As seen in the figures, the primary functional driver, performance driver and functional variable are defined as *relationship, effectiveness* and *service customisation*.

Since the emergence of modern marketing management theory during the 1950s, there have been significant developments in the field. Early concepts, based around the marketing of consumer goods, led to the development of many generic marketing concepts and tools. Traditionally, marketers have assumed and played an important role as the boundary spanner for the organisation by promoting the organisation's interactions with the market through its products. However, due to the growing trend of servitisation of many businesses, marketers now face substantially different management challenges in the role. They are expected to take a more active role in initiating and supporting an organisation's effort to develop mutually beneficial exchange relationships with customers, despite their declining direct influence over the interactions.

This challenge is most readily evident in the marketing of services where the customer enters into, or participates in, the value-creation process, or the service delivery system, as a direct input and/or as a wider input resource, and interacts with the service organisation's personnel and service production facility. As marketing managers have no direct control over the interaction process, this 'interactive' operational model poses a significant challenge to marketers and, more broadly, to the organisation – that is, the systemic management of

Figure 5.1 The integrated services management (ISM) model

Process customisation

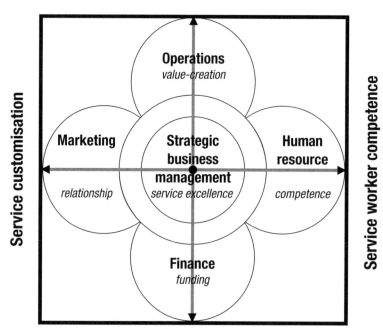

Service infrastructure

Figure 5.2 The functional services management (FSM) matrix

'personnel, physical/technical resources and operational routines' involved with the interaction process (Grönroos, 1983, 1991, p. 435). In the service-based competition that characterises the service economy, the *how* (that is, functional quality – interaction experiences with service infrastructure, technologies and staff) of a market offering often becomes a more important determinant than the *what* (that is, technical quality) of the customer's evaluation of a given market offering (Grönroos, 1983). However, the management of the service delivery process and resource allocations fall outside marketers' locus of decision making. It is this gap between their marketing domain and locus of decision making as a boundary spanner that underscores the associated problem of the traditional functionalistic management approach, and this issue calls for the application of an integrated marketing and a holistic management paradigm built on organisation-wide systemic strategic thinking.

What is marketing?

'Marketing' has been a familiar term in everyday use for some time. It is increasingly used in the media and elsewhere, reflecting the fact that contemporary economic and social life has come to be shaped by marketing decisions and consumption choices. According to Levy (2000), a renowned marketing theorist, marketing 'is the core dynamic mechanism of the social system. Marketing comes into being with the offering of something and the wanting of something' (p. 300). Think about the following. On the way to university or work, how many advertisements can you spot as signage along the roadside or on commercial vehicles, or hear on the car radio? Have you ever had a call from your bank, made from a call centre in India? Do you watch out for coupons that entitle you to purchase two burgers or pizzas or drinks for the price of one? Have you ever been asked to participate in a taste test of a product? Do you have a friend or relative who works in a marketing department? Have you ever filled in a customer survey at a hotel and restaurant you visited? Is the new Internet banking facility the reason why you have stopped making bill payments at your local post office? Are you a member of a customer loyalty program, such as FlyBuys, KrisFlyer, or the Priority Club of the Intercontinental Hotel Group? Do you value home loan lenders who come to you? Why do some private hospitals have a hotel-like, luxury building design and facility? What do you think of recent TV advertising campaigns for 'Quit Smoking', 'Work Safe' or '5 Veggies & 2 Fruits'? These examples taken from our everyday life all relate to some aspect of companies' marketing practices.

Contrary to the popular use of the term 'marketing', however, there is great confusion about what it really means. Its meaning has broadened over many years in response to the dynamic evolution of business management thinking and practice; in some cases, its meaning has even been stretched to include opportunistic, smart or pushy sales talk. Divergence of definitions can be readily found in the pedagogical marketing literature and professional marketing bodies across the world. Too often, these definitions attempt to encompass too many aspects of marketing and, as a result, provide somewhat esoteric descriptions of marketing (Morgan, 1996).

According to Philip Kotler, the father of modern marketing theory, there are four common interpretations of the term 'marketing':

- an organisation's selling (that is, promotion and distribution) function;
- an organisation's continuous process of evaluating and re-evaluating the marketplace through marketing research, segmentation, positioning and coordination of an interdependent marketing mix (that is, controllable marketing variables such as product, price, place, promotion and others);
- an organisation's department in charge of the management of the 'marketing' activities; and
- an organisation's corporate philosophy of creating customer value and satisfying customers. (Kotler, 1994).

This multiplicity of meanings underscores the context-specific nature of the interpretation of marketing. Central to the development of an adequate understanding of marketing and its strategic management is this notion of a different definitional context. Notably, the different definitional contexts have evolved in relation to the historical development of business management thinking and practice. Thus, the key to understanding strategic business management thinking and practice lies in the interdependent development of business management and marketing theory and practice.

The following section reviews the evolving history of management and marketing thinking and practice in the United States. The US context is chosen for the following reasons:

- The United States saw the birth of the marketing concept and practice.
- The United States is regarded as a leader in business management, and marketing thinking and practice.
- The US management model has been most widely disseminated across the world.

Evolving business management and marketing theory and practice in the United States

The marketing concept was developed by Peter Drucker, the father of modern business and management, over half a century ago. In *The Practice of Management* (1954), Drucker describes the purpose of a business and the marketing concept:

> There is only one valid definition of business purpose: to create a customer. It is the customer who determines what a business is. For it is the customer, and he alone, who through being willing to pay for a good or service, converts economic resources into wealth, things into goods. What the business thinks it produces is not of first importance – especially not to the future of the business and its success. What the customer thinks he is buying, what he considers 'value', is decisive.
>
> The customer is the foundation of a business and keeps it in existence. . . . Because it is its purpose to create a customer, any business enterprise has two – and only these two – basic functions: marketing and innovation. . . . Marketing is the distinguishing, the unique function of the business. . . . Marketing is so basic that it is not just enough to have a strong sales department and to entrust marketing to it. Marketing is not only much broader than selling, it is not a

specialized activity at all. It is the whole business seen from the point of view of its final result, that is, from the customer's point of view. Concern and responsibility for marketing must therefore permeate all areas of the enterprise. (pp. 37–39)

As clearly illustrated, the original conceptualisation of marketing was as a business management philosophy, which posits marketing as being organisation-wide activities and involving the responsibility to create customer value and satisfied customers, as well as being one of two key organisational functions to achieve the organisational goals. Drucker's early marketing definition appears to have been inspired by General Electric's management practice, which was to restructure the organisation by appointing the marketing department as a coordinator of other operational functions (that is, design, engineering and manufacturing) based on market knowledge underpinning the premise of the marketing concept. Here readers should be aware of the unique historical context at the time. When Drucker advocated the above ideas, there was no, or little, management realisation of the strategic significance of supporting organisational functions, such as financial and HR management. Such a realisation did not occur until the 1970s for the former idea and the 1980s for the latter. Thus, Drucker's notion of marketing as involving 'two basic functions' needs to be interpreted with caution and refers only to the organisation's subsystems concerned with customer value creation (for example, design, engineering, manufacturing and selling).

As a basis for the following discussions, Table 5.1 summarises core business philosophies across six different historical time spans over the past 150 years and provides key descriptions of their respective planning, or strategic management, drivers, characteristic market conditions and associated management challenges.

The production and sales era

In essence, throughout the first two eras (production and sales), managers were driven by the logic of scale-based production economies. Since the Industrial Revolution, production efficiency increased progressively through the development of mass production technologies and, later, the scientific management movement (see Chapter 1). When supply dominated the market, business organisations had little trouble finding buyers for cost-effective, mass-produced goods. Those with superior production capability enjoyed better profit margins. However, a fundamental change began to emerge towards the end of the 19th century with the emergence of the concept of competition, and the supply curve began to shift as a result of the oversupply of products.

Before the turn of the 20th century, management realised that demand was not a sole function of purchasing power; it also depended on buyers' desire (Bartels, 1976). This understanding led to a shift in management focus from an internal orientation (that is, production) towards an external one (that is, sales). Driven by this external management focus, organisations began to seek knowledge and the means to stimulate consumers' desire for product consumption, marking the foundation of 'marketing thought' (Bartels, 1976). Many organisations found that their survival depended on their ability to create market demand for their products through aggressive 'hard' selling activities (that is, promotion and distribution). This approach was further reinforced from the late 1920s when consumer demand subsided further during the Great Depression (Sheth and Parvatiyar, 1995) and after the Second World War

Table 5.1 Transitions of core business philosophies

Core business philosophy	Time span (strategic management driver)	Market characteristics and management challenges
Production	Throughout the second half of the 19th century (Production)	• Strong market demand for commodities and manufactured goods • Growing market • Increasing operational efficiency through capable production technologies
Sales	The beginning of the 20th century to the early 1950s (Sales)	• Increased operational efficiency through capable production technologies and scientific management movement • Subsiding consumer demand • Need for aggressive selling efforts (especially mass advertising, sales promotions and distribution networks)
Functionalistic marketing	The mid-1950s to the late 1970s (Customer orientation)	• Shift in social aspirations from quantity to quality • Intensifying competition in a saturating market • Realisation of the need to produce what customers want, rather than what the organisation can produce • Intensifying competitive pressure from overseas competitors
Integrated marketing	The early 1980s to the mid-1990s (Quality/ Process management)	• Quality as the driver of intensive global competition • The rise of the service economy fuelled by servitisation of market offerings • Realisation of the strategic need for product and service quality in the organisation's market offerings • Information technology evolution • Business process management (for example, business process reengineering)
Holistic strategic business management	The late 1990s – (Value innovation)	• Knowledge economy, which accommodates both ongoing continuous and rapid discontinuous changes • Hypercompetitive market • Realisation of the strategic need for process innovation in addition to product innovation for value creation

when production capacity exceeded market demand (Caswell, 1964). Under the wing of a sales department, so-called marketing activities extended to include market research, advertising, personal selling, sales promotion and mass distribution, but marketing was viewed as a supporting function of an organisation's sales function (Webster, 1994). Nonetheless, the fundamental management logic in this era was not so different from its predecessor. Management theory and practice were still largely based on the scale-based economic logic – that is, selling to the mass market whatever the efficient production machine can produce cost-effectively.

The functional marketing era

Following the end of the Korean War, economic scarcity waned into the mid-1950s. Competition intensified, and the proliferation of consumer goods and emerging services necessitated paying greater attention to the specific needs of customers (Assael, 1993; Sheth, Sisodia and Sharma, 2000). Marketing became accepted as a new business philosophy, as a prescription for successful business built around three key management principles: customer focus, an integrated organisation-wide marketing effort, and responsibility and profit direction (Bell and Emory, 1971; Raymond and Barksdale, 1989). This shift laid the foundation for modern marketing management. Management's realisation of the need to look to the customer as being a critical input for the organisation resulted in increased management devotion to marketing (market and consumer) research, market segmentation and product positioning, as well as product planning. In particular, marketing research, as a means to connect market needs to the organisation's production capability, gained increased attention (Webster, 1992). The emergent management thinking at the time can be best described as 'we will produce what consumers need', in contrast to 'we will sell what we produce', to convert the good into cash (Levitt, 1960).

Ideas from economics, psychology, social psychology, sociology, mathematics, statistics and operations research were applied to aid marketing planning and decision making through the use of analytical marketing tools and techniques. 'Marketing activities' came to be managed in a more systematic manner around 'the idea of integrated marketing mix, blending product, pricing, promotion, distribution policies, and conscious strategic analysis of the interactions among them' (Webster, 1994, p. 6). The growing recognition of marketing management as a distinctive business function prompted many organisations to set up a marketing department as an extension of the sales department (Webster, 1992). With this background, marketing's strategic responsibilities were expanded into the corporate level with the creation of chief marketing executive posts (McNamara, 1972). By the mid-1960s the management function had established a strong status as a strategic function at the corporate level (Day and Wensley, 1983).

Notably, the organisational arrangement of the marketing department to emerge was, in fact, contradictory to the management philosophy behind Peter Drucker's marketing concept – that is, marketing is not a specialised business function, but involves the whole organisation. Behind this controversial organisational arrangement was the management fear that if marketing is everyone's job, then no one will be responsible for 'market information, market analysis, and integrated marketing – coordination of the parts of the marketing mix and of marketing with other functions, especially manufacturing and distribution' (Webster, 1994, p. 24). And the marketing department assumed the responsibility.

Management's customer orientation and the rise of consumerism led to the creation of a dynamic, competitive marketplace. In an intensifying competitive market context, it was soon learned that market success rarely failed to attract competitors (that is, 'me-too' products and/or 'second-but-better' products) (Buzzell and Gale, 1987). Market pioneering organisations, or so-called first-movers, are commonly believed to enjoy sustainable competitive advantages. In fact, these advantages are not something to be taken for granted. Their sustainability is largely dependent on management's efforts and competence (Lieberman and Montgomery, 1988). (See this challenge in the following illustrative case on Singapore Airlines.) This highly competitive reality necessitated a more rigorous approach to the evaluation and re-evaluation of the market, product and brand management through aggressive positioning strategies (Urban and Hauser, 1980). Many organisations experienced deteriorating financial performance under overly enthusiastic market segmentation and the diversification of market offerings, which, in turn, added substantial costs and complexity to the value creation processes. Unfortunately for the marketing department, these deteriorating outcomes contributed to scepticism about customer-centric management, especially in the absence of clear evidence of marketing's financial business contribution. Thus, during the 1970s, at the corporate level, strategic planning departments began to replace the marketing department's key role and status (Clayclamp, 1985) and the marketing concept was somewhat overshadowed by a new management emphasis on strategic and financial planning (Webster, 1988).

Box 5.1   Singapore International Airlines (SIA): Rigorous service design and development

Twenty years ago Lyn Shostack complained that service design and development was usually characterised by trial and error. Unlike manufacturing organisations, where R&D departments and product engineers were routine, systematic testing of services, or service engineering, was not the norm. Things appear to have changed little since then. SIA, however, has always regarded product design and development as a serious, structured, scientific issue.

SIA has a service development department that hones and tests any change before it is introduced. This department undertakes research, trials, time-and-motion studies, mock-ups, assessment of customer reactions – whatever is necessary to ensure that a service innovation is supported by the right procedures. Underpinning continuous innovation and development is a culture that accepts change as a way of life. A trial that fails or an implemented innovation that is removed after a few months, is not seen as a problem. In some organisations personal reputations can be at stake and so pilot tests 'have to work'. At SIA a failed pilot test damages no one's reputation.

In some organisations, service – and, indeed, product – innovations live beyond their useful date because of political pressure or the lack of resource investment. SIA, however, expects that any innovation is likely to have a short shelf-life. The airline recognises that, to sustain its differentiation, it must maintain continuous improvement and be able to kill programs or services that no longer provide competitive differentiation.

According to Yap Kim Wah, senior vice-president, product and services, 'It is getting more and more difficult to differentiate ourselves because the airline is doing the same thing . . . the crucial fact is that we continue to say that we want to improve. That we have the will to do so, And that every time we reach a goal, we always say that [we've] got to find a new mountain, or hill, to climb . . . you must be able to give up what you love.' 'Customers adjust their expectations according to the brand image. When you fly on a good brand, like SIA, your expectations are already sky-high. And if SIA gives anything that is just OK, it is just not good enough,' says Sim Kay Wee, senior vice president, cabin crew.

SIA treats this as a fundamental resource for innovative ideas. Weak signals are amplified. Not only written comments, but also verbal comments to the crew, are taken seriously and reported back to the relevant sections of the airline. An additional source of intelligence is SIA's 'spy flights', where advisers travel with competitors and report on their offerings. Finally, SIA recognises that its competition does not just come from within the industry. As a rule, SIA sets its sights high; instead of aiming to be the best *airline*, its intention is to be the best service organisation. To achieve that, SIA employs broad benchmarking, not just against its main competitors, but against the best services companies.

(*Source*: L. Heracleous, J. Wirtz and R. Johnston, 'Cost-effective service excellence: Lessons from Singapore Airlines', *Business Strategy Review*, vol. 15, no. 1, 2004, pp. 34–35)

During the early 1970s, US businesses, predominantly manufacturing organisations, began to experience intense competitive pressure from foreign competitors. The Japanese, in particular, proved to be a real threat as they continued to erode the market share of US businesses in both domestic and international markets through superior manufacturing and, more notably, marketing skills (Kotler and Fahey, 1982). (See Box 5.2 for an account of the Japanese approach to marketing.) In some cases, it was not just organisations, but entire sectors, that were in jeopardy. Nonetheless, in hindsight, the painful experience was a catalyst for change in American businesses. The problems inherited in the conventional US manufacturing management model were evident when, for example, US-manufactured auto and electronics products were compared to those produced by their Japanese counterparts, who had transformed themselves from producers of 'cheap and shoddy' products to ones capable of offering superior 'customer value' (that is, better product quality at a lower price).

Box 5.2   Classic Japanese marketing in action

Ironically, Japanese marketing strategy is not based on the discovery of new and fresh marketing principles. Japan's secret is that the Japanese thoroughly understood and applied the existing textbook principles. They came to the United States to study marketing, and went home with a better understanding of the principles than most US companies had.

Japanese companies place a heavy weight on two variables in selling to new buyers – quality and service. They design and produce products of high quality (reliability). Japanese cars, for example, need substantially fewer repairs than American cars. The Japanese use more automated methods of production (to reduce human error), and they implement more quality assurance systems, to the point where the rejection rate in a typical Japanese factory is substantially lower than in comparable US factories. The Japanese also establish an adequate number of service centres, so that their products can be quickly repaired. American buyers have found service from Japanese manufacturers to be at least as good as that provided by American manufacturers. The Japanese are highly service-minded and go out of their way to accommodate customers who have a service problem. At the same time, by building better products, they don't have to invest as much in service centres.

Having established a good product, service, and price, the Japanese carefully work on the other marketing mix variables. They place a heavy emphasis on integrating distribution into the marketing mix. They develop markets region-by-region, lining up strong distributors in each location. They will help the distributors sell to the first few customers. They will pick the largest customer and offer a low price to get his business. They will give him excellent service, and then sell to other customers on the strength of their reputation with the first customer, rather than price. They frequently offer higher middleman commissions than competitors to generate product push. They encourage joint promotional efforts with distributors/dealers and typically support their products with heavy regional advertising.

(*Source*: Adapted from P. Kotler and L. Fahey, 'The world's champion marketers: The Japanese', *Journal of Business Strategy*, vol. 3, no. 1, 1982, pp. 3–13)

As Japanese companies achieved enviable market successes in the United States, stories emerged about the substantial early investment that the Japanese companies made in R&D. Japanese company representatives spent significant time in major American cities painstakingly observing, for example, the local cultural behavioural patterns associated with car usage. Observations such as how women get in and out of car doors with stiletto-heeled shoes had implications for door design. Similarly, the fashion of painted and long nails had implications for window opening design. This deeper consumer knowledge was then applied innovatively to product design and engineering under the unique Japanese quality management philosophy of 'market in', which will be discussed in the following section.

The integrated marketing era
Quality/process management: Total quality management
The unprecedented success of Japanese companies in the quality-based competition triggered a re-evaluation of conventional management thinking and practice among US business scholars and practitioners. The strong emphasis on systemic quality control (QC) among Japanese manufacturers and their organisation-wide pursuit of quality management were identified to be major sources of their competitive advantage. A series of academic studies began to unveil unique components of their quality-centred business model, such as cross-function

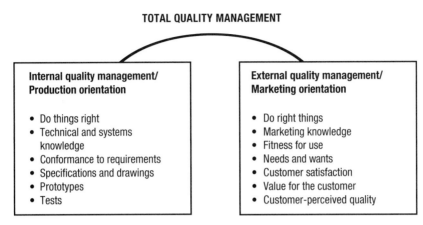

Figure 5.3 Total quality management

management, market-in, *kaizen* (that is, continuous improvement in products and business processes through company-wide efforts, as opposed to radical improvement, or innovation, by fewer specialists in the United States), quality function deployment, QC circles, employee empowerment, automation, the JIT system, job rotation and the collaborative inter-firm network in the supply chain (that is, vertical *keiretsu*), among others (see Cole, 1979; Ishikawa, 1985; Imai, 1986; Dore, 1987; Mizuno, 1988; Womack et al., 1990; Clark and Fujimori, 1991; Smitka, 1991; Fruin, 1992; Sako, 1992).

Collectively, over the coming decades these concepts contributed to the reshaping of US management thinking and business practice. In essence, the Japanese practice triggered growing management attention to a systemic, or process-oriented, view of an organisation, as well as the human side of the organisation and its management, which, since the Industrial Revolution, had been collectively neglected in the overzealous pursuit of scientifically determined economic efficiency. In particular, during the 1980s, the Japanese notion of total (that is, systemic) quality control was not only the initial driver of the later development of the process management movement, but it also renewed management interest in the marketing field.

The Japanese systemic business model is built on the following management ideal: 'to develop, design, produce and service a quality product which is most economical, most useful, and always satisfactory to the consumer' (Ishikawa, 1985, p. 44). It is concerned with the integrated management of an internal focus on operational efficiency and an external focus on market effectiveness (that is, customer value) (see Figure 5.3).

Japanese QC is a company-wide, or systemic, practice that involves all organisational members across divisions and ranks working together in pursuit of a common goal: to create satisfied customers. This organisation-wide perspective was distinctively different from its US counterpart, 'total quality control', which Armand Feigenbaum developed based on his early experience at General Electric. Contrary to Japanese QC, TQC essentially left the job of QC to the QC specialists and their department (Ishikawa, 1985). However, in the Japanese QC model (referred to as total quality management, or TQM, in the West), the organisation's market offerings are viewed as a manifestation of the quality of the whole organisation as a system (that is, quality of product, process, management, employees, resources and so forth). Thus, quality, cost (profit) and delivery are regarded as system-level (that is, strategic business units, or the organisation as a whole) outcomes that warrant system-wide attention, dedication and effort. To counteract the cross-departmental communication and cooperation problems, and the 'turf battles' commonly associated with the conventional functional department-based organisational structure, an innovative management mechanism – *cross-function management* – was devised which integrates vertical, functional management of tasks with the horizontal process management of the organisation-wide functions (Ishikawa, 1985; Mizuno, 1988). The next section discusses cross-function management and the important difference in management thinking and practice between 'cross-function' and 'cross-functional' management.

Cross-function management

Cross-function management addresses the problems associated with sequential hand-offs and chimney-like structures by creating a new category of functions that threads across traditional departmental boundaries – thus the term 'cross-function'. Note that the term 'cross-function' is used here to distinguish it from 'cross-functional'. The latter term is used in the US business literature as a general reference to multidisciplinary temporary project teams. These are usually collages of vertical chimneys, not the recognition of a new horizontal category of functions. The concept of a cross-function adds a critical dimension to total quality practices by linking divisional and departmental activities through horizontal communication. This dimension is what is missing in many Western companies' conception of TQM.

Cross-functions are introduced into a company for the purpose of optimising performance company-wide. Without them, performance, in the eyes of the customer or shareholder, is sub-optimised because specialised departments plan and execute policy insulated from one another. One department's activities may work at cross-purposes with those of another. Without cross-function management, things such as quality, cost and delivery characteristics are rarely optimised. The most common example is the cost involved in servicing an automobile for a defect covered by a warranty. The customer wastes time taking the car to be serviced. The car company loses because parts must be replaced, mechanics paid, and future goodwill lost with a customer. Warranty control is an example of a cross-function with the goal of minimising cost and maximising customer satisfaction.

Figure 5.4 illustrates that the objective of a cross-function is to focus on critical process issues that cut across the whole enterprise. These issues include such things as quality, cost control and delivery, but also a variety of others that are equally important, such as purchasing, personnel training, research, and information management. Each of these is treated as a horizontal cross-function. This emphasis on process, or on *how* to align all the activities of the company, complements traditional results-minded management, which is concerned with *what* is produced and in what quantities.

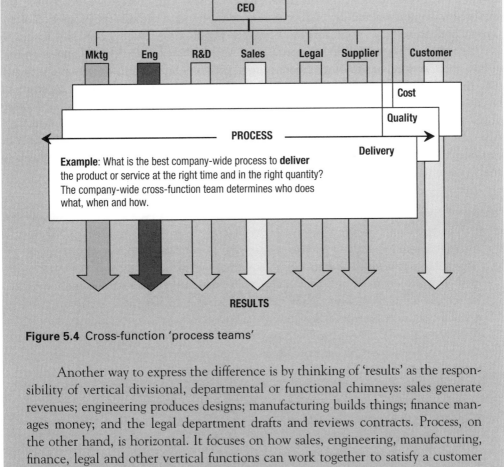

Figure 5.4 Cross-function 'process teams'

Another way to express the difference is by thinking of 'results' as the responsibility of vertical divisional, departmental or functional chimneys: sales generate revenues; engineering produces designs; manufacturing builds things; finance manages money; and the legal department drafts and reviews contracts. Process, on the other hand, is horizontal. It focuses on how sales, engineering, manufacturing, finance, legal and other vertical functions can work together to satisfy a customer requirement. Underlying this approach is a belief that attending to how one designs things is a precondition to building customer confidence. Market share and profitability follow. The combination of vertically managed results and cross-function process control is at the heart of any effort to implement the TQM paradigm (see Figure 5.4).

(*Source:* Adapted from D. Dimancescu, *The Seamless Enterprise: Making cross functional management work*, Oliver Wight Publications, Inc., Essex Junction, VT, 1992, pp. 13–16)

In addition to cross-function management, there are two other hallmarks to the systemic quality control management model. The first emphasises the value of a shared QC philosophy and practice. Its essence is succinctly captured in the phrase 'the next process is your customer' (Ishikawa, 1985, p. 107), which has been used to describe the essence of the concept of 'internal marketing'. (See the next section for a discussion on internal marketing.) This approach was introduced by Ishikawa during the early days of QC development in Japan with the aim of tearing down worker sectionalism (that is, sectional myopia) enabling smooth workflows across sections in the organisation's processes. The purpose was to replace the sectional and functional mindset with a more systemic mindset through the promotion of the vertical and lateral flows of information across the organisation. More specifically, it aims to nurture 'systemic' strategic thinking among employees – worker awareness and understanding of how their work relates to other organisational processes and other workers, and why and how they can potentially contribute to enhanced value creation in a broader spectrum of business processes – and promote their systemic strategic actions. The important implication of systemic strategic thinking is explained by popular US writers on services management, Albrecht and Zemke (2001) as 'even the most enthusiastic workers cannot deliver superior customer value if they don't know what it is or don't have the resources or support systems to enable them to do it' (p. 7).

Internal marketing

Internal marketing is about gaining recognition in both the academic and commercial arenas as a means to enhance both customer satisfaction and employee satisfaction. The services marketing and quality management literature stresses the importance of building quality into every step of the service delivery process. This area of research identifies internal customers and suppliers along the value-adding chain of the company and has been proposed as a means of managing the quality of the interactions between these. Internal marketing, therefore, aims to ensure that the internal notion of customer satisfaction and quality is progressively built into the product, or service, as it passes through the company so that the external customer is satisfied. It ensures that every department and every person within the organisation acts as both a supplier and a customer, and that the staff work together in a manner that supports the company strategy and goals.

Several principles relate to this concept:

- Each process receives inputs from the internal supplier (the previous operation), does work on it, adds value, and converts it to an output to the internal customer (the next operation).
- The internal customer's requirements and expectations need to be communicated to the internal supplier.
- The internal customer's evaluation of the service provided needs to be communicated to the internal supplier.
- The consequences of meeting, or not meeting, the internal customer's requirements must be translated into rewards and punishments.
- The process aims at continuous, never-ending improvements.
- Employees must be made partners with management for the system to work.

If an outstanding service is to be provided to external customers, then personnel who have contact with these customers need to have the necessary support from other functions to achieve this. For example, if computer programs are difficult to use, or networks constantly fail, customer contact personnel will be unable to perform well, no matter how much they wish to do so. Support services, such as training and IT, need to accept that they have an impact on the quality of the service provided to the external customer, which in some cases may be equally as important as the effect that customer contact personnel have. In this example, customer service could be improved if the support service providers, IT and training recognise their internal customers, research their needs – in this case, for reliable systems and targeted training – and provide these services, as would be the case if these support functions were contracted out to external suppliers. Internal market research, using similar tools to those used to analyse the external customer, can identify the exact needs of the internal customer and how well these needs are being met.

(*Source*: Adapted from I. N. Lings, 'Managing service quality with internal market schematics', *Long Range Planning*, vol. 32, no. 4, 1999, pp. 452–63)

The third hallmark of the Japanese QC management was the concept of the 'market in' – the management principle of market-driven new product development. This market-based QC concept means that the marketing division plays a critical role 'at the entrance and exit of quality control' (Ishikawa, 1985, p. 176).

The basis of QC is market in, that is to say, to create products that are sought by consumers. The division which has the closest contact with consumers is the marketing division. It is also the division which is best equipped to discern and discover the needs of consumers. This division must catch the trends and discover the needs of consumers ahead of competitors. It must translate the needs into new ideas and then actively participate in planning and developing new products. It is the responsibility of the marketing division to draft a new product plan that is expressed in the language of the consumer.

It is true that the ideas and plans for new products must come from all divisions of the company, but from the perspective of TQC, the one which must shoulder the main burden is the marketing division because it maintains constant contact with consumers. . . . Therefore, marketing must be an integral part of TQC. (p. 176)

These statements capture the essence of the Japanese approach to business management and marketing implementation. As is clear now, Japanese organisations view marketing as an organisational function performed by members of the entire organisation who share 'the company's philosophy and the logic of the marketing concept' (Lazer et al., 1985, p. 76).

It is noteworthy that these QC management principles, which were developed primarily in the Japanese manufacturing sector, also laid the foundations for a services marketing and management philosophy. Albrecht and Zemke (2002) define service management as being: 'A total organizational approach that makes the quality of service, as perceived by the customer, the number one driving force for the operation of the business' (p. 50). Similarly, Normann (2000) critically underscores the holistic nature of the Japanese approach to 'quality' (that is, quality as a corporate philosophy which permeates the entire organisation) and, hence, considers it to be an appropriate model for many organisations that now operate in service-centred markets. According to authorities in service marketing (for example, Lovelock, 1988; Grönroos, 1982, as cited in Grönroos, 1994, p. 13), the shared management principle between the marketing concept and service management are not at all coincidental. This is most evident in the following Grönroos (2000) notion:

> Often the term 'service management' is used instead of the term 'service marketing'. Sometimes the phrase 'service marketing and management' is also used in the literature to describe the field. The use of the term 'service management' indicates the cross-functional nature of marketing in service contexts. Marketing is not a separate function, but in the management of all business functions the interests of the customers, i.e., a marketing aspect, has to be taken into account. (p. 195)

Although this concept of marketing was relatively new to many North American services organisations, some innovative services organisations in Nordic countries were beginning to experiment with integrated marketing management, based on systemic management thinking, some decades ago. (See Box 5.3 for a good example.)

Box 5.3　The Cleaning Company

The Cleaning Company is very large and operates all over the country. In the beginning of the 1970s, no marketing was needed. All that was needed was someone to answer the telephone when potential customers called. However, in the mid-1970s competition increased, and it was decided that some active marketing had to be done. The company established a marketing department responsible for marketing, planning, sales, advertising and sales promotions. And on this occasion, the company also divided the operations department into several regional organisations, a personnel department and a finance department. All the departments were on the same hierarchical level.

The company employed a marketing manager, who realised that the marketing department was in an off-side position and that the firm would remain production-oriented if marketing and sales activities were expected to be implemented by the people in the marketing department. He therefore kept his department very small. Because of his personal qualifications, however, he succeeded in developing informal contacts with people in the operations department at the regional level, which gave him much more authority than the formal organisational structure did. Despite having a formal off-side position, the marketing manager's strategy was possible because it was supported by the managing director.

The regional managers were made responsible for sales, advertising and public relations at the regional level. The central marketing department did not include any salespeople. Only corporate advertising and sales promotion materials were developed and, to some extent, implemented by the central department. The marketing department also started to develop internal marketing and training programs that were to be used locally, in order to support the market orientation and customer-consciousness among contact personnel and supervisors.

During the last few years, the company has also developed some new service businesses outside the cleaning area. This year the organisation of the company has been changed further. The marketing department has been removed from the organisation, and the company has been divided into three divisions, one for the traditional cleaning business, and two others for two new service businesses. The division managers are responsible for operations, personnel, and marketing and sales, including the traditional marketing as well as interactive marketing function. They are expected to perform the same marketing and sales tasks as the former marketing manager, as well as to be in charge of operations. They are also responsible for internal marketing. They report directly to the managing director. On the same hierarchical level there is a personnel support department and a finance department.

The cleaning division is divided into regional organisations, which operate as profit centres. The regional managers have a responsibility for sales, traditional and interactive marketing, and operations and personnel. They are also free to develop new services, which can be marketed regionally. Marketing is implemented on the regional level, whereas the division manager only develops and gives external and internal marketing support. He is also responsible for service development on the divisional level. As a result of these changes, the cleaning company has been very successful and profitable.

(*Source:* Adapted from C. Grönroos, 'Innovative marketing strategies and organization structures for service firms', in C. H. Lovelock, *Services Marketing*, 2nd ed., Prentice Hall, Englewood Cliffs, NJ, 1991, pp. 443–4.

In response to the Japanese competitors, US managers began to review their business practices and the strategic implementation of marketing (Kotler and Fahey, 1982; Pelham and Wilson, 1996). The more they learned about their competitors, the greater was their awareness of the need for integrated marketing thinking and practice. In Japanese organisations, 'marketing as an area of decision making' was closely linked to other organisational functions, and a marketing culture prevailed (Kotler and Fahey, 1982, p. 10). However, in the United States its important conceptual attributes, or dimensions, were lost in translation. First, the marketing specialists and department were assumed to take primary responsibility for the implementation of marketing, just as the QC specialists and department were responsible for the QC program. The functional specialisation of marketing led to accumulation of expertise in specialist marketing activities and customer-based market information and knowledge. Nevertheless, the vertical departmental organisational structure made it difficult for many US businesses to disseminate the information and knowledge *across* the organisation, as an input critical to coordination and integration of business processes beyond the elevated functional walls for effective creation of superior customer value.

> The original marketing concept saw it as pervading all aspects of the business, putting the customer in the centre of all operational and strategic decision making. The objective was to do the best possible job of satisfying customer needs. . . . Instead of a blurring of the boundaries between the traditional management functions (sales, finance, manufacturing, engineering, etc.) called for by the move to total customer orientation, the functional boundaries grew higher and stronger. (Webster, 1994, pp. 15–16)

In support of the integrated approach to marketing management for holistic business management, Box 5.4 identifies how, in an increasingly complex services provision context, the myopic, functionalistic management approach fails to achieve an organisation's customer-focused service objectives. This case resonates with the complex and interrelated marketing and management challenges associated with managing customer relationships in a range of services such as banking, insurance, investment, tourism and education. It also emphasises the value of systemic management thinking and practice for superior customer value creation and customer relations based on a comprehensive understanding of the other organisational subsystems and business processes concerned.

Box 5.4   Service with a smile: Organised chaos

This illustrative case outlines the cross-function knowledge management (KM) challenges faced by a large government agency. Some 3,500 call centre representatives in this organisation fielded millions of calls a year. Many were seasonal workers, and turnover was high – about 50 per cent. To assist callers, the service representatives used manual bulletins, policy directives, websites, software applications, directories and lists of contacts, and other tools. Their primary reference manual, which contained the strict legal and policy regulations that governed their work, was 45 centimetres thick.

The reps used complex software applications to access caller data and to address more than 40 types of caller questions and problems. Each software application had a different interface, and some even used different labels for identical data. So much effort went into teaching employees how the applications were structured and how to navigate through them, that little time was left for reps to become familiar with the other aspects of their jobs. Still, the reps were expected to internalise the organisation's mandated best-practice approaches to numerous tasks and questions. Management made it clear that quality must be of paramount importance, and that one employee should be able to resolve all of a caller's questions and issues. But the high turnover, and the number and complexity of the questions and problems involved, in fact, made this impossible.

The consultants Integrated Solution Management put together a team of business analysts, trainers and KM professionals to address the business's customer relations problem. They developed realistic descriptions of the situation, scrutinised tasks and goals, and identified the way real callers ask questions and the mix of problems they called about. They mapped tasks, knowledge resources and tools to individual roles. After comparing possible solutions, they concluded that continuing the pattern of independent activity was simply not going to work. The organisation needed an integrated portal solution co-sponsored by its various functional groups. After initial design prototypes showed that training time could be reduced dramatically by providing just-in-time, just-enough, just-right knowledge, management agreed to sponsor the project. The portal was designed to accomplish some traditional and some innovative goals while fulfilling a number of needs, such as ease of use, ease of communication and built-in guidance.

The portal transformed training and workflow. Building knowledge resources into the task wizard largely eliminated the need to train people on software and business processes. The wizard masks the software, so the service reps see only the wizard interface. Since task-related knowledge and agency best practices are structured into the tools, reps can focus on listening, gathering information and interacting with callers, guided by the software. The interface also permits the reps to change roles as needed. In the end, the portal reduces complexity, structures processes, and delivers the ability to provide timely, high-quality services.

(*Source*: Adapted from G. Gery, 'Service with a smile', *Knowledge Management*, vol. 4. no. 7, July 2001, http://web5infotrac-college.com/wadsworth/sessions/512/816/.../4!xrn˙10_0_A7755625, retrieved 31 July 2002)

As Box 5.4 demonstrates, in adopting a systemic management philosophy and practice, many organisations encounter various problems – most profoundly, cognitive challenges (Cole, 1998). Many managers experience growing internal pressures derived from the overwhelming challenges associated with TQM-driven 'organisational transformation'. This organisational transformation can contribute to 'Profound, fundamental changes in thought and actions, which create an irreversible discontinuity in the experience of a system' (Adams, 1984, p. 278). Poor leadership, management intervention and change management collectively contribute to poor TQM implementation and failure. The TQM initiative is often developed at the top management level, but fails to gain acceptance at the operational level (Harvey and Brown, 2001) and management fails to understand the full extent of required changes (Grant et al., 1994). Given that the process of TQM transformation is an extended journey that requires fundamental changes across the organisation, most notably in management practice and culture (Beer, 2003), a high TQM drop-out rate among US companies is not a wonder. It is useful to note here an observation of the US companies' TQM endeavour by George Day, one of the world's leading marketing scholars: 'Regrettably, TQM faces many of the same acceptance and implementation problems as the marketing concept' (Day, 1994, p. 46).

Given the fact that TQM and integrated marketing practice are more-or-less two sides of the same coin (that is, marketing with an innate outside-in approach and TQM with an outside-in emphasis in a holistic business management philosophy), the following common challenges to US companies in the TQM journey can also be viewed as imperatives in change management for successful implementation of the integrated marketing practice:

- sustained top management leadership for the quality initiative and active application to their daily management activities;
- relentless focus on the customer, both in setting strategic objectives and in building organisational routines, to link as many units and levels in the firm as possible to identifying and meeting customer needs;
- systematically improving the quality of all business processes from an internal and (especially) external customer perspective;
- decentralisation of decision-making responsibility to a well-trained problem-solving labour force (that is, employee participation in decision making);
- breaking down the organisational barriers between departments and levels so that cross-function management becomes normal operating procedure;
- combined emphasis on both incremental and continuous improvement and breakthrough strategies; and
- realigning of reward and measurement systems, both formal and informal, to support these new directions. (Cole, 1993, pp. 7–8)

The critical implication drawn from the above list is that systemic business management, where organisational processes are coordinated and integrated effectively through cross-function management and with the support of top management as well as employees' systemic strategic thinking, is instrumental for the successful implementation of TQM and integrated marketing.

It is worthwhile to draw attention again to the universal nature of systemic quality control management philosophy and practice, irrespective of industries and context. This universality implies a disregard for particular customer specificities – that is, values, practices and needs. Some services managers strongly object to a TQM approach to services management, as being a 'highly mechanistic', 'number-based, command ideology' (Albrecht and Zemke, 2002, p. 6). It is true that TQM tools, on the surface, look overly scientific and may appear like a suppressant of innovative thinking and creative problem solving of employees. Nevertheless, it cannot be denied that the TQM model offers rich management tools to support the promotion and institutionalisation of systemic strategic thinking among employees. It presents both cognitive and behavioural frameworks for the development and promotion of employees' systemic strategic thinking to guide effective problem-solving skills considered instrumental to an organisation-wide pursuit of the creation of 'delighted' and 'loyal' customers. The applicability of quality/process management to service organisations is well supported by award-winning services organisations, such as AT&T Universal Card Services (now part of Citigroup), Federal Express Corporation, Merrill Lynch Credit Corporation and The Ritz-Carlton Hotel Company, LLC, among others (National Institute of Standards and Technology, n.d.) This is not to imply, however, that the value of the single, universal TQM model is successfully applicable for all. The most discernible challenge is the development of service quality measurement systems that encompass both internal and external, and hard and soft, measures of the tangible and intangible aspects of the service (Silvestro et al., 1990; Collier, 1990) (see also Chapter 6).

Emergence of the relationship marketing paradigm

The rise of the TQM movement, and the growing trend of servitisation of many businesses during the 1980s, warrants some discussion of the emergence of a new marketing paradigm, relationship marketing. These developments in the quality and process management movement coincided with the dramatic rise of the service economy, which added further understanding about the complexity of customers and markets. Since the late 1970s, there were nine prime drivers of the services sector:

- changing patterns of government regulation;
- relaxation of professional association standards restricting overt marketing communication efforts;
- privatisation of public corporations and non-profit organisations;
- computerisation and technological innovation;
- the growth of franchising;
- expansion of leasing and rental businesses;
- creation of service profit centres within manufacturing firms;
- financial pressures on public and non-profit organisations; and
- the internationalisation of service businesses. (Lovelock, 1991, p. 2)

In addition to these, there was increased emphasis on the service dimensions of manufacturing organisations, or the servitisation of market offerings. A good example is the car manufacturing industry. As noted earlier, the US car industry struggled in the emerging quality-based market competition when faced with their Japanese counterparts. Initially, the Japanese car makers enjoyed a distinctive market position for their superior customer value. In addition to lower price for superior quality, they also offered an extended warranty (that is, service) based on their confidence in their 'built-in quality' cars. Redefining this with a marketing term, they were superior on all 'determinant attributes' (Hansotia et al., cited in Hutt and Speh, 1995, p. 305) that are both important to customers and differentiating product attributes. The early offensive strategy of the US car makers was to improve product quality (that is, reliability of the car) and lower costs, so that they could match market offerings of their Japanese rivals. When they achieved this goal through the practice of TQM, they were standing on an equal footing with their once-invisible competitors in the market; no cars stood out for superior value along those 'determinant attributes' in the eyes of customers. All the cars came on to the market with similar quality, price and service warranty. This elevated their competition to a higher level, where the identification of new determinant attributes became a top marketing priority. Many car makers responded to the increased competition by expanding their marketing scope to incorporate more services, such as credit, transportation, delivery and maintenance.

Markets for computers, and electrical and mechanical equipment are another familiar example where service attributes became not only part of the determinant attributes, but also an important source of profit. In association with capital goods and expensive consumer durable goods, a 'system selling' marketing approach was adopted where a good is packaged with services (that is, sales of parts, supplies and maintenance) based on increased concern for customers (Sheth and Parvatiyar, 1995). (See the Skippers example discussed in Chapter 4.)

Evolution of these business practices led to an important development in marketing thinking and practice where the notion of 'transactional' was replaced by the concept of 'relational' for the assumption behind the central marketing concept of 'market exchange'. Interestingly, the origin of relationship marketing goes back to early works on (1) services marketing (Berry, 1983; Gummesson and Grönroos, cited in Gummesson et al., 1997), and (2) industrial marketing (Arndt, 1979; Ford, 1978; Häkansson, 1982; Jackson, 1985). The adoption of TQM and the servitisation of market offerings are attributed to the dynamic paradigm shift in marketing among other macro-environmental drivers (Sheth and Parvatiyar, 1995) (see Chapter 2).

In essence, a relationship can be viewed as a pair of evolving commitments of buyer and seller (Jackson, 1985) which manifests as a series of interactions where buyer and seller act, react and re-react to each other (Ford et al., 1986). The relationship marketing paradigm posits customers as an important co-creator of value, and advocates an organisation's pursuit of mutually beneficial, long-term exchange relationships with individual customers. More specifically, relationship marketing, which has gained a strong foothold in marketing, customer service and quality management domains, can be contrasted with the conventional marketing paradigm in terms of its:

- focus on customer retention rather than acquisition;
- greater customer service emphasis;

- greater customer commitment;
- more intensive interaction; and
- greater emphasis on quality. (Christopher et al., 1991)

In principle, the extent and intensity of the reciprocal nature of the exchange relationship is determined by the effectiveness of the exchange parties in facilitating meaningful interactions, based on their relationship-building competence and willingness to support and enhance the further development of the relationship (Rexha and Miyamoto 2000). As for the relationship-building competence, which is largely built on a deep understanding of the exchange partner's needs and wants, there are three types of relationship-building behaviours – namely, responding, initiating and alerting (that is, informing the exchange partner of any foreseeable problem that would affect the partner, so that the partner can make any necessary prior arrangements in case the problem eventuates) (Miyamoto and Rexha, 2004). Box 5.5 outlines some prescriptions for relationship marketing strategy in the banking sector.

Box 5.5 How banks can keep and build their relationships with seniors

The seniors market has changed. It has grown in size, with people living longer, enjoying better health, and having a younger state of mind. The average life expectancy in the United States has increased to 77, up from 47 in 1900. Today, 64.2 million Americans are over age 50, and this group controls 43 per cent of the country's US$300 billion in discretionary income, according to Primelife, a consulting firm in Orange, California.

Seniors represent a group of consumers with particular life-stage needs and, in turn, specific financial services needs. They are less likely to carry debt, but are very concerned about funding their retirement years, covering escalating health-care costs and not becoming a financial burden to their children. Other issues seniors may face are completing payments on their children's college or graduate school education; convenient bill payment and banking while travelling; rolling over pension plans; and estate planning. They are also looking for convenience while pursuing active lives.

Here are some things banks can do to reach this important market segment.

- *Consider new product offerings:* Direct deposit (payroll or pension cheques), investment services, life insurance and coverage for long-term care benefits are just a few new product areas banks could consider providing. Fixed-income mutual funds, reverse mortgages and annuities are others. Also, many seniors travel or spend periods of time at a second home. Debit and ATM cards, and bill payment and home banking by phone or the Internet give them the convenience to keep their banking relationships no matter where they go.
- *Add a seniors club:* Package together appropriate services and benefits to attract and retain mature customers. Such programs include special travel discounts or planned group trips, newsletters, discounts or free services, bonus rates on time deposits, and social events. There are a number of firms that will private label their program for use by banks. If banks have a seniors program, they could review

its benefits and consider other features they could add. They might even come up with a premium package to complement their 'standard' seniors club.

- *Watch what they say:* Image is important here. The individuals in this market segment do not consider themselves 'elderly'. Also, the term 'retired' may be limiting, since many people aged in their mid-sixties and beyond continue paid or volunteer work. Banks should refer to them as 'mature' or 'senior', and use images that represent young-looking older people for their marketing materials.

- *Present a seminar:* Offering a seminar is a great way to reinforce current relationships or attract new customers to the bank. There are a number of topics to choose from, such as health, financial planning, personal investing, travel, tax, and even computer skills. It is likely that banks already have staff with expertise in one of these areas who could put together a program. Or they could work with professionals in the community. The seminar could be timed to coincide with the launch of a new seniors program that can be promoted at the event.

- *Find ways to listen:* Hearing from seniors is the best way to determine what services to develop and offer them. Banks could set up a feedback system, either through regular surveys (mail, phone or focus groups) or by creating an advisory body. They could then use what they learn to fine-tune their existing programs. Whatever their strategies, they should be sure that their seniors program has established goals that coincide with the bank's objectives. And they should look for ways to bridge their relationships with seniors to their children and grandchildren – the bank's next generation of customers.

(*Source:* Adapted from M. Hanis, 'Reaching maturity', *Independent Banker*, vol. 48, no. 1, 1998, p. 80)

However, seldom is there a pure transactional exchange or a pure collaborative exchange in market exchange. As with the good–service continuum presented in Chapter 1, market exchange is better viewed as two anchor points delineating a transactional–relational exchange continuum (Dwyer et al., 1987; Anderson and Narus, 1991; Webster, 1994). See Figure 5.5, which depicts the 'bandwidth' of each of three types of industry groups: consumer goods, consumer services, and industrial goods and services. The bandwidth of each industry group is more or less defined by the organisation's willingness and/or requirement to identify and meet customer-specific exchange problems. As seen in Figure 5.5, the consumer goods industry group – in particular, the consumable, packaged-goods marketers – has the most transactional marketing orientation as it deals with the faceless mass market. However, since the 1980s, which saw an increase in management's interest in customer service, and the subsequent establishment of customer call centres, an organisational system has been created to facilitate direct interactions between customers and the organisation. The aim of this strategy is to respond to customers' problems and unmet needs more effectively and faster, thus expanding the organisation's bandwidth towards a pure collaborative exchange point through value-adding exchanges.

The consumer services sector, more often than not, requires direct and/or repeated interactions between customers and service organisations (that is, service staff and service delivery systems). This not only emphasises the importance of relationship marketing, but also makes

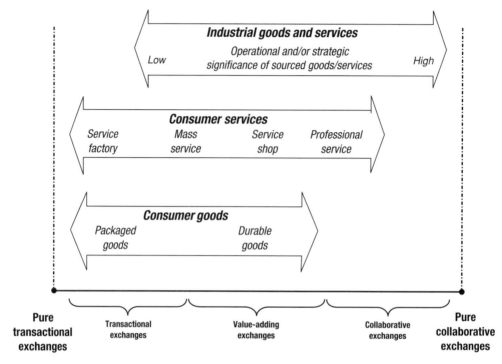

Figure 5.5 A continuum of transactional and relational exchange

service businesses a fertile field of relationship marketing. Nonetheless, as seen in Figure 5.5, it is an industrial goods and services sector that has the greatest inclination towards the pure collaborative exchange point because of the inherent nature of long-term, interactive exchange relationships in the industrial market, as discussed earlier.

Each business organisation strategically manages a portfolio of customer relationships ranging from more transactional to more collaborative exchange-based relationships within market segments. For instance, mass service, service shop and professional services organisations may choose to go beyond their industry relationship reach by redesigning their service delivery system. Thus, organisations may choose to build a more 'professional service' approach by introducing, or increasing, labour intensity, customer interaction, and service customisation in their 'relationship'-oriented marketing strategy. Alternatively, organisations may transform their existing system into more of a 'service factory' type of operation through the restriction of customer interaction and customisation, and the automation of the system to pursue a 'transaction'-oriented marketing strategy. In recent years, banks have adopted the latter 'service factory' approach. In an aggressive rationalisation effort, banks have been pushing customers away from over-the-counter, face-to-face services and towards an automated services delivery system, such as ATMs, and telephone and Internet banking. There, strategic marketing, operations and HRM decisions and actions are made reactively, or in a deductive manner, driven by financial pressures, instead of inductive, cross-function, strategic management decisions and actions being made on the basis of superior customer value creation and customer relationships.

The significant shift in the management of customer relationships within market segments has been supported by developments in new information management and communications technology. Powerful information technologies have dramatically enhanced the organisation's capability to elicit, store, analyse and manipulate customer information, opening avenues for one-to-one marketing to the traditional marketers. These developments have been especially valuable for the consumer goods and services marketer. With the support of technologies, specialist areas of database marketing, customer relationship management (see Pine et al., 1995; Rigby et al., 2002), and customer defections management (see Reichheld and Sasser, 1990) have emerged.

Customer databases and direct marketing

Peppers and Rogers (1999) list the main differences between mass marketing and one-to-one marketing (see Table 5.2). Companies that know their individual customers can customise their product, offer, message, shipment method and payment method to maximise customer appeal. Today's companies are building customer databases to support this strategy:

- A *customer database* is an organised collection of comprehensive data about individual customers or prospects that is current, accessible and actionable for such marketing purposes as lead generation, lead qualification, sale of a good or service, or maintenance of customer relationships.
- *Database marketing* is the process of building, maintaining, and using customer databases and other databases (products, suppliers, resellers) for the purpose of contacting and transacting.

In business marketing, the customer profile contains the products and services the customer has bought; past volumes, prices and profits; team member names (and their ages, birthdays, hobbies and favourite foods); status of current contracts; an estimate of the supplier's share of the customer's business; competitive suppliers; assessment of competitive strengths and weaknesses in selling and servicing the account; and relevant buying practices, patterns and policies. In consumer marketing, the customer database contains demographics (age, income, family members, birthdays), psychographics (activities, interests and opinions), past purchases, and other relevant information about an individual. For example, the catalogue company Fingerhut possesses some 1,400 pieces of information about each of the 30 million households in its massive customer database.

Database marketing is most frequently used by business marketers and service retailers (hotels, banks, airlines and, in particular, Internet retailers). It is used less often by conventional packaged-goods retailers (Coles and Woolworths) and consumer-packaged goods companies, though some (Quaker Oats and Nabisco, among them) have been experimenting in this area. A well-developed customer database is a proprietary asset that can give the company a competitive edge.

(*Source*: Adapted from P. Kotler, *Marketing Management: The millennium edition*, Prentice Hall, Upper Saddle River, NJ, 2000, pp. 652–4)

Table 5.2 Mass marketing versus one-to-one marketing

Mass marketing	One-to-one marketing
■ Average customer	■ Individual customer
■ Customer anonymity	■ Customer profile
■ Standard product	■ Customised market offering
■ Mass production	■ Customised production
■ Mass distribution	■ Customised distribution
■ Mass advertising	■ Customised message
■ Mass promotion	■ Customised promotion
■ One-way communication	■ Interactive communication
■ Economies of scale	■ Economies of scope
■ Share of market	■ Share of customer
■ All customers	■ Profile of customer
■ Customer attraction	■ Customer retention

Source: Adapted from D. Peppers and M. Rogers, *The One-to-one Manager: Real-world lessons in customer relationship management,* Random House, New York, 1999.

A wide range of customer relationship management technology has been developed to assist organisations to get closer to their customers, to understand their customers' needs and, hence, to support strategies designed to exceed customer expectations. However, according to Rod Bryan, a corporate leader in CRM in the Asia-Pacific region, the all-or-nothing part of CRM is about committing to a way of doing business, not to a set of tools. 'The key to business success lies in the strategy, not the software. It's absolutely not about technology. . . . But you need the technology to realise the strategy' (Bryan, cited in Bennett, 2002, p. 14).

Bryan offers the following example to illustrate the gulf between CRM technology and a strategy. Two competing organisations, such as banks, may be exactly the same size and offer more or less the same services product set and customer base. The two banks might both install exactly the same CRM technology, but if they are using different CRM strategies, they will get very different results. Research findings in 2001 indicate that more than half of CRM projects fail to measure up to expectations (Connors, 2002, p. 16).

A recent Merrill Lynch survey of Chief Information Officers in the U.S. found that 45% were not satisfied with their CRM installations. These findings are supported by plenty of anecdotal evidence. There is no shortage of explanations as to why disappointment is so common. CRM is as much a business strategy as a technology. The software requires a company to have its customer data bases in order and to ensure the right access for the right people. This is no easy task, but ensuring an entire organisation adopts a CRM mindset, where all activity really does revolve around the customer rather than long-entrenched work habits, is a lot harder. (Connors, 2002, p. 16)

These perspectives place emphasis on the crucial importance of the strategic business management approach to building the multifaceted management and marketing capacity required to build and sustain a specific customer base. Table 5.2 highlights the different customer- and

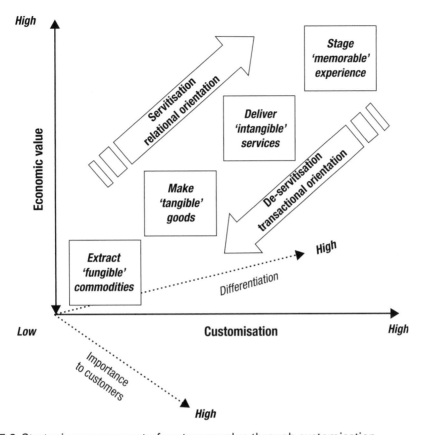

Figure 5.6 Strategic management of customer value through customisation

product-oriented mindset strategies applied in mass marketing, and the one-to-one marketing approaches used in goods and services industries.

Strategic management of customer value creation through customisation
The growing attention to individual customers and their needs, backed with enabling mass customisation technologies, has founded a platform of new market competition. In the influential book, *The Experience Economy*, Pine and Gilmore (1999) suggest the dawn of a new type of economy, the experience economy, in a framework of the progression of economic value. They explain the core economic function of the new economy as the staging of memorable memories in relation to those of its preceding economies – namely, the extracting of fungible commodities of the commodities economy, the making of tangible goods of the goods economy, and the delivering of intangible services of the services economy.

Partly drawing from Pine and Gilmore's conceptualisation of the progression of the economic value, Figure 5.6 illustrates a model of the strategic management of customer value creation through successful customisation, in relation to the preceding discussions on servitisation of businesses and relationship marketing. For operationalisation of the model, some additional explanations would be beneficial. First, Figure 5.6 treats the four economies as alternative core business functions of an organisation. Second, it should be stressed that economic value is not synonymous with customer value. While the former can be viewed as the cost to a customer incurred by the purchase of a given product, the latter involves the customer's perceived benefit associated with the purchase as well as the purchase cost. More commonly, it is understood as either a ratio or a subtraction between the two. The customer's perception of product benefit may vary; thus, enhanced economic value of a market offering does not necessarily denote enhanced customer value to everyone. It is because of this customer idiosyncrasy that some customers find greater customer value in deservitised, low economic value market offerings, while others equate high economic value, servitised offerings with greater customer value. Finally, Figure 5.6 illustrates the criticality of customisation (and sometimes its absence) to the above 'determinant' attributes (that is, both important to customers and differentiated from competitors) for the strategic management of customer value.

The following box demonstrates the progression of core economic functions, as well as strategic alternative in customer value management through servitisation by customisation and deservitisation by standardisation.

Box 5.6   The changing nature of weddings in Japan

Traditionally in Japan, a wedding ceremony was religious. It was performed by a Shinto priest of a local shrine in accordance with a Shinto rite, in the presence of close family members of the groom and bride. Often the ceremony was accompanied by a reception party for local community members, as well as the relatives of the two families, to introduce the bride to the local community of the groom as a new member and to initiate kinship and social networks between the two families. Instrumental in ensuring the success of the ceremony was the labour and skills of those volunteering female community and family members who made the wedding outfit (*kimono*) and catered for the reception.

Nonetheless, this tradition is increasingly becoming a thing of the past as a result of the country's economic and social development – in particular, Japanese young adults' affection for Western culture – since the Second World War. Rapid urbanisation, and the emergence of catering service providers in the large cities (such as hotels and specialised wedding function service providers), have made the wedding ceremony and reception less a community-based event and more the province of commercial service businesses. In addition, Japanese youth's preference for Western culture has meant that many newlyweds wear Western-style wedding outfits in addition to traditional outfits during the reception. Some couples are converting to Christianity solely for the purpose of having a formal Western-style wedding ceremony.

By the 1980s, Japan had firmly established itself as an economic superpower. The country's prosperity manifested itself as increased earnings and spending among the Japanese. Operators of luxury hotels were quick to capitalise on the emergence of wealthy Japan and began to market wedding services and lavish receptions that were intended to provide memorable wedding experiences for everyone in attendance. Some hotels installed an in-house chapel, in addition to a Shinto altar, so as to be able to offer one-stop, full wedding service in both the traditional and Western styles. In addition, they provided dress hire, professional photo and video-recording services, reception catering, a professional facilitator and musicians for the reception, a selection of souvenirs, and accommodation options for the newlyweds and their guests.

Since the 1990s, however, a new development has taken place on the weddinsg scene as a result of both the arrival of the 'second baby boomers' (born in the mid-1970s) in the wedding market and the country's prolonged economic recession. These young adults are liberal and embrace more individualistic values. They are largely uninterested in the traditional Japanese wedding, and demand the right to plan their own wedding ceremony and reception. Simply stated, they want a wedding ceremony and reception not for their parents and relatives, but for themselves. They are less concerned with the religious aspect of the wedding, and find the Western-style wedding more romantic and fashionable than the traditional Japanese style. Due to the prolonged economic recession, the operators of luxury hotels have begun to lose their dominance in this market due to their strategic focus. Young Japanese adults today view the conventional wedding services provided by those hotels as somewhat generic, laboured and expensive.

Proving popular among the new generation of customers are those wedding service providers that have adopted a strategic decision to create customer value either through servitisation via enhanced customisation, or through deservitisation around the concept of do-it-yourself. For instance, Watabe Wedding Corporation in Kyoto has established a strong market position by promoting overseas wedding services as a co-producer, coordinator and facilitator of customers' dream wedding experiences with their intimate relatives through its overseas subsidiaries in popular holiday destinations in North America, Europe, Australia, Indonesia and China. With its integrated services system, even those Japanese who cannot speak a local language can stage their wedding ceremony and reception overseas without difficulty. Another strategic move that is prevailing among specialised wedding services providers is to dispense with non-value-adding services and, instead, leave the responsibility for these service functions to the customer.

Although not all customers require an organisation's dedicated customer-specific attention and marketing effort, the following list of research findings confirms the value of the management orientation to relationship marketing, or effective customer relationship management.

- Sixty-five per cent of the average company's business comes from its present, satisfied customers.
- It costs five times as much to acquire a new customer as it does to service an existing customer.
- A business that loses each day for one year one customer who customarily spends $50 a week will suffer a sales decline of $1 million the next year.
- Ninety-one per cent of unhappy customers will never again buy from a company that has dissatisfied them, and will communicate their dissatisfaction to at least nine other people. (Vavra, 1992, p. 14)

Quality/process management: Business process reengineering

In the early 1990s, many managers realised that an increasingly mobile labour market and short-term profit-making shareholder pressure placed a substantial strain upon their TQM ventures. Management's frustration with slow progress in their TQM journey, and concern about a potential trap of the TQM game (that is, catching up to the Japanese through additive improvements) called for a new management tool. Against this background, business process reengineering (BPR) (see Davenport and Short, 1990; Hammer, 1990; Hammer and Champy, 1993) was introduced and was open-handedly welcomed by US managers as an offensive strategic management weapon. Reengineering is 'the fundamental rethinking and radical redesign of business processes to achieve dramatic improvements in critical, contemporary measures of performance, such as cost, quality, service, and speed' (Hammer and Champy, 1993, p. 32). It focuses on 'innovation' in business process based on management's 'strategic' systemic thinking, in contrast to 'incremental' process refinements and improvements through systemic business management, TQM.

After reaching its prime in 1994, the initial popularity of BPR began to wane as management's frustration with disappointing BPR performance grew. In addition to management's high expectation for BPR benefits, failures of BPR are attributed to two main factors: an overemphasis on IT as an enabling agent; and desktop process designing by a few corporate process architects (Davenport and Stoddard, 1994; Davenport et al., 2003). More specifically, the initial BPR focus failed to give due consideration to the key components of the organisation – the people. It failed to engage the people who bring the process alive for value creation, by participating in and interacting with it (see Chapter 8). In response to this realisation, a renewed interest in BPR emerged based on a more holistic view (which echoes more or less Davenport and Short's version of BPR): BPR is one of the tools of process management – such as TQM, enterprise resource planning and benchmarking – and should be applied eclectically across situations, either independently or jointly with other tools. This realisation of the complementary natures of BPR and TQM implied the emergence for the 21st century of truly holistic strategic business management paradigm, built on strategic systemic management thinking and employees' systemic strategic thinking.

Value innovation

In the 21st century, organisations operate and compete in the knowledge economy where knowledge has emerged as the most significant driver of wealth creation. Value innovation has emerged as a new driver in strategic management thinking and practice. Value innovation offers customers 'fundamentally new and superior values in traditional businesses through innovative ideas and knowledge' (Kim and Mauborgne, 1999, p. 46), rather than competing head-to-head with competitors through imitations and incremental improvements. As examples, CNN, Singapore Airlines, Bendigo Bank (Australia), Watabe Wedding Corporation and 7-Eleven (Japan) are among those organisations that have built a competitive market position through value innovation. As indicated, it is not all about 'technology' innovation. The focus is on innovation in conception and the creation of value, or the identification of a customer value need. 'Value innovation links innovation to what the mass of buyers value. To value innovate, companies must ask two questions: (1) Are we offering customers radically superior value? (2) Is our price level accessible to the mass of buyers in our target market?' (Kim and Mauborgne, 1999, p. 45).

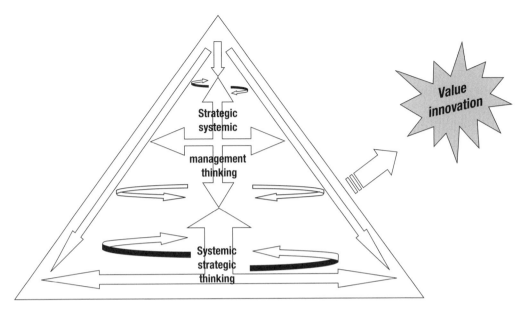

Figure 5.7 Strategic business management and value innovation

Instrumental to value innovation is strategic business management, which is built on management's and their employees' systemic strategic thinking. If an organisation lacks either of these components, its value creation effort will fail to go beyond TQM or BPR. Figure 5.7 depicts the interdependent nature of the strategic systemic management thinking of management, and employees, for value innovation.

Box 5.7 presents an example of value innovation processes pursued under the strategic business management philosophy.

Box 5.7   Scandinavian Airlines System's service development: Strategic systemic operationalisation of customer needs and wants

This illustrative case outlines the first two phases of Scandinavian Airlines System's (SAS) four phases of service development (that is, the idea phase, the project formation phase, the design phase and the implementation phase).

The fundamental or basic needs that SAS has to deal with are safety, getting passengers' luggage to the right place, and punctuality. SAS must meet these basic requirements before it can climb the pyramid of customer wants or unmet customer needs. These activities have, however, been a focus of the airline over a long period of time. In order to become more competitive, SAS must now focus on the activity support – that is, supporting its customers through the process, helping them to do what they want and need to do, and delighting them by tailoring the travelling process for each individual. This cannot be achieved by just meeting customer requirements. One must probe and seek to understand why something is important, why customers do this or that, why something is a problem. A company must understand how big a problem something is and how it may affect their customers. An environment must be visualised to discover the value that a company can provide. It is the discovery of value that must happen, and anything that helps in realising value that can differentiate a company from the competition (in a very positive way) is good. It is not sufficient to look at the conventional dimensions of competition in an industry. These dimensions are most often well understood by all the players. Instead, companies must seek to understand the problems and needs of the customers who use their products and services and create a competitive advantage.

Success in customer-focused service development requires a deep understanding of:

- customers' needs, requirements, expectations and preferences;
- customer service systems – that is, the technical infrastructure, and customers' knowledge of and ability to use services;
- customer values and cognitive structure;
- customers' behaviour when using services, and customers' usability processes (focus both on what the customer does and what he wants to do!); and
- customers' quality perceptions, such as ease of doing business, reliability, and methods of handling customers' dissatisfaction or complaints.

SAS studied customers in the environments that comprise the entire travel process – or, as it will be called, the travel experience. The travel experience was divided into five phases – check-in, lounge, gate, in-flight and baggage claim – each phase roughly representing a physical location or a function that the passenger has to pass through. Together they include all parts of the interaction between SAS and the customers. Studies of the customers were carried out partly by using on-site observation, but foremost by using video cameras documenting the customers' travel process. Video cameras were set up in different locations throughout the travel process. In all, SAS amassed thousands of hours of video and photographic data of the customers on the ground and in-flight. The video data were then studied in detail to identify recurring passenger needs and concerns. Close to 3,500 hours of video data were studied in sequences as short as five seconds, in addition to 3,600 still images taken in different situations. This conscientious analysis of data forms the basis for establishing an understanding of the passengers, drawing from actual behaviour and how customers perceive different activities. Furthermore, five weeks of in-depth interviews were carried out with various unions, in-flight staff and ground staff.

This marked the end of the idea phase. Next, the project formation phase was entered and the project team finalised. It consisted of representatives from the top management, SAS's product development organisation, and a cross-functional team with both front-line and corporate participants from technical services, marketing, and flight and ground personnel. It also contained external design and advertising resources and external marketing resources. This can be characterised as being a multi-team, or more demanding than the cross-functionality, because experts – not just personnel – from different areas are included. In the formulation phase, the various workshops to help analyse the material were planned. The people involved in these workshops were mostly executives and front-line staff. Another round of interviews was also planned.

(*Source*: Adapted from A. Gustafsson, F. Ekdahl, and B. Edvardsson, 'Customer focused service development in practice: A case study at Scandinavian Airlines System (SAS)', *International Journal of Service Industry Management*, vol. 10, no. 4, 1999, pp. 344–58)

More than half a century ago, Peter Drucker noted: 'Because it is [the business] purpose to create a customer, any business enterprise has two – and only these two – basic functions: marketing and innovation' (1954, p. 38). Given that value innovation is built on effective integration and coordination of the two functions, value innovation should not be viewed as a new management challenge. The important challenge, in searching and continuously improving customer-focused value and innovation, lies in an organisation's ability to institutionalise a strategic systemic business management philosophy, which manifests itself as management's and employees' systemic strategic thinking, in the ever-changing environment.

Convergence between marketing theories and practice

The preceding sections have reviewed key historical perspectives that have contributed to the evolving development of business management and marketing thinking and practice over the last 150 years. Table 5.3 provides a historical summary of the theoretical side of the development of the marketing discipline.

Table 5.3 draws special attention to the notion of a 'market orientation'. Simply stated, 'market orientation' refers to the implementation of the marketing concept. It reflects the characteristic traits of organisations that, to some extent, implement a holistic and integrated concept of marketing. More specifically, the term has been defined as follows:

> The organisation-wide generation of market intelligence pertaining to current and future customer needs, dissemination of the intelligence across departments, and organisation-wide responsiveness to it. (Kohli and Jaworski 1990, p. 6)

and:

> The culture that (1) places the highest priority on the profitability creation and maintenance of superior customer value while considering the interest of other key stakeholders; and (2) provides norms for behavior regarding the organizational development of and responsiveness to marketing information. (Slater and Narver, 1995, p. 67)

Renewed interest in the marketing concept during the 1980s meant that by the 1990s marketing scholars began to devote research attention to the challenges and issues associated with the practice of integrated marketing management. Consensus emerged about marketing as a corporate philosophy, and the rationale of an integrated organisational process designed to create superior customer value and sustainable relationships also gained support. Research findings contributed to discourse on the role of the marketing management function, or department, within the organisation. In line with the earlier discussions on the

Table 5.3 Schools of thought and their influence on marketing theory and practice

Timeline and stream of literature	Fundamental ideas or propositions
1800~1920: Classical and neoclassical economics	
Marshall (1890); Say (1821); Shaw (1912); Smith (1776)	Economics became the first social science to reach the *quantitative* sophistication of the nature sciences. Value is embedded in matter through manufacturing (value-added, utility, value in exchange); goods come to be viewed as standardised output (commodities). Wealth in society created by the acquisition of tangible 'stuff'. Marketing as matter in motion.
1900~1950: Early/formative marketing	
• Commodities (Copeland, 1923) • Institutions (Nystrom, 1915; Weld, 1916) • Functional (Cherington, 1920; Weld, 1917)	Early marketing thought was *highly descriptive* of commodities, institutions and marketing functions: commodity school (characteristics of goods), institutional school (role of marketing institutions in value-embedded process) and functional school (functions that marketers perform). A major focus was on the transaction or output, and how institutions performing marketing functions added value to commodities. Marketing primarily provided time and place utility, and a major goal was possession utility (creating a transfer of title and/or sale). However, a focus on functions is the beginning of the recognition of operant resources.*
1950~1980: Marketing management	
• Business should be customer-focused (Drucker, 1954; McKitterick, 1957) • Value 'determined' in marketplace (Levitt, 1960) • Marketing is a decision-making and problem-solving function (Kotler, 1967; McCarthy, 1960)	Firms can use *analytical techniques* (largely from microeconomics) to try to define marketing mix for optimal firm performance. Value 'determined' in marketplace; 'embedded' value must have usefulness. Customers do not buy things, but need or want fulfilment. Everyone in the firm must be focused on the customer, because the firm's only purpose is to create a satisfied customer. Identification of the functional responses to the changing environment that provide competitive advantage through differentiation begins to shift towards value in use.

Table 5.3 (cont.)

1980~2000 and forward: Marketing as a social and economic process

- Market orientation (Kohli and Jaworski, 1990; Narver and Slater, 1990)
- Services marketing (Grönroos, 1984; Zeithaml, Parasuraman and Berry, 1985)
- Relationship marketing (Berry, 1983; Duncan and Moriarty, 1998; Gummesson, 1994, 2002; Sheth and Parvatiyar, 2000)
- Quality management (Hauser and Clausing, 1998; Parasuraman, Zeithaml and Berry, 1988)
- Value and supply chain management (Normann and Ramirez, 1993; Srivastava, Shervani and Fahey, 1999)
- Resource management (Constantin and Lusch, 1994; Day, 1994; Dickson, 1992; Hunt, 2000; Hunt and Morgan, 1995)
- Network analysis (Achrol, 1991; Achrol and Kotler, 1999; Webster, 1992)

A dominant logic begins to emerge that largely views marketing as a continuous social and economic process in which *operant resources* are paramount. The logic views financial results not as an end result, but as a test of a market hypothesis about a value proposition. The marketplace can falsify market hypotheses, which enables entities to learn about their actions and find ways to better serve their customers and improve financial performance.

This paradigm begins to unify disparate literature streams in major areas such as customer and market orientation, services marketing, relationship marketing, quality management and network analysis. The foundational premises of the merging paradigm are: (1) skills and knowledge are the fundamental unit of exchange, (2) indirect exchange masks the fundamental unit of exchange, (3) goods are distribution mechanisms for service provision, (4) knowledge is the fundamental source of competitive advantage, (5) all economies are services economies, (6) the customer is always a co-producer, (7) the enterprise can only make value propositions, and (8) a service-centred view is inherently customer-oriented and relational.

---

* *Operant resources* are either tangible or intangible and employed to act on those resources that are used to create an effect, or *operand resources* (for example, machinery and raw materials). Operant resources can take various forms, from human skills and knowledge, and market knowledge, to core competence and organisational process.

Source: S. L. Vargo and R. F. Lusch, 'Evolving to a new dominant logic for marketing', *Journal of Marketing*, vol. 68, no. 1, 2004, p. 3.

---

implementation of a marketing concept or the integrated marketing practice, some scholars (Webster, 1989; Doyle, 1995; Montgomery and Webster, 1997) suggest that there is declining marketing department influence over an organisation's so-called marketing activities and, correspondingly, an increasing dispersion of marketing activities beyond the departmental boundary to, for example, temporary cross-functional project teams, a permanent cross-function, an existing organisational unit (for example, sales) and a new organisational unit which focuses on customer information and customer service (Homburg et al., 2000).

Figure 5.8 depicts this declining responsibility and control of the marketing department in the marketing function in the face of the rise of management recognition of integrated marketing. Box 5.3 examined an extreme case of this form of transition. The Cleaning Company ended up removing the formal marketing department from the organisation altogether.

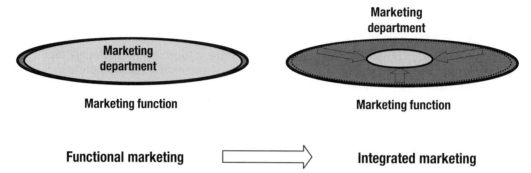

Figure 5.8 The declining role of the marketing department in the marketing function (functional to integrated marketing)

Day (1997, p. 89) offers some guidance in defining the future organisational role of the marketing department, with the following question: 'What are the core processes, and what is the contribution of the marketing function to the direction and integration of these processes?' In response, three key business processes are suggested: (1) the product development management process; (2) the supply chain management process; and (3) the customer relationship management process (Srivastava et al. (1999). A future departmental role is conceived around three customer connections: (1) the customer–product connection; (2) the customer–service delivery connection; and (3) the customer–financial accountability connection (Moorman and Rust, 1999). Kotler calls for rekindled management attention to marketing as the driver of business strategy (Crainer, 2004). These views are especially relevant to service organisations. Service organisations need to keep in mind when organising marketing within the organisation that 'a central marketing staff of *full-time marketers* may sometimes also be required to take responsibility for centrally implemented marketing activities as well as to act as internal consultants to top management in customer-related issues and in internal marketing' (Grönroos, 2000, p. 311).

While the ever-evolving business environment continues to create a new set of challenges to the marketing management of services, there appears to be a universal principle for effective management of the marketing function. That is the effective generation, sharing and utilisation of customer and market information knowledge across the organisation so as to facilitate alignment of functional strategies under the holistic logic guiding strategic systemic business management (see Figure 5.8). The successful value innovation organisations discussed in this and the previous chapter are managed by managers who apply strategic systemic management thinking, which is supported by employees' systemic strategic thinking and actions. In these organisations, operant resources are continuously upgraded and strategically invested to innovate superior customer value with customer and market information and knowledge as critical inputs to strategic decision making. Box 5.8 describes how a successful retailing organisation manages customer and market information – and, thus, market knowledge – to strategically integrate its operand and operant resources and innovatively apply its strategic systemic management thinking to a broader context – a value chain – for competitive advantage building.

Box 5.8   7-Eleven Japan

7-Eleven Japan is considered to be setting standards in efficiency worldwide. The perpetual redesign of 7-Eleven's business model has made the company the most profitable retailer in Japan, both in absolute and sales-profit ratio terms. In 1973, Ito-Yokado, a Japanese supermarket chain, and Southland Corporation, the operator and franchiser of 7-Eleven convenience stores in the United States, reached a licensing agreement. Ito-Yokado established 7-Eleven Japan and opened the first 7-Eleven stores in 1978. In 1991, it acquired the Southland Corporation. 7-Eleven Japan is a franchiser. It does not sell goods (although it runs several stores for experiments). 7-Eleven capitalises on market knowledge by managing knowledge-creation contexts. The company charges its franchisees for the services it provides them, royalties for trademarks, and leasing fees for such equipment as the information systems, display racks and refrigerated cases. Each 7-Eleven store sells some 3,000 items, of which about 70 per cent change every year. Out of total sales, 77 per cent is foods; about 40 per cent is processed foods (for example, snacks and cup noodles) and about 20 per cent is fast food, such as rice balls and box lunches. To sustain this stream of innovations and provide new services to the franchisees, 7-Eleven makes extensive use of explicit knowledge, such as manuals for store operation, employee training and franchisee recruiting/training. This heavy reliance on explicit knowledge differentiates 7-Eleven from most Japanese companies rather dramatically. 7-Eleven's outstanding success is largely based on leveraging over market knowledge (Okamoto, 1998; Usui, 1998). By striking a balance between enabling technologies, contexts, resources and processes, it has realised a dynamic system for creating knowledge.

- *Processes:* 7-Eleven uses several contexts for knowledge sharing. For example, knowledge about customers' emerging needs is captured through dialogue with customers at its 8,000 stores. Local employees' knowledge of and insights into such needs are shared with other employees as well as field counsellors and owner consultants, who visit stores frequently to consult. The market knowledge and insights are also shared in the weekly face-to-face meetings, in which managers from all the stores get together to share their views and feelings. As a result, all decisions are based on sharing knowledge of customers and on a continuous flow of feedback from the shop floor.

- *People and relationships:* 7-Eleven's system utilises the knowledge of people – that is, employees, suppliers and customers – to sustain the consistency of the offer. Field counsellors augment and concentrate the knowledge in meetings in which intensive dialogue is practised. Seven-Eleven's managers meet every Monday in Tokyo to discuss problems and possible changes. The president of the company, Mr Suzuki, expects those managers who are facing problems to leave the meeting to solve their problems immediately (by improvising) and then to return to the gathering and report on the strategies implemented, the actions taken and the early results. Thus, Suzuki triggers immediate action by synchronic face-to-face communication and improvisation.

Further, all field counsellors meet in Tokyo every Tuesday to attend a meeting aimed at synchronising 7-Eleven's market knowledge. Suzuki addresses this meeting, improvising on urgent issues and on the company vision, and creating a shared sense of urgency. Representatives from all areas in Japan have to attend the lTuesday meeting. 7-Eleven covers their travelling expenses in order to foster dialogue and the sharing of knowledge in a shared context (time and space). This weekly event emphasises the relevance of 7-Eleven's vision and design for solving everyday problems in the local 'here and now'. The regular 'lunch meeting' at which top managers try out all new products is another synchronic and direct experience. Here, dialogue and actual testing of new products help new ideas to emerge.

Another important medium for the accumulation of tacit knowledge is on-the-job training (OJT), which is stressed throughout the career path at 7-Eleven. New employees follow a career path that starts on the shop floor, as the place of their first learning experiences (internalisation) and leads up to management positions. Every member of higher management has similar experiences and has internalised the knowledge on different levels of the organisation and the market. This enables them to fully identify with and maintain the design identity of 7-Eleven. New relationships are important for the development of new knowledge. An instrument used to explore new relationships is the *burabura shain* ('walking-around employee'). These employees have the task of wandering around. They socialise with customers in stores. They might notice a problem with food freshness and report it to a field counsellor, who will then share his insights in the store and at the meetings in Tokyo.

Team merchandising projects are shared contexts for intensive interaction with suppliers. 7-Eleven leads team members with very different backgrounds, from sometimes competing companies, in a joint product development process. A successful product innovation institutionalises the work relationships in supplier–buyer cooperations. In February 2000, 7-Eleven established the joint venture SevenDream.Com to carry out e-commerce. 7-Eleven's partners from different industries include NEC, Nomura Research Institute, Mitsui & Co., Sony Corporation, Sony Marketing, Japan Travel Bureau Inc. (JTB) and Kinotrope Inc.

- *Technology and methods*: Digital technology, in particular the (point-of-sale (POS) system, offers a diachronic base of explicit knowledge. The POS system and its partly automated nature induce reflection upon important profitability listings and offer options on how to analyse and understand the current situation. Such explicit knowledge is used to identify and replace products that perform below expectations. Bad performance quickly triggers replacement with new products. Tools with graphical user interfaces are used by headquarters for analysing POS data, and building and testing hypotheses. Thus the POS system plays an important part of the knowledge creation system at 7-Eleven. Continuous testing of new ideas is the key to fast innovation. In effect, 7-Eleven has designed its systems to establish creative routines for knowledge conversions, where data induce hypotheses and intuitions of the employees (digital and analogue technologies); IT triggers the generation of hypotheses. Each hypothesis is then tested by actual orders and confirmed by POS data. The so-called action-reflection-trigger system (Nonaka et al., 1998) collects and disseminates successful hypotheses throughout the company. The system creates and utilises distributed responsibility for new idea development and proposals beyond a single department, such as a development or design department.

In 1998, a series of small items – from scissors, pencils and erasers, to toothbrushes, all designed by Philip Starck – was introduced into the market, responding to an emergent hypothesis. After the launch and introduction of this series in most stores, the POS data showed that the success of the series was limited to densely populated, urban areas. After a few weeks of experimentation, the series vanished from the shelves and the remaining stock was sold. When placing orders, people hypothesise about what items would sell well, how many, and how to sell them. To make such hypotheses, they utilise their explicit knowledge or information such as POS data, advice from field counsellors and/or 7-Eleven Japan's headquarters, and tacit knowledge captured in the shop and the context of customers that would not be available in stores. In sum, the company, which operates in the dynamic, unstable retail industry, places a great emphasis on 'real-time' customer and market information and knowledge generated by capable IT and its hundreds of systemic strategic thinkers in the field as an input to its strategic systemic planning and actions that encompass the supply chain.

(*Source:* Adapted from P. Reinmoeller, 'Dynamic contexts for innovation strategy: Utilizing customer knowledge', *Design Management Journal*, vol. 2, 2002, pp. 41–44)

The case demonstrates the successful implementation of integrated marketing under the strategic business management approach (that is, systemic strategic business management and employees' systemic strategic thinking). As for the implementation of the integrated marketing, or a market orientation, there are some noteworthy points. First, a market orientation is not the single, universal-best orientation. Some businesses – for instance, brothels, and medical and legal professionals – are better off remaining production-oriented because of the nature of their products (that is, services), as their promotion activities in public are highly controversial and regulated, or even banned in some countries. Similarly, first movers and value innovators in emerging and growing markets with supply exceeded by demand could be more successful if they retain a production-oriented perspective. Second, as to the relationship between marketing and the other fundamental organisational function of customer value creation, innovation, there are some diverse views. For instance, Song and Parry (1999) explain innovation as an input to market orientation, whereas Deshpandé et al. (1993) posit market orientation and innovation as co-determinants of the organisation's performance. Finally, the marketing concept and its implementation is equally important and applicable to public and non-profit organisations whose market offerings are most commonly intangible services (see Kotler, 1972; Lovelock and Weinberg, 1984; Kotler and Andreasen, 1996; Voss and Voss, 2000; Vazquez et al., 2002). The importance of a market orientation to non-profit organisations is succinctly captured in the following statement:

Given the sheer multitude of non-profit organisations, each competing for a far from limit-less supply of funding through ever more numerous and sophisticated channels of communi-cation, and especially considering the challenging current economic climate, not-for-profits need – more than ever before – to possess some viable source of competitive advantage. (www.henrystewart.com/journals/nvsm/mission.html)

Conclusion

The marketing and management ideas presented in this chapter resonate with the discussion in Chapter 4, especially with regard to the strategic and functional management and market-ing approaches now required to build competitive market advantage under the conceptual logic of strategic business management and practice. This chapter also has highlighted the challenges now presented to marketing scholars and practitioners in defining the future role of a more integrated, systemic strategic management approach to the marketing function. More specifically, this chapter has reviewed:

- the transit of marketing practice in relation to the historical development of business man-agement thinking and practice and contextual backgrounds of four common competing interpretations of marketing in the light of the implementation of the marketing concept;
- the need for the integrated, systemic strategic management approach for a successful imple-mentation of the marketing concept in relation to TQM;
- the contextual background behind the rise of the services economy, and management's attention to services marketing and management associated with the recent paradigm shift in the marketing discipline from a transaction to a relationship orientation; and
- the changing role of the organisation's marketing management function or department in the organisation's pursuit of value innovation through holistic strategic business management.

Exercises

Key questions
1 Define the term 'marketing' in as many different ways as possible.
2 Discuss the underlying management principles of the marketing concept.
3 How do the marketing concept and TQM differ?
4 What are the unique challenges for services marketers in implementing the marketing concept?
5 Discuss possible reasons for the slow adoption of integrated marketing among services organisations.
6 Develop a similar framework to Table 5.1 for your country context.

Web exercises
5.1 The World Marketing Association, the umbrella world body of four regional marketing bodies (the American Marketing Association, the European Marketing Federation, the

Asia Pacific Marketing Association and the Federacion Latinoamericana de Marketing), defines marketing as 'the core business philosophy which directs the processes of identifying and fulfilling the needs of individuals and organizations through exchanges which create superior value for all parties' (Chapman, 2003). Go to some of the following websites of professional marketing associations, find their adopted marketing definitions (or find a marketing definition adopted by your local marketing professional body), and discuss similarities and dissimilarities among them:

- The Marketing Association of Australia and New Zealand (MAANZ): www.marketing.org.au/default.asp?q = Marketing±Defined&cid = 138&mod = a
- The Japan Marketing Association (JMA): www.jma-jp.org/
- The American Marketing Association (AMA): www.marketingpower.com/live/content4620.php
- The Chartered Institute of Marketing (CIM), UK: www.cim.co.uk/cim/ser/html/infHow.cfm?objectID = 4662E5C1-3594-4647-89822CA45E53C642 &displaytype = full

5.2 Access the websites of two or three international non-profit organisations (for example, World Vision, Red Cross, Greenpeace) and evaluate their web page for strengths and weakness from a marketing perspective.

5.3 Choose several local and multinational companies across industries (for example, airline, retailing, financial, hotel, manufacturing, telecommunications). Research their organisational structures, especially the presence or absence of a marketing division/department for each organisation. Explore possible reasons for the presence or absence of the marketing department in each sample organisation.

Case study 5.1 Database marketing in relationship marketing strategy

If they are to come to terms with modern database capabilities, retailers must change their typical business habits. Over the years, retailers have tended to focus on selling the product; in the process, they have concentrated on advertising to create demand, and neglected to build and maintain knowledge-based relationships with customers. Once customers made a purchase, typically they were ignored until the next ad campaign. Companies had no feedback on why customers made purchases, whether or not they returned for subsequent purchases, and the reasons why they did or do not return. This lack of customer knowledge was very evident when the marketing manager of a retail chain confessed that the company had done almost nothing to make use of its gigantic database of current, past and prospective customers. Some time ago, they had compiled a list of hundreds of thousands of names, largely derived from a co-branded marketing effort. These names and addresses were lying idle, because even shipping and invoice procedures were computerised without thought being given to coordinating them with a database. It was surprising to discover that this otherwise very progressive company was so far 'out of the loop' in terms of database development and marketing, especially since it had expanded to become a leading seller of fast-moving items involving more than a thousand brands.

(*Source:* Adapted from M. Muhamed, 'India: Customer management made easy', *Businessline*, vol. 16, August 2001, p. 1)

Student projects

1 Compare database marketing and relationship marketing.
2 In general, how can database marketing be integrated into the organisation's relationship marketing strategy?
3 Using Illustrative case 5.8 as a model, how would you devise a marketing strategy under the holistic strategic business management philosophy?

References and further reading

Adams, J. D. 1984, *Transforming Work*, Miles River Press, Alexandria, VA.

Albrecht, K. and Zemke, R. 2002, *Service America in the New Economy*, McGraw-Hill, New York.

Anderson, J. C. and Narus, J. A. 1991, 'Partnering as a focused market strategy', *California Management Review*, vol. 33, no. 3, pp. 95–113.

Arndt, J. 1979, 'Toward a concept of domesticated markets', *Journal of Marketing*, vol. 43, no. 4, pp. 69–75.

Assael, H. 1992, *Consumer Behavior and Marketing Action*, 4th ed., PWS-Kent Publishing Company, Boston.

Bartels, R. 1976, *The History of Marketing Thought*, 2nd ed., Grid Inc., Columbus, OH.

Beer, M. 2003, 'Why total quality management programs do not persist: The role of management quality and implications for leading a TQM transformation', *Decision Sciences*, vol. 34, no. 4, pp. 623–42.

Bell, M. L. and Emory, C. W. 1971, 'The faltering marketing concept', *Journal of Marketing*, vol. 35, no. 5, pp. 37–42.

Bennett, B. 2002, 'Business reluctant to make the big leap', CRM special report, *Australian Financial Review*, 18 July, p. 14.

Berry, L. L. 1983, 'Relationship marketing', in L. L. Berry, G. L. Shostack and G. D. Upali (eds), *Emerging Perspectives in Services*, AMA, Chicago, pp. 25–28.

Buzzell, R. and Gale, D. 1987, *The PIMPS Principles*, The Free Press, New York.

Caswell, W. C. 1964, 'Marketing effectiveness and sales supervision', *California Management Review*, vol. 7, no. 1, pp. 39–44.

Christensen, C. M. 2000, *The Innovator's Dilemma: The revolutionary national bestseller that changed the way we do business*, HarperCollins, New York.

Christopher, M., Payne, A. and Ballantyne, D. 1991, *Relationship Marketing: Bringing quality, customer service and marketing together*, Butterworth-Heinemann, Oxford.

Clark, K. B. and Fujimori, T. 1991, *Product Development Performance: Strategy, organization, and management in the world auto industry*, Harvard Business School Press, Boston.

Clayclamp, H. J. 1985, 'Strategic management fundamentals', in H. Thomas and D. Gardner (eds), *Strategic Marketing and Management*, John Wiley, New York, pp. 9–16.

Cole, R. E. 1979, *Work, Mobility, and Participation: A comparative study of American and Japanese industry*, University of California Press, Berkeley, CA.

Cole, R. E. 1998, 'Learning from the quality movement: What did and didn't happen and why?', *California Management Review*, vol. 41, no. 1, pp. 43–73.

Cole, R. E., Bacdayan, P. and White, B. J. 1993, 'Quality, participation, and competitiveness', *California Management Review*, vol. 35, no. 3, pp. 68–81.

Collier, D. 1990, 'Measuring and managing service quality', in D. E. Bowen, R. B. Chase, T. G. Cummings & Associates (eds), *Service Management Effectiveness*, Jossey-Bass, San Francisco, pp. 234–65.

Connors, E. 2002, 'Beware of sky-high expectations: CRM special report', *Australian Financial Review*, 18 July, p. 16.

Crainer, S. 2004, 'Interview: Philip Kotler', *Business Strategy Review*, vol. 15, no. 2, pp. 25–28.

Davenport, T. H. and Short, J. E. 1990, 'The new industrial engineering: Information technology and business process redesign', *Sloan Management Review*, vol. 31, no. 4, pp. 11–27.

Davenport, T. H. and Stoddard, D. B. 1994, 'Reengineering: Business change of mythic proportions?', *MIS Quarterly*, vol. 18, no. 2, pp. 121–7.

Davenport, T. H., Prusak, L. and Wilson, H. J. 2003, *What's the Big Idea? Creating and capitalizing on the best new management thinking*, Harvard Business School Press, Boston.

Day, G. S. 1994, 'The capabilities of market-driven organizations', *Journal of Marketing*, vol. 58, no. 5, pp. 37–52.

Day, G. S. 1997, 'Aligning the organization to the market', in D. R. Lehmann and K. E. Jocz (eds), *Reflections on the Futures of Marketing*, Marketing Science Institute, Cambridge, MA.

Day, G. S. and Wensley, R. 1983, 'Marketing theory with a strategic orientation', *Journal of Marketing*, vol. 47, no. 3, pp. 79–89.

Deshpandé, R., Farley, J. U. and Webster, F. E. Jr. 1993, 'Corporate culture, customer orientation, and innovativeness in Japanese firms', *Journal of Marketing*, vol. 57, no. 1, pp. 23–27.

Dimancescu, D. 1992, *The Seamless Enterprise: Making cross functional management work*, Oliver Wight Publications, Inc., Essex Junction, VT.

Dore, R. P. 1987, *Taking Japan Seriously: A Confucian perspective on leading economic issues*, Stanford University Press, Stanford, CA.

Doyle, P. 1995, 'Marketing in the new millennium', *European Journal of Marketing*, vol. 29, no. 13, pp. 23–41.

Drucker, P. E. 1954, *The Practice of Management*, Harper & Row, New York.

Dwyer, F. R., Schurr, P. H. and Oh, S. 1987, 'Developing buyer–seller relationships', *Journal of Marketing*, vol. 51, no. 2, pp. 11–27.

Ford, D. 1978, 'Stability factors in industrial marketing channels', *Industrial Marketing Management*, vol. 7, pp. 410–22.

Ford, D., Hakansson, H. and Johanson, J. 1986, 'How do companies interact?', *Industrial Marketing & Purchasing*, vol. 1, no. 1, pp. 26–40.

Fruin, W. M. 1992, *The Japanese Enterprise System: Competitive strategies and cooperative structures*, Clarendon Press, Oxford.

Garvin, D. A. 1998, 'The processes of organization and management', *Sloan Management Review*, vol. 39, no. 4, pp. 33–50.

Gery, G. 2001, 'Service with a smile', *Knowledge Management*, vol. 4, no. 7, July, http://web5infotraccollege.com/wadsworth/sessions/512/816/.../4!xrn_10_0_A7755625, retrieved 31 July 2002.

Grant, R. M., Shani, R. and Krishnan, R. 1994, 'TQM's challenge to management theory and practice', *Sloan Management Review*, vol. 35, no. 2, pp. 25–35.

Grönroos, C. 1978, 'A service-oriented approach to marketing of services', *European Journal of Marketing*, vol. 12, no. 8, pp. 588–601.

Grönroos, C. 1991, 'Innovative marketing strategies and organization structures for service firms', in C. H. Lovelock, *Services Marketing*, 2nd ed., Prentice Hall, Englewood Cliffs, NJ, pp. 433–48. (This work was first published in L. L. Berry, G. L. Shostack and G. D. Upah (eds), *Emerging Perspectives in Services Marketing*, American Marketing Association, Chicago, 1983, pp. 9–21.)

Grönroos, C. 1994, 'From scientific management to service management: A management perspective for the age of service competition', *International Journal of Service Industry Management*, vol. 5, no. 1, pp. 5–20.

Grönroos, C. 2000, *Services Management and Marketing: A customer relationship management approach*, 2nd ed., John Wiley & Sons, Sussex, UK.

Gummesson, E. 2002, *Total Relationship Marketing: Marketing management, relationship strategy, and CRM approaches for the network economy*, Butterworth-Heinemann, Boston.

Gummesson, E., Lehtinen, U. and Grönroos, C. 1997, 'Comment on "Nordic perspectives on relationship marketing"', *European Journal of Marketing*, vol. 31, no. 1/2, pp. 10–16.

Gustafsson, A., Ekdahl, F. and Edvardsson, B. 1999, 'Customer focused service development in practice: A case study at Scandinavian Airlines System (SAS)', *International Journal of Service Industry Management*, vol. 10, no. 4, pp. 344–58.

Häkansson, H. (ed.). 1982, *International Marketing and Purchasing of Industrial Goods: An interaction approach*, Wiley, New York.

Häkansson, H., Johanson, J. and Wootz, B. 1977, 'Influence tactics in buyer–seller processes', *Industrial Marketing Management*, vol. 5, pp. 319–32.

Hammer, M. 1990, 'Reengineering work: Don't automate, obliterate', *Harvard Business Review*, vol. 68, no. 4, pp. 104–12.

Hammer, M. and Champy, J. A. 1993, *Reengineering the Corporation*, HarperCollins, New York.

Hanis, M. 1998, 'Reaching maturity', *Independent Banker*, vol. 48, no. 1, p. 80.

Harvey, D. and Brown, D. 2001, *An Experiential Approach to Organization Development*, 6th ed., Prentice Hall, Upper Saddle River, NJ.

Heracleous, L., Wirtz, J. and Johnston, R. 2004, 'Cost-effective service excellence: Lessons from Singapore Airlines', *Business Strategy Review*, vol. 15, no. 1, pp. 33–38.

Homburg, C., Workman, J. P. Jr and Jensen, O. 2000, 'Fundamental changes in marketing organization: The movement toward a customer-focused organizational structure', *Academy of Marketing Science*, vol. 28, no. 4, pp. 459–78.

Hutt, M. D. and Speh, T. W. 1995, *Business Marketing Management*, 5th ed., Dryden Press, Chicago.

Imai, M. 1986, *Kaizen: The key to Japan's competitive success*, McGraw-Hill, New York.

International Journal of Nonprofit and Voluntary Sector Marketing, www.henrystewart.com/journals/nvsm/mission.html.

Ishikawa, K. 1985, *What is Total Quality Control? The Japanese way*, Prentice Hall, Englewood Cliffs, NJ.

Jackson, B. B. 1985, *Winning and Keeping Industrial Customers: The dynamics of customer relationships*, Lexington Books, Lexington.

Kim, W. C. and Mauborgne, R. 1999, 'Strategy, value innovation, and the knowledge economy', *Sloan Management Review*, vol. 40, no. 3, pp. 41–54.

Kohli, A. K. and Jaworski, B. J. 1990, 'Market orientation: The construct, research propositions, and managerial implications', *Journal of Marketing*, vol. 54, no. 2, pp. 1–18.

Kotler, P. 1972, 'A generic concept of marketing', *Journal of Marketing*, vol. 36, no. 2, pp. 46–54.

Kotler, P. 1994, 'Reconceptualizing marketing: An interview with Philip Kotler', *European Journal of Management*, vol. 12, no. 4, pp. 353–64.

Kotler, P. 2000, *Marketing Management: The millennium edition*, Prentice Hall, Upper Saddle River, NJ.

Kotler, P. and Andreasen, A. P. 1996, *Strategic Marketing for Nonprofit Organizations*, Prentice Hall, Englewood Cliffs, NJ.

Kotler, P. and Fahey, L. 1982, 'The world's champion marketers: The Japanese', *Journal of Business Strategy*, vol. 3, no. 1, pp. 3–13.

Lazer, W., Murata, S. and Kosaka, H. 1985, 'Japanese marketing: Towards a better understanding', *Journal of Marketing*, vol. 49, no. 2, pp. 69–81.

Levitt, T. 1960, 'Marketing myopia', *Harvard Business Review*, vol. 38, no. 4, pp. 24–47.

Levy, S. J. 2002, 'Revisiting the marketing domain', *European Journal of Marketing*, vol. 36, no. 3, pp. 299–304.

Lieberman, M. B. and Montgomery, D. B. 1988, 'First mover advantages', *Strategic Management Journal*, vol. 9, Summer, pp. 41–58.

Lings, I. N. 1999, 'Managing service quality with internal market schematics', *Long Range Planning*, vol. 32, no. 4, pp. 452–63.

Lovelock, C. H. 1988, *Managing Services: Marketing, operations, and human resources*, Prentice Hall International, London.

Lovelock, C. H. 1991, *Services Marketing*, 2nd ed., Prentice Hall, Englewood Cliffs, NJ.

Lovelock, C. H. and Weinberg, C. B. 1984, *Marketing for Public and Nonprofit Managers*, John Wiley & Sons, New York.

McNamara, C. P. 1972, 'The present status of the marketing concept', *Journal of Marketing*, vol. 36, no. 1, pp. 50–57.

Miyamoto, T. and Rexha, N. 2004, 'Determinants of three facets of customer trust: A marketing model of Japanese buyer–supplier relationship', *Journal of Business Research*, vol. 57, no. 3, pp. 312–19.

Mizuno, S. 1988, *Company-wide Total Quality Control*, Asian Productivity Organization, Tokyo.

Montgomery, D. B. and Webster, F. E. Jr 1997, 'Marketing's interfunctional interfaces: The MSI workshop on management of corporate fault zones', *Journal of Market-Focused Management*, vol. 2, pp. 7–26.

Moorman, C. and Rust, R. 1999, 'The role of marketing', *Journal of Marketing*, vol. 63, Special Issue, pp. 180–97.

Morgan, R. E. 1996, 'Conceptual foundations of marketing and marketing theory', *Management Decision*, vol. 34, no. 10, pp. 19–26.

Muhamed, M. 2001, 'India: Customer management made easy', *Businessline*, 16 August, p. 1.

National Institute of Standards and Technology, n.d., 1988–2004 Award Recipients' Contacts and Profiles, www.quality.nist.gov/Contacts_Profiles.htm, retrieved 26 August 2004.

Normann, R. 2000, *Service Management: Strategy and leadership in service business*, 3rd ed., John Wiley & Sons, Sussex, UK.

Pelham, A. M. and Wilson, D. T. 1996, 'A longitudinal study of the impact of market structure, firm structure, strategy, and market orientation culture on dimensions of small-firm performance', *Journal of the Academy of Marketing Science*, vol. 24, no. 1, pp. 27–43.

Peppers, D. and Rogers, M. 1999, *The One-to-one Manager: Real-world lessons in customer relationship management*, Random House, New York.

Pine, B. J. and Gilmore, J. H. 1999, *The Experience Economy: Work is theatre & every business a stage*, Harvard Business School Press, Boston.

Pine, B. J. II, Peppers, D. and Rogers, M. 1995, 'Do you want to keep your customers forever?', *Harvard Business Review*, vol. 75, no. 2, pp. 103–14.

Raymond, M. A. and Barksdale, H. C. 1989, 'Corporate strategic planning and corporate marketing: Toward an interface?', *Business Horizons*, vol. 32, no. 5, pp. 41–48.

Reichheld, F. F. and Sasser, W. E., Jr. 1990, 'Zero defections: Quality comes to services', *Harvard Business Review*, vol. 68, no. 5, pp. 105–11.

Reinmoeller, P. 2002, 'Dynamic contexts for innovation strategy: Utilizing customer knowledge', *Design Management Journal*, vol. 2, pp. 37–50.

Rexha, N. and Miyamoto, T. 2000, 'Relationship-building supplier behaviors for winning customer trust: New insights from case research with nine leading Japanese manufacturers', in R. B. McNaughton and S. T. Cavusgil (eds), *Developments in Australasian Marketing and Advances in International Marketing*, Supplement 1, JAI Press, Inc., Stamford, CT, pp. 77–94.

Rigby, D. K., Reichheld, F. F. and Schefter, P. 2002, 'Avoid the four perils of CRM', *Harvard Business Review*, vol. 82, no. 2, pp. 101–9.

Sako, M. 1992, *Prices, Quality, and Trust: Inter-firm relations in Britain and Japan*, Cambridge University Press, Cambridge.

Sheth, J. N. and Parvatiyar, A. 1995, 'The evolution of relationship marketing', *International Business Review*, vol. 4, no. 4, pp. 397–418.

Sheth, J. N., Sisodia, R. S. and Sharma, A. 2000, 'The antecedents and consequences of customer-centric marketing', *Academy of Marketing Science*, vol. 28, no. 1, pp. 55–66.

Silvestro, R., Johnston, R., Fitzgerald, L. and Voss, C. 1990, 'Quality measurement in service industries', *International Journal of Service Industry Management*, vol. 1, no. 2, pp. 54–60.

Slater, S. F. and Narver, J. C. 1995, 'Market orientation and the learning organization', *Journal of Marketing*, vol. 59, no. 4, pp. 63–74.

Smitka, M. 1991, *Competitive Ties: Subcontracting in the Japanese automotive industry*, Columbia University Press, New York.

Srivastava, R. K., Shervani, T. A. and Fahey, L. 1999, 'Marketing, business processes, and shareholder value: An organizationally embedded view of marketing activities and the discipline of marketing', *Journal of Marketing*, vol. 63, Special Issue, pp. 168–79.

Urban, G. L. and Hauser, J. R. 1980, *Design and Marketing of New Products*, Prentice Hall, Englewood Cliffs, NJ.

Vandermerwe, S. and Rada, J. 1988, 'Servitization of businesses: Adding value by adding service', *European Management Journal*, vol. 6, no. 4, pp. 314–24.

Vargo, S. L. and Lusch, R. F. 2004, 'Evolving to a new dominant logic for marketing', *Journal of Marketing*, vol. 68, no. 1, pp. 1–17.

Vavra, T. G. 1992, *Aftermarketing: How to keep customers for life through relationship marketing*, Irwin, Chicago.

Vazquez, R., Alvarez, L. I. and Santos, M. L. 2002, 'Market orientation and social services in private non-profit organisations', *European Journal of Marketing*, vol. 36, no. 9/10, pp. 1022–46.

Voss, G. B. and Voss, Z. G. 2000, 'Strategic orientation and firm performance in an artistic environment', *Journal of Marketing*, vol. 64, no. 1, pp. 67–83.

Webster, F. E., Jr 1988, 'The rediscovery of the marketing concept', *Business Horizons*, vol. 31, no. 3, pp. 29–39.

Webster, F. E., Jr 1988, 'It's 1990 – Do you know where your marketing is?', *Marketing Science Report No. 89–123*, Marketing Science Institute, Cambridge, MA.

Webster, F. E., Jr 1992, 'The changing role of marketing in the corporation', *Journal of Marketing*, vol. 56, no. 4, pp. 1–17.

Webster, F. E., Jr 1994, *Market-driven management: Using the new marketing concept to create a customer-oriented company*, John Wiley & Sons, Inc., New York.

Womack, J. P., Jones, D. T. and Roos, D. 1990, *The Machine That Changed the World*, Rawson Associates, New York.

6
Strategic operations management in services

Learning objectives

After studying this chapter, readers will be able to:
- discuss the nature, scope and significance of operations management within services
- define the concept of operations management and explain its various functions and dimensions
- explain a variety of operations management concepts and theories
- discuss the main issues and challenges associated with managing the operations of services.

Introduction

The previous chapters have presented the nature and scope of the strategic management of services. The two interdependent, but discrete, domains of management – the *corporate* (or *strategic*) domain, and the *functional* (or *operational*) domain – are both needed for the management of organisational efficiency and effectiveness, and hence survival. The special vulnerability to external pressures and influences when managing services (as discussed in Chapters 2 and 3) makes strategic management especially important (as discussed in Chapters 4 and 5). However, the management of the service delivery process (a significant component of the service 'product') is of equal importance. This chapter will provide an overview of services operations management in a cross-functional management context. This integrated approach to the management of services will examine the issues and challenges significant for those dealing with operations management.

The functional management domain, as discussed in Chapter 1, presents the concept of management of an organisation's marketing, operations, finances, and human resources as being significant for organisations involved in services. Figure 6.1 indicates that at the macro-level, each area is focused on a particular series of outcomes (for example, finances: profitability; operations: efficiency; marketing: effectiveness; and human resources: productivity), as well as focusing attention to micro-level service delivery issues. This chapter dissects the specific issues and practices required for successful operations management within the functional management domain.

Figure 6.1 The integrated services management (ISM) model

The nature of operations management

The term 'operations management' is traditionally associated with manufacturing and production management functions. Even today, some manufacturing sector organisations still use the term 'production management' to cover their operational activities. As presented in Chapter 1, a growing number of manufacturing businesses, or secondary sector industries, are including an increasing number of services in their product offerings, with many incorporating ancillary services business units. With this increased range of production/services delivery, the manufacturing–services swing has broadened the management functions included in the discipline of operations management to incorporate many of the aspects and activities related to the entire supply chain, not just the production system (Waller, 2003).

The term 'operations management' is now used across the full spectrum of industries involved with the manufacture of products and delivery of services. This increasingly diverse spectrum of industries providing both goods and services to varying degrees has developed a continuum from purely manufacturing organisations, to those providing both goods and services in differing combinations, right through to the other end, of those providing pure services (Sutherland and Canwell, 2004). Operations management can include activities such as: purchasing or procurement involved in obtaining inputs for a production system; shipping and distribution, which are sometimes considered marketing activities and sometimes operational activities; and skills training of staff for new projects, which is often considered to be HR management. Thus, due to the interdependencies of these activities, many organisations manage the above activities as one process in the operations management area, often employing the concept of *supply chain management*. These changes in operations have resulted in many organisations developing new organisational structures based on business processes instead of traditional functional areas.

Operations management is defined as: 'the activities associated with transforming inputs into useful outputs in order to create a result of value' (Meredith and Schafer, 2002, p. 2); 'the set of activities that creates value in the form of goods and services by transforming inputs into outputs' (Heizer and Render, 2004, p. 4); or 'the actual production system in terms of environment, inputs, transformation system, outputs, and the mechanisms used for monitoring and control of the system' (Meredith and Schafer, 2002, p. 2). Research indicates that specific and evolving definitions of operations management have implications for further theory building research for specific areas of operations management and practice (Wacker, 1998). With this in mind, it is necessary to remember throughout this chapter that theories with examples are provided to reinforce the concept that 'the domain of the theory is the exact setting, or circumstances, where the theory can be applied' (Wacker, 1998, p. 363). Therefore, this chapter examines the particular special requirements for operations management within the domain of the services. More specifically, *service operations management* is the set of processes, activities and resources (including stakeholders, as discussed in Chapter 3) that create value in the form of goods, services or experiences, by transforming a range of both tangible and intangible inputs and resources into outputs of value. These outputs of value can be both tangible and intangible, but increasingly, when discussing services, they are a combination of both.

The scope of operations management for the manager

The essential functions of an operations manager dealing with services include:

- creating the product/service/experience (the supply) through a transformation process;
- involvement with the marketing area in relation to generating demand;
- involvement with the finance/accounting area to track organisational performance, pay bills and collect money;
- involvement with the HR area, which manages the staffing of the organisation; and
- management of the customer and/or other relevant stakeholders involved in the delivery process. (Fitzsimmons and Fitzsimmons, 2001; Bucher et al., 2004; and Heizer and Render, 2004)

The diverse and organisation-wide scope of these functions supports an integrated approach to services management as presented in Figure 6.1.

At a more detailed level of day-to-day activities, an operations manager is involved with numerous activities across the organisation. These can include such activities as:

- deciding on site location, facilities layout and space utilisation for the organisation;
- investigating appropriate technologies and their methods to support the activities of the organisation;

Table 6.1 Operations management from stakeholder perspectives

The business	The customer
Ensuring that quality standards are as high as possible within the resource constraints	Optimising quality regardless of costs
Minimising operating costs such as labour and energy	Maximising quality of service and optimising customer enjoyment of services
Problems solved as quickly and as cheaply as possible	No problems occurring in the first place, but if they do, being solved quickly without regard to the cost to the business
Compliance with the law – social obligation	Social responsibility and social responsiveness
Looking after the needs of those groups of customers who are considered 'special', such as loyalty groups, people with disabilities	Treating every customer as if they are unique and special
Maximising capacity, processing of customers, and providing opportunities for customer spending	Minimising delays, crowding and queuing
Safety and security of customers and staff	Safety and security of customers

Source: Adapted from J. Swarbrooke, *The Development and Management of Visitor Attractions,* 2nd ed., Butterworths-Heinemann, Oxford, 2002, p. 290.

- gaining an understanding of the customer and deciding appropriate service delivery systems and levels;
- ensuring that issues of productivity and quality improvements are closely monitored and controlled;
- evaluating the organisation's core capabilities and competencies in relation to the business's strategic management direction;
- monitoring cost and inventory control issues; and
- tracking increasing global competition.

In addition, the issue of response time is assuming greater importance along with team development. This is particularly the case in high service customer interaction zones within high service delivery organisations. Table 6.1 provides some interesting examples of services operations management being viewed from often quite different perspectives by the various stakeholders involved. While this set of examples is by no means comprehensive, it does illustrate the constant dilemma of the operations manager, who often not only has to manage their own conflicting objectives, but in addition must manage the possible conflict between their business and their customers' objectives. The basis of many of these conflicts comes in the decisions to be made between quality and costs tradeoffs, and the subsequent outcomes from these decisions from an operations perspective (Swarbrooke, 2002).

Operations management is often thought of in the context of large organisations involving many business units and linked with a number of locations, and the processing of large volumes of goods or customers. However, changes in the role of operations managers are not limited to large organisations; small and medium enterprises also 'are faced with a number of challenges if they wish to gain competitive benefit from their production/operations function' (Sohal et al., 2001, p. 437).

The significance of operations management

The essential reason why the study of operations management in services is important is because it is one of the four main functions (marketing, finance, operations, HR management) of any organisation, whether it be a primary-, secondary- or tertiary-sector industry. Organisations need to know how the various goods and services they are involved with are produced and delivered; and how the various processes, tools and activities for operations need to be established; and to recognise that operations management is a costly part of every organisation, constituting up to 54 per cent of its costs (Heizer and Render, 2004).

Waller (2003, p. 5) supports the logic of an integrated and holistic approach to business functions in the study of operations management based on the following:

- Operations must also work within the external environmental context, such as working within political systems, economic environments, and technology and social contexts. Another important consideration for the sustainability of any organisation is the ecological business environment (see Chapter 2).
- Particularly in the services, where operations often involve a range of participation by customers, the various stakeholders' interests need to be acknowledged (see Chapter 3).
- Operations are derived from the strategy of the organisation; thus, there is a need for the organisation's strategic management and operations management to be connected (see Chapter 4).
- Marketing provides the links to products and services produced or delivered by operations that must satisfy customer needs (see Chapter 5).
- Costs need to be controlled in operations, and as investment is required in all operations for such items as plant, equipment, buildings, and information and communication (ICT) systems, financial accounting is important (see Chapter 7).
- HR management provides the link for the provision of appropriately skilled, productive, motivated staffing (see Chapter 8).

Operations management in the service sector

In economic terms, services are currently the largest economic sector in developed economies (see Chapter 1); a similar trend is emerging in some developing nations. Hence, it is necessary to briefly review the different attributes that services and goods exhibit, so as to understand the associated changing role of operations management. This review enables the operations manager to understand how operations processes and functions can become more integrated with other management functions when working in a services operations context. It also provides a basis for increased efficiency when adopting this approach.

The key difference between services and manufacturing, from an operations management perspective, is that there is no real transformation of physical material in the former's operations system. Some of the processes that occur in services include: information or knowledge transformation, the distribution of information, financial activities, the movement or transportation of goods and people, and the generation of experience. Thus organisations

Table 6.2 Attributes of services and goods

Attributes of services	Attributes of goods
A process, an activity, information or knowledge	A physical product
Intangible	Tangible
Includes extensive contact with customer	Requires minimal or no contact with customer
Simultaneous production/delivery and consumption	Separation of production, delivery and consumption
Customers participate in production/delivery	
Immediate consumption	Delayed consumption
Labour-intensive production	Equipment-intensive production
Service is often difficult to automate	Automation or production is easy
Heterogeneous	Homogeneous
Often unique	Often mass production
Difficult to be inventoried	Product can be inventoried
Provider, not product, is often transportable	Product is transportable
Site of facility is important for customer contact	Site of facility is important for cost
Reselling a service is unusual	Product can be resold
Quality is difficult to measure	Quality is easily measured
Productivity is difficult to measure	Productivity is easily measured
Revenue is generated primarily from the intangible services	Revenue is generated primarily from the tangible product

Sources: Adapted from J. Heizer and B. Render, *Principles of Operations Management*, 5th ed., Pearson/Prentice Hall, Upper Saddle River, NJ, 2004, p. 10; J. Meredith and S. Shafer, *Operations Management for MBAs*, John Wiley & Sons, Danvers, MA, 2002 p. 8; and S. Desmet, B. Van Looy and R. Van Dierdonck, 'The nature of services', in B. Van Looy, P. Gemmel and R. Van Dierdonck (eds), *Services Management: An integrated approach*, Prentice Hall, Harlow, UK, 2003, p. 11.

with a high number of services include operations management – for example, emergency services, such as fire or health departments; transportation services, such as air charters for oil riggers or school buses for remotely located students; information services, such as postal or telecommunications; education services, such as virtual universities; not-for-profit organisations, such as art galleries or museums; and community service organisations, such as welfare groups or religious groups. Table 6.2 summarises the differing attributes of services and goods.

Chapter 1 explained that many organisations now provide products that are a combination of both physical goods and intangible services. Thus, in this case the operations manager is not only dealing with the transformation process on the shop floor, but integrating these across the functional areas of the entire organisation. The dispersal of activities across traditional functional areas can be seen to change when considering a range of organisational charts that depict the differing levels of manufactured products and services delivery systems involved. While activities in traditional production industries can be clearly grouped to fit into functional areas, such as operations or finance, activities within each of these functional areas are becoming less able to fit into a single area when dealing with services and are becoming more integrated across traditional functional boundaries. Scheduling activities

Table 6.3 Classification of the economic offerings of the four business sectors

Economic offering	Commodities	Goods	Services	Experiences
Economy	Agrarian	Industrial	Service	Experience
Value added by	Extracting	Producing	Delivering	Staging
Form of output	Fungible	Tangible	Intangible	Memorable
Key attribute	Natural	Standardised	Customised	Personalised
Method of supply	Stored in bulk	Inventoried after production	Delivered on demand	Revealed over a duration
Seller	Trader	Manufacturer	Provider	Stager
Buyer	Market	User	Client	Guest
Features of demand	Characteristics	Features	Benefits	Sensations

Source: Adapted from B. J. Pine II and J. Gilmore, *The Experience Economy: Work is theatre & every business is a stage,* Harvard Business School Press, Boston, 1999, p. 6.

could be grouped under the operations functional area in a clothes dryer manufacturing company; however, in a pharmaceutical company some scheduling activities could be grouped in operations and some in marketing. Due to these changes in operations, many organisations have developed new organisation structures based on business processes, as opposed to traditional functional areas.

It is interesting to notice the significantly shifting emphasis between the various functional areas and the changing roles and activities of operations management in the various examples used throughout this chapter. This is important to remember when considering that operations management is a value-adding process involved with efficiency outcomes. In *The Experience Economy,* Pine and Gilmore (1999) propose a quaternary sector of industries defined as being organisations that produce 'experiences'. The four sectors are differentiated by a classification of their economic offerings. Clearly distinct characteristics in the four sectors are identifiable across the following dimensions of the economic offering: the economy type, the value added, the form of output, the key attributes, the methods of supply, the seller, the buyer, and the features of demand. It is apparent that these ideas have significant implications for operational management theory and practice. They are summarised in Table 6.3.

When looking at the operations activities of organisations classified according to the four business sectors presented in Table 6.3, it can be seen that most are involved to some extent in service operations. The degree to which service operations involvement occurs increases as one moves across the table, depending on the combination of product/service offerings.

Significant events in operations management

The developments in the area of operations management can be divided into three significant eras, each with a number of events that define its significance (Heizer and Render, 2004). The initial focus of operations management was the investigation into labour specialisation and the standardisation of parts. This initial focus was followed by the scientific management era (see Chapter 1) where time and motion studies produced outputs such as Gantt charts, process analysis and queuing theory. The turn of the 20th century witnessed the development of mass production with a moving assembly line. Together these three eras resulted in an overall focus described as the *Cost Focus Era* (1776–1980). More recently, the *Quality Era* (1980–95) emerged, with post-Second World War productivity and quality issues playing important roles in the evolving operations management focus in which many internal organisational changes were sought and implemented. The third stage of development, *Customisation Focus* (1995–2005), derives from the dramatic changes instigated by the external environment that include globalisation, the Internet, International Quality Standards, and the increased realisation of the need for, and the implementation of, supply chain management aided by rapid changes in technologies.

The impact of these various factors has been discussed in Chapters 2, 3, 4 and 5. Each of these management eras is represented in Table 6.4, which briefly indicates their legacy to operations management along with the key contributors to its current body of knowledge. Drawing on this evolving conceptual legacy, the key focus of service operations management is to identify the cross-functional efficiencies (HR, finance, marketing, operations) when transforming a bundle of complex inputs (both tangible and intangible) into either a valuable or value-added output. These outputs can be tangible or intangible, or a combination of both. This more complex approach to the services production process is usually referred to as a 'systems approach'.

The 'production' system

This section describes key production concepts currently associated with cross-functional operations management activities in relation to other functional areas – in particular, in relation to efficiency (Figure 6.2). Using a systems approach, these include the ideas of inputs, the transformation systems, outputs, and monitoring and control within a given external business environment and internal organisation context. Bundles of *inputs* used in a production system can be complex, and typically involve inputs from a number of functional areas within the organisation, including marketing, finance, engineering and human resources. Some typical examples of inputs include facilities, labour, capital, equipment, raw materials, supplies, knowledge and time. Raw materials and supplies are both listed as inputs, with the difference between them being that raw materials are used in the process, whereas supplies are usually used to denote those inputs required to aid the process, but which are not a part of the final good or service being delivered. A raw material input could be the utilities, such as electricity and water, and knowledge required by the dentist to provide an examination; while the supplies could be the instruments, such as drills, used in the examination process.

Another important input in many services is knowledge, or information. This is an interesting input, as it can be used and re-used as many times as is appropriate until it is no longer relevant and needs to be updated. Information is therefore an increasingly valued intangible input that does not become depleted, and can be used in many locations at the same time in the service operations management system. Additional to these organisationally controlled inputs are the inputs from the external environment, such as economic or political considerations. The significant challenge to services provision is when another external factor – that of 'the customer' – becomes a significant input into the system creating the situation of

Table 6.4 Significant events in operations management

Cost focus	Quality focus	Customisation focus
Early concepts, 1776–1880 Labour specialisation (Smith, 1776; Babbage, 1852) Standardised parts (Whitney, 1880)	**Lean production era, 1980–95** Baldrige quality awards (Baldrige, 1980) Just-in-time Electronic data interchange Total quality management	**Mass customisation era, 1995–2005** Globalisation (1992) Internet (1995) Enterprise resource planning Learning organisation
Scientific management era, 1880–1910 Time and motion studies (Frank & Lillian Gilbreth, 1922) Process analysis Queuing theory	Empowerment Kanbans Computer integrated manufacturing (1990)	International quality standards Finite scheduling Supply chain management Agile manufacturing
Mass production era, 1910–80 Coordinated assembly line (Ford/Sorenson/Avery, 1913) Gantt charts (Gantt, 1916) Quality control (Shewhart, 1924; Deming, 1950) Computer (Atanasoff, 1938) CPM/PERT (DuPont, 1957) Materials requirements planning (Orlicky, 1960) Computer aided design (CAD) (1970) Flexible manufacturing system (FMS) (1975) Statistical sampling Economic order Linear programming PERT/CPM		

Source: Adapted from J. Heizer and B. Render, *Principles of Operations Management*, 5th ed., Pearson/Prentice Hall, Upper Saddle River, NJ, 2004, p. 8.

simultaneity, a distinguishing characteristic of services. This is the situation when the customer or client becomes involved in the production or consumption of services in real time; this situation presents a real challenge to operations management.

The *transformation system* is the part of the system that adds value to the inputs. This can be done by applying a number of techniques such as collating, processing, transporting, storing or inspecting. Courier services are an example of transportation companies that have shown rapid growth over the last few decades. These services can be provided in the form of cyclists delivering documents around CBD areas of large cities, or in the form of daily delivering of fresh produce, whether garden vegetables from local growers to local restaurants or fresh, live yabbies from outback Australia to restaurant tables in Paris, or the much-cited

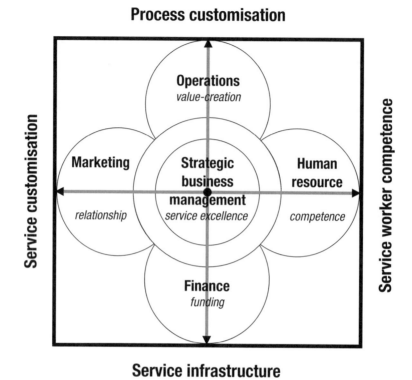

Figure 6.2 The functional services management (FSM) matrix

example of the FedEx company global courier network. Other examples of transformational value-adding services include the slicing and dicing of raw vegetables for making a salad, the processing of credit card applications, or the inspections undertaken by quality assurance service organisations when businesses undertake a quality assurance accreditation.

Transformation systems have to operate within the constraints or limitations imposed by the external environment, such as government regulations or political situations. Again, depending on the nature and strategic choice of the business, the customer can be a key component of the transformation system. A group of visitors to a zoo can watch feeding performances all day beyond the boundaries of the enclosures, or at certain planned times the zoo keepers may invite visitors to go into the enclosures and become involved in the feeding of the animals. The involvement of the customer may be a permanent part of the organisation's operations, or it may be temporal according to the type of operations the business has developed from their strategic plans regarding customer involvement.

According to Pine and Gilmore's model (1999), there are four types of economic outputs from a system. These are usually referred to as commodities, goods, services or experiences. While this may be an appropriate classification for economic purposes, from an operations management perspective it is becoming increasingly difficult to distinguish businesses' outputs as 'goods or services' and 'services or experiences' in this simple way. Thus the classification of outputs may depend on the degree of the product/service/experience combination offered to the customer by the organisation. In addition, this classification may not be strictly the same every time the output is considered. For example, it may also change according to the differing levels of customer interaction or involvement in the delivery of the output or final product/service/experience. If a customer has to re-fuel their car by placing the petrol in the car themselves, as opposed to having a service attendant fill it with petrol, then the customer may not consider the business a service provider and just consider the fuel as the product. However, from a management planning perspective, the organisation is a service organisation; it has just decided that as part of the service operations strategy, the customer will be part of the service operations delivery and output. Outputs involving services may include a document such as a passport/visa delivery to a consulate, an airline flight, a medical examination, an insurance policy being completed, a police sergeant providing a driver's licence examination, or a student graduating with a degree. The results of many of these services are often in the form of 'memorable experiences'.

Monitoring and control are the processes involved where the activities and components of the system are examined to see if they are carried out according to plan, and to recognise when significant changes occur in the various stages of the production process. If changes are observed, it is then the responsibility of the operations manager to decide if the changes to the planned outcomes are significant and thus require attention, or if they are within expected limitations and thus require no further attention. If the changes are significant, then either the inputs or the transformation system may be altered, or a combination of actions applied to both may be required to maintain acceptable quality and productivity parameters. *Control* is the ability to change a system when required – that is, to amend, or correct, the differences in the system's expectations, as opposed to its actual workings. Inspections undertaken by customs and immigration officials monitor visitors to a country to check that immigration regulations are being followed by the arriving passengers. If, for example, one of the customs regulations prohibits the import of food products, and a food article is found in the luggage of a passenger, then the control process must be implemented whereby the law must be put into action, which in this case may result in a legal prosecution.

A challenge for the services operation manager is a requirement to monitor the transformation process and output concurrently due to the characteristics of simultaneity in services. Also, external environmental attributes, such as weather, economics or political controls, may occur while the service process is in progress, and so the manager must deal with the concurrency of these situations in order to maintain quality and efficiency of services. An example may be that a country bids to stage an international games event three or four years in advance. It then markets the games according to expected pricing from financial and marketing decisions. Shortly before the games are ready to be staged, the world currencies may change dramatically, or terrorist attacks may occur. This, in turn, would have significant flow-on effects.

These events will inevitably influence visitors' decisions to attend, thus impacting on the expected number of visitors to the games and, subsequently, the projected revenue expected to be generated from the event. Thus the operations manager would be working very closely with the marketing manager, financial manager and HR manager to deal with the situation in order to achieve the best possible outcomes for the organisation and the stakeholders involved. One of the key variables to manage cross-functionally in services is pricing. While many goods can be priced once they have been manufactured, many services are priced *before*

Table 6.5 Four industry examples of the systems approach to operations

Inputs	Transformation	Outputs	Monitor/Control	Environment
Primary sector: Mining				
Machinery	Transportation	Minerals	Weather	Transportation
Plans	Alteration	Gas	Production	networks
Facilities	Extraction	Petroleum	volumes	PEST
Utilities	Design			
Secondary sector: Manufacturer				
Materials	Cut	Machines	Material flows	Economy
Equipment	Join	Consumer	Production	Commodity prices
Labour	Form	goods	volumes	Consumer market
Technology		Chemicals		
Tertiary sector: Education				
Student	Study	Marks	Demographics	Tax system
Attitude	Read	Knowledge	Parents	Program
Money	Go to class	Attitudes	Money	availability
Time	Examine	A4 sheet of	Time	Costs
IQ/EQ		paper		
Quaternary sector: Wine festival				
Wineries	Staging	Experience	Location	PEST
Event	Participation	Wine	Timing	environment
management		consump-	Cost	
Visitors		tion	Status	

they go to market, making variation in price difficult to operationalise by both operation and marketing managers. Table 6.5 presents examples of various primary, secondary, tertiary and quaternary industry production systems.

Key areas in services operations management

Many of the processes and activities encompassed in the area of service operations are integrated in real life and cannot really be separated. However, in order to study these, it is easier to group similar activities and processes together under a number of headings in order to build knowledge of the overall complex and interdependent aspects of the discipline of service operations management. Hence, to promote understanding of the various activities in each of the key topic areas in services operations management, the topic discussions have been grouped under 12 key headings:

1 Developing a services business and global strategy
2 Service and product design
3 Quality management

4 Location and site planning
5 Layout planning
6 Human resources management
7 Supply-chain management
8 Inventory and capacity management
9 Schedule management
10 Project management
11 Maintenance
12 Managing innovation in service operations

Depending on the nature of the business and the type of organisation and industry sector, the relationship, autonomy and emphasis of each of these topic areas in operations management can vary greatly.

Developing a services business and global strategy

When describing a business and its services, it is assumed that there is a particular reason, or purpose, for that business to provide that service. The goal may be, for example, to provide an upmarket 'wellness' program for women in the local community, or to provide a reading program for special needs students. These goals imply awareness of marketing and financial considerations – that is, they indicate what services and/or goods these defined markets want (wellness program, or reading program), and where they are aimed at in the marketplace (women, or special needs students) and imply the monetary value to which they are pitched (upmarket cost, or student cost). The HR needs are also implicated in the skill, or ability, required in providing these services at the operational level, or the point of service delivery. However, without the organisation being able to operationalise these goals – that is, to actually deliver these services from available resources with an appropriate transformation process – then there will be no business. It is necessary, therefore, to gather information from selected research and development teams to establish an organisation's business strategy and then determine the critical operations tasks required to support the organisation's overall stated mission and objectives.

Thus, a firm's business strategy provides the information and actions required to design the processes, actions and activities for the organisation to achieve its specific goals. Depending on the structure of the organisation, the type of business strategies may vary. For instance, if the organisation's business units are structured in a functional way, a marketing strategy, an operations strategy, a finance strategy and an HR strategy may be developed to support the overall business strategy. However, if the organisation is designed on a matrix structure of business units based on processes, then instead a strategy for how each business process unit supports the overall business strategy could be developed (Meredith and Schafer, 2002). A golf club may have the golf course, the members' club facilities in the form of clubhouse, food and beverage areas, and additional recreation areas. At certain low usage times the club may hire out the food and beverage areas to the public for functions. Thus, the organisation could have an overall business strategy for the club, and then a business strategy for the members' facilities, the golfing facilities and the functions area. These operations strategies could be developed on the basis of the specific specialised requirements for the processes of each of the different areas, rather than the traditional functional area requirements of a business.

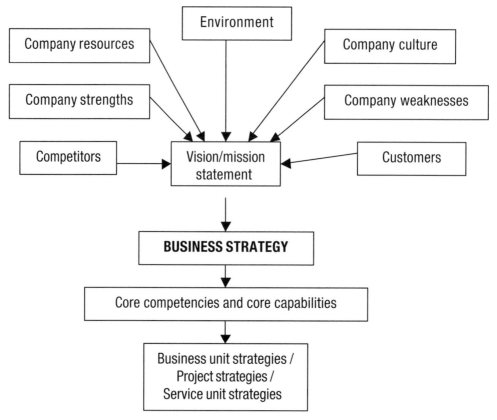

Figure 6.3 Strategy formulation

Source: Adapted from J. Meredith and S. Schafer, *Operations Management for MBAs*, 2nd ed., John Wiley & Sons, Danvers, MA, 2002, p. 24

The key *inputs* to the *strategic planning process* are the goods and services needed by the customers; the strengths and weaknesses of the competition; the environment in general; and the organisation's own strengths, weaknesses, culture and resources (see Figure 6.3).

Chapter 4 discusses business strategy in detail. This section indicates how business strategy is then translated to the area of services operations management. One of the key areas of business strategy is dealing with global competitiveness and the crucial role of operations in achieving this. Examples of these activities include factors such as: the efficiency and effectiveness of domestic production in comparison to outsourcing; the appropriate locations of international facilities; the output capacities needed by various plants; and the labour–machinery tradeoffs in each facility (Meredith and Schafer, 2002). As an additional example in developing economies, when investigating the establishment of a service sector business there may be a surplus of low-cost labour and a high cost of capital to purchase equipment, indicating that the transformation system should be designed to be more labour-intensive than in a developed nation operational context. For example, a company setting-up 'eco-lodges' in remote African regions may find that outsourcing the laundry services to local labour pools may be more appropriate than operating expensive machinery and maintenance schedules. This strategy may embed the operation more effectively into the local economy, making a better contribution to goodwill through the promotion of local social and economic development along with the potential to improve local environmental practice and, hence, creating a more stable environment for a sustainable system of operations.

Meredith and Schafer (2002, p. 46) describe six critical characteristics of the transformation system when considering operations and global competitiveness. These are:

1 *Efficiency:* Usually measured as output per unit of input. The key challenge is to choose relevant measures for both inputs and outputs. This is a challenge when managing intangible components of services.
2 *Effectiveness:* This is making sure that the right set of outputs is being produced, while focusing on the right tasks. This is a challenge when customers' expectations and perceptions are involved in determining the 'right' outputs of services.
3 *Capacity:* Specifies the maximum rate of production for products, or the amount of services that can be sold at a given point in time. Capacity is closely related to efficiency, and is a difficult challenge in services due to the finite capacity and perishability of services.
4 *Quality:* The required time and level of service specified in the business strategy must be upheld. The challenge in services is to identify, maintain and measure quality.
5 *Response time:* This refers to how quickly an output can be produced. It is a challenge due to simultaneity in services, technology and globalisation.
6 *Flexibility:* This refers to how easily and quickly the degree of change required for a transformation produces other, different outputs. It includes the degree of variety and customisation. The challenge is to standardise service for quality and efficiency, while at the same time wanting to customise service for all stakeholders.

Service and product design

An organisation's strategic plan provides direction for achieving its goals. Within this context, it then guides the determination of the actual services the organisation will offer. As has been previously discussed, many organisations provide both services and goods; therefore, their interrelated production and delivery processes must be designed to meet consumer needs and exceed expectations. More particularly, the organisation needs to determine the design of the services and goods so as to efficiently and effectively operationalise the production and delivery of the goods and services.

Designing goods and services is usually considered as being a three-stage business process. Stage one involves the research for new services and/or goods; stage two is the design and development of the chosen services/goods; and stage three is the design of the transformation system required to produce or deliver them. While this three-stage process is clearly seen as a formal process when undertaken by manufacturing or product firms, it is often seen as a less formal process when undertaken in service-oriented businesses. However, it is of equal importance for the process to be undertaken by *all* organisations when considering new services or goods.

Stage one of the product/service selection and design process is the research process required before the design of the good or service takes place. At this stage the critical importance of stakeholders must be acknowledged. Chapter 3 indicated why stakeholder research must include those external to the organisation, such as the customers, and those internal to the organisation, such as marketing and financial areas, particularly due to the integrated nature of functional areas in operations management.

The ISM model (see Figure 6.1) illustrates the overlapping nature of the interrelationships between the functional areas during this stage of service design, and this book emphasises the critical value of integration, especially at this early stage of the goods and services production design. New service and product ideas can be derived from a range of stakeholders. These can include ideas generated from past, or potential, customers through direct feedback or market research, internal organisational R&D departments, and partners along the supply chain or competitors. Once ideas are generated, a screening and selection process must take place (Meredith and Schafer, 2002). This includes market analysis, forecasting of customers' needs, assessments of competitor reactions, and analysis of economic viability, technical feasibility studies and checklists for organisational fit. Upon selection of the idea, it will then move to the design stage.

At *stage two* a number of major questions need to be answered before a prototype, or simulated service process, can be developed. Some of these questions are required to determine the physical materials the good may be constructed from, the amount of human process delivery required versus the amount of automation used, aesthetic considerations versus functionality, quality versus cost tradeoffs, the amount of customer participation versus staff delivery of service, and the location of service delivery elements in the customer interaction zone or the customer-free zone of the organisation.

Once these design criteria have been determined, a prototype can be developed. This can be a physical good, or it may be a service delivery system. At this stage of the design of the production process the various aspects of efficiency and effectiveness of the service can be monitored, amended, simplified and tested according to various permutations of characteristics of the service or good. The results of the testing of the prototype or service simulations will inform the final design, which will be documented through specifications, drawings, costings, policies and procedures.

Stage three encompasses the transformation system design. At this stage the production system is designed to enable a new good to be produced, or a new service delivered, according to the requirements of stage two. This stage should not be left to the end of stage two. Moreover, the organisation capabilities and competencies in this stage should be simultaneously considered with stage two of the goods and services design. This interrelated approach reinforces the concept of cyclical (or concurrent) engineering as opposed to linear processing. Many reasons for adopting this cyclical approach include:

- the current increase in a process orientation of organisations in preference to a functions orientation;
- the increased use of teams instead of traditional linear and hierarchical organisation structures;
- the decreased time organisations have to get their goods and services to market;
- the benefits of increased quality controls throughout the design process;
- the ability to design-in the components of overlap developmental stages, as opposed to developing whole products and services; and
- the employment of new technologies at various stages when required and the outsourcing of various stages for external expertise. (Meredith and Schafer, 2002)

Box 6.1 presents an example of a product and services review by airlines to highlight a push factor – the internal need for change – and the implications in the areas of operations.

Box 6.1   Airlines check out DIY check-ins to reduce costs

The airline industry had been forecast to post a profit this year for the first time in four. Revenue has been on the rise as passenger numbers recover from the devastating effects of the September 11 terrorist attacks, the Iraq war and the outbreak of severe acute respiratory syndrome in Asia.

But as quickly as one crisis subsided, another appeared to push many carriers back into the red. Mr Bisignani, IATA (International Air Transport Association) chief executive, said that airlines had to remain focused on stripping out costs – a process already well under way in the Asia-Pacific region.

Qantas is in the middle of a $1.5 billion cost-cutting drive implemented in response to the low-cost Virgin Blue and the volatile international airline market. Across the Tasman, Air New Zealand has rescued itself from the brink of collapse through a radical overhaul of its domestic operations, which includes removing business class and meals, adding more seats and cutting cabin crew numbers.

So strong is this relentless drive to cut costs that many executives at IATA's annual general meeting held [in 2004] in Singapore heralded the end of the budget airline, believing it will become the norm rather than the exception. Low-cost carriers have caused a shake-out in the global aviation industry, stripping customers from the flagship carriers by offering cheap tickets with no added extras. But now it's the likes of Ryanair and easyJet that are facing a profit crunch as full-service carriers return to the game with a cheaper cost base – or at least a better product. In Australia, Qantas has launched its own low-cost airline, Jetstar. Many believe it will become Qantas's main domestic airline within the next few years, circumventing many of the union cost-related issues with the main carrier.

(*Source:* T. Harcourt, 'Airlines check out DIY check-ins to reduce costs', *The Weekend Australian*, 12–14 June 2004, p. 11)

Quality management

Quality is an area which operations continually strive to improve. Several chapters in this book have discussed various aspects of the importance of quality within services. One of the challenges in quality management in services is due to the diverse range of stakeholders involved in the entire services supply chain and the variability in the external environment within which the service operation activities are taking place. The resultant measure of quality is thus represented by the cumulative quality from the supply chain stakeholders, the variability of the environment when the operations are being undertaken, and simultaneity, or the involvement of the customers in the operations processes. For example, the freshness of the fish from a quality fishery (the physical product), the timely delivery of the seafood to the chef (the transforming component), and the service skills of the wait staff (service quality aspects) will all impact on the quality rating of a seafood cafe. Additionally, the experience the diners have will also impact on the overall quality rating – for example, if the people seated at a nearby table are loud and raucous, the dining experience will not necessarily be a quality experience and will influence the overall quality rating. While in manufacturing businesses many quality attributes and variables are easy to control, both the quality attributes and variables in service operations are much more difficult to identify and control due to the issues of variability, supply chain issues, simultaneity and customer involvement. Therefore, the challenge is to determine who is responsible for quality within the service organisation's supply chain, as well as how the service organisation defines or determines their key quality attributes when considering the intangibility of the 'service/good' it is delivering and the level of customer involvement, which may influence service quality.

Quality has been a focus in manufacturing operations management since the 1950s; hence, there is a large body of research and theoretical knowledge developed based on manufacturing industries (Sohal, 1995). While many of the fundamental issues of quality can be assigned across industries, there is a need for research relating to services. However, due to this imbalance towards manufacturing in the research, the implementation and measurement of quality in services deserves much greater attention by researchers. The increasing contribution of services to gross national employment indicates the scale of the need for research into quality issues within the services sector (Beaumont and Sohal, 1999).

There are many approaches to managing and measuring quality. The focus on quality really became visible in operations management when the Japanese invited W. Edwards Deming to lecture on quality and then subsequently developed Deming's 14-points strategy. This was followed by J. M. Juran's three tenets of quality, focusing on quality planning, quality control and quality improvement. Juran differed from Deming primarily in his increased focus on the customer and quality, in terms of its appropriateness for use, not just its adherence to the written specifications. Other methods and approaches to quality were developed in the United States and Japan with often similar objectives and differing names. *Kaizen* is the Japanese word used to describe the continuous process of unending improvement, similar to TQM and zero defects, terms used in the United States to describe the continuous approach to managing quality. Six sigma is also a term used to denote very high achievement and continuous quality improvement. Operations managers are a key ingredient in quality management as the facilitator for the organisation and the nexus between the senior levels of management and the functional levels in the provision of facilities and culture that supports, and thus enables, achievement of the quality goals. Increased employee involvement in quality management has seen the development of such approaches as 'quality circles'. Most of these former studies and approaches were focused in manufacturing.

While many organisations recognise the importance of quality, the *world* also recognises its importance. The International Organization for Standardization (ISO) 9000 quality assurance standards were developed by 91 member nations in 1987, and are the only quality standards with international recognition. The ISO 9000 standards were revised in 2000. ISO 14000 accreditation is more recent. It is an environmental management standard which focuses on environmental business practices such as environmental management, auditing, performance evaluation, labelling and life-cycle assessment of an organisation (Heizer and

Render, 2004). With the inclusion of both economic and environmental goals in quality, some organisations are moving to sustainable approaches to management requiring the addition of a social element to complete the triple bottom-line equation.

The implications of quality strategy operate at a number of levels. It is important for the individual service to be recognised as attaining a particular level of quality, as the reputation of the organisation then develops and becomes known for the delivery of quality services. Thus the sector can collectively become identified as producing quality services within a destination or region, and hence have implications for national economies. As the global economy is more and more reliant on revenue generation from services, the significance of quality for organisations and countries becomes paramount in the execution of operations management strategies. Due to the importance and value that organisations and industry sectors place on quality, a number of awards have been developed. These include well-known awards such as the European Quality Award, the Deming Award (usually used in Japan), and the Malcolm Baldrige National Quality Award (see www.quality.nist.gov) established in the United States.

SERVQUAL (Parasuraman et al., 1988), while receiving much discussion and criticism, 'remains the most commonly used diagnostic model for evaluating service quality and the development of service quality strategies' (Soutar, 2001, p. 103). The basic premise of the SERVQUAL model is that it adheres to the assumption that quality is not a finite measure; it is the gap that results from customers' expectations and their end measure of the service performance. Thus, quality is measured external to the operations of the business, a shift from the internal quality measurement focus of manufacturing. Thus, a definite need is presented for further research in this area of quality and services.

This presents the challenge to somehow broaden the scope of quality measurement in service organisations to allow the quality performance measure to encompass a more complete quality evaluation to be undertaken according to all stakeholders' measures of quality – that is, not just end users such as the customers, but also other stakeholders such as the organisation itself. The enormity of this challenge arises from many of the inherent characteristics of services, such as the simultaneity of the production and consumption of services, the involvement of various stakeholders such as the customer in the production and delivery of services, and the issues of homogeneity and heterogeneity within the services. While a full-service French restaurant may be able to determine the quality of its food because it has total control over the production and service delivery of the meal, a Korean barbecue restaurant would find quality far more difficult to measure as the customers choose the combination of ingredients and then cook their own food at their tables. Thus, if unique service characteristics can be defined, relative quality issues can then be ascertained. Following this step, instruments can then be developed to measure and monitor these significant attributes and thus provide firms with valuable information for strategic decision making.

Location and site planning

Location planning and/or site selection is required when an organisation plans to commence operations in a new area or at a new site. In addition, location planning may derive from the need to expand current operations, and involve the purchase of an existing premises and detailing it to suit the specific needs of an organisation according to its services/goods provision requirements. These decisions are instigated by growth in the business of the organisation, an increase in its customer base, or possibly by technological changes that require location changes.

Hence, it is apparent that there is a diverse range of factors required for consideration when selecting a business location. These can include: construction feasibility; environmental conditions; political and economic stability in relation to the needs, capabilities and time-frames for the organisation's operations; local conditions, such as taxation; building regulations; financial considerations; proximity to and quality of stakeholders in the supply chain, such as suppliers; outsourcing availability; staffing; customers; availability of utilities and raw resources; and appropriate transportation services (Heizer and Render, 2004). One of the key considerations in services' location decisions is the relative importance of the location of the customer and the location of the business.

Location planning decisions have long-term implications for business operations. Thus, they are considered as strategic decisions usually conducted at the level of senior management. However, operations managers are often included in the decision making, as they will be responsible for the operations, once the services are established. The ISM model provides a multifunctional approach on which the organisation needs to base decision making for location planning. The complexities involved in the site location process highlight the need for cross-functional decision making, which links the strengths and goals of the inner circle of business strategy with the opportunities and the risks of the outer circle of the external business environments. Thus, it is critical that the operations management team considers the context of the environment within which the site will be located; the organisational needs for the physical premises as determined by both the needs for labour, and customers; and the specific needs of customers within the characteristics of services operations. An evaluation of these issues enables the operations management team to develop the appropriate criteria to determine an optimum site selection based upon their cross-functional investigations.

In manufacturing industries, traditionally, key decisions included how large the required facility should be (that is, the physical space requirements for the operations), and how the facility should be arranged according to production requirements. However, in services, the nature of facilities management – in particular, how facilities management decisions influence the customer – highlights that operations management is not made up of purely technical or even operational decisions, but must involve HRM and marketing decisions as well. Table 6.6 indicates the shift in focus associated with decisions concerning the facilities and layout design associated with goods and services organisations.

Some of the key characteristics of services, such as simultaneity between production and consumption, represent important considerations for operations and facilities management. The customer is often present in the 'service factory' and participates in the service delivery process. This means that decisions regarding location of the business, the physical setting, and ambient decisions must include explicit and implicit customer needs and expectations. Facilities also indirectly affect customer perceptions of convenience, accessibility and functionality, all key features that contribute to the competitive advantages of many service organisations. The intangibility aspect of a service 'product' is compounded through specific experience/ credence attributes, and in the customer's evaluation of quality. Therefore, in

Table 6.6 Organisational focus shift in location planning decision making

Manufacturing environment	Services environment
Location planning/ *Facilities management*	*Location planning/* *Facilities management*
◑	**◑**
Plant location	Organisational structuring
Process choice/design	Marketing
Automation	Organisational behaviour
Process layout	Product/service/experience development
Activities and tasks design	Operations management
	Staff involvement
	Customer involvement
	Other stakeholder involvement
	Financial capabilities in relation to relative goals of quality standards
Domain	**Domain**
Production management/ Operations management	HRM/Marketing/Operations management/Finance management

services, the additional crucial element of customer perceptions must be added into location decisions and facility management decisions.

Thus, the goals of operations in facilities management include: controlling costs; improving efficiency by ensuring the proximity of operationally related tasks in layout decisions; achieving economies of scale or logistics in location decisions; and enhancing safety, security, environmental impacts and standardisation in work design locations. Without the inclusion of the customer as a key focus in an organisation's location and layout planning, the result is often a very confused customer who is unnecessarily shunted around the premises, who ends up finding the facilities unattractive and inconvenient, which often results in them finding employees unresponsive to their individual customer needs (Van Dierdonck, 2003, p. 320).

Students have to wait for a significant length of time at the enrolments counter at their institution of study. When they finally reach the front of the queue, they may be given a form that required the signature of a lecturer, whose office was located in a building on the other side of campus. After the lecturer is tracked down the form has to be taken to the course controller in the faculty located in an adjacent building. If the form wasn't completed accurately or another unit needed to be added to the study plan, the student may have had to complete this circuit again. The challenge of the operations manager in services is thus to recognise the customers' needs within the operations and physical layout of the organisation as they, the customer, become part of the organisation's operations. Former Scandinavian Airlines CEO Jan Carlzon (1989) succinctly illustrated this concept in his much quoted 'We fly people, not airplanes.'

Many site-planning decisions in services are based on achieving a balance between a range of factors that influence general choice and site selection. Depending on the nature of the organisation and the contact levels required between the various stakeholders up and

Table 6.7 Factors influencing the general area location planning decisions of a range of service firms

	General area decisions	
Factors (ranked in order of importance)	*Services for which higher-than-average influence*	*Services for which lower-than-average influence*
Good infrastructure	Transportation – warehousing, wholesaling	Education – social
Proximity to consumers and buyers	Auto-sales service Banking Hospitals Retailing Wholesaling	Education – social Professional service Utilities
Ability to attract good labour	Hospitals Personal-business services	Retailing Utilities
Attractive place to live	Personal-business services	
Low rents, building costs		Banking Hospitals Utilities
Favourable taxes	Auto-sales service	Banking Education – social Hospitals Personal-business services
Favourable governmental policies	Transportation – warehousing	Personal-business services
Proximity to suppliers and services	Transportation – warehousing	Retailing
Labour costs	Transportation – warehousing, wholesaling	Amusement Personal-business services Utilities
Labour 'climate'	Personal-business services Restaurants Wholesaling	Amusement Utilities
Proximity to competitors	Auto-sales services Banking	Amusement Education – social Personal-business services Utilities
Being near other company facilities		Hospitals Personal-business services

Source: R. W. Schemmer, 'Service firm location decisions: Some mid-western evidence', *International Journal of Service Industry Management*, vol. 5, no. 3, 1994, p. 49.

down the supply chain, senior-level management, in conjunction with operations managers, will consider many of the factors listed in Table 6.7 as being significant to their location planning decisions.

The key challenge for the operations manager is to balance customer service with operational efficiency and employee satisfaction. Thus, decisions relating to site selection are

Table 6.8 Factors influencing particular site location planning decisions of a range of service firms

	Particular site decisions	
Factors (ranked in order of importance)	Services for which higher-than-average influence	Services for which lower-than-average influence
Adequate parking	Restaurant – retailing	Construction Wholesaling
Attractive building	Banking Insurance – real estate	Construction Utilities
Attractive rent cost	Retailing	Banking Construction Hospitals Hotels Utilities
Specialised space needs met here	Transportation – warehousing	Retailing
Easy commute for employees	Professional service	Auto sales-service Education – social Hotels
High customer traffic in area	Auto sales-service Banking Hotels Restaurants Retailing	Construction Professional service Utilities Wholesaling
Easy commute for managers and owners	Professional service	Auto sales-service Education – social Hospitals
Favourable governmental policies (zoning/traffic/etc.)	Restaurants – wholesaling	Professional service
Favourable taxes at site	Auto sales-service Wholesaling	Hospitals Professional service
Proximity to suppliers and services		Utilities
Proximity to competitors	Auto sales-service Banking	Amusement Education – social Personal business service Utilities
Being in fully developed site	Wholesaling	Construction Insurance – real estate Restaurant Utilities

Source: R. W. Schemmer, 'Service firm location decisions: Some mid-western evidence', *International Journal of Service Industry Management*, vol. 5, no. 3, 1994, p. 52.

important from both a strategic as well as an operational perspective. While the operations manager provides detailed information that relates to the organisation's operational needs, Table 6.8 indicates that factors such as human resources and distribution are also important inputs to site planning decisions. Hence, the ISM systemic model (Figure 6.1) provides the organisational framework for interactions between the operations, HRM, marketing and finance managers in order to facilitate good decision making.

Layout planning

The key decision in developing a layout strategy for services organisations is to determine the activities and tasks involving the customer, and hence, the activities to be placed in zones with customer access and those in customer-free zones. Customer-free zones are areas designed to accommodate activities either physically and/or temporally separate from the customer. The customer-access zones are areas where tasks and activities that require explicit customer involvement are performed, or which involve tasks and activities that are part of the strategic advantage of an organisation, and thus are performed in the presence of the customer. These various high/low-contact areas are termed, for example: back-stage or front-stage (McColl-Kennedy, 2003); front-office or back-office (Van Dierdonck, 2003); front- and back-room operations (Haksever et al., 2000); or front-of-house functions versus back-of-house functions (Kandampully, 2002).

Across the range of services organisations, the number and types of activities performed in front of the customer vary according to the nature of the business and the business strategy adopted by the organisation (Grainger and Taylor, 2003). Many characteristics of service providers – such as process design choices, scheduling decisions, seasonality demands, worker skills, quality control, time standards, occupational health and safety issues, and capacity planning – are taken into account in various services stakeholder interactions and directly affect layout decisions (Van Dierdonck, 2003). Moreover, key operational layout decisions based on the determination of customer-free zone activities and customer-access zones also involve input from finance, HR and marketing areas. This need for multiple inputs into decision making emphasises the value of an integrated decision-making approach. Some major physical design variables that require analysis include the size of the customer-access zone relative to the customer-free zone, and the relative number of activities to be performed in direct contact with the customer, in contrast to the number deemed unnecessary for customer involvement. The findings of this analysis are then translated into specific decisions concerning physical space allocations, process design and environment design.

Van Dierdonck (2003, p. 321) has classified service delivery systems on a scale of *high-contact* to *low-contact* systems (see Chapter 1). Some major design considerations in customer/non-customer zones, from a facilities and operations perspective, include:

- locating near resources and/or customers;
- economies of scale through centralisation/decentralisation of activities;
- social and communication skills base/needs of labour force;
- demand fluctuations in relation to production levels; and
- investments in 'visual amenity' of the customer-free zone versus the considered design of a customer-access zone.

An organisation may choose to adopt two different operations strategies within the customer-access and customer-free zones. A strategy of cost leadership in the customer-free zone allows for increased standardisation of processes by minimising uncertainties in operations. It also provides a barrier zone around the core operations areas, thus isolating it from environmental fluctuations. Collectively, these add to the increased production efficacy of the customer-free zone activities. An organisation chooses a differentiation strategy in the customer-access zone to achieve an increase in customer satisfaction through the customisation of delivery and increased interaction with customers. The design of the customer-access zone can critically influence customer expectations, behaviours and satisfaction. If performed well, the customers' perception value, or perception of quality, can also be affected, both during (simultaneity) and after the service process (Van Dierdonck, 2003).

The process design for the efficient operation of the business has significant implications for the design of the physical layout, or setting, for the business. Moreover, because of the inherent characteristics of services, the environment in which they are being delivered becomes an integral part of the service (the product). Thus, in achieving good design, the service provider is not only addressing the 'substantive' needs of the customer, but is also addressing an entire bundle of customer needs and perceptions.

Transaction volume is usually the key determinant in choosing the process type for a manufacturing organisation. Examples of process type range from the specific needs of projects, to job shop, batch production, line production and continuous production. Process types for services can be based on a number of variables, which together produce three constructs that result in three types of services processes. These are professional services, service shops and mass services. A fourth process type, the 'service factory', is similar to mass services, but differs due to the high degree of required capital intensity.

Various specialists, from ergonomists to operation managers, have undertaken research on the overall envelope, or environment, in which the service delivery process takes place. Ergonomics is the study of the relationship, or the interfacing, of all the essential factors required to create a satisfying, productive, safe and secure physical work environment (Quible, 2001). Ergonomics integrates theories from the disciplinary areas of psychology, physiology, sociology and communication. While the concept of ergonomics has been applied widely to employees and the work environment, the inclusion of the customer-access zones into many areas of the operating work environment indicates that a more inclusive design approach is required for services. The term 'servicescape' (Bitner, 1992) is used widely to describe and discuss the physical and psychological design of service layouts or the service delivery environment. The key environmental elements of the servicescape include:

- *Aesthetic or ambient conditions*: such as lighting, colour scheme, air quality, acoustics, music, odour and furnishings.
- *Ergonomic considerations*: such as space utilisation, equipment, fixtures, fittings and furnishings, safety and security provision, vibration, and energy conservation management.
- *Information and interpretation considerations*: such as signage, style and landscaping.

Collectively, these elements generate a perception of the overall servicescape. Both staff and customers have cognitive, emotional and physical responses to the servicescape. Thus the servicescape can contribute to positive and negative behaviours from staff and customers. En masse the servicescape produces social interactions between, and among, customers and employees (Bitner, 1992).

In summary, the servicescape directly affects business results, and hence it is important for the operations management to understand how this complex set of interactions benefits the organisation and ensures that the business strategy is being achieved through good location and layout planning for their services.

Human resource management

HRM is no longer a stand alone functional area in many industries, and is more closely interlinked to the area of operations and marketing, particularly in services (see Chapter 8). As discussed, this interdependent functional relationship underscores effective decisions in, for example, the area of layout. The provision of suitable work environments for staff and operations efficiencies is not only an important HRM issue, but also has operational implications for process efficiency, along with marketing implications relating to customers and service worker interactions in the delivery of services. Issues associated with stakeholders, such as customers and suppliers, should be integrated in many HRM decisions and processes within service firms (Johnson and Clark, 2001). Korczynski (2002) states that a key operational issue derives from the challenge to manage staff and customers within a simultaneous operation and quality standard context of service delivery, where the customer becomes part of the employment relationship. Box 6.2 shows the close link between operations and HRM.

Box 6.2   Aviation

In November 1922, at Longreach, Queensland, Qantas co-founder Hudson Fysh climbed into the cockpit of an Armstrong Whitforth FK8. He took off carrying outback pioneer Alexander Kennedy – the first Qantas passenger. Fast-forward 82 years and Qantas is not only still flying, but has more than 2,100 pilots operating 130 aircraft. Since the 1960s, Qantas has run a cadet pilot program that takes about three years and is designed to equip graduates with the qualifications, experience and skills necessary for future entry into Qantas as a second officer on any of its wide-body international flights. Acceptance into the cadet program does not guarantee employment at Qantas; this is only offered once the cadet has successfully completed the program and has been through a final assessment process. The training throughout the program is intensive. It includes ex-Roulettes (the RAAF formation aerobatic team) teaching aerobatics; ex-Qantas flight engineers teaching systems – how jets work and how planes fly; and ex-airline pilots teaching standard operating procedures. A second officer's duties include monitoring and assisting the operation in all respects. This requires the second officer to have a good working knowledge of all Qantas policies and procedures. Flying is not the only option for pilots at Qantas. They can also do office-based work in operations, as some roles require flying as well as managerial skills. 'Cadets, being people of high ability and motivation, have contributed in many areas of the company beyond being a pilot. Many have become involved in the training area, technical projects, management and safety. The current chief pilot and deputy chief pilot are both former cadets,' says First Officer Hind, who manages pilot recruitment for Qantas.

(*Source*: R. Cartwright, 'Aviation, QANTAS: The Australian way', *Inflight Magazine*, July 2004, p. 32)

Supply chain management

The *supply chain* refers to all activities involved in supplying an end user with a product or service (Meredith and Schafer, 2002, p. 259). For Slack et al. (2004, p. 163), a supply network 'means setting an operation in the context of all the other operations with which it inter-acts, some of which are its suppliers and its customers'. For example, a university provides health professionals with medical degrees; hospitals provide the internships for graduands; the examination and accreditation panels provide an official approval service; the medical equipment technicians provide the skills; the manufacturers produce medical equipment; the equipment wholesalers provide the equipment; the retailer sells the equipment; the health service provider supplies private-sector consultancies; the marketing firm provides awareness of the services available to the public; and the customer is the user of the health system. This example develops the image of a link, or chain, of organisations. However, it is not only services and goods that flow up and down the 'chain', but also information, people and finance. In addition, the supply chain involves all functional areas. The integration of activities and areas builds a complex network of activities and flow and counter-flow processes, rather than a linear chain of effects (Slack et al., 2004).

Supply chain management (SCM) is the process of appropriately managing this net-work of activities and flows. The aim of SCM is to coordinate and integrate all the sup-ply chain activities into a seamless process linking all the partners in the chain, including the internal organisational departments along with the external suppliers, carriers, third-party companies and information system providers. SCM enables manufacturers to actively plan and collaborate across a distributed supply chain to ensure that all parties are aware of their commitments and schedules. By actively collaborating as a virtual corporation, manu-facturers and their suppliers can source and deliver products with minimal lead time and expense. Thus, the goal of SCM is to optimally deliver the right product to the right place at the right time, while yielding the greatest possible profit (Meredith and Schafer, 2002, pp. 259–60).

The contemporary importance that supply chain management holds within operations management has been derived from the strategic advantages of SCM that have been gained by businesses, with total supply chain costs representing some 50–75 per cent of total oper-ating expenses for most organisations (Quinn, 1997, cited in Meredith and Schafer, 2002, p. 260). These expenses include the supply, storage, and movement of resources, informa-tion, personnel, equipment and finished goods within the organisation itself, and between the organisation and markets. The basic tenet of strategic SCM is that it holistically assesses how an organisation can apportion these costs over the entire supply chain, instead of each segment acting separately to optimise its own value, often creating discontinuities at the interfaces that result in unnecessary costs. The increasing support capacity of informa-tion and communications technology (for example, bar coding, Internet, enterprise resource planning (ERP) systems, electronic funds transfer (EFT), and customer relations manage-ment software) is making this holistic and integrated approach more feasible (Meredith and Schafer, 2002).

Outsourcing is one of the most important elements of SCM, and hence has implications for a firm's competitiveness. Activities such as human resource development (HRD), R&D and accounting, which are not part of an organisation's core competencies, may be performed more efficiently and effectively outside the organisation, and at a lesser cost. The outsourcing of service activities accounts for significant growth in services. Outsourcing affects services in two ways. First, it provides an increase in the types and numbers of service firms required. Second, it provides a real challenge to organisations to provide an inclusive 'face' to their market when goods/services are provided by multiple firms under the umbrella of one organisation. This multiple organisational model raises important quality issues. Service firms, such as hotels, may decide to outsource entire areas such as their food and beverage departments, or laundry services. While this is more efficient in terms of operations for the business, the guest views all the services in the hotel room compendium as being provided directly by the hotel itself. Thus the challenge for the operations manager is to ensure efficiencies and quality across the entire supply chain so that there is a seamless delivery to the guest.

Purchasing and procurement are two key activities of SCM. *Purchasing* implies monetary transactions, whereas *procurement* is the responsibility for acquiring the necessary goods and services by any means, which may include scrap, recycled, remanufactured as well as purchased materials. Procurement by an organisation is similar to purchasing by an individual consumer, except for the following differences:

- The volume and dollar amounts are larger.
- The buyer may be larger than the supplier, whereas in consumer purchases the buyer is typically smaller than the supplier.
- Very few suppliers exist for certain organisational goods, whereas many suppliers typically exist for consumer goods.
- Certain discounts may be available for organisations, depending upon things such as volume or turnover. (Meredith and Schafer, 2002, p. 265)

The key elements of effective purchasing include leveraging buying power, committing to a small number of dependable suppliers, and working with and helping suppliers to reduce total costs.

Another SCM area to develop significantly with services is in managing the role of information and communication technologies (ICT). E-commerce and m-commerce (mobile-commerce) are developing at a rapid pace with the use of mobile phones, electronic data interchange (EDI), bar coding and scanning, databases, email, EFT, intranets, Internet, websites, point of sale terminals (POS), ERP, and terms such as B2B (business-to-business) and B2C (business-to-customer) transactions. These technologies have important support and performance implications; they also have additional operational and cross-functional management implications.

Inventory and capacity management

In manufacturing firms, 'inventory' refers to the stock of materials, while in services the term refers to stored capacity. The functions of inventory are to:

- 'decouple' or separate various parts of the production process;
- provide a stock of goods that will provide a 'selection' for customers;
- take advantage of quantity discounts; and
- hedge against inflation and upward price changes. (Heizer and Render, 2004)

However, the disadvantages of inventory must be weighed against the perceived benefits of holding inventory. These include the higher operation costs to the organisation; holding costs associated with holding or 'carrying' inventory over time; ordering costs associated with costs of placing the order and receiving the goods; set-up costs to prepare a machine or process for manufacturing an order; administrative costs such as forms and clerks' wages; and space costs such as building leases, insurances and taxes. Inventory can be difficult to control and can inadvertently hide production problems.

Inventory can be held, or stored, at four different stages in operations. These inventories include: raw materials, work-in-progress (WIP), maintenance/repair/ operating supply, or finished goods and services. The characteristic of perishability is of significance to services inventory. Many raw materials – such as time in a professional service, food at a cafe, and cabins on a cruise ship – are perishable if not used within a finite time-frame. WIP inventory often suffers in relation to the characteristic of heterogeneity. Due to many services functioning over long opening hours, often 24/7, maintenance and repairs need to be carefully scheduled to minimise disruption to customers, while maintaining quality for the organisation. Thus, it is important to have an inventory of the required items available in a timely manner and in an accessible location at all times. As discussed previously, many services produced are intangible; therefore, output inventories are not often 'real' in terms of a list of physical products in services, and therefore they do not need to be managed in the same way, in a real sense, as a list of physical products. Techniques for controlling service inventory include: good personnel selection; training and discipline; tight control of incoming raw materials or capacity; and effective control of all services and goods leaving the business.

In services, capacity and inventory are often linked. Capacity is defined as the 'throughput or number of units a facility can hold, receive, store, or produce in a period of time' (Heizer and Render, 2004, p. 276). The key challenges of capacity management in services are: to decide how much capacity to make available (capacity planning), and how to utilise existing capacity (capacity scheduling); managing capacity as part of the 'service product' (demand management); and using capacity as a strategic weapon. Capacity planning involves deciding the capacity level of the organisation. The immigration department, for example, decides on the number of immigration booths required at the international airport. Once these have been constructed, the most effective approach for utilising the booths will need to be determined. For example, factors such as the frequency and size of arrival aircraft and the range of immigration entry documentation will determine the immigration staffing levels and number of booths to be opened. Additional factors, such as entry documentation requirements or queuing in regions according to arrival passenger documentation (for example, Australian passport holders and Others), will also determine the arrangement of booths.

When managing capacity in services, there are a few key characteristics of services that require attention. First, intangibility means that excess capacity cannot be stockpiled, or inventoried for use at another time. Thus, capacity planning and demand have to be part of an integrated management system. Similarly, the simultaneity of production and consumption means that inventories cannot be used to balance supply and demand. Uncertainty in demand and in service patterns is termed 'stochastic'. This statistical variation results in the heterogeneity of services.

Thus, in managing capacity and capacity planning, issues such as capacity level, service level and waiting times are key factors to be understood. Increased numbers of studies are being conducted on the psychology and managerial consequences of waiting. The times people are prepared to wait for particular types of services vary considerably. As you will know, you are prepared to wait for differing times in supermarkets, banks, clothes shops, cafes, airplanes, art galleries or a doctor's surgery. In all these examples, research has found that the waiting time as measured by the consumer is usually different from the actual time they were waiting – that is, the perceived waiting time for a service is usually overestimated by the customer. Therefore, it is the role of the operations manager, often in conjunction with the marketing manager, to investigate ways to minimise perceived customer waiting time, according to the directive of the service concept.

Another approach that an operations manager may incorporate when designing capacity and the associated wait-time for service relates to unoccupied time feeling longer than occupied time. This context is where the layout of the physical environment and process is very important. By including the customer in the processing operation, the wait-time for the core service will appear to be smaller. This also helps to decrease pre-process waits, which feel longer than process waits. People like to know why they have to wait, as anxiety makes waiting feel longer. Therefore, strategies such as keeping the customer informed of their order in the queue, or the length of time it may take to get to the front of a phone queue, are reassuring for customers. Unexplained waits are less tolerable than explained waits, again emphasising the importance of communication in services (Van Dierdonck, 2003).

The lower the degree of personal control, the less tolerance there is for waiting. The increased involvement of the customer in customer-access zones increases their levels of perceived personal control. Good operations will provide a fair system of waiting, as unfair waits appear longer than equitable waits. This can be done by the use of physical queuing systems or numbering systems. The more valuable the service is, the higher the tolerance for waiting. Solo waits feel longer than group waits. Managing the perception of waiting time is important for all services and is becoming increasingly so with the essence of time being more and more valued in today's society of 'busy' people.

The characteristic of simultaneity (that is, the direct interaction of the customer and capacity supply) has important implications for the organisation's capabilities associated with managing the demand side of services. This is best achieved when the organisation understands, and then influences, the demand patterns. The basic aim is to shift the demand by levelling out peaks and troughs in the demand pattern. Fluctuations in demand patterns may be due to seasonality (for example, September is the busiest month for babies to be born in Australia, taxis are busy on Friday and Saturday nights, and hotel rooms can remain empty in July in Hong Kong due to the typhoon season).

The introduction of price incentives can help to manage capacity by shifting peak demand to shoulder zones and thus increasing usage in undercapacity utilisation times. Hong Kong is very busy with conventions in July and August when seasonal tariffs are low. Hotels can offer lower-priced rooms and services as incentives for the corporate traveller where seasonality is not a key decision influencer. Promoting off-peak demand by using price can also be a strategy (for example, electricity consumption costs are lower at night than in the day; and summer hiking holidays in mountain regions are good value, as opposed to skiing in the peak winter season.) Offering alternative services can fulfil some of the demand for prime services. Movies on board ship can be offered when the cabaret dinner seating has been filled. Altering the product can also help to manage demand. Singapore Zoo has breakfast with the orang-utan and evening zoo safaris, as well as the ever-popular day zoo offerings. Through the elevation of awareness (that is, through various types of advertising) of busy, or peak, times to potential markets, businesses can help to spread demand to times that are not so busy. Installing reservations systems allows management to schedule demand according to capacity. With the increasing use of technology by customers, businesses can include the customer in another operating area of the organisation by providing a virtual customer-access zone. For example, by introducing a booking system on a website for hotels, the organisation is thus providing access to the organisation's capacity inventory through its reservations system, thus allowing the customer to see the availability of various types of rooms, the dates they are available and the relative costs of those rooms.

'No-shows' is a term coined in the airline industry when passengers make a reservation, purchase a ticket, and then do not turn up for their flight. So as not to constantly waste available capacity, many airlines have adopted the practice of overbooking a certain number of seats to compensate for those no-show passengers. Many other services also use this no-show, or overbooking, approach to counteract potentially unused capacity. These services include hotels, car hire companies and live-performance theatres.

While operations managers are seeking to maximise capacity by employing strategies such as overbooking, they are also trying to achieve an acceptable rate of return from their business outputs; hence, the concept of yield has received attention in many services. 'Yield management is the process of allocating the right type of capacity to the right type of customer at the right price, so as to maximise revenue or yield. . . . Yield is the ratio of revenue realised over revenue potential' (Van Dierdonck, 2003, p. 304). Yield management is an issue when an organisation is operating with a relatively fixed capacity and cannot sell more than the available capacity and has to leverage revenue by varying price. As many services are intangible, the firm cannot change the physical features of the service to generate more revenue, so changes must come from providing more, or restricting, certain benefits of the service. Airlines are good at applying this capacity-related management strategy. On any flight, a number of passengers will have paid very different prices for their tickets despite being seated in the same row on the aircraft; however, they will have a range of restrictions associated with their tickets, such as restriction to certain times or airlines or non-refundable payments. While the tangible parts of the service may be the same, the payment conditions and restrictions associated with the airfare may vary widely.

Yield can also be increased if an organisation can segment its markets – for example, hotels may have a leisure rate, a corporate rate and a last-minute Internet rate for its different customer groups; and a health club may have a members' rate and a casual visit rate. Due to the perishability of many services, capacity sold is better than capacity not used. Therefore, many service organisations are willing to sell capacity deemed unsellable at very short time-frames – for example, concert tickets for West End shows sell at a greatly discounted rate in ticket booths in Piccadilly Circus, London, after 4 pm, and airline seats can be purchased via airline websites or hotel capacity from websites such as www.lastminute.com. The emerging trend for managing capacity is for service organisations such as hotels, airlines, trains, car hire companies, drycleaners and entertainment venues to use this approach of releasing unused capacity very close to the consumption time of the service at very low cost to the consumer. To facilitate access to this inventory of unused capacity, many businesses are using the Internet as the method for people to access the information and make purchases, as opposed to the location of physical outlets of intermediaries where people have to be close in order to enable

Level	Staff	Horizon
Strategic	HR planning	Multi-year
	Workforce staffing	Yearly
	Workforce scheduling	Monthly
Operational	Daily assignment	Daily

Figure 6.4 An integrated HR planning, staffing and scheduling framework

Source: Khoong, 1996, cited in R. Van Dierdonck, 'Capacity Management', in B. Van Looy, P. Gemmel and R. Van Dierdonck (eds), *Services Management: An integrated approach*, Prentice Hall, Harlow, UK, 2003, p. 297

the purchase to take place. Thus a virtual customer-access zone managed directly by the business has been created to facilitate capacity utilisation, with the necessary financial/accounting e-commerce facilities also being operated for accepting payments and bookings in a timely way. Thus, technology is vital in aiding organisations in capacity and inventory with last-minute sales of many services, through providing a virtual customer-access zone within the service operations of the business.

Schedule management

'The problems with productivity are often attributable, in large part, to poor management of the schedule: ensuring that the right tasks are conducted at the right time on the right items to produce the output' (Meredith and Schafer, 2002, p. 231). While scheduling is without a doubt an important part of the supply chain at the operational level, aggregate planning is also important from a strategic perspective. From a strategic perspective, a long-term view is required in conjunction with daily short-term decisions. Some examples of scheduling include the university operations administrator scheduling appropriate lecture rooms, subject lecturers and students to meet for the required lecture time across the semester; an airline scheduling its flights according to passenger numbers, aircraft size, gate availability at the departing airport and curfew times at the arrival airport.

One of the areas that require detailed scheduling in services is the scheduling of staffing in a service environment. Some issues to consider in workforce scheduling are the available staff, the wishes of the individual employees as to when they want to work, and the demand pattern for services over a shorter cycle of a week or a day. Figure 6.4 presents an integrated framework for HR planning, staffing and scheduling from a strategic level through to a short-term operational level.

Good operational scheduling benefits daily operations, and has implications for strategic advantage. With the implementation of effective scheduling, businesses use resources, or assets, more effectively, and thus create greater capacity per dollar invested. This, in turn, lowers cost, and with the increased capacity and related flexibility, provides faster delivery and, therefore, better customer service. Good scheduling is a competitive advantage that also contributes to dependable delivery. Scheduling must be viewed at all levels within the service organisation, and then be broken down into its sub-areas, according to time and service needs. Three levels of scheduling can be developed across the time-frame of long-term through to short-term scheduling requirements. These groupings include capacity

LONG TERM
Capacity planning
 1 Facility size
 2 Equipment procurement

> **MEDIUM TERM**
> **Aggregate scheduling**
> 1 Facility utilisation
> 2 Personnel needs
> 3 Subcontracting
> **Master schedule**
> 1 Materials requirements planning
> 2 Disaggregation of master plan

> > **SHORT TERM**
> > **Scheduling**
> > 1 Work centre loading
> > 2 Job sequencing

Figure 6.5 The three levels of scheduling

Source: Adapted from J. Heizer and B. Render, *Principles of Operations Management*, 5th ed., Pearson/Prentice Hall, Upper Saddle River, NJ, 2004, p. 561

planning, aggregate scheduling, master scheduling and short-term scheduling (as indicated in Figure 6.5).

Scheduling can be undertaken using either quality or numerical methods. Some examples of scheduling methods include:

- Qualitative criteria:
  - number and variety of jobs;
  - complexity of jobs; and
  - nature of operations.
- Quantitative criteria:
  - average completion time;
  - utilisation (percentage of time facility is used);
  - WIP inventory (average number of jobs in the system); and
  - customer waiting time (average lateness). (Heizer and Render, 2004)
    Some of the pertinent goals in scheduling for services include:
- minimise completion time issue (recognise that customers will require varying service times);
- be clear on customisation versus standardisation issues (apply strategic objectives);
- maximise utilisation (make effective use of personnel and equipment);
- minimise WIP inventory (keep inventory levels low); and
- minimise customer wait time (manage the psychology of waiting).

This last point highlights the interrelatedness of many functions in services management, with waiting being considered an important function of both scheduling and capacity management.

Project management

'Project management involves: the planning, organizing, controlling and directing of usually one-off activities' (Sutherland and Canwell, 2004, p. 191). A team of people, with specialised technical and functions skills, will be put together to manage a project, and will use the program evaluation and review technique (PERT) or the critical path method (CPM) to manage the activities of the project. The usual characteristics of projects include: a single unit encompassing many related activities, difficult production planning and inventory control, and the use of general-purpose equipment, but requiring high labour skills. There are many services that have these characteristics and would benefit from project management. Some complex examples include organising large events such as the Olympic Games, or corporate events such as world expos or international conferences. Location planning and layout design of amusement parks, golf courses and resorts involve specific project management skills. Large environmental awareness campaigns, ICT roll-outs in a new building, emergency services operations, and pyrotechnic displays all support a project management approach.

The three key management functions undertaken by project managers include:

- *Planning*: goal setting, project definition, team organisation, resources, and work breakdown schedule.
- *Scheduling*: relating people, money and supplies to specific activities; sequencing activities to one another; determining start and end times; developing networks; and determining critical activities.
- *Controlling*: monitoring resources, costs, quality and budgets; revising plans and shifting resources to meet time and cost demands; and developing appropriate action plans. (Heizer and Render, 2004)

Project management is ideally suited to work when:

- the work can be defined with a specific goal and deadline – that is, the project has a finite lifetime and limited resources;
- the job is unique or is somewhat unfamiliar to the existing organisation;
- the work contains complex interrelated tasks requiring specialised skills and is often subject to uncertainties;
- multiple stakeholders have vested interests in the project;
- there is a matrix structure, which may conflict with the formal organisational structure. It is said that while project managers are often held accountable for the success of the project, they are not always given full control of project resources; and
- the project is temporary, but critical to the organisation. (Metters et al., 2003)

Project management techniques include Gantt charts, CPM and PERT. Figure 6.6 presents an example of a Gantt chart showing a service schedule for a jet during a 60-minute layover. It provides a simple visual output for staff to easily read and obtain information in sequential order with appropriate time-frames related to the activities and tasks to be completed.

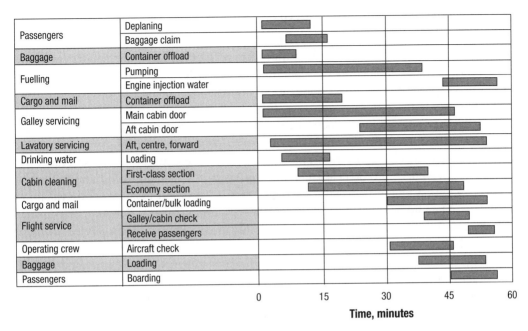

Figure 6.6 Service activities for a jet during a 60-minute layover

Source: J. Heizer and B. Render, *Principles of Operations Management*, 5th ed., Pearson/Prentice Hall, Upper Saddle River, NJ, 2004, p. 59

The number of projects and project management activities is growing on a global basis, probably at the same rate as services. A number of reasons attributed to this project growth include:

- higher productivity;
- faster response to customers;
- greater customisation for customers; and
- increased accountability. (Meredith and Schafer, 2002, p. 362)

Maintenance

Maintenance management encompasses all activities involved in keeping a system's equipment working, with the core objective being to maintain system capability and minimise total costs. While maintenance is considered very much an operations management function, the strategic importance of maintenance and reliability is significant in terms of the firm's operations, reputation, profitability, customers, product and services, employees and profits. An efficient and effective maintenance and reliability strategy requires employee involvement, and maintenance and reliability procedures to yield reduced inventory, improved quality and capacity, reputation for quality, and continuous improvement. High utilisation of facilities, tight scheduling, low inventory and consistent quality demand reliability – the key to which is total preventive maintenance. Challenges for maintenance in services include:

- how to measure system reliability;
- how to improve maintenance; and
- how to evaluate maintenance performance.

Managing innovation in service operations

In reviewing many successful companies' practices, with particular regard to their specific competitive strategies, it is apparent that they focus on four key areas: continuous configuration, innovation, development of outsourcing, and knowledge management practices. Innovation includes product or service innovation, and can also include 'innovating processes at the business units, activities, processes, functional, or transfunctional level' (Bounfour, 2003, p. 5). Innovation for manufacturing tends to be sequential, or a linear innovation process. The current emphasis in innovation process is on the *concurrency* of various phases. This starts with an idea generation phase, followed by the concept definition phase, the problem-solving phase, prototype–design–test–correct cycles, manufacturing, and finally, the commercialisation phase. Between each phase, stop–go decision moments and evaluation take place (Meredith and Schafer, 2002). This process is more of a cyclic spiral, or a concurrent process, and is a more appropriate contemporary innovation process for services than the traditional linear approach.

This process approach has resulted in each innovation stage becoming modularised. This is done through the development of small-scale prototypes that can be designed, quickly 'built', and then upgraded to full-scale developments. At each stage, the refinement of specifications and functionalities between design groups and users can be undertaken concurrently, thus producing savings in time and costs. The key to this reiterative approach is the rapidly developing new meta-technologies. Thus, this innovation spiral, or continuous sequence of iterations, refines and articulates the organisation's product, services and process platforms to allow for innovation across and within service lines, and enables interrelated innovation of the service, product and/or process. In services, customer needs and associated problem solving are often the core drivers of innovation. Thus, the involvement of the customer in the innovation process should not be limited to assessment of customers' needs. The intangibility and simultaneity of many services implies a need for real involvement of customers in the design and development phases of services.

Innovation fosters endogenous firm growth through competence-enhancing products, services and processes, thus consolidating and optimising commercial and technological capabilities within the service firm by incremental innovation to the services, products or processes. However, it can also be highly disruptive, destroying a firm's existing technological and commercial capabilities. The dual constructive and destructive nature of innovation requires careful management within services. Management must balance the need for short-term incremental improvement of its existing service-market platforms, and the more long-term fundamental need for new business development. There is a risk of becoming locked into a particular technical path/platform associated with technologies involved along the supply chain. Hence, an innovation portfolio for service businesses allows for a more controlled approach to innovation. An innovation portfolio forces management to make the mission and nature of the organisation's innovation activity explicit. It enables operations managers to distinguish between research, breakthrough, platform and derivative projects. These different projects support different missions entailed in the firm's innovation efforts.

As Figure 6.7 shows, the relationship between the content of service offerings and the service delivery process provides three types of innovation projects:

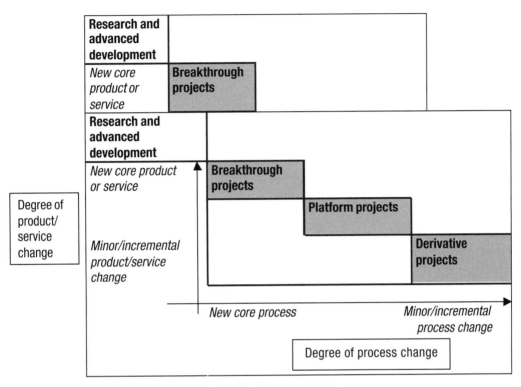

Figure 6.7 A process-orientation to innovation management

Source: K. Debackere and B. Van Looy, 'Managing innovation in a services environment', in B. Van Looy, P. Gemmel and R. Van Dierdonck (eds), *Services Management: An integrated approach*, Prentice Hall, Harlow, UK, 2003, p. 410

- *Derivative projects* usually consist of small or incremental changes and improvements to either the service itself, the service delivery process, or both – for example, a frequent flyer program for passengers or a drycleaning pick-up service within a 3 kilometre radius of the drycleaning depot.
- *Breakthrough projects* usually consist of radical changes to existing services, as well as to the delivery process. For example, global electronic classrooms are changing the face of international education. By using technology, students living in different locations can link into live lectures being streamed from a campus in another country, and undertake tutorial sessions through various e-learning programs at any time during the week with a group of students from around the world all logged on for as long as the participants are willing.
- *Platform projects* in between breakthroughs and derivatives. Originating in breakthroughs, they imply significant product-market extensions and the developments of new services, both in terms of the service itself and the service delivery process, or both. For example, with electronic ticketing for theatre and sporting venues, spectators can purchase tickets via the Internet, choosing seats according to a virtual image of the venue and printing out tickets on their own home printer. Not only does this facilitate the distribution of tickets and payment systems, but it also acts as part of the security system for the venues (Debackere and Van Looy, 2003, p. 411).

Innovation management: A summary

Innovation management may be summarised as follows:

1 Strategic and operational imperatives are involved in products and services innovation.
2 Innovation should be aimed at providing solutions to customers and organisational needs and problems.
3 Innovation is a paradox: it can be both competence enhancing and competence destructive.
4 The development of combined product/service offerings is imperative to successful services portfolios.
5 Services innovation requires balanced portfolios.
6 Portfolio management requires a balance between longer-term (breakthrough) projects and the shorter-term (derivative) projects.
7 Management needs to plan a strategic vision as to the sequence and the timing of the development of new product and service platforms.
8 Management needs to foster self-discipline among staff to prevent chaos in innovation.
9 A sense of ownership among staff needs to be created to encourage entrepreneurial effort.
10 A strong, supportive organisational culture is required to sustain project innovation, with both a strong competence component and a strong operational component. (Botten and McManus, 1999; Debackere and Van Looy, 2003).

Box 6.3 presents an example of an operations management product and services review showing savings worth billions achieved through the increased use of technology both by the consumer and by the provider.

Box 6.3   Airline company needs to simplify business

The airline industry has survived SARS, the conflict in Iraq, terrorism and the economy. However, with the price of oil fluctuating greatly, profitable years in the early 21st century for airlines may be an unachievable goal.

Overall, there is no single state that describes the air transport industry. The challenges are as great as the opportunities. However, it must be recognised that air transport is the economic lifeblood of a community. Governments must stop milking the industry to solve their inefficiencies or a city's budget problems. Thus, change is urgently needed. We must recognise the complexity of the traditional model. The challenge is to retain the value of the network system but eliminate the costs of complexity. I believe the term 'low-cost carrier' is absolutely wrong. Our future structure is a 'low-cost industry' with some airlines offering network services at a premium the consumer is willing to pay. How do we get there from here?

The key new element is 'simplifying the business'. For example, paper costs money. A paper ticket is US$9 (A$13) more expensive than an e-ticket. IATA distributes 300 million paper tickets each year. You don't have to be a rocket scientist to understand that up to US$3 billion in savings is possible.

Technology can also make us more efficient. We need to look for opportunities throughout our business, such as radio-frequency baggage tags, bar-coding technology and self-service check-in kiosks. The agenda to 'simplify the business' also includes safety and security. Safety and security is the promise we make to 1.6 billion passengers each year. Simplifying our approach to security, with standardisation of rules, is essential. We need to battle terrorism, not the paperwork.

By 2010, we will have 600 million more passengers and seven million more tonnes of cargo than today. If we don't make fundamental changes to simplify our business, our future is at risk.

(*Source:* Excerpts from Giovanni Bisignani's address to IATA, Singapore, 2004, 'Industry news, QANTAS: The Australian Way', *Inflight Magazine*, July 2004, p. 24)

PAST	⇨	CAUSES OF CHANGE	⇨	FUTURE
Local or national focus	⇨	Low-cost, worldwide communication and transportation networks	⇨	Global focus
Batch (large) shipments	⇨	Short product life cycles and cost of capital put pressure on reducing inventory	⇨	Just-in-time shipments
Low-bid purchasing	⇨	Quality emphasis requires that suppliers be engaged in product improvement	⇨	Supply-chain partners, enterprise resource planning, e-commerce, m-commerce
Lengthy product development	⇨	Shorter life cycles, Internet, rapid international communication, computer-aided design, and international collaboration	⇨	Rapid product development, alliances, collaborative designs
Standardised products	⇨	Affluence and worldwide markets; increasingly flexible production processes	⇨	Mass customisation with added emphasis on quality
Job specialisation	⇨	Changing socio-cultural milieu; increasingly a knowledge and information society	⇨	Empowered employees, teams and lean production
Low-cost focus	⇨	Environmental issues, ISO 14000, increasing disposal costs	⇨	Environmentally sensitive production processes, green manufacturing, recycled materials, remanufacturing
Economic system of productivity	⇨	Increase in services sector; increase in knowledge societies	⇨	Development of new models for service sector productivity

Figure 6.8 Changing challenges and trends for operations management

Source: Adapted from J. Heizer and B. Render, *Principles of Operations Management*, 5th ed., Pearson/Prentice Hall, Upper Saddle River, NJ, 2004, p. 12

New trends in operations management

Figure 6.8 summarises the evolution of approaches to operational management and highlights the future directions for the area. When comparing the past linear and manufacturing industry-oriented approaches to the more complex and interdependent future services-oriented approaches, it is apparent that the role of operations management becomes critical. Moreover, the more complex role and tasks of operations management must be strategically integrated with all the other specialist functional management areas in order for services businesses to effectively and efficiently meet their customer-focused performance objectives.

Conclusion

This chapter provides a broad overview of the key areas within the operations management domain of services organisations. The management area of strategy has more recently gained considerable attention. However, the importance of operations management is underestimated in most services organisations. The area of operations management has the capacity to translate the visions and goals of strategic management into the processes and activities required in services. The powerful legacy of the traditional silos approach to the function management areas, along with the operations management legacy of traditional linear manufacturing production processes, means that currently the area is frequently treated too superficially, or too technically.

While operations management is the translation of the organisation's strategic decisions into meaningful outputs for the organisation, the distinction between strategic and operational management is often not so clear. Operations have both long-term and short-term management implications. For example, quality management is a long-term activity, but in addition it involves day-to-day attention; environmental management is a long-term strategy, but it involves day-to-day management activities; facility layout is considered operational, but also as strategic due to the costs and strategic marketing decisions involved; and project management is a day-to-day activity, but projects can be long-term (Waller, 2003).

Thus, operations management decisions must consider the financial capabilities of the organisation. The operations decisions interact with marketing decisions to establish the appropriate services and processes to attract a specific customer target. In addition, interactions are required with human resources to enable the organisation to provide the appropriate labour force with specific knowledge and skill requirements suitable for the particular service delivery approach. This emphasis on the interrelated and interdependent nature of functional decisions highlights the importance of operations management. Moreover, a collaborative and interdisciplinary approach is now required to further develop and implement the integrated management model to successfully achieve the delivery of quality services across the diverse range of services.

Exercises

Key questions
1 Discuss the reasons for the change in thinking from production management to operations management. What are some of the key characteristics of services that make operations activities more integrated with other areas such as marketing, finance and human resources?

2 Why is the concept of supply chain management so effective in operations management when dealing with services?

3 What would be some of the considerations an operations manager would undertake when deciding on the activities to place in customer-access zones, as opposed to customer-free zones of the organisation? List some business examples you are familiar with, and compare and contrast the operational activities undertaken in these two zones. How does customer involvement in these examples vary?

4 How important is innovation for both the short-term and long-term survival and growth of services? Explain why, using examples of services businesses.

Web exercise 6.1

Students should search for a services organisation of their choice and access the relevant website. You may find some interesting examples by looking at the finance and banking sector, tourism sector, health sector, education sector or the ICT sector; all of which are major growth areas within services. Using the information provided, identify the operations areas of the organisation. Discuss how the financial, marketing, operations and HRM areas operate in an integrated mode. It will be helpful to use the ISM model (Figure 6.1) as the basis for your consideration. How does the inclusion of the customer as a key stakeholder influence the operations of your organisation in relation to quality and productivity goals? What suggestions would you provide your organisation in regards to the provision of customer-access zones and customer-free zones in light of their current operations and potential operations?

Case study 6.1 Operations for a holiday island

'There are a lot of reasons why people visit Rottnest Island. These include relaxing in a coastal setting; enjoying its scenic natural beauty; taking part in a special event; carrying out a research project, as part of a school camping trip or participating in a conservation initiative. These different areas of interest reflect the wide range of people who enjoy Rottnest Island's facilities and services, and who want to ensure it is effectively managed in the future. The Rottnest Island Authority has a commitment to maintain the Island's environmental, social and economic values for the coming years.' The Honourable Clive Brown, Minister for Tourism, wrote these words in the foreword to the *Rottnest Island Management Plan 2003–2008*.

Introduction
The Rottnest Island case study provides an overview of an iconic island destination for local and international visitors. It provides a background to the island (also visit the website for more information and many visual displays of information – www.rottnest.wa.gov.au), then looks at the strategy development of the island, the policy context within which it operates, its financial position, stakeholders and then operational management planning.

Brief description
Rottnest Island is one of the most popular recreation and holiday destinations for Western Australians, and is also a popular destination for interstate and international visitors.

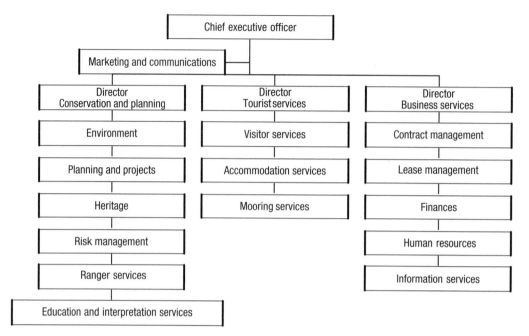

Figure 6.9 Rottnest Island Authority organisation structure

Source: Rottnest Island Authority, *Rottnest Island Management Plan 2003–2008*, Rottnest Island Authority, Fremantle, 2003, p. 4

Approximately half a million people visit Rottnest Island every year, arriving primarily by commercial ferries (a 20-minute trip from the local port of Fremantle) but also on 10-minute charter flights from Perth. Additionally, a significant number of visitors travel to Rottnest in their own pleasure craft, usually in the warmer season of the year.

Rottnest Island is located on the southwest coast of Western Australia at latitude 32°00′ South and longitude 115°30′ East. It is 18 kilometres long and less than five kilometres wide at its broadest point. It is an A-class reserve declared under the *Land Administration Act 1997*. The boundary of the Rottnest Island Reserve contains the terrestrial component of the island itself and the surrounding sea. (See www.rottnest.wa.gov.au for charts.) The terrestrial area is approximately 1,859 hectares in area, containing 200 hectares of classified 'Settlement' area and 200 hectares of salt lakes and swamps. The marine portion of the reserve constitutes approximately 3,810 hectares of sea surrounding the island and includes several smaller islands and exposed rocks adjacent to the coast.

Organisation structure and power

The *Rottnest Island Authority Act 1987* created the Rottnest Island Authority (RIA) as a statutory body to control and manage the island, reporting to the Minister for Tourism. The CEO is responsible for the administration, subject to the control of the Authority, of the day-to-day operations and management of the island. The CEO is supported in these operations by a staff of 117 people, most of whom live on the mainland and commute daily to the island. The staff numbers may vary due to seasonal requirements. The RIA organisation structure (Figure 6.9) provides an outline of the key areas within the RIA.

The scope of operations of the RIA is highlighted through the definition of the area covered by the spatial boundary of Rottnest Island. The *Rottnest Island Authority Act 1987* states that the reserve is the land, comprising 1,859 hectares; the waters as defined by the Rottnest Island Reserve Boundary, including the sea-bed and subsoil beneath such waters; and all jetties apart from the Green Island Jetty at Nancy Cove. While the airspace above the reserve is not vested in the RIA, the RIA has an interest in influencing users of that airspace.

Rottnest Island strategic plan

The RIA operates under the guidance of its strategic plan, which incorporates the organisation's vision, mission, goals and strategies. This plan may be viewed on the Rottnest Island website: www.rottnest.wa.gov.au.

The vision *Rottnest: Forever Magic* reflects the community's wish that the unique Rottnest Island experience be preserved for future generations of Western Australians.

The mission is: 'Rottnest Island provides holidays for Western Australians and other visitors while sustaining the Island's natural environment and unique heritage.'

The Authority has three goals:

- Rottnest Island provides a unique holiday experience that is accessible to Western Australian and other visitors.
- Rottnest Island's environment and heritage are conserved and enhanced as a model of sustainability.
- The Authority conducts its business responsibly and in a way that is sustainable and beneficial to the island.

Fifteen strategies have been adopted to meet these goals in line with the mission and vision. See the website for further details.

Financial position

The financial provisions of the *Rottnest Island Authority Act 1987* are framed in the expectation that the Authority is self-sufficient. In other words, sufficient revenue is to be generated from operations to meet expenses. Financial pressures over many years have caused loans to be raised that are now in the process of being repaid. These loan repayments have added to the financial pressures and losses in recent years.

Policy context

The operations management functions of the island must operate within the external environment (Figure 6.1) for all strategy development and implementation. The following information provides an idea of the complexities of managing the island given the policy contexts at the international, national and state levels which have to be adhered to in all operations of the island:

1 *International policy:* Key international policies that influence Rottnest Island operations include:
   - ICOMOS International Cultural Tourism Charter;
   - agreements between the governments of Australia, Japan and China for the protection of migratory birds and birds in danger of extinction and their environment (JAMBA

and CAMBA), and the Convention of the Conservation of Migratory Species of Wild Animals (CMS or Bonn Convention);
- Convention of Wetlands of International Importance (Ramsar Convention);
- Convention of Biological Diversity (Rio Convention); and
- International Charter on the Protection and Management of Underwater Cultural Heritage (ICOMOS).

2 *Australian policy*: Key national policies that influence Rottnest Island operations include:
- National Strategy for the Conservation of Australia's Biological Diversity;
- National Ecotourism Strategy;
- The Burra Charter;
- Native Title; and
- *Commonwealth Disabilities Discrimination Act 1992*.

3 *Western Australian state policy*: Key state policies that influence Rottnest Island operations include:
- Western Australian Sustainability Strategy;
- Nature-based Tourism Strategy, 1997;
- Western Australian Volunteering Compact;
- State commitment to a new and just relationship between the government of Western Australia and Aboriginal Western Australians; and
- *State Disability Services Act 1993*.

Stakeholders

The range of stakeholders involved in the operations of the island is comprehensive and includes numerous government departments as well as private businesses. The private businesses include bike hire, hairdresser, dive shop, ferry operators, bakery, grocery store, one fast-food outlet, the tearooms and coffee shop, the hotel and the clothing store. The list below provides information on the government bodies that have a particularly relevant role in the management of Rottnest Island. The roles and responsibilities of Western Australian government bodies include:

1 *Department for Planning and Infrastructure* – is responsible for all boating regulations, ensuring safety of all vessels, management of marine pollution, and management of all gazetted roads on the island.

2 *Department of Health* – monitoring environmental health standards on the island, environmental monitoring, pollution control, food safety, disease control, health education, waste disposal, chemical control and building management.

3 *Western Australian Police Service* – is responsible for the application of a number of Acts, including the *Police Act 1892*, on Rottnest Island; the lead agency in the enforcement of law and emergency management procedures.

4 *Department of Environment, Water and Catchment Protection* – controls the marine and terrestrial pollution, several operations on the island such as water supply, wastewater treatment, landfill site operations and protection of groundwater.;

5 *Department of Conservation and Land Management* – administers the *Wildlife Conservation Act and Regulations 1950* that aims to conserve Western Australia's native flora and fauna.

6 *Department of Fisheries* – responsible for the management of Western Australia's fish, marine and aquatic resources, and pearling industry, while protecting and conserving the various related ecosystems.

7 *Western Australian Museum* – major functions are to preserve significant and representative examples of Western Australian heritage for the enrichment of present and future generations, investigate the natural and cultural world, and share ideas and information through a variety of public programs.

8 *Department of Indigenous Affairs* – responsible for the administration of Aboriginal sites of significance and of indigenous material culture.

9 *Heritage Council of Western Australia* – encourages and provides for the conservation of places that are significant to the cultural heritage of Western Australia and thus is responsible for the conservation of a large number of significant cultural heritage places representing the layers of historical use of the island.

10 *Tourism Western Australia (TWA)* – a statutory authority and pre-eminent body responsible for the promotion, development and marketing of tourism in Western Australia, as Rottnest Island is considered an icon of Western Australian tourism. The RIA works with TWA to liaise with transport providers, facilitating visiting journalists and agent familiarisation tours, and providing opportunities for positive tourism development and growth.

11 *Department of Industries and Resources* – administers the *Petroleum Act 1967* and the *Mining Act 1978*. Although it is highly unlikely that significant mining would occur on Rottnest, there needs to be an organisation that monitors and assesses these activities.

12 *Disabilities Services Commission* – provides information and advice to the RIA to assist the development of the island as a universally accessible island.

13 *Department of Fire and Emergency Services* – provides training for the emergency services on the island, and fire and public safety advice on facilities for the protection of residents and visitors.

Some significant service operations management considerations

The elements of sustainability have always been a dominant factor in the management of the island, with the RIA wanting to develop Rottnest as a model of sustainability. This raises discussion on potential co-existence and conflict with regards to location, site usage and layout issues from the multitude of stakeholders with invested interests and responsibilities on the island. From a services operations management perspective, the initial key question to explore is the delineation of the island into visitor-access zones and visitor-free zones. Table 6.9 provides a summary of the current zones based on various access levels to the public.

The servicescape of the island is unique, and provides one of the key characteristics of the island for both visual and heritage recognition and amenity. While over the years there has been a range of different styles used in the physical planning and layout of the island's infrastructure, the RIA is aware of the need to be consistent with respect to building materials used on the island and for them to be sympathetic with heritage elements. Other operations areas designated as requiring attention include public furniture, settlement vegetation (landscaping), the use of colour (the use of the Rottnest ochre colour is a highly recognisable

Table 6.9 Activities and development permitted in the Rottnest Island terrestrial zones

Activity	Settlement zone	Natural zone	Activity nodes	Environmental exclusion zone, permanent	Environmental exclusion zone, temporary
Public access[1]	Yes	Yes	Yes	No	No
Escorted access[2]	Yes	Yes	Yes	Special[4]	Special[4]
Accommodation	Yes	No	No	No	No
Built facilities (other than accommodation)	Yes	No	Yes	Special[4]	Special[4]
Vehicle access (on designated roads and tracks only)	Yes	Yes	Yes	Special[4]	Special[4]
Approved events and functions[3]	Yes	No	Yes	No	No

1 Public access – available to the public.
2 Escorted access – access only permitted while in the company of an RIA officer.
3 Approved function or event – including weddings, parties, conferences, festivals and sporting events.
4 Limited for the purpose of conservation and risk management.

Source: Rottnest Island Authority, *Rottnest Island Management Plan 2003–2008*, Rottnest Island Authority, Fremantle, 2003, p. 20

element, as it dominates the colour-scape of the island), lighting, quality of accommodation facilities, and quality of day-visitor facilities.

From an environmental operations management perspective, the issues requiring management include geological, landforms, soil, groundwater and surface water. Other issues include the management of landscape and vista, and atmosphere conditions such as air pollution, odour and noise. Terrestrial flora and fauna are significant environmental management areas on the island and require dedicated operations of these habitats. The marine environment is also unique and provides a range of uses for many stakeholders. The operations of these zones need to be monitored and controlled due to the exacerbating effects of the high level of seasonal usage.

The holiday and recreation services and facilities have been managed for over 95 years, with recreational pursuits only stopping briefly for short periods during the First and Second World Wars. One of the areas presenting operational challenges is that of capacity management. The core of this challenge resides in the fact that the RIA does not have the power to limit entry into the reserve. Currently, 500,000 people visit the island each year, with approximately 350,000 arriving by commercial ferry or aircraft and the remainder by private pleasure craft. The six-month period from November to April shows very high levels of occupancy in accommodation facilities (90-plus per cent), while during the other six months of the year it drops below 40 per cent. Thus, this marked seasonality is an issue for management. Since 2002, visitors have been charged an admission fee. There has been minimal research undertaken on Rottnest Island visitor numbers and behaviour, and the environmental, social and economic impacts on the island.

Other operation management challenges resulting from the unlimited supply of visitors and financial constraints have resulted in poor customer service quality and accommodation quality issues. Quality management on the island is a significant challenge when considering the range of stakeholders involved.

Source: Adapted from Rottnest Island Authority, *Rottnest Island Management Plan 2003–2008*, Rottnest Island Authority, Fremantle, 2003.

Student projects

1 After considering the organisation chart for RIA (Figure 6.9), provide a detailed expansion of the chart, including the functions and operational roles each of these areas would cover. What are some of the significant issues associated with operations management within the visitor-free zones and visitor-access zones within each of the three areas (Conservation and Planning, Tourist Services, Business Services) of the island? How could you develop an appropriate strategy that provides guidelines for materials use on the island so as to emphasise the overall ambience and recognition of the island while considering the characteristics of uniqueness and authenticity in the approach? What services and issues along the supply chain would have potential impact on the island's operations due to its unique location and site requirements?

2 While the financial situation, as discussed previously, in previous years has not been adequate for the island's operations, the need to provide a quality destination is obvious. One of the suggestions for addressing potential revenue generation is in the hosting of events on the island. From an operations perspective, discuss the challenges this would present to the director of visitor services, the director of business services and the director of conservation and planning. Some of the issues you may wish to consider include social issues of increased visitor numbers and the impact of this on other people holidaying on the island and compromising their holiday experience; the scale of events allowed and the ensuing operational requirements; seasonality and capacity planning issues; and the relevance of events on the overall mission of the island, its ethos and cultural history. Would project management provide a good basis for the operations of the island's day-to-day activities and/or its event activities?

References and further reading

Beaumont, N. and Sohal, A. 1999, 'Quality management in Australian service industries', *Benchmarking*, vol. 6, no. 2, p. 107.

Bisignani, G. 2004, 'Industry news, QANTAS: The Australian way,' *Inflight Magazine*, July 2004, p. 24.

Bitner, M. J. 1992, 'Servicescapes: The impact of physical surroundings on customers and employees', *Journal of Marketing*, vol. 56, April, pp. 57–71.

Botten, N. and McManus, J. 1999, *Competitive Strategies for Service Organisations*, Macmillan, London.

Bounfour, A. 2003, *The Measurement of Intangibles: The organisation's most valuable assets*, Routledge, London.

Bucher, P., Lee, G. and Sohal, A. S. 2004, 'The changing roles of production and operations managers in Britain from the 1970s to the 1990s', *International Journal of Operations and Production Management*, vol. 24, no. 3/4, p. 409.

Carlzon, J. 1989, *The Moment of Truth*, Harper and Row Publishers, New York.

Cartwright, R. 2004, 'Aviation, QANTAS: The Australian way', *Inflight Magazine*, July 2004, p. 32.

Debackere, K. and Van Looy, B. 2003, 'Managing innovation in a service environment', in B. Van Looy, P. Gemmel and R. Van Dierdonck (eds), *Services Management: An integrated approach*, Prentice Hall, Harlow, UK.

Desmet, S., Van Looy, B. and Van Dierdonck, R. 2003, 'The nature of services', in B. Van Looy, P. Gemmel and R. Van Dierdonck (eds), *Services Management: An integrated approach*, Prentice Hall, Harlow, UK.

Fitzsimmons, J. A. and Fitzsimmons, M. J. 2001, *Service Management: Operations, Strategy and Information Technology*, 3rd ed., McGraw-Hill, New York.

Grainger, R. and Taylor, R. 2003, 'A model for the tourist/business zone of interaction within service operations management', *Refereed Proceedings of the First Asia Pacific CHRIE Conference*, Seoul, Korea, 21–23 May.

Haksever, C., Render, B., Russell, R. and Murdick, R. 2000, *Service Management and Operations*, 2nd ed., Prentice Hall, Upper Saddle River, NJ.

Harcourt, T. 2004, 'Airlines check out DIY check-ins to reduce costs', *The Weekend Australian*, 12–14 June, p. 11.

Heizer, J. and Render, B. 2004, *Principles of Operations Management*, 5th ed., Pearson/ Prentice Hall, Upper Saddle River, NJ.

Johnson, R. and Clark, G. 2001, *Service Operations Management*, Pearson Education, Harlow, UK.

Kandampully, J. 2002, *Services Management: The new paradigm in hospitality*, Pearson Education, Sydney.

Korczynski, M. 2002, *Human Resources in Service Work*, Palgrave, Basingstoke, UK.

McColl-Kennedy, J. 2003, 'Introduction to services', in J. McColl-Kennedy (ed.), *Services Marketing: A managerial approach*, John Wiley, Brisbane.

Meredith, J. and Schafer, S. 2002, *Operations Management for MBAs*, 2nd ed., John Wiley & Sons, Danvers, MA.

Metters, R., King-Metters, K. and Pullman, M. 2003, *Successful Service Operations Management*, Thomson South-Western, Cincinnati, OH.

Nankervis, A., Compton, R. and Baird, M. 2001, *Strategic Human Resource Management*, 4th ed., Thomson, Melbourne.

Parasuraman, A., Zeithaml, V. and Berry, L. 1988, 'SERVQUAL: A multiple-item scale for measuring consumer perceptions of service quality', *Journal of Retailing*, vol. 64, spring, pp. 12–37.

Pine B. J. II, and Gilmore, J. 1999, *The Experience Economy: Work is theatre & every business is a stage*, Harvard Business School Press, Boston.

Quible, Z. 2001, *Administrative Office Management*, Prentice Hall, Upper Saddle River, NJ.

Rottnest Island Authority, 2003, *Rottnest Island Management Plan 2003–2008*, Rottnest Island Authority, Fremantle, March.

Schemmer, R. W. 1994, 'Service firm location decisions: Some mid-western evidence', *International Journal of Service Industry Management*, vol. 5, no 3, pp. 49–52.

Slack, N., Chambers, S. and Johnson, R. 2004, *Operations Management*, 4th ed., Pearson Education, Harlow, UK.

Sohal, A. S. 1995, *Quality Practices in Australian Manufacturing Firms*, Ernst & Young, Melbourne.

Sohal, A. S., D'Netto, B., Fitzpatrick, P. and Noori, H., 2001, 'The roles and responsibilities of production/operations managers in SMEs: Evidence from Canada', *Technovation*, vol. 21, no. 7, p. 437.

Soutar. G. 2001, 'Service quality, customer satisfaction, and value: An examination of their relationships', in J. Kandampully, C. Mok and B. Sparks (eds), *Service Quality Management in Hospitality, Tourism and Leisure*, Haworth Hospitality Press, New York.

Sutherland, J. and Canwell, D. 2004, *Key Concepts in Operations Management*, Palgrave Macmillan, New York.

Swarbrooke, J. 2002, *The Development and Management of Visitor Attractions*, 2nd ed., Butterworth Heinemann, Oxford.

Van Dierdonck, R. 2003, 'Capacity management', in B. Van Looy, P. Gemmel and R. Van Dierdonck (eds), *Services Management: An integrated approach*, Prentice Hall, Harlow, UK.

Wacker, J. 1998, 'A definition of theory: Research guidelines for different theory-building methods on operations management', *Journal of Operations Management*, vol. 16, pp. 361–85.

Waller, D. 2003, *Operations Management: A supply chain approach*, 2nd ed., Thomson, London.

Financial management in services

Learning objectives

After studying this chapter, readers will be able to:
- appreciate the importance of financial management
- understand the underlying principles and concepts of financial management
- discuss the financial manager's responsibilities
- explain some of the main financial management objectives and concepts
- identify some of the key functions of financial management (for example, financial analysis, planning, control and sourcing for funds), and analyse each function from a services perspective
- apply a selection of financial management techniques to the services environment (for example, activity-based costing, financial risk management)
- examine contemporary issues in financial management of services.

Introduction

This chapter highlights the underlying principles and contemporary importance of financial management with particular reference to its implications for services. In general, the study of finance consists of three interconnected areas:

1 *Capital and money markets*, which deals with securities markets, banks and financial institutions.
2 *Investments*, which includes the decision making of individuals and organisations with respect to securities (shares and bonds) for their respective investment portfolios.
3 *Financial management*, which involves the acquisition, management and financing of resources for organisations.

The broad nature and characteristics of the global finance environment will be discussed first.

Financial management has undergone significant changes in recent years. The focus of financial management has changed dramatically from the historical emphasis on legal aspects such as mergers, acquisitions, consolidations, the formation of new organisations, and the various types of securities (shares and bonds) issued by corporations in the early 1900s. In the

1960s and 1970s the emphasis was on the emergence of 'portfolio' theories. More recently, in the 1980s and 1990s, the emphasis shifted to the importance of inflation and its effects on interest rates and the deregulation of the financial institutions. Arguably, financial management has become more sophisticated since its emergence as a separate branch of study, and it continues to develop.

Increased economic activity, financing innovations, new theoretical developments, and improvements in technology and communications are constantly reshaping financial ideas. For example, the growth of funds management, the emphasis on risk management, and corporate governance and transparency issues have all received increasing attention recently to complement the increased volume and complexity of global economic activity. In addition, the economic recession and the slowdown of the world economy in the 1990s created new challenges for the financial manager to keep organisations afloat, by rationalising operations and cutting costs so as to leave organisations in a more viable position to recover and benefit from the renewed global economic growth. However, despite continued record profits posted by banking – one of the largest service subsectors – major corporate crashes in ancillary service sectors have occurred. Between 2001 and 2003, examples such as HIH Insurance, Ansett Airlines, Impulse Airlines, and One.Tel in Australia further highlight the importance of rigorous financial management practices. (See Case study 7.2, at the end of this chapter, on the collapse of HIH Insurance.)

During the last decade, most economies have become globally oriented, and cross-border trade and investment flows have reached new heights. Global organisations are increasingly making decisions with little or no regard to national boundaries. The opening of markets abroad has created new, exciting and profitable opportunities for the internationalisation of organisations' operations. This optimism, however, has been overshadowed by major economic crises such as the financial 'meltdown' of the Asian economies in 1997, and the 'fallout' from the information technology and telecommunications 'slump' in the late 1990s. Just as the world economy was starting to improve, the September 11 attacks sent capital markets spiralling with a consequential gloomy outlook for economic global stability predicted. As discussed in Chapter 2, the travel and tourism industry has been struggling ever since and has not yet fully recovered from terrorism attacks in Bali in 2002, and SARS and the bird flu epidemics in Asia in 2003. The opening up of foreign markets, the deregulation of sectors such as finance and telecommunications, and the privatisation of former government-controlled entities have exposed world markets to increased overseas competition (Jeanett, 2000).

Peacock et al. (2003, p. 6) note that 'this two-way globalisation has, in turn, created a need for financial managers to better understand the financial systems of other countries and the role of the financial manager in assessing the risks of international operations'. Thus, managers in banks and financial institutions, airlines, legal organisations, restaurants, hotels, recreational services, information technology and communications, as well as all other service subsectors, need to appreciate the importance of the role of financial management in the day-to-day functioning of business. It should, however, be noted that to achieve efficiency, profitability and service excellence leading to sustainable competitive advantage, financial management must be effectively integrated with the management of operations, marketing and human resources, as illustrated in the following

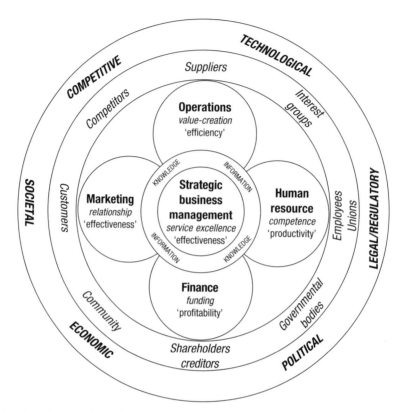

Figure 7.1 The integrated services management (ISM) model

ISM model. (See Chapter 4 for a discussion on the strategic integration of the services function.)

As Figure 7.1 indicates, the primary objective of the financial management function in the service sector is 'funding', with the purpose of ensuring an organisation's 'profitability'. As the functional driver of the finance function, 'funding' covers two facets: fundraising and allocation. *Fundraising* deals with the sourcing of funds from various internal and external sources after examining the associated costs and risks with each available source. *Allocation* deals with the actual disbursement of the funds to services operations, marketing and HR areas after employing budgeting, costing and planning (short- and long-term) procedures. Hence, effective financial management, in conjunction with the effective management of the industry's operations, marketing and human resources, is crucial to ensure that service operations are efficient, transparent, profitable and sustainable, and meet the expectations of the various stakeholders. (See Chapter 3 for a discussion of stakeholder issues.)

Why is financial management important?

The historical trends highlighted have greatly increased the contemporary importance of financial management. Brigham and Gapenski (1994, p. 8) point out that 'in earlier times, the marketing manager would project sales, the engineering and production staff would determine the assets necessary to meet those demands, and the financial manager's job was simply to raise the money needed to purchase the required plant, equipment, and inventories'. This simple approach is now inadequate to deal with the complexities of today's fast-paced competitive world. Decisions are now made in a much more centrally coordinated manner, and the financial manager generally has direct responsibility for the financial control process. Banks, education providers, airlines, tourism agencies and other service-oriented organisations employ financial managers who, in liaison with other organisational functional managers, are accountable for the various financial decisions taken in their respective organisations.

The collapse of HIH Insurance, Ansett Airlines and One.Tel in Australia, and an earlier bankruptcy scandal in energy giant Enron in the United States, are all examples of poor financial management and reporting. The global accounting and consulting organisation Arthur Andersen was blamed for employing 'window dressing' strategies and projecting positive financial reports when, in fact, Enron was close to bankruptcy. The HIH collapse was blamed on poor auditing and financial reporting; Ansett on poor financial planning, budgeting and strategy; and One.Tel on poor forecasting. These are among many examples that have emphasised the importance of the role of financial management in the overall running of the day-to-day activities of organisations worldwide. The ramifications of one wrong financial decision can affect the future viability of the organisation. For example, poor budgeting decisions led to the dot.com 'bubble bust' in India in the late 1990s. Thus, it is also becoming increasingly important for staff in the various other functional areas such as accounting, marketing, operations and human resources to understand the principles of finance in order to work efficiently in their respective areas. Illustrating the need for this, accountants must understand how the day-to-day accounting data is used in financial planning and budgeting. Human resource staff must understand how their decisions on recruitment, staffing, and the inter- and intra-departmental transfer of staff affect, and are affected by, funds availability and organisation capacity. Similarly, marketing staff must understand how various marketing decisions affect, and are affected by, inventory levels, plant capacity levels and funds availability.

Given that virtually all business decisions have financial implications, the smooth functioning of the organisation entails encouraging all staff (including non-financial executives) to learn the principles of finance and to know enough about finance to understand the implications of the financial decisions of the organisation.

Responsibilities of the financial manager

Financial management involves the acquisition, management and financing of resources for organisations. Hence, the financial manager's responsibility is to acquire and use the funds required so as to maximise the profitability and enhance the future viability of the organisation. Four specific financial manager responsibilities – *forecasting and planning, major investment and financial decisions, coordination and control* and *liaising with financial markets* – are outlined below.

1 *Forecasting and planning:* The firm's financial future and viability depends largely on the financial decisions made. The financial manager has the responsibility to liaise with other functional area executives to draft the firm's short- and long-term financial plans. Well-managed firms set growth targets whenever they are able to, and use devices such as budgets to plan and control the process.

2 *Major investment and financing decisions:* A successful firm usually has rapid growth in sales, which requires investments in plant, equipment, inventory and services. The financial manager must help to determine both the optimal sales growth rate and the ideal way to finance and obtain those assets by minimising risk and maximising returns. For example, should the firm finance with debt, equity or some combination of the two? If debt, how should it be used, and should short-term or long-term debt be acquired?

3 *Coordination and control:* Any business, whether old or new, needs to plan and control its operations on an ongoing basis. All business decisions have financial implications, and financial executives must liaise with executives from other functional areas to coordinate the smooth and efficient running of the firm. If the firm is not well coordinated and controlled, returns of projects and, ultimately, the wealth of the various stakeholders could be jeopardised.

4 *Liaison with financial markets:* The financial manager must deal with money and capital markets. Each organisation affects and is affected by the general functioning of the financial markets where funds are raised, organisation's securities are traded, and investors make or lose money. (Adapted from Brigham, 1989; Brigham and Gapenski, 1994)

In summary, the financial management of services requires crucial decisions regarding how to raise, manage and distribute funds to acquire assets and resources in the most efficient manner. If these responsibilities, along with the coordination and control of the day-to-day financial activities of the organisation, are managed optimally, financial managers will help to maximise the *value* (explained in the next section) of their organisation and the *welfare* of employees (see also Chapter 8), consumers and stakeholders (see also Chapter 3), and ensure the long-term *viability* and *sustainability* of the organisation in today's competitive world. (See Chapter 4 on the implications of long-term strategy.)

Financial objectives and concepts

The financial objective is the same, whether the focus is on the manufacturing organisations that trade goods, service organisations that provide services, or financial organisations that trade financial services. Financial management is about making decisions that support the underlying organisational principles of 'profit maximisation' or 'maximisation of shareholder wealth' (Brigham, 1989; Pinches, 1992; Brigham and Gapenski, 1994; Peacock et al., 2003). This section explains some of the key financial management objectives and concepts that managers in non-financial functional areas need to understand before they are able to apply them in their respective areas while keeping in mind the organisation's underlying principles.

Profit maximisation is the measure of the change in the *market value* of the organisation. More specifically, the objective of an organisation is to maximise the value of the organisation's ordinary shares (equity). Organisations in the services sector also have wealth maximisation as their internal goal, and this goal is pursued through their unique operations in providing quality services, enhancing goodwill and expanding their consumer base. Specific services sector examples follow. Banks and finance institutions maximise shareholders' wealth by providing, arranging or facilitating the flow of financial resources from surplus (*savers*) to deficit units (*borrowers*). Insurance providers enhance goodwill and maximise shareholders' wealth by returning premiums earned to customers on claims and providing excellent after-sales service. Hotels and hospitality organisations enhance goodwill by providing comfortable facilities at competitive rates, and a range of 'extra' services that serve as 'value-additions' and help to retain customers.

As illustrated above, all organisations are in a position from time to time where they need to make decisions with respect to financing, investments or dividend/interest payments to share/debt holders. It is vital for managers in all functional areas in services to understand the basic financial concepts of direct and indirect financing, value, time and uncertainty, market efficiency and asset pricing, arbitrage, and agency relationships. Moreover, managers need to understand how these financial concepts apply in day-to-day operations in order to make the management and operations of service organisations, as providers of financial, health, tourism, recreation and other services, efficient and effective.

Direct (disintermediation) and indirect (intermediation) financing

First, a distinction needs to be made between 'direct' and 'indirect' financing, and the various activities and types of financing available to Australian and Southeast Asian service organisations. In 'debt' markets (financial markets where debt instruments such as bonds, bills, notes, commercial papers and bankers' acceptances are traded), service organisations might go directly to the financial markets for their funding (thus avoiding the financial institutions) and issue debt instruments to savers and investors. This process is described as *disintermediation*, because it does not involve the financial institution in lending money (that is, it avoids an intermediate institution). When borrowers seek funds from financial institutions, this process is known as *intermediation* and this is described as indirect financing. Figures 7.2 and 7.3 show the direct (disintermediated) and indirect (intermediated) financial flows.

The direct finance model represented in Figure 7.2 indicates that organisations needing funds can opt for loans with collateral security (assets pledged by a borrower of a loan to secure it, which are subject to seizure in the event of default) in the borrower's name.

Brokers and dealers (financial specialists acting as middlemen between lenders and borrowers for a commission) do not accept deposits and make loans in their own names, but act as agents for borrowers and lenders, and arrange loans with other financial service providers who lend on, or off, balance sheet. Examples of deposit-taking institutions in Australia and Southeast Asia are listed in Table 7.1. They include banks (for example, global banks such as National Australia Bank, Hong Kong Shanghai Banking Corporation), building societies (for example, in Australia, Newcastle Permanent Building Society Ltd, Heritage Building Society Ltd) and credit unions (for example, Australian National Credit Union, Members Australia Credit Union, Central Credit Union in Singapore). Examples of

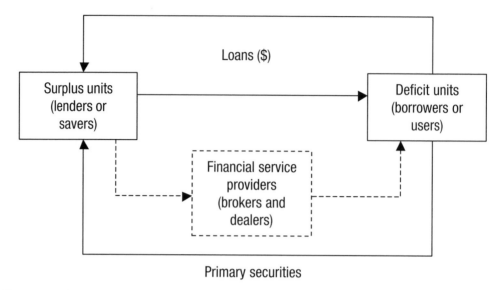

Figure 7.2 Direct (disintermediated) financial flows

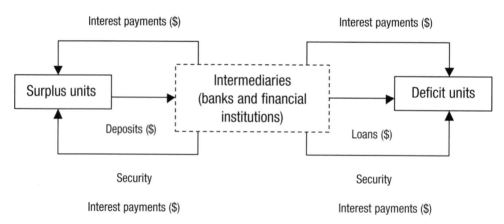

Figure 7.3 Indirect (intermediated) financial flows

Source: Figures 7.2 and 7.3 contributed by Dr John Simpson, Curtin Business School.

non-deposit-taking financial institutions that can, on occasion, make loans from their balance sheet are insurance organisations (for example, Allianz Group, QBE Insurance Group) and superannuation organisations (for example, ING Group, AXA Group).

Value
The value of an organisation is determined by the value of its equity (ordinary shares or ownership equity) plus the value of its debt (loans). The value of equity and debt varies as equity (ordinary shares) and debt instruments (bonds, bills, notes, commercial papers) gain/lose

Table 7.1 Financial institutions in developed economies

Type of institution	Main activity	Type of financing
Banks:		
Majors	All activities	Both direct and indirect
Regionals	Retail banking	Mostly indirect
Investment*	Wholesale banking	Mostly direct
Non-banks:		
Building societies	Retail banking	Indirect
Credit unions	Retail banking	Indirect
Merchant banks	Wholesale banking	Mostly direct
Finance companies	Retail and wholesale banking	Indirect
Fund management:		
Superannuation funds	Fund management	Direct
Insurance offices	Life and general insurance	A distinctive blend of direct and indirect
Unit trusts	Fund management	Direct

*Investment banks are also called merchant banks. Their principal operations include the provision of takeover and investment advice, dealing in the short-term money market and the underwriting of debt and equity issues. (The money market is regarded as a market trading in short-term debt and investment instruments with less than a year to maturity – for example, commercial bills. The capital market deals in debt and investment instruments with maturities in excess of one year – for example, corporate bonds. Underwriting is a function where an underwriter – a financial services provider such as a merchant bank – guarantees to provide the unsubscribed portion of a debt or equity issue (capital raising) by a deficit unit organisation. The unsubscribed portion is the amount of capital planned to be raised from investors less the actual amount raised.)

Source: B. Hunt and C. Terry, *Financial Institutions and Markets*, 3rd ed., Nelson Thomson, Melbourne, 2002, p. 87.

value on the markets. This depends on numerous internal factors such as organisation profitability and performance, dividend/interest payments, and external factors such as consumer confidence and sentiment, and economic booms/recessions. In summary, the value that financial markets ascribe to the debt and equity depends on the risk and expected return on investment in debt and equity instruments. The major issue is whether or not the instruments will be successful. (In other words, will they add value to the organisation by generating more cash than was laid out in the investment originally?) An organisation's value depends on the growth opportunities available to it (airlines expanding operations to connect to new destinations, banks providing diversified services, food chains expanding their franchise to overseas locations), which in turn depends on the organisation's ability to attract capital. Corporations are better able to take advantage of growth opportunities, as they are in a position to obtain funding more easily than unincorporated businesses. For example, because of their successful track records, it would be easier for a well-established banking corporation such as National Australia Bank (NAB) or Australia-New Zealand Banking Corporation (ANZ), or airline giants Qantas or Singapore Airlines, to source funds and increase in value, compared with an unincorporated small funeral company, a restaurant or a new Internet service provider.

Time and uncertainty

Time and uncertainty are fundamental concepts in finance theory. An investment's value is determined by the amount and timing of cash flows that are generated for the debt and/or equity holders from the investments. The main issue is how timing and uncertainty of cash flows will affect those decisions. The amount and timing of cash flows are not known with certainty, because (as noted earlier) of the influence of numerous internal and external factors. In addition, the assumption in finance theory is that investors are risk-averse (that is, they prefer to minimise risk for a given level of return). This assumption is universal and is applicable to all sectors of the finance industry. Part of the role of the successful financial manager is to assess and manage credit and minimise risk, while maximising returns for the organisation.

Market efficiency and asset pricing

The concepts of market efficiency and asset pricing are important for managers in all functional areas in various industries. In finance theory it is anticipated that securities and other assets should be fairly priced when their expected risk and returns are taken into consideration. Higher risk should be rewarded with higher expected returns. For example, it is commonly felt that shares in an organisation are more risky than debt, and therefore that the expected return on equity is greater than that on debt. The challenge for financial managers is to ascertain the tradeoff between risk and return.

The capital asset pricing model (CAPM) has been developed to assist financial managers to find the optimal tradeoff between risk and return. Under this model, *total* risk is made up of a *systematic* and an *unsystematic* component. The systematic component is described as *market* risk, which derives from market-wide factors such as changes in interest and exchange rates, the general economic situation, social changes, major political events and crises such as September 11 and SARS (see Chapter 2). This component of risk cannot be avoided, and therefore cannot be diversified away – the process of diversification is the spreading of risk between 'risky' and 'non-risky' assets to reduce the total amount of risk for a given level of expected return. The *unsystematic* risk is the unique risk of a single organisation within an industry, such as a union strike, a bad takeover bid, or a change in the composition of the board of directors. This risk is avoidable because it can be diversified. The arbitrage pricing model (APM) also describes the tradeoff between risk and return, and both the CAPM and APM emphasise that the financial market will only reward investors with higher expected returns for systematic risks. Financial managers need to focus on the systematic risk when they make decisions on investments with a given required *rate of return* (RoR). This is because service organisations also have their own levels of acceptable risk and return tradeoffs depending on their present levels of operations and future expectations, which will be affected by the risk and return tradeoff of various stakeholders.

Arbitrage

Financial managers are always looking to increase the value of the organisation. One commonly adopted strategy, known as arbitrage, involves the exploitation of the price differences of identical or similar financial instruments, on different financial markets or in different forms. An *efficient market* is defined as a market in which the values of all assets and securities at any point in time fully reflect all the available information – that is, there is no *information asymmetry*. (A situation where some participants in the market – buyers/sellers of assets and securities – have more information than others is known as 'information asymmetry'.) It should be noted that in markets that are information efficient, the prices of assets adjust instantaneously to new information (such as the news of a new venture, a new merger or an acquisition). In reality, markets are not perfectly efficient and it is possible therefore to buy an asset at a low price and quickly sell the same asset at a higher price in order to arbitrage a profit. Because markets have a degree of informational efficiency (where the participants are fully informed), this situation would not persist as informed traders/participants push up the lower-priced asset until the prices of the assets reach parity. Financial managers in all industries need to fully understand the logic of arbitrage and efficient markets in order to comprehend the working of the stock markets, which is a source of finance for routine activities and investments.

Agency relationships

The 'agency problem' is a major area of research in finance theory and is applicable to all industries. The problem relates to the conflict of interest that derives from the separation of ownership and control in an organisation. The managers of an organisation are the agents, while the shareholders are the principals. Managers (controllers) have a natural tendency to maximise their own level of satisfaction, whereas shareholders (owners) have a natural tendency to maximise the value of their equity. These goals are clearly in conflict. If managers go too far in pursuit of their own vested interests, lower profitability and, ultimately, loss of wealth to shareholders could result. For example, a large organisation may be run by professional managers who have little or no ownership position in that organisation and might invest in non-profit artwork ventures such as theatres or museums to satisfy self-interests, which might be seen by shareholders as a wasteful expenditure (see also Chapter 3).

The costs associated with the agency problem are difficult to measure and have been subject to ongoing arguments by scholars and practitioners. Occasionally, however, this conflict is resolved in the share market. For example, if the market feels that the management of an organisation is damaging shareholder wealth, there might be a positive reaction to the share price once the shareholders dismiss the management at the annual general meeting (AGM). A common solution to this conflict is to give the managers a stake in the ownership of the organisation in the form of shares or stock options. Usually given to employees, stock options are an opportunity to purchase stock in the organisation at a future date. The price of the option is established (that is, determined on the issue date). Thus if the organisation's stock price rises above the option price, the owner is able to take advantage of the stock increase (that is, current stock price – established stock price). The manager now has an incentive to increase his or her own share wealth and thereby to establish some commonality of interest with the ordinary shareholders. Financial managers need to be aware of any agency problem, as it clearly affects the profitability of the stakeholders and, ultimately, the profitability of the organisation.

Golden handshakes: Cost or benefit?

When senior executives of organisations have their employment terminated, they often receive a substantial payout – a 'golden handshake'. To many members of the public, this may seem excessive, unreasonable and unwarranted. But it may – for example, in hindsight – be of benefit to the organisation to rid itself of under-performing executives, allowing the organisation to perform better and increase the share price. This is particularly so in the case of a takeover of one organisation by another; the golden handshake can be used to remove managers who might other-wise be hostile and react detrimentally to the organisation's performance.

(*Source:* Adapted from R. Peacock, P. Martin, M. Burrow, J. W. Petty, A. J. Keown, D. F. Scott, Jr and J. D. Martin, *Financial Management*, 3rd ed., Pearson Education Australia, Sydney, 2003, p. 8)

Moral hazard

This aspect of financial theory has immense relevance in public-sector service organisations – in particular, to central banks (for example, Reserve Bank of Australia, Bank of Indonesia, Reserve Bank of India). Central banks are charged with the responsibility of administering and implementing *monetary policy* (the regulation of the money supply and interest rates by a central bank in order to control inflation and stabilise currency) and *fiscal policy* (policies involving the collection and spending of revenue – that is, a 'tax and spend' policy) to control inflation and maintain systemic safety and stability. Financial service providers such as banks need to understand the concept of 'moral hazard'. This concept describes the process where banks, knowing that they can be rescued by governments (seeking to maintain systemic sta-bility) in the event of failure, take higher-than-acceptable risks in their lending portfolios. This may result in substantial non-performing loans and lower profitability and, ultimately, contribute to a reduction in shareholder equity value. Other public and private-sector service organisations are also subject to government bailouts from time to time due to unwarranted risks derived from the problem of 'moral hazard'.

Vaknin (2004) explains that a moral hazard infringes upon both transparency and accountability, arguably a key factor in the 1997 Asian 'economic crisis'. He further contends that moral hazard is never explicit or known in advance. It is always arbitrary, or subject to political and geopolitical considerations, hence increasing uncertainty rather than decreasing it. In addition, by protecting private investors and creditors from the outcomes of their errors and misjudgments, it undermines the concept of liability.

This section has discussed the important roles and responsibilities of financial man-agers to ensure the financial viability and successes of the organisation. The primary focus for managers in the various organisational functional areas (marketing, operations and human resources) is to understand how the basic principles of financial management (direct and indirect financing, value, time and uncertainty, market efficiency and asset pricing, arbitrage, the agency problem and moral hazard) are fundamental in achieving the financial goal of the organisation (the maximisation of wealth of the organisation's shareholders or owners). The maximisation of shareholder wealth reflects the impact of all financial decisions. Shareholders react to poor investment or dividend decisions by causing the total value of the organisation's shares to fall. They react to good decisions by pushing up the price of shares. The growing awareness of the need for good corporate governance and transparency has increased the contemporary importance of stakeholder theory. Organisations now have an obligation not just to shareholders, but also to other stakeholder groups such as government, environmental groups, creditors and suppliers. A more detailed discussion on the various stakeholders of the organisation is provided in Chapter 3.

Functions of financial management in the services sector

As previously discussed, modern financial management provides a conceptual and analytical framework for prudent financial decision making. It defines the finance function to include both the acquisition of funds and the efficient allocation of those funds. It is an integral part of overall management, and its scope for the services sector may be defined in terms of the following critical questions adapted from Ezra Solomon's (1963) conception of financial management discussed in his classic work, *The Theory of Financial Management*:
- What should be the composition of the organisation's assets (fixed assets, current assets financed by debt, equity)?
- What should be the mix of the organisation's financing (short-term, long-term)?
- How should the organisation analyse, plan and control its financial affairs?

   The important functions of financial management in the services sector, as related to the central concerns noted above, may be categorised as: *financial analysis, planning and control; sourcing for finance;* and *financial risk management*. These are explained in the following way.
1 *Financial analysis, planning and control*
   - Analysis of financial condition and performance: assessing the financial performance and condition of the organisation.
   - Financial forecasting and planning: estimating the future needs of the organisation.
   - Activity-based costing: effective control mechanism to evaluate the effectiveness of resource utilisation.
2 *Sourcing for finance*
   - Identification of sources of finance and determination of financing mix (working capital management, short- and long-term financing).
3 *Financial risk management*
   - Managing risk in an uncertain environment (business, credit, market, operational, liquidity and legal risk).

   These functions are now discussed in detail, with consideration of the implications for the operations of the management of services.

Financial analysis, planning and control
Analysis of financial condition and performance
Major management decisions are determined by the analysis of financial information. Careful scrutiny of the alternative choices, based on the results of projected information comparing

each project/venture, is needed before deciding on the most favourable choice for eventual implementation. This assessment of an organisation's past, present and anticipated future financial condition is known as *financial analysis*. The main objective of financial analysis is to determine the organisation's financial strengths and identify its weaknesses.

Organisations generally report their financial performance through the use of three basic financial statements:

- the profit and loss statement (also known as *statement of financial performance*) (reveals the operating results of the business activities of the organisation);
- the *balance sheet* (also known as *statement of financial position*) (a statement of the financial position of the organisation, identifying the assets, liabilities and owners' equity at a particular point in time); and
- the *statement of cash flows* (a statement providing details of the accounting of cash inflows and outflows during a specific period).

Though not obliged to do so by corporate law or accounting standards, organisations may also complete a *funds statement*, which provides an account of the resources allocated during the specific period and their uses. It should be noted that financial reporting formats vary from industry to industry. Thus the financial statements of banks and financial institutions would be different from those of airlines or hotels, for example, because of differences in revenue, expense, asset and liability items.

Financial reporting in industries across countries is governed by accounting standards. For example, financial reporting in Australia is governed by the International Financial Reporting Standards (IFRS) under the guidance of the Australian Accounting Standards Board (AASB) from 1 January 2005. Financial reporting in India is governed by the Accounting Standards Board under the guidance of the Institute of Chartered Accountants of India (ICAI). However, the number of organisations worldwide listed on the National Association of Securities Dealers Automated Quotation system (NASDAQ) or the New York Stock Exchange's (NYSE) adopting double reporting standards – that is, reporting as per the local accounting board as well as the US Generally Accepted Accounting Principles (GAAP) (a requirement by US regulation to be listed on US stock exchanges) – has become common. In 2004, CEO of media giant News Corporation, Rupert Murdoch, announced that the Australia-based News Corp. would shift its headquarters to the United States in order to simplify its operations and reporting measures.

According to CPA Australia CEO Greg Larson, cited in a CPA Australia media release (2002):

> People are entitled to believe that companies publish credible financial reports. Quality financial reporting needs good directors, good management, good financial accounting, good internal auditors and good external auditors. We believe there is generally too much mystique surrounding financial reporting, and to be effective the financial reporting system must be transparent, credible and easily explained.

(See Chapter 3 for a discussion on transparency.)

Financial ratios are the principal tools of financial analysis. Financial ratio analysis is the calculation and comparison of ratios, which are derived from the information in a company's financial statements. The level and historical trends of these ratios can be used to make inferences about a company's *financial condition* (for example, a bank loan officer considering the application of a two-year loan might want to gather information about the solvency and liquidity condition of the organisation), its *operations* (for example, the internal financial analyst might employ financial turnover measures to show how efficient a company is in its operations and use of assets), and investment attractiveness (for example, a potential investor in the organisation's ordinary shares might want to get a historical account of the profitability of the organisation). Answers to questions about a company's financial conditions, operations and investment attractiveness can be found through the analysis of financial ratios.

Financial ratio analysis groups the ratios into categories, which tell us about different facets of an organisation's finances and operations. While a detailed analysis of the ratios is beyond the scope of this chapter, following is an overview of some of the categories of ratios:

- *Leverage ratios* (operating leverage, financial leverage, combined leverage), which show the extent of the use of debt in an organisation's capital structure.
- *Liquidity ratios* (current ratio, acid-test ratio), which give a picture of an organisation's short-term financial situation or solvency.
- *Solvency ratios* (debt to equity ratio, debt to assets ratio, coverage of fixed assets, interest coverage), which give a picture of an organisation's ability to generate cash flow and pay its financial debts.
- *Operational ratios* (inventory turnover ratio, debt turnover ratio, accounts payable and receivable turnover ratios), which use turnover measures to show how efficient an organisation is in its operations and use of assets.
- *Profitability ratios* (profit margin, return on assets, and return on equity), which use margin analysis and show the return on sales and capital employed.

Financial ratios attempt to standardise financial information to facilitate meaningful comparisons. It should be noted that an organisation's financial ratios can be compared with two types of standards. The first consists of similar ratios for the same type of organisation from previous financial statements, known as *trend analysis*. The second norm employs ratios from other organisations that are considered comparable in the same industry or sector, generally involving the use of published *industry or sector-average ratios*.

Financial forecasting and planning

Financial forecasting and planning plays a crucial role in ensuring the financial viability of an organisation's future. It describes the process by which organisations think about and prepare for the future. The forecasting process provides the means for an organisation to express its goals and priorities and to ensure that they are internally consistent. It also assists the organisation to identify the asset requirements and needs for financing from external sources. Forecasting in financial management is required when the organisation is ready to estimate its future financial needs. The impact of computers, financial software and the communications revolution on the practice of financial forecasting, planning and budgeting has been dramatic. Nowadays, spreadsheets can be linked to databases and the Internet. Vast amounts of data can be stored on databases and retrieved in the future to facilitate meaningful comparisons.

Organisational planning and financial forecasting go hand in hand. Planning generally includes setting goals and objectives for the organisation, identifying and estimating the probable future environment of the organisation (that is, forecasting), and devising means by which the organisation may reach its goals in the future. Cheng (1986) points out the implicit relationship between planning and forecasting whereby planning inevitably deals with adapting to likely future conditions.

A financial forecast is an estimate of the predicted results of the operations of a business for a future period. Financial forecasts are an essential part of any organisation from the conception of a business idea. A bank or other potential funding source will require detailed profit and expenditure forecasts, which should form a central part of a business plan. It is essential for new venture organisations to ensure that their business idea will produce sufficient profits to make the venture viable before seeking financial backing. Once a business has been established, financial forecasts remain an important part of planning and control. Regular and prudent budgeting, which is later compared with the actual results of the business, will quickly highlight areas where costs require attention, or a particular product or service line is in trouble. This facilitates taking remedial action before the organisation reaches a crisis point or ends up in bankruptcy.

As previously explained, forecasting in financial management is required when the organisation is ready to estimate its future financial requirements. Financial forecasts are particularly needed for many corporate long-range planning decisions and for the preparation of operating budgets, and they also serve as guideposts directing actions when exceptions and new situations develop (Cheng, 1986).

Data and information used in the preparation of forecasts may be many and varied, from factual data embodied in contracts to pure surmises (depending on managers' professional experience and judgment). The forecaster needs to pay attention to the dynamic nature of the service organisation's environment. (See Chapter 2 for a discussion on environmental factors that impact on an organisation.) The forecaster must be aware of a variety of external environmental factors, including economic and political uncertainty, economic crises, and increased competitiveness in a period of rapid globalisation, international competition and price stability, taxation, inflation and government intervention. In general, forecast sources should fall into the following categories:

- management's policies and the operation plan, which are expected to govern corporate activity during the period of the recast;
- budgets, which have been approved by management's detailed operating plans;
- individual forecasts and estimates of future operations obtained from operating departments;
- studies of past experience from organisation records from which trends may be determined;
- analyses of statistical data from outside sources, used to determine trends of sales, salary scales and prices; and
- information available from statistical bureaux and government databases on exogenous factors that may affect operations, such as government policies, tax laws and exchange rates. (Adapted from Robertson, 1948)

How long should a period of forecast cover? There is no one answer to this question. The period covered will vary, depending on the nature of the business, its needs, and the length of time it is possible to forecast accurately. Industries that operate in a relatively stable market are able to make forecasts well into the future. Alternatively, an organisation that operates on a contract basis may find it impossible to forecast beyond the date of expiration of current contracts (for example, dot.coms, start-up service organisations and joint ventures). The length of a forecast can also be determined by a particular situation or event, such as the expiration of a bank loan or share issue. Nevertheless, as a general rule, a reasonable forecast should cover at least one year but not extend so far into the future that it is unrealistic. Forecasts are also revised from time to time, depending on additional information obtained in the future. Generally, forecasts of service organisations consist of two schedules: a profit and loss statement and a cash statement. These forecasts are illustrated below.

Profit and loss forecast

Particulars	Amount ($)
Sales (goods and/or services)	XXX
Less: Cost of sales	XXX
Gross profit	**XXX**
Less: Expenses	
Salary expenses: Basic pay plus overtime	XX
Payroll expenses: Including paid holidays, sick leave, health insurance, unemployment insurance	XX
Outside services: Include costs of subcontracts, one-time services	XX
Supplies: Services and items purchased for business (not for resale)	XX
Repairs and maintenance: Regular maintenance and repair, including periodic large expenditures such as renovation	XX
Car, delivery and travel: Include charges if personal car is used in the business. Include parking, tolls, repairs	XX
Advertising: TV, radio, Internet commercials, directory listing	XX
Accounting and legal: Outside professional services	XX
Rent for real estate	XX
Telephone	XX
Utilities: Water, heat and light	XX
Insurance: Fire or liability on property, workers' compensation	XX
Taxes: Inventory, sales, excise, real estate	XX
Interest	XX
Depreciation: Amortisation of capital assets	XX
Other expenses: Leased equipment and tools, small expenses	XX
Total expenses (sum of above expenses)	**XXX**
Net profit before tax	**XXX**
Less: Tax @ company rate of taxation	XX
Net profit after tax	**XXX**

The profit and loss forecast matches the income and expenditure of the organisation to the period in which goods and/or services were provided. Generally, organisations prepare monthly profit and loss forecasts for the first year of operation, followed by monthly or quarterly projections for subsequent years. The profit forecast not only enables all functional areas of the business to assess if the organisation's operations are viable and sustainable in the future, but also provides a clear guide for potential investors when seeking initial or additional funding. It also keeps the various stakeholders informed of the performance of the organisation.

(A typical profit and loss statement appears on p. 267.)

Cash flow forecast

The cash flow forecast measures the anticipated flow of payments received against the products and/or services suppliers. This forecast will differ from the profit and loss forecast, as payment is not always received in the same month as the income is accounted for in the profit forecast. Most organisations use the *accrual* method of accounting (income when earned and expenses when incurred), as opposed to *cash basis* accounting (which reports income when received and expenses when paid).

The organisation's operations can be illustrated through the use of a 'cash flow cycle' diagram. Figure 7.4 explains the organisation's operations as a large 'pump' that injects the flow of cash through various 'reservoirs', such as accounts receivable and inventories, and disburses cash for interest and principal payments on debt, taxes and dividends. It is not an easy task to predict the exact amount of cash inflows and outflows at a particular point of time given that a number of internal and external factors impinge on the organisation from time to time. Hence, financial forecasting is a difficult task, especially in a highly competitive, volatile and globalised world. (See Chapter 2 for discussion on the changing economic environment.)

Any estimate of the future using forecasts should be compared over time with the actual results. Regular comparisons will reveal how reliable the forecast may be as a guide, and indicate how actual results can be brought closer to management objectives. The adoption of a coordinated approach by the planners and forecasters ensures the future viability of the organisation. The use of financial forecasts by all functional areas of an organisation is vital to the organisation's performance. For example: forecasts assist HR managers to make recruitment decisions; marketing managers can decide on the feasibility of marketing plans; and operations managers are able to prudently plan various operational areas. Furthermore, accurate forecasts keep the various stakeholders informed of the future direction of the organisation. (See Chapter 3 for stakeholder expectations.)

Activity-based costing

Activity-based costing (ABC) is a cost accounting system used by numerous private- and public-sector companies today, across a variety of industries that include manufacturing, services and government. ABC was first developed as various commercial businesses began to experience difficulties in accounting for indirect and overhead costs (for example, Pneumatic Bellows (pneumatic controls), Mueller-Lehmkuhl GmbH (clothes fasteners) and

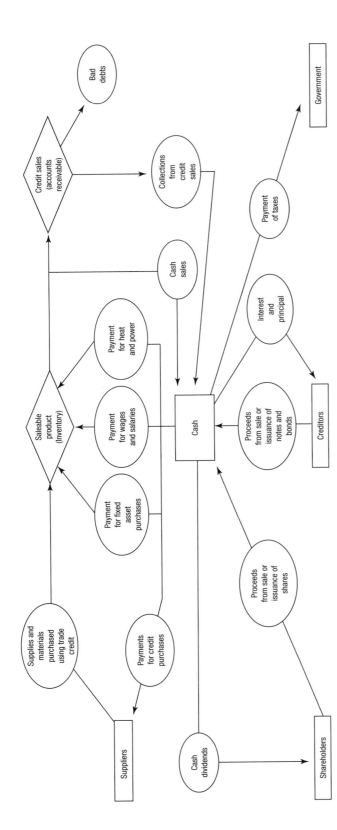

Figure 7.4 The cash-flow cycle

The organisation's cash-flow cycle is a continuous ongoing process and begins with the organisation's cash reservoir, which includes the owner's investment (funds raised through issue of equity) and funds borrowed from banks, financial institutions and other creditors. This cash is utilised to acquire plant, equipment (if any), other infrastructure, as well as supplies and materials. It is also used to pay wages, salaries, overheads such as head and power, and other ongoing costs. Sales of goods and/or services are made for cash, or on credit (where some are permanently written off as bad debts). Inflows to cash flows account from the sale of assets and securities. In the final phase of cycle, cash is disbursed to pay off obligations to suppliers for credit purchases, income taxes to government, interest and principal payments to creditors, and cash dividend to owners. Retained earnings after payments made are then reinvested back into the organisation to become part of owner's investment.

Source: R. Peacock, M. Burrow, J. W. Petty, A. J. Keown, D. F. Scott Jr and J. D. Martin, *Financial Management*, 3rd ed., Sydney, Pearson Education Australia, 2003, p. 140

American Bank (retail banking). ABC helped to solve this problem by directly tracing overhead costs to the processes that generate goods and services (outputs). By providing accurate and reliable cost information and measures, ABC has helped to improve product costing, strategic pricing, profit planning and the overall control of the various activities of the organisation.

ABC is a powerful tool used to measure performance by identifying, describing, assigning costs to and reporting on organisational operations (The Learning Source, 2002). ABC is considered to be a more accurate and reliable cost management system than traditional cost accounting. 'ABC identifies opportunities to improve business process effectiveness and efficiency by determining the "true" cost of a product or service' (The Learning Source, 2002, p. 2). Management across organisations is particularly interested in ABC principles as it clearly defines processes, identifies the cost drivers of those processes, determines the *unit costs* of various products and services, and creates various reports on organisational components that can be used further to prepare activity- or performance-based budgets. In other words, ABC generates reports on how money is being allocated or spent, and whether individual departments are being prudent (that is, cost effective), as well as benchmarking reports that facilitate comparisons to enable quality control.

ABC works on the principle that *when employees understand the activities they perform, they can better understand the costs involved.* For example, bank employees who approve loans, and real estate agents, would have an understanding of stamp duties and other taxes; and employees working in call centres would be better equipped to provide details on costs associated with telephony. Hence ABC endeavours to clearly project the activities of the various functional areas of a business and, thus, is crucial for service organisations to apply.

> Some ABC systems rank activities by the degree to which they add value to the organisation or its outputs. This helps managers identify what activities are really value-added – those that will best accomplish a mission, deliver a service, or meet customer demand, thus improving decision-making through better information, and helping to eliminate waste by encouraging employees to look at all costs. (The Learning Source, 2002, p. 3)

ABC and the services sector

Service organisations have modelled their cost accounting systems on those used by manufacturing organisations. Manufacturing organisations emphasise the value of stock (inventory), which does not apply to some service organisations (for example, transport, insurance), and use standard costing techniques for direct materials and labour. (Direct cost is defined as expenditure that can be economically identified and specifically measured with respect to a relevant cost object.) Service organisations, where direct materials and direct labour costs are less relevant, calculate standard costs in that setting. Thus there may be conflicts for service organisations in terms of the applicability of the manufacturing cost accounting techniques. Nonetheless, as pointed out earlier, service organisations do need to know accurate costs for profitability analyses. In particular, the following factors need to be assessed:

- What goods and/or services are profitable?
- What goods and/or services should be emphasised?
- What are the trends in goods and/or service profitability over time?
- What are the goods and/or service costs as a basis for setting prices?

This means that service sector costing needs to be forward-looking, and ABC is a tool for such analysis.

Service organisations are becoming more interested in accurate costing in order to make long-term strategic decisions as well as day-to-day operating decisions (Ruhl and Hartman, 1998) (see Chapters 4 and 6). Accurate costs are crucial in making product pricing, staffing and resource allocation decisions. The resources allocated will depend on the needs, tastes and preferences of service customers. Reports on accurate costs, along with the quantities and patterns of resource consumption (for example, airlines need accurate costing information of aviation fuel consumption; food-service organisations need accurate costing information on electricity, gas and other overhead cost consumption), give managers the necessary information to charge the appropriate price for the various services. Ruhl and Hartman (1998) contend that ABC is difficult to implement in service organisations since employees often work on many projects in a day and for different amounts of time. This makes it difficult to trace the resources used by various elements.

How ABC works

ABC focuses on the activities of a production cycle. This is based on the premise that outputs (goods or services) require activities to produce, and that activities consume resources. An output is defined as something 'put out' at the end of a production process (see Chapter 6). It can be a good or a service, and it must be measurable or quantifiable. An organisation's output is determined by its core activities or processes – that is, the main things that the organisation does or provides. For example, an output at a health-care facility can range from the provision of anaesthetics, to nursing services; at a financial institution, from credit card issue to home loan applications; at an undertaker, from the provision of crematorium services to catering; at an offshore call centre, from debt collection to contract renewals; and at a legal services organisation, from insurance fraud cases to advice on estate duties. As noted, the activities of service organisations are often complex and involve the production of more than one output.

Outputs have the following general characteristics:

- produced to satisfy customer wants;
- distinctly quantifiable, measurable and auditable;
- should be consistent between fiscal periods to facilitate cost comparison;
- should be incorporated into existing or modified financial management systems; and
- should be separately identifiable so that costs can be more easily allocated.

The unit cost formula

The ABC system uses cost 'drivers' to assign the costs of resources to various activities. It can employ unit cost as a means of measuring output. Unit cost is simply the 'average total cost' of producing one unit of output. It is calculated by dividing the total cost of production by the total number of units of output produced. For example, if a

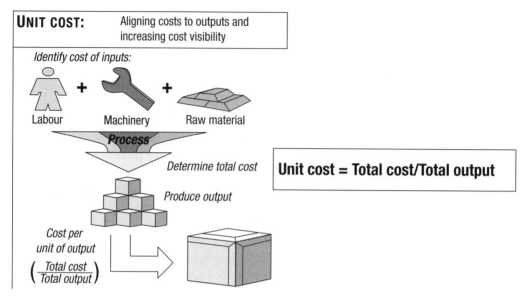

Figure 7.5 Unit cost determination

Source: The Learning Source, 1992 'Activity Based Costing – Accounting for Operational Readiness', Concept Paper published at the OSD Comptroller I-Centre, USA.

consulting organisation provides 10 consultancy services for a total cost of $100,000, then cost per unit (service) is $10,000. Figure 7.5 provides a generic illustration of unit cost determination.

ABC adopts the aggregated method for unit cost methodology for organisations with more than one output. As previously noted, because there is not always a physical good provided to customers, the unit cost activities in service organisations are more complex. For example, a research and development activity may be utilised by one of the health-care organisations to test a specific drug in addition to its basic research mission. Arguably, a tested drug is a valid output. However, the diversity of services offered to customers requires that a more common output be identified. In this particular case, the direct labour hours expended in the accomplishment of a task as a 'proxy' (or substitute output measure) can be adopted.

Making clear connections between costs and outputs creates total *cost visibility*. A clear picture of the costs incurred by the various functional areas is essential to the prudent allocation of resources. It also facilitates quick comparisons against benchmarks and effective cost management and control across the organisation. Some of the benefits of employing ABC in service organisations are identified later in this chapter.

Steps to ABC implementation in service organisations

This section examines the current practices and recent developments in two particular parts of the services sector – banking and health care – with respect to the application and implementation of ABC. Other sectors may also use similar approaches.

Banking

Globalisation and the telecommunications revolution have led national governments in Australia and Asia to open up their economies to overseas competitors, which has implications for the banking sector. Multinational banking corporations such as Citibank, HSBC and ANZ have now established themselves beyond national boundaries with worldwide branches. During the previous decade, the significant increase in competition among banks, owing to the large-scale effects of globalisation, has resulted in significant improvements in the quality and quantity of services.

Cost accounting has played a fundamental role in ensuring the viability and long-term sustainability of banks worldwide. Notably, costs incurred by banks are not driven by the volume of customers, but rather by the number of transactions processed. Previously, various banks employed traditional volume-based costing techniques, but the current technological developments in information and communications have rendered the traditional approach less useful owing to increased cross-border volumes. Banks are adopting the concept where the user pays for the cost of the services they use, so that all users do not share the bill evenly in adherence with the principle of fairness. Online banking, any time banking with ATMs, e-banking and telephone banking have all contributed to the increased volume of transactions, and enable more accurate tracking of individual customer services. In order to keep track of the individual's particular use of the various services, an accurate reflection of the cost of services is required. This is where ABC becomes useful.

Sharma (1992) describes step-by-step how banks should implement ABC:

- Split the bank into profit centres.
- Prepare a list of goods and/or services associated with each profit centre and a list of product-related and non-product-related activities.
- Divide non-product-related activities into activities with unit-specific significance and activities with organisation-wide significance. The former activities are spread across all products produced by the unit. The latter category should include as few things as possible.

Health care

The following section examines in some detail various perspectives on hospital cost accounting systems. Health-care providers across regions previously had the autonomous authority to increase their prices for services provided and to increase revenues and profitability. Today, Medicare or managed care organisations essentially set revenues with their prospective payment system (PPS), whereby Medicare pays a fixed fee per patient day based on the level of the patient to cover the agreed level of hospital and post-hospital extended care routine service costs (for example, Medicare Top Cover patients). For Medicare patients not receiving post-hospital extended care services (for example, Medicare Other patients), reimbursements for ancillary services, including rehabilitation services, are made as per government schedules under the guidance of the local medical associations and are limited to a pre-decided amount or beneficiary cap. Prior to PPS, Medicare reimbursement was made primarily based on the provider's cost of services. Health-care providers can improve profitability by making prudent decisions with accurate cost information. PPS has improved the sophistication of cost accounting systems in health care.

Table 7.2 A four-step hospital cost accounting process

Stage type/(Responsibility)	Information used	Key activities	Managerial uses
Stage 1: Improving the full cost system (accounting staff)	Direct and indirect costs	Choice of cost object. Assignment of costs to cost centres. Choice of allocation bases. Allocation of service centre costs to revenue centres.	Product-line profitability. Strategic decisions (programs, facilities, personnel to support product lines).
Stage 2: Assessing cost behaviour (accounting staff)	Fixed and variable costs	Analysis of cost behaviour by Diagnosis Related Groups (DRG). Contribution analyses.	Special price offerings. Contracts for services. Retention or discontinuation of unprofitable centres.
Stage 3: Controlling costs (senior management)	Patient- and DRG-related costs	Determination of cost drivers. Budget development using cost drivers. Determination of responsibility centres. Assignment of variances to controlling agents.	Cost control. Motivation. Performance measurements. Involvement of physicians in cost management.
Stage 4: Designing administrative systems (senior management)	Process-related costs. Non-financial measures of performance.	Definition of administrative systems. Calculation of costs by administrative systems. Development of non-financial measures of performance.	Performance measurement across functional boundaries. Shift of measurement focus to cross-functional groups.

Hospital administrators' survey responses (Ruhl and Hartman, 1998) indicate that the following information was needed to manage effectively:

- the cost of an episode/event of care;
- an accurate allocation of administrative costs to goods and/or services;
- a comparison of costs and their causes over time; and
- information regarding the cost of various activities.

All of this information can be determined by an ABC system. Young and Pearlman (1993) indicate that a hospital's cost accounting system evolves in a four-step process (see Table 7.2).

Young and Pearlman (1993) list some of the cost drivers (instrumental to ABC) in a hospital setting, illustrated in Table 7.3.

Ramsey (1994) argues that hospital cost accounting should serve three main purposes:

1 It should promote cost efficiency without sacrificing the quality of goods and services.

2 It should allow the organisation to maximise its resources through goods and services line management.

Table 7.3 Cost drivers in a hospital setting

Cost driver	Example
Case type or diagnosis	Acute myocardial infarction (MI); influenza; pneumonia; phlebitis.
Number of cases	300 acute MI cases; 200 influenza cases; 100 pneumonia cases; 50 phlebitis cases.
Resources per case	For acute MI cases: 10 inpatient days, 5 X-rays, 10 complete blood counts (CBCs). For influenza cases: 5 inpatient days, 1 X-ray, 5 CBCs. For pneumonia cases: 6 inpatient days, 2 X-rays, 3 CBCs. For phlebitis cases: 7 inpatient days, no X-rays, 7 CBCs.
Input unit prices (or factor prices)	Cost per minute for nurses; cost per minute for laboratory technicians; cost per unit of routine care supplies; cost per unit of X-ray film and other supplies; cost per unit of CBC supplies.
Input efficiency	Number of nursing minutes needed per patient day, by diagnosis; number of technician minutes needed per X-ray; number of technician minutes needed per CBC. Number of units of inpatient supplies per patient day; number of units of X-ray and CBC supplies per procedure/test.
Fixed facility costs	Equipment depreciation in inpatient ward, radiology and laboratory; administrative salaries in ward, radiology and laboratory; overall hospital administration: hospital-wide (that is, non-departmental) depreciation.

3 It should highlight areas for continual improvement, all of which are enabled with the application of ABC.

The following are some of the benefits of applying ABC to most types of service organisations:

- makes it possible to determine total costs traced to outputs ('tagging');
- targets areas needing management attention;
- encourages the consideration of alternative methods of service delivery;
- highlights operational efficiency and inefficiency;
- identifies money-makers and money losers;
- identifies financial benchmarks for activity performance (finds an economic breakeven point);
- generates more information to measure and reward performance, and prioritises activities for cost reductions;
- provides a common managerial framework among support activities; and
- facilitates opportunities for cost improvement and strategic decision making.

The application of an ABC model to an international insurance services organisation is provided in Case study 7.1 at the end of this chapter.

Sourcing for finance

From their inception, service organisations need funds to operate in both the short and long term. One of the most difficult tasks a financial manager faces is to determine short- and long-term funding sources. Various criteria – such as the cost of funding, associated risk and return, and future performance and expectations – need to be considered. Some of the sources of short- and long-term funding available to service organisations are now discussed.

Short-term finance is essential to provide business with funding for a short-term period of a year or less. These funds usually run their day-to-day operations, including payment of wages to employees, overhead expenses, raw materials, inventory and supplies. Retail service organisations such as Coles and Kmart, which place orders for supplies for which they pay for with finance (short-term credit) and which they anticipate repaying by selling the goods over the period of a year, are examples of firms using short-term financing. In contrast, long-term financing decisions include investment in plant and machinery and telecommunications infrastructure, the benefits of which extend beyond a year. For example, Qantas's purchase of new aircraft and Telstra's investment in laying fibre-optic cables in Australia will be financed by long-term sources that will provide benefits for the next several years.

Financial managers in services understand the importance of net working capital management and the use of short-term funding to run the day-to-day operations of the organisations. *Net working capital* is defined as the organisation's investment in current assets minus its current liabilities (that is, the organisation's liquidity management). Current assets include assets that are liquid (can be converted to cash within the financial year) such as cash, marketable securities, accounts receivable and inventories. Alternatively, current liabilities include all debts that the organisation needs to repay within the financial year, such as accounts payable, and loan principal and interest due within the financial year. Financial managers face the dilemma of increasing the organisation's liquidity by investing in current assets while knowing that the greater reliability on short-term debt or current liabilities in financing its assets investments will lower its liquidity. So, how do financial managers decide on the optimal level of working capital at a given point of time? The answer is not simple. Managing the organisation's net working capital (liquidity) involves simultaneous and interrelated decisions regarding investment in current assets and the use of current liabilities (Peacock et al., 2003). The hedging principle, or the principle of self-liquidating debt, 'provides a guide to the maintenance of a level of liquidity sufficient for organisations to meet [their] maturing obligations on time' (p. 168).

Hedging principle
The hedging principle involves matching the cash-flow-generating characteristics of an asset with the maturity of the source of financing used to finance the asset. For example, Kmart's expansion of inventories of umbrellas, raincoats and rain boots during the rainy season and of sweaters, jackets and other warm clothing in winter should be financed using short-term loans or current liabilities. This is because the funds are needed for a limited time, and after that time has elapsed the cash needed to repay the loan would have been generated by the sale of the extra inventories. Using long-term sources of finance (more than one year) for the above orders would mean that Kmart would still have the funds after the sale of the inventories which they helped finance. In this case, Kmart would have extra liquidity, which it would hold in cash or invest in low-yield short-term marketable securities until the seasonal change occurs again and the funds are needed. This would result in an overall lowering of Kmart's profitability (the hedging principle).

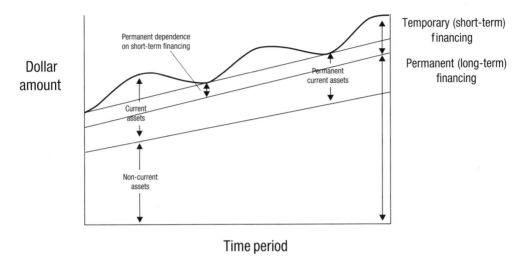

Figure 7.6 Conventional hedging financing strategy

Source: Adapted from R. Peacock, P. Martin, M. Burrow, J. W. Petty, A. J. Keown, D. F. Scott Jr and J. D. Martin, *Financial Management*, 3rd ed., Sydney, Pearson Education, 2003

Alternatively, if Kmart proposes to install automated check-out counters that are expected to produce cash savings by eliminating the need for five employees, and consequently their salaries, these savings would result in $50,000 per annum with the automated check-out counters estimated to cost $250,000 to install and with a life of 15 years. If Kmart decided to finance the automated check-out counters with short-term (one-year) finance, it could not repay the loan from the cash flow generated by the asset installed. The hedging principle states that Kmart should finance the automated check-out counters with a source of finance that matches the expected life and cash-flow-generating characteristics of the asset. Hence, Kmart should utilise a 10- to 15-year loan to finance the asset.

Thus, the 'maturity matching' concept under the hedging principle states that short-term (temporary) assets such as working capital requirements must be financed by short-term sources, whereas long-term (permanent) assets such as plant, machinery and infrastructure should be financed by long-term sources. The conventional hedging financing strategy is illustrated in Figure 7.6.

In Figure 7.6, total assets are broken down into temporary (short-term) and permanent (long-term) asset investment categories. The organisation's permanent investment in assets such as plant, machinery and telecommunications infrastructure is financed by the use of permanent sources of financing (intermediate and long-term debt, equity and preference shares). Its temporary investments in assets for day-to-day operations are financed with temporary finance (unsecured loans, commercial bills, promissory notes, inventories and loans secured by accounts receivable).

Recently established service organisations and 'start-ups' such as dot.coms follow a more cautious hedging financing strategy where permanent sources of financing exceed permanent assets, so that excess cash is available to be invested in low-yield short-term marketable securities. The excess liquidity reduces the risk of falling short of cash in the initial years of operation, while compromising profitability by investing in low-yield marketable securities. Alternatively, well-established organisations follow an aggressive hedging finance strategy from time to time, where parts of their permanent assets are financed with temporary or short-term funds. Such organisations face increased liquidity risks in terms of cash shortfall in a time of crisis. The tradeoff, however, results in the savings resulting from the use of lower-cost short-term debt (as opposed to long-term debt).

Organisations across various industries follow different financing strategies from time to time depending on their needs, expectations, associated costs, risks, trade cycles and the performance of the economy.

Short-term finance

Financial management experts suggest three main factors that should be considered in selecting a short-term finance source:

- the cost of credit (total cost to borrow the funds);
- the spontaneity of availability of credit when funds are required; and
- the after-effects of the use of the credit source (that is, the cost it imposed on other sources of funds).

The sources of short-term finance available to service organisations range from unsecured sources (credit on borrower's faith, no collateral involved) such as trade credit, promissory notes and bills of exchange, to secured sources (borrower pledges assets as collateral) such as bank and finance company loans.

Trade credit

Trade credit is the most flexible and common source of short-term financing available to service organisations. It is defined as the credit made available by an organisation's suppliers in connection with the acquisition of materials, supplies and inventory. Trade credit arises with the organisation's purchase of goods and services. When Kmart places an order for bottled mineral water with Spring Valley, the Spring Valley credit department will check Kmart's credit rating and, if favourable, will despatch the order of bottled mineral water on the premise that Kmart will honour its credit terms and pay for the bottled mineral water in due course. Trade credit has a number of advantages, in that it is conveniently obtained as a routine part of an organisation's operations without any formal agreements involving credit. Trade credit also enhances the goodwill and credit rating of the borrowing organisation if it is able to honour all its payments as per the credit terms.

Promissory note

A promissory note is a short-term financial instrument where the borrower (issuer) promises to pay back the face value at a fixed date (maturity) to the investor (holder). There is an interest component involved, which is the face value less the sum borrowed (principal amount). Promissory notes are generally issued by leading public and private service organisations and semi-government authorities with excellent credit ratings. Since promissory notes do not contain any promise to repay other than the promise of the borrower, they are also known as one-name paper or commercial paper.

Promissory notes generally have a 30- to 180-day maturity and are normally issued in multiples of $100,000. They are generally negotiable (that is, they can be sold by the investor before the maturity date). Merchant banks are often involved in managing a promissory note issue on the borrower's behalf. They are normally issued as unsecured, but may sometimes involve collateral as security.

Bills of exchange

A bill of exchange (commercial bill) is a written order requiring payment, either on demand or at a specified time. They can be drawn by individuals or banks and are generally transferable by endorsements. The difference between a promissory note and a bill of exchange is that the latter is transferable and can bind one party to pay a third party (endorsement) that did not exist at the time the bill was created. If these bills are issued by a bank, they can be referred to as bank drafts. If they are issued by individuals, they can be referred to as trade drafts. Bills of exchange are convenient as they do not involve collateral as security and are commonly used by service organisations to raise short-term finance.

Bank and finance company loans

Service organisations can also opt for secured loans which involve the pledge of specific assets as collateral in the event that the borrowing organisation defaults on payments of the principal borrowed or periodic interest payments. On default of the principal or interest amounts, the lender can claim the pledged assets. Hence, secured credit arrangements offer an added element of safety to the lender. Banks and finance institutions are the primary sources of supplying secured credit. Generally, the sources of security pledged as collateral include specified assets, property, accounts receivable, inventories, or a charge over the assets of the borrower. Borrowing interest rates vary, depending on the amount required and the overall economic environment, but are generally competitive.

Long-term finance

Service organisations invest in long-term projects and initiatives from time to time and these investments need financing. For example, retail organisations such as Coles Myer and Kmart need finance to open new branches; airlines such as Qantas and Virgin Blue need to purchase aircraft to expand their services to reach new destinations; and telecommunications service organisations such as Telstra need finance to constantly upgrade their infrastructure in order to provide better services (fibre-optic cables to provide broadband Internet services in Australia). The life expectancy of the benefit accruing from the above ventures is generally for a long time (10 years and over). According to the hedging principle (discussed earlier), organisations must raise long-term finance in order to invest in long-term ventures. Generally, service organisations raise long-term finance through share capital, retained earnings, loan capital or a suitable combination of these.

Share capital

Share capital is the most important source of long-term finance for a listed organisation. Share capital is raised from the owners of the organisation (that is, from its shareholders). Share capital is raised through the sale of shares to individuals or institutions who, in return for their investment in the organisation, receive a share of the profits in the form of a dividend. Listed companies such as Qantas, Telstra and National Australia Bank raise long-term finance through the issue of share capital. There are two main types of shares that are commonly issued by service organisations:

- *Equity shares:* The majority of share capital is raised through the issue of ordinary/equity shares. Equity shareholders receive full voting rights at AGMs and are entitled to receive dividends on the shares invested. However, the organisation has no obligation to pay equity shareholders any dividend. Equity shareholders, however, face the risk of non-payment on their invested amount in the form of shares if the organisation is declared insolvent.
- *Preference shares:* Organisations also issue preference shares from time to time. Preference shareholders are not the real owners of the organisation; hence, they do not have voting rights at AGMs. However, they are entitled to guaranteed dividends and have a greater claim on the organisation's assets if it is faced with the threat of liquidation.

Retained earnings

Another major source of long-term finance for a service organisation is retained income – that is, profit that is not distributed to the shareholders in the form of dividends at the end of the financial year, but instead retained and ploughed back into the business. One of the advantages of this form of internal finance is that it costs far less than external sources of finance, which normally entail an additional interest payment. Retained earnings also provide flexibility in the use of funds to the organisation – that is, the organisation is not answerable to external financial institutions for the application of such funds.

Dividend or capital gain: What do shareholders want?

There has been an ongoing debate in corporate finance theory as to whether shareholders prefer to receive a share in the profits of the company on an annual basis, in the form of dividends, or whether they would rather that the profitable organisation not distribute dividends annually, but plough back the profits (that is, reinvest the retained earnings) into further profitable ventures. Prudent reinvestment of the organisation's profits in profitable ventures generally entails an appreciation in the share price of the organisation over a period of time. Shareholders would benefit by selling the appreciated shares in the future and receive a lump-sum capital gain (after taxing the capital gain at the appropriate rate), which could be significantly greater than all the annual dividends (indexed) received over the same period.

This debate about shareholders' preferences between dividends (a short-term perspective) and capital gains (a long-term perspective) has interested a number of strategic management scholars. Strategic management models developed around this shareholder preference dilemma are constantly striving for shareholder value maximisation strategies. For example, the Virgin group of companies, under the leadership of Sir Richard Branson, adopts a shareholder maximisation strategy with a long-term perspective for shareholders, whereby a fair percentage of the profits are distributed as dividends on an annual basis, and the remainder is reinvested into expanding the existing business. (See Chapter 4 for a more detailed discussion on the Virgin Group's competitive strategy.) Given the dynamics of the services environment, as outlined in the earlier chapters, and the growing emphasis on stakeholder theory, it is imperative that service organisations align their strategies with the needs and requirements of its various stakeholders (including shareholders) in order to remain competitive and sustainable. This further reinforces the importance of integrating exploratory and innovative strategies and applying them to each unique service organisation, rather than employing a 'one size fits all' strategy. A detailed discussion on alternative stakeholder value maximisation strategies is presented in Chapter 3.

Loan capital

Besides raising long-term finance from internal sources through the issue of share capital and retained earnings, service organisations also look to external long-term finance sources to raise funds. Finance that is generated through long-term borrowing from external sources is often referred to as loan capital. Generally, debentures, mortgages, long-term bank loans, venture capital and private investment (business angels) are the common sources of loan capital.

- *Debentures:* Debentures are normally associated with public companies. A service organisation offers potential investors the opportunity to invest in the organisation through the purchase of debentures. The investors (debenture holders) are creditors to the organisation (and not owners, as in shares), and receive periodic fixed-interest payments from the organisation until, at an agreed date (maturity date), the loan is redeemed (that is, repaid in full). Most debentures are secured, whereby the holder of the debenture will have a claim either over specified assets of the organisation should it default on interest payments, or over general assets of the organisation up to the value of the debenture loan.
- *Long-term bank loans:* Standard long-term bank loans with a maturity of between five and 20 years are another source of long-term finance available. Interest rates charged by banks vary and are competitive.
- *Mortgages:* Service organisations take out mortgages from banks to purchase assets such as land and buildings, which form the collateral for the loans. Mortgages can prove to be expensive, especially in a volatile economic environment where property prices are uncertain, with rising interest rates being the main concern.
- *Venture capital:* Venture capitalists offer capital, normally $500,000 and upwards, to business ventures that other banks, financial institutions and investors might consider too risky. The dot.com boom of the late 1990s saw the emergence of venture capitalists that were instrumental in funding a range of risky start-up business ventures, including dot.coms. To protect their investment, the venture capital organisation will require shares in the business and influence in the running of the company at a strategic level, usually in the form of a non-executive position on the board. Their main aim is to increase the net worth and value of the shares of the organisation in which they have invested capital, as a return for investing in a risky venture.
- *Business 'angels':* Business 'angels' are private investors who invest directly in private organisations in return for an equity stake and a seat on the company's board. Investments generally range from $50,000 to $500,000. Business 'angels' are motivated by capital gains arising from their investment, and the donor organisation can benefit from the entrepreneurial expertise of the private investor.

Financial risk management

Globalisation has made the world a riskier place. As discussed in Chapter 2, the economic environment has become very complex, with increased volumes of cross-border trade, technological innovation, and the move towards a unified world market. The changing business environment has made risk and its management an important aspect of managing a business. Today, organisations face risks in every stage of their business operations, from inception to demise. Managers realise that eliminating risk completely is a myth. Hence, the challenging task is how to deal with and minimise risks. Managing risk, or risk management, has gained enormous contemporary importance across industries operating in today's dynamic business environment. The insurance business has thrived on this renewed focus on risk management in every facet of the organisation's business life. This section concentrates on the financial risks the services sector faces, and presents some strategies for financial managers having to deal with risk.

Organisations today employ 'risk managers', who are specialists in forecasting and mitigating risk. They work within the finance department and constantly liaise with the financial manager. In fact, Craig Gass, vice president of the New York-based insurance firm Alexander & Alexander, recently suggested that the 'risk manager's job will continue to evolve and, because of new responsibilities, a more appropriate title for the function may be *financial service advisor*'. He further added that:

> Risk management will encompass much more than insurance-buying in the future, include risk funding, quality assurance and insurance management. As a result [of this shift], risk managers will need to have a strong understanding of their companies' business and to keep in step with the financial services industry. (Risk Management, 1995, p. 11)

This contemporary dual role for risk managers emphasises the need for financial managers to understand the importance of risk management.

Figure 7.7 highlights the broad types of financial risks that service organisations face today. Organisations across the services sector face similar risks, and their managers must decide how to deal with them. The risks organisations face are broadly categorised as business risk, credit risk, market risk, liquidity risk, operational risk and legal risk. Each type of risk has implications for the roles and responsibilities of the financial manager in liaison with the risk manager.

Business risks

Business risks are those risks that are specific to the industry and to the market in which an organisation operates. If the organisation operates, for example, in the tourism industry, its business risks would be those specific to the industry and market for tourism (for example, terrorist threats, environmental degradation, and epidemic breakouts such as SARS and bird flu). If the organisation operates in the banking industry, its business risks would be specific to the industry and market for banking (for example, central bank regulations, economic recession and the Asian financial crisis).

Numerous types of business risks affect organisations from time to time. Risks such as an environmental or a war/terrorism risk are beyond the control of the financial manager. Other types of risks (for example, resources risk) can be forecast beforehand using financial analysis

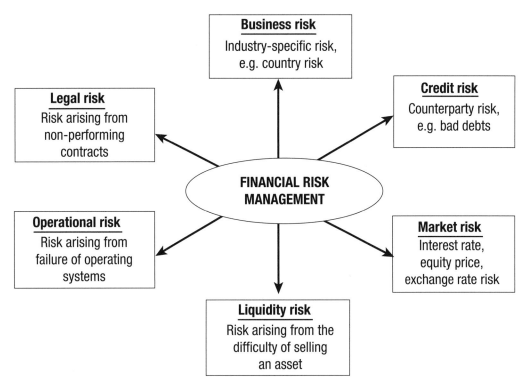

Figure 7.7 Financial risk management – types of risk

and forecasting techniques, which will be discussed later. Table 7.4 summarises the different types of business risks that service organisations face today.

The onus of forecasting and managing risk lies with the risk manager, who works closely with the financial manager. The financial manager has a deep understanding of the financial operations of the business and works closely with managers in other functional areas such as marketing, operations and human resources (see Chapters 5, 6 and 8). Hence, financial managers are in a central position to forecast and respond to the various types of business risks in conjunction with the various other managers of services.

Credit (counterparty) risk
Credit risk is the risk of loss arising from the failure of a counterparty to honour their obligations (that is, the failure to pay for, or deliver, goods and services) or to repay a borrowing. All types of businesses face credit risk. Generally, counterparties are unable to honour their commitments due to any, or a combination, of the following factors (Holliwell, 1997):
- They have been let down by a third party.
- They cannot obtain the resources necessary to honour the transaction.
- They are prohibited from making payments (for example, foreign exchange controls) or from meeting their obligations (for example, the introduction of a ban on transfer of technology).
- They have become insolvent.

Table 7.4 Types of business risks with implications for the financial manager

Types of business risk	Definition	Steps for handling and managing risk
Competitor risk	Risk arising from competitors taking over market share.	Understanding of competitors' marketing and management strategies.
Country risk	Risk arising from characteristics of specific countries; political, social, cultural and economic.	Thorough understanding of the political, social, cultural and economic characteristics of particular countries.
Criminal risk	Risk arising from criminal damage, including computer hacking, fraudulent transactions.	Information systems safeguard measures to prevent unauthorised use and verification steps at every stage.
Economic risk	Risk arising from cyclical trends in the global economy.	In-depth knowledge of the economic trends with the help of financial forecasting techniques.
Environmental risk	Risk arising from environmental degradation, litigation from environmental stakeholder groups, etc.	Environmental assessment and audit.
Information risk	Risk arising from the obtaining, processing and circulating of inaccurate information.	Verification of accuracy of information at every stage, use of 'value networks'.
Personal risk	Risk arising from personal liability of the organisation and its managers.	Understanding of personal liability scope, limitations and implications with financial advice.
Political risk	Risk arising from decisions taken by national- and sub-national-level governments – taxation, interest rates, grants, subsidies.	Thorough understanding of the economics of decisions taken by governments at all levels.
Product/industry risk	Risk that the primary product or service would go out of demand.	Studying demand estimates, market estimators, trends.
Public relations risk	Risk from media, environmental and other pressure groups.	Transparency of documentation and representation, regular meetings with stakeholder groups.
Resources risk	Risk of the availability of resources: land, labour, capital and organisation.	Accurate forecasting using financial forecasting techniques, costing techniques.
Technological risk	Risk that new ways of doing business will destroy the demand for existing products/services.	Liaison with R&D department and updates on competitors' use of technology in the production of goods and delivery of services.
War/terrorism	Risk from hostile acts and insurgency which disrupt business operations.	Adequate insurance and post-event crisis management initiatives.

As pointed out earlier, financial managers have responsibility for financial planning, analysis and control, along with sharing the risk management function with the risk manager and other functional managers. Credit or counterparty risk is a major risk facing service organisations, and financial managers must exercise stringent controls to check the creditworthiness of the counterparty before entering into any contract. The following general steps to mitigate credit risk are recommended:

- *Select the counterparty carefully:* Strong liaison with old contacts, and references for new contacts, is advisable.
- *Exercise an appropriate level of due diligence at all times:* Due diligence is often undertaken as a necessary evaluation procedure with the assistance of merchant bankers, lawyers and accountants. Credit rating agencies such as Credit Rating Information Services of India Ltd (CRISIL), Malaysia Rating Corporation (MARC) and Taiwan Rating Corporation (TRC) provide up-to-date reports on credit rankings of individuals, partnerships and corporations.
- *Apply appropriate financial analysis techniques:* Ratio analysis can be used to ascertain the creditworthiness of counterparties.
- *Spread your risks over a group of counterparties* (that is, don't put all your eggs in one basket).
- *Keep informed of the extent of the credit exposure and the movements of the counterparties, their performance and commitments.*
- *Review credit approval procedures on a regular basis.*

Market risk

Market risks are the risks of losses from adverse movements in market prices (equity share prices) or market rates (interest or exchange rates). In other words, market risk is the risk that investments will lose money based on the daily fluctuations of the market in which it is traded. Risk on the bond market results from fluctuations in interest; stock prices are influenced by factors ranging from company performance to economic factors, to political news. Market risk can be subdivided into interest rate risk, exchange rate risk and commodity price risks. These risks are very common. A US Treasury Management Association survey indicated that over 90 per cent of organisations polled faced interest rate risk, 75 per cent faced foreign exchange risk, and over 33 per cent faced commodity price risk (Field, 1995, p. 2). A brief description of each type of risk is provided below:

- *Interest rate risk:* Organisations across the services sector are exposed to interest rate fluctuations. Airlines, banks and insurance organisations are all exposed to interest rate variations, primarily due to their financing, investing and cash management activities, which include short- and long-term debt to maintain liquidity and fund their business operations. Interest rate risk (also known as price risk) represents an asset's price movement in response to changes in market interest rates. A rise or fall in interest rates will cause a bond's price to fall or rise. Interest rate swaps (agreements between two parties who exchange interest payments, based on a notional principal amount, over an agreed period of time) are the most common interest rate risk management methods offered by banks and financial institutions. Swaps are used to assist in the management of interest rates and cash flows.
- *Exchange rate risk:* Service organisations operate on a global scale and hence their operations are affected by foreign exchange fluctuations. The risk that a business's operations or an investment's value will be affected by changes in foreign exchange rates is known as

exchange rate risk. For example, if Australian dollars (A\$) must be converted into Indian rupees (INR) to make a certain investment, changes in the value of INR relative to the A\$ will affect the total loss or gain on the investment when the money is converted back. This risk, also known as currency risk, usually affects businesses, but it can also affect individual investors who make international investments. One of the financial manager's responsibilities includes foreign exchange risk management (that is, to stabilise the cash flows and reduce uncertainty from financial forecasts). Two common hedging (minimising risk) instruments, known as 'spot' and 'forward' foreign exchange contracts, help the financial manager's cause.

A spot foreign exchange contract refers to the 'immediate' exchange of currencies at the prevailing market rate as determined by the size of the transaction. Banks and financial institutions offer a competitive foreign exchange dealing service for the professional needs of importers and exporters. In the wholesale foreign exchange market, settlement occurs two business days after the transaction has been concluded. This is the technical meaning of the term 'spot'.

A forward foreign exchange contract is an agreement between the organisation and the bank, in which the bank agrees to buy or sell foreign currency to the organisation on a fixed future date, or during a period expiring on a fixed future date, at a fixed rate of exchange. The organisation undertakes to pay the bank, or receive from the bank, the overseas currency in terms of the contract in exchange for the settlement currency (A\$ in Australia).

- *Commodity price risk:* Service organisations in aviation, travel and tourism purchase certain raw materials, such as natural gas, propylene and acetone, under short- and long-term supply contracts. The purchase prices are generally determined based on prevailing economic conditions. Changing raw material prices can have serious impacts on the company's earnings and cash flows, and can continue to have significant impacts on future earnings and cash flows. The risk resulting from the possibility that the price of the commodity may change in the future is known as commodity price risk. Financial managers in service organisations use hedging instruments such as commodity forward and future contracts, options, commodity swaps, swing contracts and average price options to minimise the effects of commodity price risks.

Liquidity risk

Liquidity refers to the ability to get cash when an organisation needs it. Additionally, counterparties and stakeholder groups must perceive that the organisation has the ability to raise cash immediately. Liquidity risk is financial risk from a possible loss of liquidity. There are two types of liquidity risk: specific liquidity risk and systematic liquidity risk. *Specific liquidity risk* is the risk that a particular organisation will lose liquidity. This might happen if the organisation's credit rating fell, or experienced a loss of goodwill, which might cause counterparties to avoid trading with or lending to the organisation. *Systematic liquidity risk* affects all organisations. It is the risk that an entire market will lose liquidity. Financial markets tend to lose liquidity during periods of crisis or high volatility.

Liquidity risk tends to supplement other risks and can be most damaging for organisations that are experiencing the financial difficulties that create an immediate need for cash bailouts. Financial managers understand that, in particular, the effects of credit (counter-party) risk and market risk complications are multiplied when combined with liquidity risk. Conversely, other risks can lead to liquidity risk. For example, credit risk can make funding a difficult task. If the counterparty defaults, the organisation in question may be deprived of cash earmarked for current operating expenses and liabilities.

An excellent example of the perils of liquidity risk is the downfall of Long-Term Cap-ital Management (LTCM). Established in 1994 by John Meriwether, a renowned Salomon Brothers bond trader, the hedge fund LTCM seemed destined for success. Meriwether had assembled an all-star roster of top-notch traders and experts, including Nobel Prize winners Myron Scholes and Robert Merton. Investors eagerly contributed a combined US$1.3 billion of capital. They believed that LTCM's financial strategy was bound to be profitable. Through convergence trades, LTCM took large and highly leveraged positions, but demonstrated that the net risk was minimal, because their long and short positions were highly correlated. How-ever, when the Russian government defaulted on its debts in 1998, liquidity suddenly evap-orated from the international financial markets, and asset prices plummeted. LTCM suffered massive losses because it could not liquidate its assets before the value of its portfolio dropped. By the end of the year, LTCM had been all but destroyed, a victim of 'flight to liquidity' ('Liquidity risk' case study, 2004).

To manage liquidity risk, the service organisation's finance department must be diligent in monitoring potential liquidity. Essential steps include closely noting cash flow, diversify-ing funding sources, and ensuring quick access to liquid assets. A number of organisations employ 'stress-testing' measures to estimate their liquidity risk under potentially stressed mar-ket conditions – that is, under hypothetical situations, which can in future become a reality. 'Stress-testing' a portfolio (group) of assets can prepare the organisation for possible liquidity problems (Dowd, 1998).

Operational risk

Operational risks can vary from the failure of internal systems to the people who operate and interact with the systems. Virtually all aspects of an organisation are exposed to oper-ational risk from numerous sources. These risks cover a huge variety of specific risks: 'Risks from unauthorised trading, fraud, and human error, loss of personnel, communications fail-ures and breakdown of control systems, problems with valuation and simulation models, com-puter breakdowns and other technological problems, failures of suppliers and/or customers and many others' (Dowd, 1998, p. 191).

Generally speaking, there are two key areas of operational risk: people risk and process risk. The first, *people risk*, is the risk of loss associated with human interaction (see Chapter 8). Examples include incompetence and fraud. The second, *process risk*, encompasses three more specific types of operational risk: model risk, transactional risk and operational control risk. All three represent forms of human error, such as misuse of financial models, execu-tion and booking errors, and exceeding the set or established limits. Operational risks can be very minor (breakdown of a printer, scanner or photocopier) through to very critical (risks of bankruptcy owing to loss of managerial control) (see also Chapter 6).

An example of operational risk management is the Walt Disney Company's treatment of weather risk. In 1965, as Disney searched for a location for DisneyWorld, it considered the effects of weather on theme-park visitors. As inclement weather discourages people from visiting theme parks, both Disney and the vacationers are exposed to considerable weather risk. To reduce this risk, DisneyWorld was built at a warm, sunny location in Orlando, Florida. However, this decision rendered Disney vulnerable to other forms of operational risk. At the time of the establishment of DisneyWorld, Orlando was a relatively remote locale, thus increasing Disney's exposure to fuel prices, the cost of air travel, and fluctuations in the economy. To counterbalance this risk exposure, Disney could develop an alternative operational model consisting of multiple theme parks, located in densely populated areas. Disneyland Paris is an example of such a counterbalancing theme park. It draws largely upon single-day visitors, rather than traditional vacationers. If bad weather occurs, visitors may simply postpone their trip to Disneyland Paris, allowing Disney to reduce the risk of lost customers (Pickford, 2001, p. 68, cited in 'Operational risk', 2004).

A second example of operational risk is the infamous case of the rogue trader Nick Leeson. Appointed as the general manager of Barings Futures in Singapore in 1993, he quickly established himself as a very profitable trader, earning over £10 million that year. He achieved such immense profits through unauthorised and very risky trading, made possible because top management poorly understood trading in Asian markets and did not closely supervise Leeson. A lack of internal checks and balances exposed Barings to operational risk. The next year, a downturn in the Japanese economy spurred by the Kobe earthquake prompted Leeson to conceal his losses in an error account. The losses only continued to grow as Leeson resorted to even riskier practices, and by February 1995 amounted to over £800 million, almost the entire assets of the bank. Barings' collapse was finalised when the Dutch group ING purchased it for £1 in March 1995 (BBC News, 1999, cited in 'Operational risk', 2004)

The collapse of HIH Insurance in Australia (see Case study 7.2) is an excellent additional example of the pitfalls of operational risks being overlooked.

Operations risk management poses a challenge for financial managers. A number of risk measurement frameworks have been developed, whereby financial managers obtain qualitative data via survey questionnaires. This qualitative data is then translated into quantitative data using financial management statistic analysis techniques such as Delta and Extreme Value Theory (EVT). Some explanations of risk measurement frameworks follow:

- *Control self-assessment:* The categories within this framework correspond to the departments within the organisation. Each department completes a survey instrument, normally a questionnaire, which is coded, scored and analysed to determine high-risk areas of the organisation. This framework helps to identify the organisation's important operational risks.
- *Loss categorisation* analyses the past losses incurred by the organisation. Data is collated and entered into a database, categorised as per its source (people, technology). The accuracy of this technique is limited, however, by problems of 'double counting', which can be encountered when a loss falls into overlapping categories.
- *Process analysis* framework is used to redefine and reengineer process tasks and controls. It provides a holistic view of the procedures employed within the organisation and identifies key control points and their related risks. However, it is limited in its scope and only identifies operational risks related to the procedures analysed.

- *Performance analysis* is a popular framework that uses the performance measures of an organisation to develop related risk measures. The relationship between the business activities and the earnings of an organisation is used as a basis for the link between the business activities and the risk of earnings. Its main limitation is its focus on gains, which limits its ability to identify all operational risks to which an organisation is exposed. (Holliwell, 1997; Dowd, 1998; 'Liquidity risk' case study, 2004)

Legal risk

Legal risk is the risk of loss from uncertain legal proceedings. It arises through uncertainty in laws, regulations and legal actions. Sources of legal risk include capacity and enforceability issues, as well as the legality of financial instruments and exposure to unanticipated changes in laws and regulations. Legal risks pose a significant threat today, with the number of legal actions against organisations across the globe ever increasing.

Two cases that illustrate legal risk involve the food service giant McDonald's, which had hundreds of legal actions filed against it by non-resident Indians in the United States in 2003 for allegedly including a meat component in its famous vegetarian burgers. In the mid-1990s, Bankers Trust (BT) (now part of Deutsche Bank) was sued by four of its major clients – Federal Paper Board Company, Gibson Greetings, Air Products and Chemical, and Procter & Gamble (P&G) – who asserted that BT had misled them with respect to the riskiness and value of derivatives that they had purchased from the bank. The first three cases were settled out of court for a total of US$93 million. The US$195 million P&G suit was settled at a net gain to P&G of US$78 million. The most lasting damage, however, was to BT's reputation (adapted from http://erisk.com/Learning/CaseStudies/ref_case_bankers.asp).

Legal risk often arises from an organisation's regular trading activities. This type of legal risk is called *transactional risk*, and is related directly to specific deals and not to the government or the organisation itself. Even if all transactions are documented, there is still risk associated. *Documentation risk* is the transactional risk that losses will occur if there is not adequate documentation. For example, ambiguous language creates documentation risk, which is why a lot of service organisations place clear written notices and disclaimers using footnote-style documentation in their visual and printed advertising materials. While the financial manager understands that legal risk cannot be avoided under all circumstances, a certain degree of due diligence is warranted at all times. There are no standard techniques available to measure legal risk; however, organisations use decision-tree-type analysis to look at their legal strategies employed from time to time to minimise the threat of litigation.

Conclusion

The chapter highlights the importance of the role of financial management within services, focusing on the particular responsibilities of the financial manager as an important component of the ISM model (see Figure 7.1). Services need finance managers to help design and plan the operations of the business. Working closely with managers in other functional business areas (human resources, marketing and operations), the financial manager is responsible for financial forecasting and budgeting, analysing of financial statements, employing prudent control measures, and liaising with financial markets to determine the most viable financial mix to fund the various day-to-day and long-term operations of the organisation. Managing financial risk is another key area for the financial management expertise. With a deep understanding of the underlying financial management objectives and concepts, the financial manager is responsible for the smooth functioning of the organisation, which will optimise the *value* of their organisation, maximise the *welfare* of employees, consumers and various stakeholder groups, and assure the long-term viability and sustainability of the organisation in today's competitive world.

In the wake of the recent global economic slowdown and the increasing importance given to various stakeholder groups, it has become imperative for management across all sectors and industries to install, monitor and maintain good governance practices within organisations. A recent ADB study found that poor enforcement of corporate laws and regulations, underdeveloped capital markets and a high concentration of corporate ownership were the main reasons for weak corporate governance among the Asian nations hard hit by the Asian financial crisis of 1997 (Juzhong et al., 2000). Ineffective risk management was also one of the key factors that led to the deepening of the worst financial crisis to hit the Asian region. Good financial management demands good governance, and good governance demands prudent financial control. The following chapter explores the roles of marketing and HR managers in ensuring organisational effectiveness and profitability in the services sector, along with schemas for promoting transparency and good governance, side-by-side with its financial managers.

Exercises

Web exercise 7.1

The analysis of financial statements is one of the important functions of the financial manager. Access the financial statements of National Australia Bank Ltd, Singapore Airlines Ltd and Videsh Sachar Nigam Ltd; three service organisations operating in different sectors and based in different countries, whose financial statements are available publicly. National Australia Bank Group Ltd is one of the largest banks in Australia, with branches worldwide. The group consists of five lines of business – Financial Services Australia, Financial Services Europe, Financial Services New Zealand, Corporate and Institutional Banking and Wealth Management. Full financial reports can be obtained from NAB Group's website at www.nabgroup.com/0,,32863,00.html. The Singapore Airlines Group is internationally recognised as one of the world's leading carriers; it operates over 95 aircraft across 89 destinations in 40 countries. Full financial reports can be obtained from Singapore Airlines Group's website at www.singaporeair.com/saa/app/saa?hidHeaderAction = onHeaderMenuClick&hidTopicArea = AnnualReport&currentSite = global. Videsh Sanchar Nigam Ltd (VSNL), a wholly Indian government-owned corporation, acts as the telecommunications gateway, providing retail, wholesale and corporate services to millions of Indians. It has been instrumental in transforming India into a frontrunner in information technology and communications initiatives. Full financial reports can be obtained from

VSNL's website at www.vsnl.com/channel.php?htm = aboutvsnl/investor_financialdata. htm.

1 Browse through the statements of financial performance (income statements), statements of financial position (balance sheets) and statements of cash flows of the three service organisations and identify the similarities and differences in reporting measures.

2 Compare the financial performance of the three organisations over the reported period of time (that is, 2001, 2002, 2003). Have the organisations been reporting an improvement in financial performance?

3 Would you, as a stakeholder, invest in any of the three organisations? Explain.

Case study 7.1 Application of ABC: The case of Sun Life Insurance

Background

Sun Life Insurance, an international insurance company, provides individual and corporate life insurance, group retirement services and benefit management services. The Canadian operations have offices located throughout Canada, with the head office in Toronto. The group claims division provides drug and dental claim management and claim adjudication to companies in Canada through its four main centres in Toronto, Ottawa, Edmonton and Montreal. Clients include the federal government, City of Toronto, Royal Bank of Canada and Magna International.

Business issues

Several issues have led Sun Life to undertake the implementation of an activity-based costing analysis. Increased competition, the introduction of new computing technology, and increasing client demands have caused margins to decrease and costs to rise. The increased costs and decreased per-unit revenue have pressured management to seek to reduce costs significantly in order to maintain profitable operating results. Competition and customer demands have forced the organisation to dramatically reduce the length of time taken to process a claim, while also increasing the due diligence performed on each claim. Each processing centre performs tasks using different operational processes, and standards with greatly differing processing times for various types of claims. The organisation needs to identify the best practice for each process, and to institutionalise that best practice across all its operations. To make management and strategic decisions, senior management agreed that a better set of decision-making tools was needed in the group claims division, including better costing information and better performance data.

Approach

Focused Management Information (FMI) was engaged to assist the group claims division to implement and internalise an ABC system, and then to tie this in with best-practice analysis, process improvement and budgeting. A cross-functional team of eight Sun Life employees representing all locations, including group finance, was formed and guided through the implementation process and data collection with the ongoing assistance of FMI. After thorough training in ABC concepts and implementation methodology, the team conducted activity analysis on all positions in the group claims area. Then a consolidated activity dictionary was created, along with a cost flow diagram, which represented all activities and processes within the area, as well as mapped the flow of activities throughout the area. 'One of the things we've discovered through our work with Focused Management is [that] the simple act of examining what activities occur in which department has yielded valuable insights and caused us to change the way we perform what we do,' explained Henry Kowal, senior analyst at Sun Life. The team, with the assistance of the systems department, collected resource and activity driver information and entered all the information into their ABC software. Activity, process and unit activity costs were obtained, and then validated by the team and by senior division management.

Results

The results of the ABC analysis provided a great deal of insight for the Sun Life senior management team. Additionally, it confirmed quantitatively what many managers had assumed, but could never prove. Significant differences in activity cost, process cost, cycle time, transaction volumes and unit costs were found both within locations and between the different locations. In some cases, unit costs for the same activity varied by over 300 per cent. These unit cost results varied according to type of claim, as well as according to the experience of the claims adjudicator.

When the team looked at cycle time, or the full-time equivalent (FTE), required to perform a given volume of claims, large differences were found in the efficiency of the four processing centres, as well as in the call centres. Some locations could process a similar amount of claims with a lot fewer personnel than other locations. This led to a review of the activities, tasks and workflow in each location, with a view to standardising the process steps as much as possible, as well as learning from the most efficient areas.

When compared with industry standards, outsource partners and the different claims processing centres, Sun Life has been able to perform extensive benchmarking analysis. The benchmark or best-practice data has allowed them to determine how efficient and effective they are, compared with where they can be, and has shown management where to concentrate the process improvement initiatives.

The activity cost and performance results have also allowed operations management to assess the 'value' or utility of all the activities performed within group claims. Some activities are performed that do not add any value to the process, and hence are being eliminated. Other activities have been found to be value adding, but are performed too often, or cost too much every time they are performed. These activities are in the process of being redesigned, so that they will be performed at the right time and cost.

Action steps

Faced with all this great new information, Sun Life, like all organisations, had to determine how best to use the information and analysis to make changes in the way they run the business. The first step was to present the analysis to operations management in each of the four processing locations, as well as to senior management. This was accomplished through a full-day management briefing and workshop. The workshop provided managers with an opportunity to 'dive' into the analysis and become comfortable with the results. Once this had been accomplished, the ABC project leader then led the managers through an analysis of where further detail was required and what data the managers needed to see on a go-forward basis. Management then brainstormed all the uses of the ABC results and prioritised which uses were most immediate. They then assigned responsibilities and resources, to ensure that the actions were achieved. The management workshop was found to be a critical component in obtaining management buy-in, as well as getting management to internalise the next steps with regard to the ABC analysis.

Following the ABC management workshop, the ABC team and the operations management set about taking several action steps. The first priority was to conduct best-practice analysis on their operations. Process and work steps were shared among the various locations, and best practices were implemented across these locations. This is an ongoing part of a larger process redesign and improvement project. Ongoing education has been a key component in the overall strategy to ensure that managers understand the data and know how to use the information properly to inform their decision making. The continuous training and working with management has helped management to understand the results and has promoted buy-in on a continuous basis. The ABC results have focused management's attention on the importance of measurement and the management of those measures. The time, quality, quantity and financial data provided by the ABC analysis have reinforced the concept of management through measurement within Sun Life. Decisions are now beginning to be made within an overall measurement and management framework.

A major focus for all managers within group claims is now the management of unit costs across all the activities. With claims volume increasing at a steady rate, a reduction of the unit cost of processing claims should result in an overall cost reduction for the division and an increase in profitability. By using the ABC data, managers have been able to significantly reduce the absolute activity cost, as well as the unit cost of the major claims processing activities. 'As a result of the ABC analysis, we have seen over a 10x reduction in expenses compared with the implementation costs of ABC,' explained Luc Chouinard, manager, expense management. In order to evaluate the progress being made with all these action steps, the ABC results have been updated several times, and trend analysis has been undertaken to monitor the results on an activity basis. These updates are being completed quarterly.

Next steps

As a result of the initial ABC analysis, several next steps are in the process of implementation. These include the roll-out of ABC within other divisions of Sun Life, the integration of the ABC results with ongoing NQI and ISO initiatives, and the ongoing use in process redesign initiatives. The current ABC analysis concentrated on activities by position and their associated cost, quantity, quality, cycle time and unit cost calculations. As the ABC analysis becomes further refined, individual customer profitability will be analysed. There is recognition that customers have different profitability characteristics that have an impact on service pricing and profitability. As a next step, activities will be costed at the unique customer level to determine customer profitability.

Summary

The ABC system implemented within Sun Life's group claims division has helped to realise significant reductions in operational costs within the claims processing areas. The ability to compare the activities performed in different locations has allowed operations management to install best practices observed at each location throughout all the centres. The ABC information has acted as an important driver in implementing a measurement-based management system, as well as helping to realise concrete results. ABC has been a catalyst for change within Sun Life.

(*Source*: Adapted from J. Gurowka, 'Sun Life Insurance – a case study: Activity based costing implementation', *Focus Magazine for the Performance Management Professional*, vol. 4, 2000. www.focusmag.com/back_issues/issue_04/pages/bpbpte.htm)

Student projects

1 What were the main reasons why the management of Sun Life Insurance decided to implement ABC in their organisation?
2 What were the central challenges associated with ABC implementation in Sun Life Insurance Ltd, and how were they dealt with by the management?
3 What were the benefits of ABC implementation in Sun Life Insurance Ltd? Would the ABC technique be applicable to all insurance organisations? Discuss.

Case study 7.2 HIH's failed insurance strategy

When HIH Insurance was put into liquidation on 15 March 2001, it represented one of the biggest collapses in Australian corporate history. Shares in the organisation, once the second-largest Australian insurer, had been suspended two weeks earlier after the Australian Securities and Investments Commission (ASIC) analysed organisational documents.

Through its many subsidiaries the organisation had been a key player in Australian and international general insurance, workers' compensation, public and private liability, and property, industrial and commercial insurance. While regulators quickly organised the transfer of much of the organisation's retail business to other insurers, the nightmare of disentangling HIH's accounts books was only just beginning. As the winter of 2001 progressed, the loss estimates mounted. Then, in late August 2001, the liquidator revised the estimate sharply upwards, saying that the insurer might be anything from A$3.6 billion to A$5.3 billion in the red as a result of overoptimistic valuations of assets and extensive underestimation of liabilities.

The fundamental problem was that HIH had been offering insurance at too low a price, and had not set aside enough capital to cover its future liabilities. This was exacerbated by management and 'due diligence' failures, which led HIH to acquire other troubled insurance businesses at too high a price during a period of rapid growth in the 1990s. The size of the loss is so stunning that it is predicted to have a negative impact on Australia's discretionary spending for some time to come, and insurance premiums have risen in the market sectors in which HIH was most influential.

The failed strategy

Many of HIH's difficulties can be attributed to its aggressive acquisition strategy and the creation of more than 200 subsidiaries. The strategy had the effect of increasing HIH's size by many times in the course of a decade – with premium growth averaging 26 per cent per annum – in insurance markets that were already overcrowded and competitive. In the most controversial acquisition, Rodney Adler, who later became a member of HIH's board of directors, sold his majority-owned insurance company, FAI Insurance, to HIH in late 1998. HIH borrowed heavily to pay A$300 million for the company, but the stock market did not respond well to the acquisition and FAI was later thought to be worth just A$100 million. FAI's acquisition put additional pressure on HIH's financial viability at a time when its reserving and pricing strategies, were, most likely, already compromised.

The acquisition of FAI was not the only questionable business decision. The organisation's failure can be partly blamed on its international operations, particularly those in England and the US. It also acquired subsidiaries in Thailand and Hong Kong. The strategy that HIH pursued in California, where it was a leading underwriter of workers' compensation insurance, was also flawed. HIH had been writing workers' compensation policies in California – and pocketing modest profits – until 1995 when a law setting minimum rates was scrapped. This encouraged insurers in the newly deregulated market to compete by offering lower insurance premiums. HIH believed that rates worked in three-year-cycles and left the market at the time of deregulation. It stepped back into the market three years later, at the very time that state courts were awarding large increases in benefits retrospectively and reinsurers were demanding that lead underwriters assume more of the risk. HIH committed a strategic error in re-entering the California market, and its 'three-year cycle' hypothesis seems to have led it to misjudge the inherent risks. Within the three-year gap, other leading market participants also suffered stunning losses.

HIH also encountered severe problems in the London insurance market, which it had entered in 1993, and where through the 1990s it pursued professional indemnity and public liability business. In addition to substantial losses suffered by the Lloyd's market as a whole in this period, HIH incurred certain high-profile losses associated with the film-financing sector, where it provided leading banks with insurance and reinsurance tied to that business. HIH ended up paying out claims related to a series of failed film projects.

Conclusion: A safety net with many holes

It is not unheard of for insurance companies to mis-price and under-reserve for minimising risks, to have difficulties in their mergers and acquisitions strategy, and to fail in their attempts to create or break into new markets. But it *is* unusual for them to be able to do this on the scale that HIH did, in so many markets and for such an extensive period. Many commentators believe that, if HIH's real condition had been apparent, the company would have quietly failed, and been absorbed by more successful rivals, many years before. Instead, it was able to expand in a way that leveraged all of its underlying problems and allowed a massive gap to open up between its assets and its future liabilities. Why was this? In part, it was because of the nature of many of the insurance markets in which HIH specialised. It is easy for general insurers to get their pricing and reserving wrong (and for that fact to remain obscured) in sectors that exhibit long tails of risk, such as workers' compensation and professional indemnity. Often the true price of risk in such markets is affected by social and legal trends. Companies are tempted to price keenly in order to gain market share, only to find that long-term 'tail risks' hit them with unexpected liabilities when it is too late to do much about it.

The picture is complicated even further by reinsurance strategies. Reinsurance contracts can be used not only to reshape liabilities, but also to reshape cash flows and company accounts by altering premium payment timing and loss coverage. Without a sophisticated risk measurement and reporting system across the whole enterprise that is linked to capital management strategies, it can be very difficult for those outside an organisation – and for most of those inside, too – to keep an objective eye on the extent of insurance liabilities.

Until November 2000, HIH retained a strong credit rating, and although its rating then declined, it never reflected HIH's precarious position. Like many other companies, HIH made the most of its ratings in its business literature, saying they were 'the result of a strong business franchise, sound and consistent performance, with solid profits achievements, and good capitalisation levels'.

Like their credit rating counterparts, equity market analysts did not predict losses at a level that would have made the organisation insolvent even a few months before the crash, though some observers had voiced deep concerns about the organisation many years before. As Graeme Thompson, CEO of the Australian Prudential Regulation Authority (APRA), commented in August 2001, '[I]t's instructive that after having a substantial team of experts *in situ* for a couple of months the provisional liquidator's estimate of HIH's deficit still had a range as wide as A$1.3 billion – greater than the net asset position in its last audited accounts.'

However, this difficulty of relating risk to capital wasn't HIH's only problem. There were additional mishaps and infelicities at the junction between risk reporting, corporate governance, external auditing and regulation. The detailed and complex history of HIH's key transactions between its constituent businesses and various third parties is only gradually becoming clear. Since autumn 2001, certain HIH directors have been defending themselves against legal actions brought by the ASIC in respect of possible breaches in their duties as directors.

The role of the external auditor, Arthur Andersen, has proved interesting. The HIH Group's externally audited accounts for the year ended June 2000 showed net assets of nearly A$1 billion, and solvency at almost double the statutory required level. The organisation's subsequent collapse spotlighted the fact that three of HIH's board members in 2000 were previously employed by Arthur Andersen. No evidence has been presented to suggest that this compromised the actions of the board members, or the independence of the auditor. However, an independent report commissioned by the Australian government following the failure of HIH has recommended that, in the future, audit firm partners who are directly involved in ongoing audits ought not to be admitted to the company's board for at least two years after leaving their auditing employers. The Australian regulator has acknowledged that the HIH case has raised huge issues for how much reliance it should place on information provided by companies and their auditors.

The failure of HIH is one of several remarkable failures in the Australian insurance sector in the past few years. New rules, which became effective in 2002, require organisations to set out a clear reinsurance strategy, increase capital buffers, measure risks more accurately, and link the value of assets more closely to the likely value of their liabilities. Many of these rules were being formulated well before the HIH collapse: it is thought that if the new regime had been in place, HIH might have failed to live up to its strictures as far back as 1995.

But while the new rules should mean that the capital held by organisations is more closely related to the risks they run, it is not clear that the reforms will fully answer the risk reporting concerns of corporate policyholders.

Bruce Ferguson, president of the Association of Risk and Insurance Managers of Australasia, said at the time of the collapse: 'We need a watchdog with more teeth, and one that barks a bit more often. It is futile to have a regulatory system which is either not armed with the [timely] information the market requires or is unable to pass it on to insurance buyers.'

(*Source*: Adapted from P. Cagan, 'HIH Insurance: A case study', *E-Risk Publication*, November 2001; retrieved from www.erisk.com/Learning/CaseStudies/HIHCaseStudy.pdf)

Student projects

1 What were some of the main reasons for the collapse of HIH?
2 What were some of the financial management concepts that were not adhered to by HIH's management team?
3 What were some of the financial risks to which HIH was exposed? Did its management take prudent steps to ensure that those risks were identified and controlled?
4 What are some of the lessons a finance manager might have learned from the HIH case study?

References and further reading

BBC News. 1999, 'How Leeson broke the bank', *BBC News*, 22 June 1999; retrieved from www.riskpsychology.net/FinancialRisk/OperationalRisk.jsp.

Brigham, E. F. 1989, *Fundamentals of Financial Management*, 5th ed., The Dryden Press, Orlando, FL.

Brigham, E. F. and Gapenski, L. C. 1994, *Financial Management: Theory and practice*, 7th ed., The Dryden Press, Fort Worth, TX.

Cagan, P. 2001, 'HIH Insurance: A case study', *E-Risk Publication*, November 2001; retrieved from www.erisk.com/Learning/CaseStudies/HIHCaseStudy.pdf.

Cheng, T. T. 1986, 'Financial forecasting: Throw away the crystal ball', *Management Accounting*, vol. 64, no. 11, pp. 50–52.

CPA Australia. 2002, 'CPA Australia recommends new approach to financial reporting', CPA Australia media release, 18 December; retrieved from www.cpaaustralia.com.au/01_information_centre/16_media_releases/2002/1_16_0_20020418_ mr.asp.

Dowd, K. 1998, *Beyond Value at Risk: The new science of risk management*, John Wiley & Sons, Chichester, UK.

Field, P. 1995, 'The art, not science, of risk management', cited in K. Dowd, *Beyond Value at Risk*, John Wiley & Sons, Chichester, UK, 1998.

Gurowka, J. 2000, 'Sun Life Insurance – A case study: Activity based costing implementation', *Focus Magazine for the Performance Management Professional*, vol. 4; retrieved from www.focusmag.com/back_issues/issue_04/pages/bpbpte.htm.

Holliwell, J. 1997, *The Financial Risk Manual: A systematic guide to identifying and managing financial risk*, Pitman Publishing, London.

Hunt, B. and Terry, C. 2002, *Financial Institutions and Markets*, 3rd ed., Nelson Thompson, Melbourne.

Jeanett, J. P. 2000, *Managing with a Global Mindset*, Financial Times/Prentice Hall, London.

Juzhong, Z., Edwards, D., Webb, D. and Capulong, M. V. 2000, *Corporate Governance and Finance in East Asia: A study of Indonesia, Republic of Korea, Malaysia, Philippines, and Thailand*, Asian Development Bank, Manila.

Learning Source, The. 2002, 'Activity based costing – Accounting for operational readiness', concept paper published at the OSD Comptroller I-Center, in the United States; retrieved from www.defenselink.mil/comptroller/icenter/learn/abconcept.pdf.

'Liquidity risk' case study. 2004; retrieved from www.riskpsychology.net/FinancialRisk/LiquidityRisk.jsp.

'Operational risk' 2004; retrieved from www.riskpsychology.net/FinancialRisk/Operational-Risk.jsp.

Peacock, R., Martin, P., Burrow, M., Petty, J. W., Keown, A. J., Scott, D. F. Jr, and Martin, J. D. 2003, *Financial Management*, 3rd ed., Pearson Education Australia, Sydney.

Pickford, J. (ed.). 2001, *Mastering Risk*, Pearson Education Limited, Harlow, UK; retrieved from www.riskpsychology.net/FinancialRisk/OperationalRisk.jsp.

Pinches, G. E. 1992, *Essentials of Financial Management*, 4th ed., HarperCollins Publishers, New York.

Ramsey, R. H. 1994, 'Activity-based costing for hospitals', *Hospital & Health Services Administration*, vol. 39, no. 3, pp. 385–96.

Risk Management. 1995, 'Today's risk manager . . . Tomorrow's financial service advisor', *Risk Management*, vol. 42, no. 2, p. 11.

Robertson, J. G. Jr. 1948, 'The technique of financial forecasting', *National Association of Cost Accountants, NACA Bulletin*, vol. 29, no. 23, pp. 1459–72.

Ruhl, J. M. and Hartman, B. P. 1998, 'Activity-based costing in the service sector', *Advances in Management Accounting*, no. 6, pp. 147–61.

Sharma, V. 1992, 'Determining product profitability', *The Bankers Magazine*, March/April, pp. 67–71.

Solomon, E. 1963, *The Theory of Financial Management*, Columbia University Press, New York.

Vaknin, S. 2004, 'Moral hazard and the survival value of risk', online publication; retrieved from samvak.tripod.com/pp150.html.

Young, D. W., and Pearlman, L. K. 1993, 'Managing the stages of hospital cost accounting', *Healthcare Financial Management*, April, pp. 58–80.

Human resource management in services

Learning objectives

After studying this chapter, readers will be able to:

- explain the concepts of human resource management, strategic human resource management and industrial relations
- appreciate the linkages between HRM, marketing, financial and operational management
- discuss the major internal and external labour market issues in the services sector
- understand the relevance of such HRM functions as HR planning, job design, recruitment and selection, human resource development, performance management, remuneration and career development to the services sector
- appreciate the special needs of employees in services.

Introduction

Earlier chapters of this text emphasise that the primary distinguishing feature of services is the nature of their customer relationships. This distinguishing feature is described as the 'service encounter', which can sometimes become the 'moment of truth' (Carlzon, 1987) that separates one services organisation from its competitors. Despite the particular services or products offered, organisational size, structure, or use of various technologies, the defining element of the services sector lies in its delivery systems. These delivery systems are ultimately reflective of the quality and management of the sector's employees. Thus, financial institutions, hospitals, airlines, legal offices, funeral homes, restaurants, hotels, IT and recreational services, all depend to different degrees on the capacities and skills of the people they employ.

As the other chapters indicate, service delivery systems are of course also reliant on appropriate marketing and financial systems, supported by efficient and effective operational processes. However, few service organisations will survive in today's increasingly competitive local or global business environments without a well-qualified, skilled, flexible and highly motivated workforce. The following examples indicate the complex and dynamic performance now required of the workforces of service organisations:

Figure 8.1 The integrated services management (ISM) model

- The services of Foxtel and SingTel are chosen based as much on the perceived calibre of their customer service and support staff as on their communications technology.
- Hongkong and Shanghai Banking Corporation, Virgin Blue, pharmacists and taxation consultants require employees with changing and more complex service skills.
- Motor vehicle retailers pride themselves on their personalised service.
- Flexible delivery systems in the health and education sectors require new and different employee competencies, including online services.

This chapter focuses on the management of employees as being a significant element in the overall management of services organisations. It must be recognised that, in order for service organisations to be competitive and survive in a complex and dynamic business environment, the consideration of any HRM issues needs to be integrated with the management of all functional areas – that is, operations, marketing and finance (as illustrated in Figure 8.1).

As Figures 8.1 and 8.2 indicate, the primary objective of the management of the service sector's human resources is to have a 'competent' workforce. The notion of competency indicates the multifaceted informational, practical and interpersonal skills now required to deliver high-quality customised services within the legal (or regulatory) environment in which they operate. The competency levels of a particular service organisation's workforce, combined with the effectiveness of overall management systems, will determine its 'productivity' in an increasingly competitive business environment. Figure 8.1 also shows that a competent

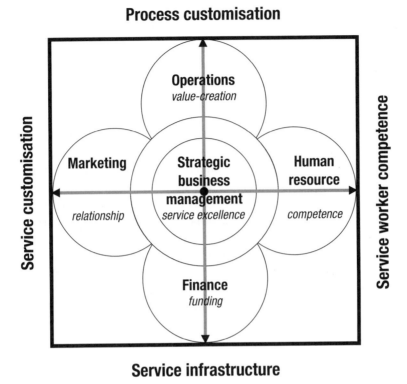

Figure 8.2 The functional services management (FSM) matrix

workforce relies on an appropriate 'service infrastructure', together with 'process' and 'service' customisation, in order to effectively deliver the desired nature and level of services. These issues have been discussed in the previous chapters. Both Figures 8.1 and 8.2 indicate that the strategic management of services demands effective HRM, in conjunction with the efficient management of the organisation's operations, finance and marketing. This integrated approach strives to ensure that services operations are continuously conducted according to the diverse expectations of *all* stakeholders so as to reduce the vulnerability of, and risk to, services and, ultimately, their competitiveness and profitability.

HRM and industrial relations

What is HRM?

HRM is a relatively new profession, having evolved over only the last 50 years from earlier management concepts such as personnel administration or personnel management. These two early concepts represent the formative development stage of a management discipline that is now regarded by many (for example, Cascio, 1999; De Cieri and Kramar, 2003; Nankervis et al., 2005) as being the key element in determining the competitiveness and survival of an organisation. Essentially, personnel administration, personnel management, and more recent notions of 'human resource management', are all concerned with ensuring that an organisation's employees contribute their labour, skills and energy according to their employers' requirements. In return, the employees receive salaries, rewards and other benefits in accordance with their efforts, and with their legal rights and responsibilities.

The 'time' and 'motion' emphasis of *personnel administration* reflects the legacy of classical scientific, or traditional management theories (as discussed in Chapter 1). Traditional management was concerned with the scientific analysis of the time and motion aspects of the manufacturing process in order to build in production efficiencies. Hence, the focus of personnel administration is on quantifying and recording administrative aspects of employment, including such functions as work schedules (punctuality, attendance) and the maintenance of accurate personnel records (personal details, leave, absence, payroll, training) for primarily operational and legal compliance (for example, salary rates, occupational health and safety) purposes. In parts of the services sector, characterised by relatively routine jobs and semi-skilled employees (for example, ancillary hospital services, retail trade, hotels and restaurants, transportation and distribution), this historic view of the management of employees still dominates management practice. This is evidenced by the existence of time clocks, strictly monitored rosters and breaks, systematic functional training, and quantified performance outputs. As examples, hospital cleaners, motor vehicle technicians, restaurant waiters, McDonald's and KFC customer service attendants, P&O and Star cruise line attendants, car park and toll booth cashiers, and furniture removalists, are often 'managed' according to this closely regulated administrative approach.

Personnel management, which developed from personnel administration during the mid- to late 20th century, has a broader perspective that emphasises the functional aspects of employee management. This management area was influenced by theoretical developments in the sociological and industrial psychology disciplines and, hence, it has more emphasis on employee behaviours. Thus, together with the administrative features, this approach stresses the importance of such specific functions as job design, recruitment and selection, training and development, performance appraisal, remuneration and career development, and techniques for developing more effective workforce performance. As such, the approach has a greater operational emphasis than personnel administration. However, the focus is essentially on the maintenance and improvement of existing employee management requirements, rather than on any future developments, or the integration of the outcomes of personnel functions with the strategic goals of organisations. Many traditional government agencies (for example, immigration, minerals and energy) and some private organisations (for example, shipping, airline, retailing and construction companies) retain such approaches. It is apparent that this approach to management in these business areas links with a strong traditional science and engineering manufacturing orientation.

Human resource management is a refinement of these earlier approaches, which incorporates them, but also suggests that not only is the management of employees the central management concern, but that it needs to be perceived as an integral component of the overall strategic management of organisations and of services as a whole. The concept of *human resources* suggests that employees should be considered not only as service providers, but also as human beings with ideas, undeveloped capacities and future potential, who, if properly managed, can contribute enormously to the maintenance and development of organisations. The terms 'human capital', 'intellectual capital' or 'human investments' are often associated

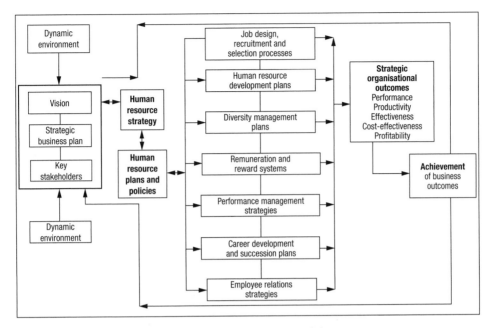

Figure 8.3 A strategic human resource management model

with this view of the potential (or actual) organisational value of employees (De Cieri and Kramar, 2003; Nankervis et al., 2005).

Taking the premise that an organisation's employees, especially in services with their heavy reliance on the employee–customer relationship, are its key to success and competitiveness, HRM theory emphasises the importance of closely aligning all HR functions (for example, job design, recruitment, selection, training, remuneration, performance management) with the overall business goals and objectives. Thus, a private hospital that fails tobreak; properly recruit qualified employees with the appropriate skills, or doesn't pay them competitively, is likely to lose valuable specialists and to incur significant replacement costs. Similarly, an IT service provider that employs systems analysts with technical knowledge, but no interpersonal skills, will quickly lose important customers.

Therefore, based on this logic, HRM theory suggests that HRM practice is only effective when its strategy and functions are directly congruent with the business strategies and objectives. Furthermore, it proposes that this alignment will only be achieved by the horizontal and vertical integration of HRM and organisational policies and strategies (see later). Figure 8.3 illustrates this desirable alignment between HRM strategies, plans and functions, and with the broad goals and objectives of organisations.

As the figure shows, *horizontal* integration is achieved when all HRM activities (for example, job design, recruitment, selection, training, performance management, remuneration and industrial relations) are compatible and congruent with each other and with the overarching HRM strategy. *Vertical* integration occurs when the outcomes or outputs of all the HRM functions meet the business needs of the organisation as a whole.

Thus, a hospital that desires high-quality clinical and nursing skills, supported by efficient and customer-responsive administrative staff, needs clear and appropriate job descriptions to attract the best professional, paraprofessional and administrative employees through the use of modern selection techniques. It will also require performance management systems that accurately chart employees' individual and collective outcomes. Additionally, the performance of employees must be adequately supported by appropriate remuneration, rewards and career development programs, in order to motivate and retain high-quality staff.

Figure 8.3 also indicates factors external to the organisation ('Dynamic environment'), such as government funding restrictions for public hospitals or shareholder pressures on expenditure for private health providers, or legislative or industrial relations requirements. These restrictions may inhibit the ability of HR professionals to offer industrially competitive salaries or essential development and training opportunities, and hence, contribute to high employee turnover or wastage rates. Within individual organisations, the application of a narrow-based fiscal management logic that results in the introduction of labour-saving technology, cost-cutting or retrenchment programs, in turn may result in the loss of talented employees to competitors, or diminish the attractiveness of the organisations to potentially valuable new recruits.

As an example, during the 1990s, facing competition from many new telecommunications providers (for example, Vodafone and Optus), former wholly owned Australian government agencies such as Telstra were forced to review the costs and effectiveness of all their services, particularly their employee costs. In response, Telstra in Australia decided to severely prune its staff numbers (from 94,000 to around 50,000), to replace some of them with outsourced services (for example, call centres, training, research and development), and to negotiate new enterprise agreements with remaining staff in order to enhance flexibility and productivity. The unintended consequences of this combination of cultural and structural change were:

- the loss of many highly qualified and experienced technical specialists to competitors;
- serious morale problems with remaining staff (the so-called survivor syndrome: Littler et al., 1997); and, perhaps more importantly,
- the loss of internationally acknowledged telecommunications research expertise, due to the closure of its R&D section.

As one observer commented, '. . . whole products walked out the door' (Bagwell, 1997, p. 1).

More recently, the disastrous merger (and subsequent de-merger) of Australia's AMP Society with a debt-ridden UK company led not only to a significant financial loss to AMP's shareholders, but also to the loss of many of its valuable potential managers through competitor 'poaching', and resignations caused by its uncertain future. National Australia Bank's 2004 foreign exchange crisis (see Chapter 7) will no doubt result in similar HRM problems.

The above examples reflect either inadequate HR planning, or short-term HRM problems brought on by inappropriate management strategies, which resulted in the loss of talented human resources. The following illustrative case demonstrates the adverse impact on service quality of the failure of many crucial and interconnected HRM functions. Centrelink is the main Australian government agency responsible for the administration and payment of social welfare benefits such as unemployment and sickness benefits, retirement pensions and disability allowances. The service 'mistakes' highlighted in this case (for example, overpayments, underpayments, inconsistent eligibility criteria, incorrect or misplaced records, duplications) clearly derived from the combined failure of Centrelink's employment conditions, training, performance review, retention and supervisory systems (HRM). Additionally there is no doubt that its internal procedures and systems (operations management) severely impacted on both the management of its finances and its customers.

The following analytical material (see Figure 8.4), derived from the report on Centrelink, presents examples that argue for a rational and systematic approach to the management of employees (human resources). This rational and systematic approach needs to take into account the external and internal environments of the services industry and its individual organisations, the business strategies and plans of the latter, and the nature of internal HRM systems, processes and functions. This more comprehensive approach is the essence of HRM.

Box 8.1   Problem? Pass it on to someone else!

If Centrelink employees did not want to do paperwork assigned to them they just put it in someone else's pigeon hole, a report commissioned by the agency found. 'Any given piece of documentation could end up doing the whole round of pigeon holes before anyone takes ownership of it,' the report by DBM Consultants said. Staff reported to DBM of colleagues filing a client's documentation in their own personal drawer, which meant that when they were away the file would not be found to deal with a client's case. 'The primary reason that payment mistakes occur centres on inconsistent information provided by staff, lost documentation, earnings not recorded accurately, or no record of information given to Centrelink at all. Records [are] not being documented at all when they should have been or the documentation [is] inadequate or incomplete.'

The report shows that staff are given problems to fix, but have inadequate information and insufficient time to read the relevant documents. Some staff use their own shorthand, which other staff cannot read when processing documents. Warnings by the computer system of wrong data entry are so often 'irrelevant that staff have learnt to disregard them'. The report found that the high turnover of staff results in customers being dealt with by officers who don't have enough experience to prevent errors from occurring. 'New and less experienced staff are over-dependent on the computer system to tell them what to do. It is often the most experienced staff who are assigned to the task of distributing the mail.' The consultants point out in their report that Centrelink staff have made an invaluable contribution to identifying ways in which the agency can reduce the incidence of mistakes. One solution suggested by staff is to assign work to teams structured by payment type. The staff also want warehouses where back-office work can be done, and dedicated days for addressing difficult paperwork.

(*Source*: M. McKinnon, 'Problem? Pass it on to someone else', *The Australian*, 14 February 2004, p. 2)

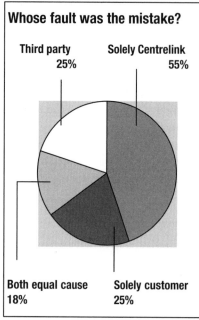

Whose fault was the mistake?

Third party
25%

Solely Centrelink
55%

Both equal cause
18%

Solely customer
25%

Type of mistake			%		
Benefit	**Employ**	**Retire**	**Disability**	**Families**	**Youth**
Payments (overpaid, underpaid, not paid at all)	46	39	47	50	43
Told you were ineligible when you thought you were eligible	10	5	8	9	11
Told you were eligible but then you were ineligible	4	3	4	13	5
Incorrect recording of personal details	15	14	11	7	12
Incorrect recording of partner/children's personal details	4	3	4	13	5
Not receiving promised information – written	9	10	11	9	13
Not receiving promised contact – telephone call or visit	7	8	9	11	8
Didn't understand correspondence	8	8	11	10	6
Received multiple copies of letters	11	11	14	14	14
Centrelink lost form or other item	18	10	21	18	21
Other	14	23	12	12	9

Seriousness of mistake			%		
Very	34	31	45	35	24
Fairly	34	31	27	35	35
Little	21	18	18	19	31
Not at all	11	18	9	11	9

Urgency of getting mistake fixed			%		
Critical	33	21	37	30	25
Fairly	50	44	48	50	54
Not very	13	20	12	13	19
Not at all	3	4	2	8	1

Number of different mistakes in past four months

■ One mistake   ■ Two mistakes
□ Three mistakes   □ Four mistakes

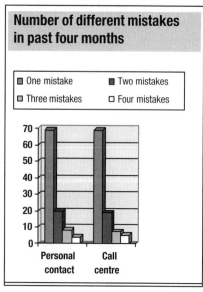

Figure 8.4 Weak link

Source: Adapted from M. McKinnon, 2004, 'Problem? Pass it to someone else', *The Australian*, 14 February, p. 2

Functions of HRM

As discussed, HRM theory and practice is concerned with the optimisation of employee skills and potential towards the achievement of organisational goals and objectives. The repertoire of HRM activities can be divided into *macro* and *micro* domains. In alignment with organisational imperatives, at the macro level HRM is concerned with the establishment and development of organisational strategies, structures and cultures. Thus, HRM professionals in, for example, police services, hospitals and retail stores are concerned to develop staff supply strategies that address labour scarcities or oversupply, or to provide for flexible employment conditions (for example, part-time, casual and on-call employee contracts) in sectors vulnerable to seasonal customer trends (for example, tourism resorts, transport services in remote regions).

The modification of organisational structures may be achieved through reducing management levels, creating cross-divisional task forces, and devolving work responsibilities (see Case study 8.1 at the end of this chapter) to line managers. These modifications are introduced to cut costs, to improve communication and consultation with employees, or to enhance the efficiency of service delivery systems and customer responsiveness (see Chapter 6). Chapter 6 also discusses the concept of 'service cultures', the essential element driving service delivery systems. Service cultures are developed and reinforced by clear links between organisational and HRM strategies and plans, by appropriate organisational structures that facilitate efficient and responsive service delivery systems, and by integrated HRM functions. When these factors are integrated together, they constantly and consistently reinforce the desired service culture. Organisations such as IBM, Genting Casino (Malaysia), McDonald's, David Jones (Australia), Tang's (Singapore), Keisu department stores, Centrelink, Virgin Blue and the Oriental Hotel (Bangkok) display distinctive service cultures built upon all these macro-level-based HRM features.

At the micro level, the focus is on the effectiveness of all HRM functions, including:

- HR planning;
- industrial relations;
- job design;
- recruitment;
- selection;
- learning, training and development;
- performance management and career development;
- rewards and remuneration; and
- HRM evaluation and accountability.

All of these micro-based HRM activities are discussed in further detail in relation to services management. However, it is first useful to discuss the concept of industrial relations and its impact on HRM in the broader community, as well as in services.

What is industrial relations?

Industrial relations is a broad and generic term that encompasses the overall legal, moral and societal relationships between employers and their employees in all countries and industries. It includes the formal rights of employees (for example, wages, conditions, health and safety, equal employment opportunities) and employer obligations enshrined in global, national, and local laws and regulations, together with the informal agreements established within particular industries or organisations. In Western nations, such as the United Kingdom, Australia and New Zealand, industrial relations has been closely associated with the establishment of formal tribunals (for example, the Australian Conciliation and Arbitration Commission, the Australian Industrial Relations Commission). These formal institutions are designed to ensure equity and fairness in employer–employee relationships, to facilitate the negotiation of ongoing employee conditions, and to provide legal mechanisms for the resolution of grievances. These industrial management systems work in close association with social welfare legislation that provides such employee benefits as unemployment, redundancy, sick leave, annual leave, maternity leave, and occupational health and safety protection.

In developing nations, this legislation may be limited or even non-existent, and hence the legal environment for HRM will differ according to the local jurisdiction, and may be more or less supportive of the HR plans of service organisations. For example, the wages and salaries of services employees differ considerably between countries and regions, and between service roles, as do employment conditions and employee expectations and rights. As discussed below, unions in Australia and New Zealand have been powerful influences on employee rights, and often confrontational and adversarial in their relationships with employers, while those in Singapore, Indonesia and Malaysia have usually supported management.

Western formal industrial relations systems derive from the perceived mistreatment of employees by employers during the Industrial Revolution. Traditionally, these systems involved tripartite relationships between the three major 'players': governments, employers (represented by employer associations) and employees (represented by their trade unions). Representatives of these three major players negotiated employer–employee relationships through a centralised system based on the relevant state and Commonwealth legislation. Regional countries such as India, Japan and China also have well-developed employment legislation within their industrial relations systems, while other regional nations such as Singapore, Malaysia, Indonesia and Thailand have less developed employee protection and welfare legislation. In addition, partly due to the less powerful position of trade unions, the industrial relations systems in these countries have been less prone to industrial conflict (for example, 'go slows', strikes, lockouts) than their counterparts in the United Kingdom, Australia and New Zealand.

Industrial action, including actual incidents of conflict (and its consequent adverse effects on productivity and profitability), was a common occurrence in Australia and New Zealand until the mid-1980s. However, a range of factors – such as the combination of global and regional competition, the rise of services, successive reformist Australian governments, a significant reduction in union membership, and more cooperative attitudes between employers associations and trade unions in both countries since then – has led to increased flexibility by both sides in the interpretation of employment conditions and attitudes to radical industrial action. Box 8.2 vividly illustrates the harm that can be caused in services organisations by 'old-style' industrial relations (IR) conflict.

Box 8.2 'Off the rails!'

This is a story about how a mishap with a modern railway locomotive was the catalyst for the resolution of a 16-year-old industrial relations issue. The locomotive was a 'state-of-the-art' vehicle. Indeed, the onboard computer system was integrated with inbuilt radar. In practice, the radar was used to determine the linear speed of the locomotive (by assessing the rate of travel by counting the track sleepers passed), and this information was linked to the computer, which calculated the peripheral wheel velocity. Subsequently, the computer adjusted the fuel flow to the engine to obtain the optimum tractive effort of the locomotive (that is, nil wheel slippage). The scheme gave fuel savings of some 30 per cent, and the improved engine efficiency enabled greater train loads (that is, number of wagons). However, these technological advances did not ensure good traffic operations.

Shortly after being put into service in a remote country region, the locomotive was seriously damaged. As a result of the locomotive crew being unaware that the railway track had been extensively washed away by the floodwaters of an electrical storm, the locomotive was derailed on to its side. After repair staff re-railed the locomotive with high-capacity cranes, the vehicle was towed to a metropolitan marshalling yard. This action began a chain of industrial events.

The first stage of this industrial sequence was the determination of who would repair the locomotive. Management argued that the locomotive should be repaired by the manufacturer, a private consortium. The unions contended that locomotives had always been repaired in the government railway workshop. They further proposed that *not* following this tradition would reduce work for their union members. These contrasted points of view resulted in the locomotive remaining in the yard for a number of weeks, until the unions declared the vehicle to be 'black' (that is, untouchable). To break the deadlock the relevant government minister arranged a meeting between management and union representatives. A compromise was reached. It was agreed that the locomotive would be repaired at the workshop with union staff, but the supervision would be provided by the locomotive manufacturer to ensure the repairs were to the standards of construction. Although it appeared that the concerns of both main groups (management and unions) had been satisfactorily accommodated, a greater industrial issue arose.

After the damaged locomotive was towed to the workshop, a major impediment to the repairs was discovered. In addition, not having plans and information about the material type of the components to be replaced, the workers determined that the locomotive body was treated with polyethylene paint. Although this material has many attractive features, such as providing a relatively low-cost, high-gloss retention surface (and hence, it is used extensively in the motor car industry), the paint also has a serious attribute. Specifically, in the drying process the paint fumes have carcinogenic properties, and during the previous 16 years the workshop management and the unions had been unable to agree on what protective equipment was to be provided. In response to this situation, there was an industrial ban on polyethylene paint at the workshop. Clearly, if this locomotive was to be repaired (as well as others in the future), a change had to be negotiated so that this industrial ban could be lifted.

The realisation that completion of the repairs hinged on how to paint the locomotive compelled a more positive re-examination of industrial relations issues at the workshops. The complexity of the paint problem, as indicated by the length of the industrial ban, was addressed by establishing a working committee. However, this group of local people soon disbanded, because agreement could not be reached. Indeed, this committee lacked the vital expertise, and perhaps the members held the memories of too many old conflicts and, hence, had 'scores to settle'.

A second committee was established with membership based on recognition of the urgency of the situation. Unlike the first committee, which was essentially 'vocal' management or union personnel, the second group was comprised of technically qualified people. This alternative stakeholder selection strategy led to an improved, more open group climate. More particularly, this group was given the power to further induct a variety of experts and practitioners from a diversity of relevant fields. For instance, health and safety matters became a priority, and any people who were involved in the painting process were required to undertake a series of medical lung function tests prior to, during and after the project completion. Even a registered nurse became a member of the repair team. After thousands of previous hours of deliberation and investigation, agreement was reached about how polyethylene would be used. Consequently, the management and unions applied to the State Industrial Court for an urgent hearing to pursue the lifting of the 16-year-old industrial ban. Shortly after this hearing, the locomotive repairs were completed.

(*Source:* Case provided by Dr Cecil Pearson)

The growing economic and social significance of services has had an enormous influence on IR systems and practice in Australia, New Zealand and the United Kingdom, where there has been a historically powerful and confrontational approach to unionism. The different nature of service work and the unique characteristics of its employees have meant that there has been a relative absence of the kinds of industrial action and conflict previously common in the primary and secondary industries. The IR implications of these issues for services are discussed in the following section.

The broad societal framework of legislation and regulations governing industrial relations provides the *context*, or business environment, within which HRM must function (see Chapter 2). More particularly, the flexibility provided by contemporary IR systems, especially their focus on enterprise-level employer–employee negotiations, ensures that the management of HRM within services generally and in individual organisations will also include the overall management of its IR processes and practices. As Mills and Dalton (1994, p. 57) note, '. . . given the relative labour intensiveness of service industries in general . . . it would seem that IR is of immediate and crucial concern in sustaining internationally competitive advantage'. The following section supports their additional assertion that the patterns of likely industrial relations disputes and their resolution are different in services.

IR in services

The growing need to be more competitive within a global economy forced countries such as Australia and New Zealand to amend their IR systems in order to facilitate a more flexible and cooperative framework. The introduction of enterprise bargaining in 1991 in Australia, for example, marked a move away from the traditional conciliation and arbitration mode of bargaining to a more consultative and uniform mechanism whereby parties were encouraged to negotiate productivity and efficiency gains at the workplace level. This change in focus was reinforced with new IR legislation in both Australia and New Zealand – the *Workplace Relations Act 1996* in Australia and the *Employment Relations Act 1995* in New Zealand. This legislation brought about a new framework for IR diminishing the roles of unions and the various Industrial Relations Commissions, and encouraging workplace-level negotiations instead. The new legislation also encouraged the use of individual bargaining between employees and employers. This further diminishes the role of unions and the Industrial Relations Commission as key players in the bargaining process.

Changes to the structure and nature of work have also impacted upon the IR framework. Following global trends, the service sector's workforce is becoming increasingly 'casualised', with a growth in part-time, contract, temporary and casual employment. Together with these changes, there is also a global trend towards increasing employment opportunities in services. This trend has brought with it a range of HR and IR challenges, including increasing skill flexibility, career mobility and new employment agreements (Nankervis et al., 2005).

As previously mentioned, enterprise and individual bargaining arrangements have changed the focus of the IR framework from an adversarial process that involved a number of external parties, including the employee and employer associations, to a more consultative one that focuses on the two main parties: the employee and the employer. With this change, in order to remain pivotal and useful, government players have also changed. Industrial tribunals and commissions are being replaced with enterprise commissioners and employment advocates, whose basic role is to scrutinise proposed enterprise agreements and to ensure that they meet particular universal minimum conditions and standards (Keenoy and Kelly, 1998, p. 146). The Australian Industrial Relations Commission (AIRC) has by no means become redundant. Apart from providing a safety net for wages and conditions of employment, the AIRC continues to assist with settling the more difficult disputes that have failed to be resolved through other mechanisms, such as the assessment of Australian Workplace Agreements (AWAs) (Nankervis et al., 2005). An increasing role for the commission lies in determining whether these fit the 'no disadvantage test', and in hearing unfair dismissal claims.

A range of bargaining arrangements provide choices for both employers and employees. These choices are either collective, in the form of awards and certified agreements, or individual, with the use of AWAs and individual contracts of employment. Individual contracts of employment are made under common law arrangements (not industrial) and, as such, are not subject to the 'no disadvantage test' mechanisms in place through the commission. These arrangements do not have to operate independently. There can be an overlap between them, such as the setting of terms and conditions using a combination of an award and a certified agreement (Nankervis et al., 2005). Moreover, while there is diversity and flexibility of choice, the degree of that choice may vary according to the relative bargaining power of the parties (Nankervis et al., 2005). If industry is to survive ever-increasing global competition, these new enterprise solutions require new forms of cooperation supporting the fundamental need for labour to be flexible, multiskilled and efficiently utilised (Keenoy and Kelly, 1998).

Labour characteristics of services

Services are not only characterised by increasing growth in employment, but also by a large number of casual, part-time and highly mobile workers. Unions have, in the past as well as currently, not been able to gain any real strength in many service sectors (Piso, 1999). These changes, coupled with the growth of services, present some interesting challenges for IR. As

Table 8.1 Pattern of labour use strategies

Labour type	Job security (tenure)	Numerical flexibility	Functional flexibility
A	Core	Low	Medium
B	Periphery	High	Low
C	Seasonal	Low	Medium
D	Retentive	High	Low

Source: N. Timo, 'The organisation of service work – a tourism perspective', unpublished paper, Griffith University (Gold Coast campus), Australia, 1994, p. 12.

an outcome of the shift towards services, labour hours are characterised by '24/7'; rates of pay in many sectors are generally seen as low; the casual nature of services reflects a highly mobile and non-unionised resource; and career paths and structures are limited. Consequently, the impact of services characteristics on IR strategy and bargaining arrangements is enormous (Farrell, 2001, p. 121). Tables 8.1 and 8.2 illustrate the various categories of service employment types (for example, 'core', 'periphery', 'seasonal' and 'retentive'), and the different ways in which employers use 'flexible' employment conditions to reduce costs and increase productivity levels.

The highly mobile and often casual nature of services employment makes it difficult to maintain a culture of commitment and loyalty among employees. For a proportion of these employees, the casual nature of the work is attractive as it allows them to commit to other 'quality of life' activities such as study, family commitments, community volunteerism, and other recreational interests, as well as being able to change jobs as it may suit them not to further develop their skills and qualifications. Less positively, the lack of job security and highly variable hours of work may be regarded as exploitation by some other employees who argue that they essentially have limited economic resources and, hence, limited opportunities to improve their circumstances. This exploitative potential of employees by services employers is frequently observed, and is exacerbated by the distinctly lower levels of union membership, which further reduce the bargaining power of employees.

For the employer, the transient sector of services employees also presents some dilemmas. Not only is there a lack of commitment, but investment in training, development and career opportunities is also difficult where employees are in casual, or short-term contractual arrangements. However, there are opportunities to introduce greater multiskilling of positions and labour flexibility initiatives, even with casual and part-time employees. Changes to the design of jobs to make them more interesting and varied will encourage the need for training and further development to build capacities, and this may encourage greater commitment from employees. Nevertheless, one of the IR challenges for employers in services is to employ staff on more fixed-term and part-time contracts. If supplemented by labour flexibility, leave entitlements, and opportunities for job and wage growth, these more stable employee relationships will result in not only more motivated staff, but also increases in productivity and efficiencies.

These changes to employment arrangements will lead to changes in the bargaining arrangements whereby employers will be required to bargain more extensively with potential and existing employees in order to achieve these productivity gains. This supports the

Table 8.2 Labour flexibility techniques

• Flexible commencing and ceasing times.
• Extending the spread of ordinary working hours on any day at a single time.
• Flexible rostering (notification of roster changes).
• Averaging ordinary hours.
• Rearranging penalty or loaded hours to a single time (for example, time off in lieu of overtime).
• Changes in the duration of working time.
• Restructuring shift arrangements (split shifts, 10-hour and 12-hour shifts).
• Reduction or elimination of breaks (between periods of work, rest pauses).
• Reducing constraints on managerial discretion regarding the scheduling of work (for example, scheduling of rostered days off (RDOs), breaks, taking of leave).
• Liberalisation of restrictions and constraints on use of labour (part-time, casual and seasonal labour).
• Reduction in rostering notice and changing of roster provisions.

Source: N. Timo, 'The organisation of service work – a tourism perspective', unpublished paper, Griffith University (Gold Coast campus), Australia, 1994, p. 13.

predictions that bargaining arrangements will need to be cooperative and unitary in nature if labour flexibility and multiskilling is to be achieved (Keenoy and Kelly, 1998).

There is also the possibility that, along with these changes, increases in the levels of union membership in this sector will occur as a result of greater negotiation opportunities. It is clear that there are already concerns among employees in this industry. A number of international studies (Price, 1994; Baum, 1996; Weiss, 1997; McShulkis, 1998) indicate that the main concerns relate to employee retention, low wages, unattractive working hours and lack of career opportunities. This situation presents challenges for employers to integrate more collaborative negotiations with staff and with their representatives, in order to address these issues and, importantly, investigate new and innovative contractual and employment arrangements that will assist the provision of more stable and productive service delivery and work performance.

HRM issues in services

Although there are, of course, many similarities between manufacturing and services, the unique characteristics of services, as discussed throughout this text, suggest that different HRM approaches are required from those used in their primary and secondary counterparts. Certainly, the repertoire of HRM functions detailed earlier (for example, job design, recruitment and selection, HR development, remuneration, performance management) are applicable in all industries.

However, the distinguishing features of services – namely, their *intangibility*, *variability*, *perishability* and *inseparability*, the customisation of service delivery processes, and the diversity of types of service providers – demand different HRM approaches, processes and techniques. As illustrations, investment advisers, nurses, dentists, funeral directors, teachers, hotel room service attendants, call centre staff, florists and airline pilots provide significantly different levels and types of services; and all specialist skill positions require different kinds of job design, recruitment and selection, training and development, remuneration, and performance management, strategies, processes and techniques. Automated services such as ATMs, food vending machines, toll booths, theatre and airline booking systems, email and voice-mail services naturally require minimal HRM support. However, in these cases, it may be necessary for the customers (as 'partial self-service employees') themselves to be trained, at least in the early stages of their implementation.

Rather than detailing each of the HRM functions (see, for example, Stone 2002; De Cieri and Kramar, 2003; Nankervis et al., 2005) in relation to services, the following sections explore their applications within the context of service delivery systems and processes.

The main HRM problems in services can be summarised as including: role ambiguity, role conflict, work overload, employee/job mismatches, a lack of common purpose (between employees and their organisations), an absence of management commitment, a focus on quantity (at the expense of quality), poor communication, and an acceptance of high employee turnover levels (Mudie and Cottam, 1999, p. 136). In some parts of services, other issues might include: low or inequitable wages, narrow or non-existent career paths, a lack of training or development, job insecurity, and abuse by colleagues and customers – issues that are often exacerbated by casual or on-call employment conditions and little or no protection from representative unions.

As examples, immigration officers and bank tellers may experience both role ambiguity and role conflict with respect to the timely processing of clients versus attention to individual needs; supermarket checkout operators and airport check-in staff may suffer from periodic work pressure or overload; traffic radar operators may lose sight of the overall objective of road safety, or simply presume that revenue (quantity) is preferable; and hotel employees may feel that their work is unrecognised, especially when their managers remind them that they can easily be replaced. Growing sectoral unemployment levels in Western developed nations such as Australia, New Zealand, and many East and Southeast Asian nations further undermine the job security of many services employees. Moreover, the importation of 'foreign' service workers, especially in the latter countries, further adds to job security issues.

All of the above issues adversely affect the practical competencies of service employees, and their real and potential productivity; consequently, more effective HRM strategies and practices – such as human resource planning, job design, recruitment and selection, human resource development, remuneration, performance and employee turnover management – need to be designed to overcome these critical employee and employer concerns. Box 8.3 provides an unusual but quite pertinent example of a comprehensive HRM strategy for addressing some of these issues.

Box 8.3 Protocol House: Modernising HR while serving the Crown

Protocol House is an impressive and grand reminder of Australia's continued allegiance to the Crown. It serves as the principal place of residence for the Governor of Australia and also houses a small team of dedicated staff whose primary function is to meet the social and legislative needs of the governor. Over the past 10 years the staff employed at Protocol House have experienced significant change, not only to their jobs, but also to their reporting structures. Historically, Protocol House has always been closely tied to the operations of the government, but this changed in 1992 with the introduction of legislation that severed those ties, making it a separate legal entity. It is also exempt from equal employment opportunity, occupational health and safety, and freedom of information legislation.

The official secretary to the governor saw this move as an opportunity to review and improve the HR operations and functions at Protocol House, whose structure, systems and procedures had remained unchanged since the early 1900s. In order for this review to be as objective as possible, expressions of interest were called and consultants were encouraged to apply. The following consultancy activities were agreed upon:

1 Review the present structure and organisational chart.
2 Review present position descriptions.
3 Evaluate the effectiveness of a range of HR functions and systems, including the recruitment, selection, induction and performance management functions.
4 Assess the overall efficacy of HRM systems and practices against modern management principles.

The appointed consultants found that the organisational culture that existed at Protocol House was a unique blend of colonial values and etiquette, with all the staff being acutely aware of their role to provide support to the governor, as one of the few remaining ties in Australia to the Crown. This culture was further reinforced by the physical location of staff in an impressive colonial estate, complete with heritage-listed furnishings, chattels and gardens.

The titles and principal functions of the staff employed at Protocol House also reinforced and reflected this unique culture. While a number of the staff carried out managerial, administrative and financial responsibilities that would be considered to be generic to any significant public or private organisation, there were also a number of quite specialised positions, no longer relevant to modern organisations. These positions, which included the roles of chauffeur, butler and aide de camp, together performed a range of duties that were designed to meet the personal needs of the governor, such as cleaning the governor's ceremonial sword and ensuring that it is worn according to etiquette. These members of staff, along with gardeners, house attendants and the chef, were also frequently exposed to high-profile members of government and the private sector, international heads of state, and royalty.

However, despite the complexities and uniqueness of the organisation and its fundamental links to the Crown, it was found that many of the present practices were reflective of modern management principles. Recruitment and selection processes were linked to merit and equity principles and associated with key competency requirements; induction and performance management programs were in place and conducted with efficiency and consistency; and communication processes were transparent and efficient. The effectiveness of the recruitment and selection processes in place in Protocol House has meant that a successful and efficient team is in place.

They have a keen understanding of the need for confidentiality at all times, as well as the requirement to be flexible and to perform a range of quite unique and different functions.

However, the confidential and strictly hierarchical organisational culture has also led to inefficiencies in some areas. There is a wide range of senior control responsibilities held by the positions of official secretary and deputy official secretary. These led to the situation where seven out of the 10 operational positions are directly responsible to the deputy official secretary. This makes it difficult for that position to operate strategically and to implement effective change. The fact that Protocol House operates as a small, isolated organisation has meant that there has been no impetus for change from outside until the appointment of consultants to review these processes.

A number of positions have also been developed around particular personalities, rather than to meet the pursuit of strategic and operational outcomes. Hence, even though some positions have changed over time, it has only been to meet the particular needs of staff within those roles, rather than the needs of the organisation. An example is the role of personnel officer, now no longer performing any HR, or personnel-related, functions.

The review made a number of recommendations with regard to the reporting relationships, span and control, training and career development opportunities for the staff employed at Protocol House. In particular, it was suggested that the official secretary be made directly responsible to the state premier on ceremonial issues, and to the CEO of the Department of Premier on administrative matters; that the official secretary supervise the butler and the aide de camp: that all job descriptions be updated on a competency basis; and that opportunities for regular staged training be made available for all relevant staff, based on identified need and budget provision. The consultants were cognisant of the unique role that staff play, particularly the historical links to the Crown. The objective of their recommendations was to assist the staff to become efficient and effective employees in an organisation whose corporate objectives involved both historical colonial values along with the provision of excellence in service and public policy.

(*Source:* Contributed by Jane Coffey, School of Management, Curtin University of Technology, Perth)

The context of services

As earlier discussions indicate, compared with counterparts in primary and secondary industries, the defining characteristics of services and their accompanying service delivery systems demand different, unique management approaches to ensure efficient, reliable solutions to complex customer requirements. In addition, services are subject to '. . . increasing competition, rapid product imitation and sophisticated customers' (Lewis and Gabrielsen, 1998, p. 64).

All of the organisational functions included in the ISM model (Figure 8.1) – namely, finances, marketing, operations and HRM – contribute separately towards the achievement of desired functional goals and outcomes, and all need careful management in order to do

		Degree of interaction and customisation	
		Low	**High**
Degree of labour intensity	**Low**	Service factory: • Airlines • Trucking • Hotels • Resorts and recreation	Service shop: • Hospitals • Auto repair • Other repair services
	High	Mass service: • Retailing • Wholesaling • Schools • Retail aspects of • Commercial banking	Professional service: • Doctors • Lawyers • Accountants • Architects

Figure 8.5 Schmenner's service process matrix 1986

(*Source:* R. Schmenner, 1986, 'How can service business survive and prosper?', *Sloan Management Review*, vol. 21, no. 3, 1986, pp. 21–32)

so. These various functions must also be integrated by senior managers, to achieve the necessary strategic alignment so that organisations are competitive within their dynamic social, economic and industry environments (see Chapter 2).

Thus, banks and credit unions, hospitals, service stations and furniture removal companies all require clearly defined customer services to be provided by means of specified delivery systems, comprised of the direct service providers (for example, tellers and financial advisers; doctors, nurses and porters; petrol pump attendants or self-service facilities, and cashiers; salespeople, van drivers and packers) who are supported by a host of 'back-room' staff. These services must be marketed and evaluated for their financial viability and competitiveness; they must also use efficient and effective operating systems that '. . . cover every aspect of a company's operations, from the design of the product or service, to how it is packaged, delivered and serviced. Even the accompanying instructions, so often forgotten by the Japanese, are part of the process' (Mudie and Cottam, 1999, p. 134).

As discussed throughout this text, the nature of services varies enormously, from the highly standardised and routinised (for example, McDonald's, or call centres), to the customised and personalised advice offered by medical specialists, career guidance professionals or tax consultants. In all cases, the management of a service organisation's human resources is often the crucial element to ensure its productivity, competitiveness and profitability. As Schneider (1999, p. 64) suggests, '. . . the connection between human resource management and customer service is conceptually (as well as physically and psychologically) . . . very strong', if only because of the inherent characteristics of the services themselves – that is, intangibility, variability, perishability and inseparability – discussed in previous chapters.

Schmenner's service process matrix (1986) (see Figure 8.5) is an example of a model used to analyse the degree of 'interaction and customisation' required in particular services, and their corresponding level of 'labour intensity'. However, in this model, 'labour intensity' primarily refers to the level of competency or skills utilised by service providers (for example, doctors, lawyers and architects), rather than the numbers of employees involved.

Like all similar models, the industry sectors included in each segment of the matrix are debatable. It could, for example, be argued that airline, hotel and resort staff may provide very personalised customer services, while doctors and lawyers may conversely delegate or outsource many of their 'intensive' services (for example, blood pressure and pathology tests, conveyancing and the preparation of client briefs) to their paramedical or paralegal colleagues. The degree of judgment exercised by service providers within highly customised service delivery processes may be as significant as the level of their specialist competencies (Lovelock, 1996, cited in Mudie and Cottam, 1999, p. 132).

Nevertheless, while such models are not precise, they do assist industry strategists to better assess the quantity and quality of employees required to effectively and efficiently deliver their service objectives to their particular customer market. In turn, operational managers and supervisors can determine the appropriate numbers, qualifications and skills of their employees, as well as their necessary staffing techniques, training and development, performance review, and remuneration policies and practices.

Even the most standardised or automated services (ATMs, Internet booking systems, supermarket self-scanning devices) rely on such human capabilities and skills as systems design, manufacture and repair in order to maintain customer satisfaction and responsiveness. Moreover, those that are considerably more customised require even greater involvement from, and management of, the relevant service providers. As an example, service provider competencies can be divided into 'low'-level, core qualities (for example, unobtrusiveness, honesty, detachment – hospital cleaners, hotel room attendants, waiters) and 'high'-level skills (for example, technical ability, professional experience, empathy – plastic surgeons, lawyers, counsellors), combined with such mutual and 'supplementary' personal attributes as confidentiality, courtesy, responsiveness and timeliness (Mudie and Cottam, 1999, p. 134).

Accordingly, the management of human resources, including HR planning, appropriate job design, effective staffing processes, timely HR development, incentive remuneration systems, planned career development, absence and employee turnover management, and the development of suitable work cultures and structures, provides the opportunity for services organisations to achieve and retain their competitive edge within their dynamic industry environments.

HRM functions and the service delivery process

As discussed throughout this chapter, HRM functions are crucial to the achievement of organisational competitiveness and profitability goals in services, as the service delivery process and its perceived quality is dependent on the individual and work team competencies, skills and behaviours of both its direct and indirect service providers. The service 'encounter' is defined as '. . . any episode in which a customer comes into contact with any aspect of the organisation and gets an impression of the quality of its service' (Albrecht, 1988, p. 26), and is the product of a managed service delivery process designed to meet the organisation's objectives through the customer satisfaction of its target markets.

Albrecht (1988) further suggests that these 'service encounters' result from a managed 'cycle of service' that encompasses '. . . technical control systems and procedures, [the] management of human aspects, and the development of a service oriented culture' (Lehtinen and Lehtinen, 1991, cited in Lewis and Gabrielsen, 1998, p. 66). These definitions imply that all management functions (finances, marketing, operations *and* HRM) are interrelated. More importantly, they also indicate that HRM is pivotal to the management of service delivery processes, and thus to services as a whole.

At the macro-level, HRM is focused on the establishment (or review) of the appropriate organisational strategies, structures, cultures and policies that will develop effective infrastructure for the achievement of corporate objectives. At the micro-level, it is concerned with the provision of suitable HRM functions (for example, HR plans, job design, recruitment and selection, HR development, remuneration, performance assessment), which will implement these objectives within service delivery processes.

As examples of the above, an e-commerce company offering health advice over the Internet may decide to outsource all its research activities to subcontractors, with only minimal staff employed at its headquarters (that is, those engaged in *strategy* and *structure* functions); many companies choose to use global call centres in India or South America for customer information services (*strategy* and *structure*); and IBM, Virgin Airlines, Deutsche Bank and Hilton Hotels are renowned for the consistent replication of their corporate *culture* in different countries. Recent reports suggest that many traditional in-house professional services, such as project management, resource management and IT vendor management, are being increasingly outsourced (or 'off-shored'). As an example, the IT&T manager of Michael Page Technology, Stuart Packham, reports that '. . . typically, the design will be done in Australia by architects, and then it will be off-shored for the coding component, which . . . will be done in large outsourced Indian development centres' (Foreshew, 2004).

The same companies use different HRM functions associated with their strategic HRM choices (Legge, 1995). Thus, an e-commerce company will be likely to develop close alliances with its outsourced service providers (for example, Amazon.com), and to ensure that its core employees are highly skilled, well-paid and have access to career opportunities. Global call centre staff need to be carefully recruited, well trained in such aspects as customer responsiveness (for example, knowledge of multi-country climates, languages and sporting results), and employed on contract, rather than permanent, bases. The following box illustrates such a case.

Box 8.4   They have to speak the lingo

His friends call him 'Yankee Pankee', because he sometimes slips into an American accent, but the taunts don't worry commerce graduate Rakesh Garg. Speaking with an accent is his job, and it fetches him a monthly salary of 12,000 rupees (S$468, or approximately A$364), much more than what a 21-year-old graduate with no special skills could expect in a bank or government office. Mr Garg is one of thousands employed at call centres across India who dish out advice on subjects as diverse as housing loans and computer crashes. Sometimes, the operators have to deal with an angry washing machine buyer hurling abuse, or an anxious businessman who has lost his credit card. A colleague with higher qualifications, such as an MBA, could outline the best stock options for a British or American investor. The workers are put through intensive training covering communication and technological skills. They have to watch the BBC and CNN, as well as British television comedies or American soap operas. 'It is a very detailed training program that makes the student aware of everything there is to know about a country and its people – their culture, their customs, their festivals and their weather,' said a spokesman for BPO (business process outsourcing) provider Wipro Spectramind.

In contrast to this corporate approach to culture, companies such as the Bank of Scotland, Braun, Qantas, Telstra and the JW Marriott Hotel chain are concerned with the development of in-house expertise on a longer-term (and potentially global) basis. Hence, they apply HRM techniques such as clear job design, international recruitment and selection techniques, criterion-based performance review, performance-based remuneration, international career development, and the management of employee turnover and absence. The following section focuses on the application of the above HRM strategies and functions to a variety of services organisations.

(*Source*: Adapted from V. Raghunathan, 'They have to speak the lingo', *The Straits Times*, 6 December 2003, p. 6)

HRM and 'strategic choice' in services

As the ISM model (Figure 8.1) illustrates, the effective management of services demands both 'strategic' and 'functional' approaches be used in marketing, financial, operations and HRM components. Other chapters discuss these approaches in relation to marketing, financial and operations management; this chapter now considers how these issues affect HRM.

HRM strategies can be defined as 'the pattern of planned human resource deployments and activities intended to enable an organisation to achieve its goals' (Wright and McMahan, 1992, p. 295). 'Strategic choice' in HRM implies that all HRM practices should therefore be designed to ensure that employees are attracted, chosen, developed, paid and managed so as to enable an organisation to achieve its competitive and profitability goals.

De Cieri and Kramar (2003, p. 50) cite the case of Boeing in the United States as being an example of a services company that failed to achieve this link between corporate and HRM strategic choice. Its Consumer Products Division chose as its corporate-level strategy a price war with Airbus Industries that led to a shift away from the focus on customer service and towards the pursuit of cost reduction. However, while it received significant new business from airline companies, the staff downsizing associated with its cost cutting meant that it had insufficient staff to meet these new orders.

On the more positive side, some multinational fast-food operators (for example, McDonald's, KFC) located in Singapore found it difficult to recruit enthusiastic and committed young service staff locally, due to their high education levels. In response, they actively attracted 'seniors' to these positions, as they were able to provide the complementary service qualities such as customer communication and problem-solving skills and experience at the same cost as juniors. Conversely, Australia Post's service diversification strategy (for example, the inclusion of banking, retailing, bill payment services) has required the recruitment of new employees and/or the retraining of existing staff to develop the appropriate skills associated with additional sales, product knowledge, and financial and computer use. It is apparent that in order to achieve organisational objectives the various levels of strategic corporate decisions made by service organisations need to be matched by parallel strategic decisions within and between all HRM strategies, practices and activities.

These HRM practices and activities include human resource planning, job design, staffing, human resource development, remuneration, performance management, absence and turnover management, and occupational health and safety.

Human resource planning in services

While it is not possible to discuss all the specific human resource planning issues and practices for service organisations here, the section raises some of the main themes and their underlying principles.

Human resource planning (HRP) is the '. . . process through which organisational goals are translated into human resource goals concerning staffing levels and allocation' (De Cieri and Kramar, 2003, p. 148), and in turn it provides the blueprint for all other HRM functions and practices. Thus, an IT company undertaking international expansion may choose an HR plan that seeks to recruit the brightest systems designers from anywhere in the world. Hence, they offer very competitive salary packages, relocation incentives, performance bonuses, and state-of-the-art development opportunities, but only on limited contract bases. The primary purpose of this (short-term) HR plan might be to rapidly enhance its intellectual capital, IT systems and market penetration. This short-term planning strategy might be followed by a longer-term plan to attract staff, who can operate the new systems and service the new clients on an ongoing basis.

The links between corporate and HRM plans are developed through an organisation's *environmental scanning process*. An environmental scanning process evaluates the likely changes in its internal and external environments, and subsequently develops appropriate business plans to address these findings. Such internal HRM factors as the numbers, skills, experience and culture of the organisation are assessed against its likely future directions. The assessment also includes developments in the industry, local, regional, national and global environments relevant to its operation. The external factors that may require responsive HRM planning strategies may include changes in the social, economic, political and technological conditions.

Following is an example of the changing impact of environmental factors. After the 1997 Asian economic crisis and later after the dramatic events of September 11 in the United States, the hotel sectors in Australia and much of Southeast Asia suffered a significant decline in occupancy levels, due to multiple factors such as currency fluctuations, customers' fears of terrorism, and political unrest. However, not all hotels in the region suffered equally. This uneven impact was due to their different local environments, more or less attractive currency exchange rates, different degrees of national security, and the specific and proactive business plans of their managers. Thus, while Singaporean hotels experienced serious reductions in their occupancy as a result of the Asian economic crisis, similar establishments in Phuket (Nankervis and Wan, 1999) and some Australian locations fared considerably better. Many Asian and Australian hotels benefited from an increase in intraregional tourism following the September 11 incident. These examples suggest that corporate and HR plans should incorporate both long- and short-term components, including contingency (or crisis) HRM planning approaches.

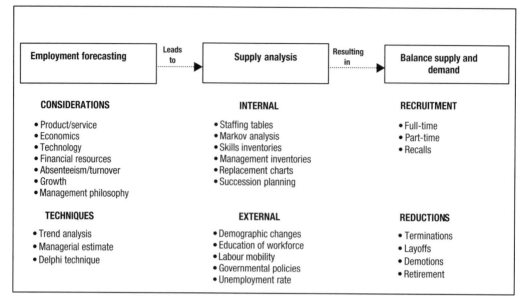

Figure 8.6 Human resources planning model

Source: A. Nankervis, R. Compton and M. Baird, *Human Resource Management: Strategies and processes*, 5th ed., Thomson Learning, Melbourne, 2005.

HRP translates the findings of specific environmental scanning processes into appropriate HRM practices through attention to *labour demand* and *labour supply* formulae. An assessment of labour demand involves decisions on the numbers and skills of employees, and the productivity levels associated with desired organisational objectives and goals. The outcomes of such analyses might include a need for more staff with specialist skills, a need for cultural change, or the multiskilling of existing staff. Conversely, a need to rationalise existing positions may involve the downsizing of some positions and the outsourcing of others. Labour supply analysis, on the other hand, suggests where and how appropriate employees might be sourced.

The various techniques for labour demand and supply are summarised in Figure 8.6.

Different services sectors experience different labour demand and supply responses, in both the short and the long term. The following examples indicate the variable demand and supply issues associated with particular occupations:

- Doctors and nurses are variously scarce or oversupplied.
- IT specialists were in demand in the early part of the new millennium, but demand has declined since the demise of many dot.com companies.
- Some Singaporean and Hong Kong hotels have been forced to hire contract workers from China or the Philippines due to a lack of interest by locals.
- Retail stores and fast-food outlets attract young and experienced employees in some countries and 'seniors' in others.

Thus, services face a myriad of choices with respect to their HRP strategies. The following HRP choices may be included:

- internal and/or external labour markets;

- local, regional, national, and/or international sources;
- young and/or mature employees;
- variable employment conditions (for example, permanent versus part-time versus contract versus casual employees); and
- downsizing and/or outsourcing.

All of these choices have consequences that need careful consideration within well-prepared HR plans.

HRM in a 'service culture'

Human resource plans, and all consequent HRM activities, are the foundations of customer-oriented organisational cultures in services, and '. . . studies show a positive relationship between what employees report about their experiences as employees and what customers report about their experiences as service consumers' (Schneider and Bowen, 1999, p. 41). It is further suggested that organisations with these types of 'climates for service' combine a focus on customer retention, supported by all organisational functions (operations, marketing, finances, HRM), along with active support to service providers in the forms of resources (for example, equipment, supplies) and '. . . management behaviour that rewards, supports, plans for and expects service excellence' (Schneider and Bowen, 1999, p. 67).

In practice, service climates in organisations are developed and reinforced through a range of activities that may include technological/information and logistics systems support, clear and accurate job design, focused recruitment and selection, appropriate employee training and development, effective supervision and performance management, and the control of undesirable employee turnover levels.

In services, where personal qualities and skills are of the utmost importance, effective job design may be the key to customer satisfaction and organisational success. Effective job design will identify the particular qualifications and competencies required for a specific job. In addition, it may identify the affective or emotional interaction dimensions to a specific customer service position. This 'emotional labour' issue is discussed later in this section, but the 'job' of a professional football player, or television newsreader, involves that the candidate have some entertainment attributes associated with their specific sporting, technical or skills requirements, in order to successfully perform for their audience. Hence, their specific job design needs to acknowledge the multifaceted nature of the skills required for a position.

Job design in services

The ways in which different jobs are designed should reflect the uniqueness of their organisations and the disparate expectations of their internal and external customers. They should also accurately indicate how discrete jobs and job 'clusters' (for example, hairdressers, accountants, and personal trainers) fit with associated jobs (for example, cashiers, administrators, personal training marketers). It should be indicated just how these discrete jobs and job clusters fit with the overall aims of their organisations, while incorporating sufficient flexibility to adapt and transform as circumstances change. In some organisations, this need for flexibility might lead to multiskilling (for example, hairdressers who also act as cashiers, and personal trainers who do their own marketing). In other organisations, service quality might demand the retention of seemingly duplicated functions (for example, maitre d' positions as well as waiters, hotel doormen and porters). These decisions will inevitably be influenced by the nature of the services offered, the targeted customer market, cost factors and strategic HR plans. Job design is often the crucial fulcrum on which all other HRM functions depend, as it translates overall organisational expectations into individual tasks and performance criteria, and thus provides the basis on which recruitment, selection, HR development, performance management, and remuneration systems and processes can be developed.

Job design comprises three related aspects: job analysis, job description and job evaluation.

1 *Job analysis* involves an examination of the job 'environment' (for example, workplace, reporting relationships), the level or grading of the particular job, the tasks, activities and functions required to perform the job, any technology or other equipment used, and any special conditions under which the job must be performed. It also involves a parallel assessment of the qualifications, work experience, competencies, skills and personal qualities required by any person appointed to the job. Job analysis can be conducted by the following activities: interviewing or surveying present job incumbents; directly observing staff performing the job; using focus groups within the work area; making comparisons with similar jobs in other organisations; or consulting generic occupational classification systems (for example, the Australian Standard Classification of Occupations). Jobs are usually analysed when organisations begin their activities, and subsequently, on an annual basis, or when significant changes are occurring in the organisation.

2 *Job descriptions* (or duty statements, or position descriptions) and *person specifications* (or person descriptions) are the outcomes of job analysis, which should accurately and succinctly describe the necessary tasks and functions of the job, and the corresponding skills, competencies and personal qualities required of job holders. Tables 8.3 and 8.4 provide examples of typical job descriptions and the person specifications in different sectors of services. The first describes a line management position and hence is broad in the expectations required of the job's occupant. The second is a lower-level position, and so the job description is considerably more prescriptive and task-focused. Such prescriptive job descriptions derive from the preferred hierarchical and authoritarian cultural practices based on the scientific management theories discussed in Chapter 1. The intention of this approach to task management is to enhance the efficiency and standardisation of service. However, arguably when educational levels in society are rising, this approach discourages employees from applying the full range of their capacities (ideas, skills and abilities), and may even contribute to work stress due to the lack of control over their jobs and low morale due to a sense of feeling not valued by their employer. There is, however, no right or wrong job description, and each must be carefully prepared to accurately and effectively reflect the competencies and tasks required to meet organisational and customer expectations.

3 *Job evaluation* completes the job design process by assigning a financial value to each job or job cluster, according to its classification level within the organisation, industrial relations determinations, award conditions, and external labour market competition issues.

Some of the main flaws in job design include inaccurate or outdated analysis and descriptions, generic rather than specific tasks and functions, an absence of either job descriptions

Table 8.3 A sample job description

	Job Profile
Title:	**Co-ordinator – Operations**
Classification:	
Position no:	
Directorate:	**Botanic Gardens, Parks and Recreation**
Branch:	**Horticulture and Assets**
Last reviewed:	**July 2000**

Job role:
Assist the Curator – Parkland to manage the Operations team and implement the operational plan for the Operations section.

Context
The Botanic Gardens and Parks Authority:
The mission of the Botanic Gardens and Parks Authority is 'to conserve and enhance Kings Park, Bold Park and the State's Botanic Garden for the Community'.
The core business of the Authority is the care, control and management of the designated lands and of plant collections, horticulture, biodiversity conservation and associated research.
To meet its mission the Authority has two outputs that are purchased by Government. Output 1 relates to visitor service and cultural heritage, and Output 2 relates to conservation and scientific research.

This directorate:
This directorate is responsible for all the on-the-ground operations and recreation services on designated lands.

Role of this job:
1. Assist with the implementation of the Operations operational plan.
2. Oversee day-to-day and short-term management of the Operations team.
3. Monitor and maintain buildings, hard landscape features, memorials, machinery, bore pumps and dams and main line.
4. Assist in the implementation of records for the machinery, vehicles and cultural heritage items within Kings Park and Botanic Garden.
5. Manage the repair and maintenance of machinery, vehicles and assets.
6. Assist with the coordination of Garden Week, Sunset Cinemas and other events.
7. In coordination with the engineer, manage the monitoring repair and maintenance of pumps, bores and irrigation supply equipment.
8. Assist with budget management – purchase officer.
9. Liaise with other teams and branches to ensure projects, machinery and works are coordinated with other works in progress.
10. As part of a team, assist with the operational and strategic planning of the branch.

Essential competencies for effective performance of this job

Technical/professional/specialist competencies (technical/specialist knowledge, skills and abilities required for effective performance of the job)
1. Demonstrated knowledge and skills in maintenance and repair of machinery, hard landscapes, signage and buildings, pumps, bores and water quality.
2. Demonstrated knowledge of public safety issues in urban parks.
3. Current B class driver's licence.
4. Experience in buildings, hard landscape, and machinery maintenance and repairs.
5. Experience in coordinating building and services work in a public park environment.

Table 8.4 Hotel room attendant job description

Position title: **Room Attendant**
Grade: 2
Incumbent:
Job tasks:
1 Collection of chemicals and tools from chemical room.
2 Sign on and collect uniform.
3 Attend briefing in housekeeping at 8 am ready for work; collect work board, keys and sign keyboard.
4 Collect trolley from the floor allocated with the most rooms. Check all 'Vacant Ready' rooms. Ensure that all TV guides, what's on, Foxtel and movie guides are the right dates and that all old ones are thrown out.
5 When on a floor, check your board for any 'Vacant Dirty' rooms that can be done first. Also check which rooms have arrivals. Do rooms with early arrivals first, following times put on sheet. Always check occupied rooms for 'make up' signs.
6 Knock on the door and say 'Housekeeping', then wait 10 seconds before knocking again if no reply. Enter cautiously in case guest is in room. If no guest, enter, and put your doorstopper under the door.

Cleaning the room:
1 Spray the shower with chemical.
2 Turn off the fridge.
3 Strip the bed.
4 Put linen in trolley linen bag.
5 Bring clean linen in for bed.
6 Clear all rubbish from room.
7 Make the bed.
8 Dust whole bedroom, damp dust.
9 Check all books and compendiums.
10 Check mini bar cupboards and wardrobe.
11 Empty water in irons and kettles.
12 Clean and wipe fridge out, removing bottles on bottom shelf and wiping up excess water.
13 Check that all pillows and blankets in the wardrobe are clean and folded neatly.
14 Vacuum the room.

Cleaning the bathroom:
1 Scrub the shower.
2 Rinse the shower, and wipe the tiles and grouting.
3 Clean the shower door.
4 Clean the toilet, inclding the back and base.
5 Check toilet rolls and change if half a roll or less.
6 Remove items from vanity, clean and wipe vanity and basin.
7 Polish taps.
8 Polish all mirrors, picture frames and glasses.
9 Wipe out bath and rinse.
10 Replace all towels and amenities.
11 Wipe floor with damp rag.
12 Make sure that areas under the vanity, behind the toilet and in corners are cleaned properly.
13 Refill ice trays.

or person specifications, a lack of prioritisation of tasks (or, simply, too many), inappropriate job grading and/or salary level, and a failure to include critical job tasks. Evidence of all of these flaws is found in many job descriptions within services, but perhaps of most concern are inappropriate job grading and the failure to include critical job tasks.

The issue of the payment of service workers, especially front-line service providers, is contentious, at both the highest and lowest levels of the industry. Doctors, lawyers, real estate agents and used car dealers are often criticised for their reported exorbitant salaries and bonuses, while nurses, schoolteachers, child-care workers and the police are often among the lowest-paid workers in the world. These differences may be justified on the basis of different qualifications and experience, relative skill levels, different accountabilities or labour market realities. It may also be true in some circumstances that the responsibilities and demands on front-line service personnel are not adequately built into either their job descriptions or their salary classifications. This argument revolves around the twin issues of the 'emotional labour' component of service, and current attempts to 'empower' front-line employees, which are discussed below.

Antecedents	Emotional labour	Consequences
• Explicitness of display rules	• Frequency of interaction	• Emotional exhaustion
• Routineness of task	• Duration of interaction	• Job satisfaction
• Job autonomy	• Emotional dissonance	• Role
• Power of role receiver		• Internationalisation

Figure 8.7 Emotional labour

Source: J. Morris and D. Feldman, 'Managing emotions in the workplace,' *Journal of Management Issues*, vol. ix, no. 3, 1997, p. 260.

Emotional labour

Service work almost inevitably engages the emotions of service providers in quite dissimilar ways to those in other industries, and this element needs to be recognised in job descriptions, rewarded and managed (Hochschild, 1983b; Morris and Feldman, 1997). Emotional labour is defined as '. . . the act of expressing organisation-desired emotions during service transactions' (Morris and Feldman, 1997, p. 257). It may be expressed in the performance of theatrical language and gestures of artists, theme park guides, or even restaurant waiters; the 'sincere' service gestures of sales assistants, real estate agents, doctors or lawyers; or as the control of negative emotions by complaints officers, call centre staff, police and ambulance employees. Hochschild (1983b) classifies these interaction performances as 'regulated displays of emotion' (p. 258) that involve face-to-face or voice-based contact, and a requirement of the service worker to evoke an emotional reaction from the customer, or to provide the employer with an opportunity to influence the employee's emotional expressions. Figure 8.7 summarises the features and consequences of the use of emotional labour within services.

As the figure illustrates, the required degree of emotional labour in a particular service job will be determined by four variables: (1) the explicitness of display rules; (2) task routineness; (3) job autonomy; and (4) the power of the role receiver. All of these variables help to assess the intensity of the emotional labour appropriate to particular service occupations. Thus, using the jobs illustrated above, artistic performers are likely to have very explicit display rules, less routine tasks, some job autonomy and considerable interpretative power over their roles. This emotional labour dimension is in contrast to theme park guides and waiters who may have less explicit requirements, more routinisation and less job autonomy. Conversely, doctors and lawyers may have fewer explicit display rules and fewer task routines, but considerably greater autonomy and power than sales assistants and real estate agents. In the case of negative emotional displays, rules may be explicit and tasks may be more or less of a routine nature, but job autonomy and role power are both considered to be paramount. The consequences of the management of the emotional labour component of service work can be both positive and negative, as Figure 8.7 illustrates.

The management issues raised by the discussion on emotional labour include the control of 'emotional dissonance' (that is, the conflict between genuine and job-related emotions); the inclusion of emotional labour as an integral part of service occupations, reflected in associated job and person specifications; and performance rewards based upon the achievement of predetermined job, section and organisational goals. However, as also indicated, the degree of emotional depth required will differ from job to job, and should be so recorded and monitored in the relevant job/position descriptions.

Where the emotional labour component of service is minimal (for example, retail checkout operators, cashiers, fast-food service providers), and where little autonomy is permitted, the standardisation of routine service delivery processes helps to ensure uniform service quality and to allow easier monitoring and management. Perhaps the most well known examples of this 'production line' approach to service delivery are McDonald's, Hungry Jack's and IKEA, which have deliberately adapted scientific management (see Chapter 1) principles and practices in order to provide greater efficiency and controls. The HRM features of these prescriptive approaches include practices such as:

- the simplification of job tasks;
- the clear division of labour;
- the use of 'scripts' (for example, McDonald's notorious 'Would you like fries with that?', 'Have a nice day!', and the cryptic hotel farewell, 'Missing you already!');
- little worker autonomy; and, where possible,
- the substitution of equipment for employees. (Bowen and Lawler, 1992, p. 31)

These applications of manufacturing processes to services have spawned the use of the term 'McDonaldisation' to describe routinised delivery systems. They are often associated with the negative features of industrialisation, including low pay, long working hours and autocratic management styles. Routinised approaches are useful in service operations with little variability or customisation. However, they are unlikely to provide either customer or employee satisfaction in more complex services. Doctors, lawyers, financial and taxation consultants, iridologists, or teachers, and their customers, are likely to be uncomfortable with such standardised processes, although the use of Internet medical diagnostic services appears to be currently popular. In these cases, while there may still be some routine procedures, their primary services involve considerable variability and autonomy. Organisations such as Virgin Blue, Shell, Air Paradise, AMEX, Federal Express, Westpac and Sydney Electricity, among others, have addressed the twin issues of employee job satisfaction and service variability through the implementation of either employee empowerment or team-based systems, which are explored in the following sections.

Table 8.5 The contingencies of empowerment

Contingency	Production line approach	Empowerment
Basic business strategy	Low cost, high volume	Differentiation, customised, personalised
Tie to customer	Transaction, short time period	Relationship, long time period
Technology	Routine, simple	Non-routine, complex
Business environment	Predictable, few surprises	Unpredictable, many surprises
Types of people	Theory X managers, employees with low growth needs, low social needs, and weak interpersonal skills	Theory Y managers, employees with high growth needs, high social needs, and strong interpersonal skills

Source: D. E. Bowen and E. E. Lawler, 'The empowerment of service workers: What, why, how and when?', *Sloan Management Review*, spring, 1992, p. 37.

Employee empowerment

Empowerment has been variously defined as 'purposeful chaos' (Tom Peters), 'directed autonomy' (Robert Waterman), or '. . . turning the front line loose' (Zemke and Schaaf, cited in Bowen and Lawler, 1992, p. 31). In essence, empowerment involves the delegation of some job responsibilities or a degree of flexibility in the interpretation of job- or customer-related decisions to front-line employees. Examples of employee empowerment might include giving hotel reservation officers some leeway in room pricing, encouraging tour operators to design individualised tour 'packages' for clients, allowing doctors' receptionists to prioritise patients, or university enrolments staff to provide academic advice on course choices.

As Table 8.5 illustrates, empowerment is useful in services that require more complex and long-term interactions with their customers, and where managers have positive perceptions of their employees' abilities and willingness to provide quality services (Theory Y, as opposed to the Theory X basis of scientific management). However, empowerment may be '. . . inappropriate or even counterproductive in situations of low service heterogeneity because flexible behaviours will disrupt the quasi-industrialised service delivery operations' (Chebat and Kollias, 2000, p. 67).

The reasons to use employee empowerment strategies include concerns for both service quality and the satisfaction of employees' needs. The assumption is that service employees desire more involvement in their jobs, and are more motivated and effective, when they are given opportunities for greater interaction with customers, and that this will lead to enhanced levels of service quality. Based on employee motivation theories (for example, Maslow, 1954; Porter and Lawler, 1968; Herzberg, 1974), it is suggested that employees require challenging and satisfying jobs as well as salaries and job security in order to perform according to required management standards. Figure 8.8 illustrates the role of employee empowerment in customer satisfaction and service quality, and some of the management techniques that may be used to support it.

Figure 8.8 Employee development in the customer satisfaction wheel

Source: P. Mudie and A. Cottam, *The Management and Marketing of Services*, 2nd ed., Butterworths and Heinemann, Oxford, 1999, p. 150.

Of course, there are many kinds and degrees of employee empowerment, appropriate to different service positions. The notion of empowerment is made up of two job dimensions – namely, involvement and control (Bowen and Lawler, 1992, p. 36). It is further suggested that these dimensions can be divided into 'high involvement' (overall organisational performance), 'job involvement' (job skills and systems), and 'suggestion involvement' (employee ideas) (Bowen and Lawler, 1992, p. 36). The HRM dimensions of empowerment techniques range from communication about organisational performance, section and job knowledge; to power to make decisions; to rewards based on enhanced service performance.

The reported benefits of employee empowerment include new service ideas, closer interaction with customers, more efficient online responses during service delivery, and better service 'recovery' outcomes (Bowen and Lawler, 1992, p. 33). In addition, employees appear to be more motivated. The problems associated with some empowerment systems include higher recruitment, selection and maintenance costs (due to more highly skilled staff); slower or inconsistent service quality (customisation); and inappropriate employee decisions (Bowen and Lawler, 1992, p. 34). Aspects concerning the latter outcome are illustrated by the case of Willie, a doorman at a Four Seasons Hotel in the United States. The doorman provided excellent service quality, but cost his employer thousands of dollars in airfares by personally delivering a lost briefcase to a customer. Similarly, Nick Leeson, a futures broker for Barings Bank in Singapore, contributed to the bank's demise in the mid-1990s through his 'rogue' trading without adequate supervision, and more recently, similar unrestricted futures traders were at work in the National Australia Bank. Hence the cautionary warning is given that:

> Empowerment and production-line approaches demand different types of managers and employees. For empowerment to work, particularly in the high-involvement form, the company needs to have Theory Y managers, who believe that their employees can act independently to benefit both the organisation and its customers. (Bowen and Lawler, 1992, p. 38)

Table 8.6 The benefits of SMWTs

For managers	For customers	For employees
• Reduced hierarchies • Less supervision • Reduced labour costs • Performance improvements	• Service quality improvements • Greater customer loyalty	• Enriched jobs • Greater quality of work life • Job satisfaction • Lower employment turnover

Another HRM technique commonly used in services for similar purposes is the formation of 'semi-autonomous' or 'self-managing' work teams, which together deliver the required services to their customers. These approaches are explored in the following section.

Work teams and service delivery systems

Similarly to the empowerment of individual service workers, the development of self-managing work teams (SMWT) in service organisations is a useful tool to promote productivity, integration and synergy within service delivery systems, and 'seamless' service for customers. SMWTs may consist of employees in similar job clusters (for example, call centre telephonists, retail checkout or sales staff, railway porters), or they may combine several different job types (for example, hospital emergency and intensive care ward teams, including administrators, nurses and medical staff; aircraft cabin crew, involving pilots, flight attendants and mechanics).

SMWTs are defined as '. . . groups of interdependent individuals that can self-regulate their behaviour on related *whole* tasks', suggesting that they can have considerable benefits for managers, customers and the employees themselves (Spreitzer et al., 1999, p. 340). These include the benefits listed in Table 8.6.

Katzenbach and Santamaria (1999) suggest that service organisations such as the US Marine Corps, 3M, the New York City Ballet, Toyota, FirstUSA, McKinsey, Mary Kay and Tupperware use SMWTs as part of their employee commitment and service quality strategies, but note the differences between 'single-leader work group(s)' and such 'team(s)' as outlined in Table 8.7.

As the table indicates, the crucial features of SMWTs lie in the rotation of leadership, the relative autonomy to determine team goals, 'mutual' accountability, and group commitment to the achievement of what is described as a 'service guarantee' (Hart, 1995) to both internal and external customers – '. . . a promise or commitment by one part of the organization . . . to deliver its products or services in a specified way and to the complete satisfaction of the customer' (Hart, 1995, p. 64). While real estate sales teams, medical centre professionals, legal firms, information systems analysts or car wash staff may find it relatively easy to establish effective SMWTs, it is obviously more difficult to do so in multifunctional services such as those provided by hospital casualty units, university business schools or whole bank branches. However, while difficult to implement in some circumstances, SMWTs can provide important changes in employees' perceptions of their roles and their relationships with other internal service providers and customers, and can result in increased initiative, more integrated and customised service, and, ultimately, enhanced efficiency and productivity.

Table 8.7 Teams and work groups: It pays to know the difference

Managers tend to label every working group in an organisation a 'team', whether it's a roomful of customer service operators or a string of assemblers on a manufacturing line. But employees quickly lose motivation and commitment when they are assigned to a team that turns out to be a single-leader work group. If executives want to spark energy and commitment on the front lines, they must know how a team differs from a single-leader work group, and when to create one or the other.

	Team	**Single-leader work group**
Run by:	The members of the team best suited to lead the tasks at hand; the leadership role shifts among the members	One person, usually the senior member, who is formally designated to lead
Goals and agenda set by:	The group, based on dialogue about purpose; constructive conflict and integration predominate	The formal leader, often in consultation with a sponsoring executive; conflict with group members is avoided, and the leader integrates
Performance evaluated by:	The members of the group, as well as the leader and sponsor	The leader and the sponsor
Work style determined by:	The members	The leader's preference
Success defined by:	The members' aspirations	The leader's aspirations
Most appropriate business context:	A complex challenge that requires people with various skill sets working together much of the time	A challenge in which time is of the essence and the leader already knows best how to proceed; the leader is the primary integrator
Speed and efficiency:	Low until the group has learned to function as a team; afterward, however, the team is as fast as a single-leader group	Higher than that of teams initially, as the members need no time to develop commitment or to learn to work as a team
Primary end-products:	Largely collective, requiring several team members to work together to produce results	Largely individual and can be accomplished best by each person working on his or her own
Accountability characterised by:	'We hold one another mutually accountable for achieving the goals and performance of the team.'	'The leader holds us individually accountable for our output.'

Source: J. Katzenbach and J. Santamaria, 'Firing up the front line', *Harvard Business Review*, May–June 1999, p. 114.

As an example, it is not unusual for hotels to form groups from employees working in their reception, concierge, rooms, or food and beverage sections, although many of these have traditionally been of Katzenbach and Santamaria's 'work group' type, with single hierarchical leadership and focused almost solely on functional activities. However, a more innovative approach might form SMWTs comprised of a selection of reception, concierge, rooms, and food and beverage staff to reflect the customer's perspective of an integrated (rather than a 'silo') service delivery system. This approach can encourage the germination of new ideas for each part of the process, and for building the linkages between parts, as well as for the process as a whole.

This section has explored the nature of job design strategies in services, including the role of emotional labour, employee empowerment and self-managing work teams. Job design strategies provide the blueprint for almost all of the other HRM functions, including staffing, HR development, remuneration, and employee retention, which are now considered in more detail.

Staffing strategies in services

Recruitment and selection

A clear and accurate job design is the starting point for the two complementary components of effective staffing in any organisation – namely, *recruitment* and *selection*. Effective HR planning, combined with appropriate job design, enables organisations to target the most suitable potential employees, to attract them, and then to choose the right ones to fit their culture and their designated jobs, in order to ensure that they have 'the right people in the right jobs'. Recruitment has been defined as 'the process of attempting to locate and encourage potential applicants to apply for existing or anticipated job openings' (Compton et al., 2003, p. 15), while selection is the process of choosing the best recruits from among those attracted in the recruitment stage. Based upon the particular kinds of job design chosen and the labour markets deemed most suitable, choices can then be made concerning the most likely sources of qualified and skilled employees, the most effective recruitment techniques and the most accurate selection tools.

In some organisations, it may be preferable to appoint employees to vacant positions by job rotation, secondment, transfer or promotion (*internal recruitment*), in order to save the greater costs of outside recruitment, or to provide career opportunities and motivational benefits to existing employees. The public sector and many private-sector service organisations choose such internal recruitment options to retain human resource expertise (Compton et al., 2003, p. 25). Conversely, other service organisations recruit applicants for specialist technical or professional positions (for example, accountants, scientists, doctors, engineers) directly from universities, and senior managers from executive recruitment consultants (for example, Michael Page International or PricewaterhouseCoopers), in order to assure appropriate expertise or to widen their labour pool globally – *external recruitment* (Compton et al., 2003, p. 26). E-recruitment, using the Internet as an inexpensive, but wide-ranging tool to broaden the available labour markets (for example, Monster.com, Seek.com), is also becoming popular, especially for new graduates, professionals and middle managers, in the IT sector.

Some organisations use both internal and external recruitment techniques simultaneously, in order to create a competitive staffing climate, or use different methods for different levels of positions. As examples, Australian federal government agencies are obliged to recruit both externally and internally, despite the costs, to assure equity and non-discrimination in their staffing processes. Retailers such as Coles, Kmart and Woolworths generally recruit externally for sales assistants, choose internal recruitment for middle and senior management positions, and may use international recruitment consultants for their senior executive positions. McDonald's and KFC rarely promote their customer service staff to more senior administrative positions, and hotels tend to segment internal recruitment within their discrete departments (for example, front office, food and beverage, housekeeping), with few opportunities for cross-skilling or promotion across the organisation.

While there is no preferred option, the recruitment choices made by service managers are inevitably reflected in organisational cultures, employee commitment and, ultimately, the quality of service provided to customers. Casual employees with little opportunity for career development cost less and provide more flexibility for the employer, but they are also likely to be less loyal to their organisations, to be less committed to service quality, and to be more easily attracted to competitors' offers of higher wages or job security. Alternatively, too much job security and a lack of external competition for jobs may lead to complacency, the failure of employees to upgrade their skills, or a decline in customer service quality.

Government services, such as railway booking offices, taxation offices, motor vehicle registration agencies and telecommunications authorities, are frequently criticised for their low levels of customer service, associated with unmotivated staff employed on permanent bases. Many of these organisations have successfully adopted contract or permanent part-time employment conditions, in order to provide a balance of job security and job challenge. This approach has been enshrined in recent European, Australian and New Zealand employment relations legislation, and has received acceptance from some unions as well.

Decisions on the appropriate recruitment sources and techniques (for example, high school, college or university 'career days'; public or private recruitment agencies; newspaper or Internet advertising) are complemented by similar decisions on the most accurate selection processes to identify the best applicants. There is a broad range of available selection tools, whether for internal or external recruits. These include, but need not be restricted to:
- application forms and/or resumes;
- background investigations (for example, police, credit and reference checks);
- selection tests (for example, ability, aptitude, competency, personality 'profiles');
- medical examinations;
- worksite tours; and
- selection interviews. (Nankervis et al., 2005)

While it is not possible to examine all of these tools in this chapter, an important theme of effective selection is that, since they all have significant inherent difficulties, it is crucial to choose a 'package' of several tools best considered to reflect the particular demands of the positions to be filled. These choices should be mindful that all techniques can only assess the applicants' competencies or skills ('can do' factors), and cannot predict their future performance in the job ('will do' factors). The latter aspect will depend on how well they are managed once they have been appointed. However, a valuable rule of thumb is that their past performance is the best indicator of their future performance.

Application forms (designed by the employer) facilitate the collection of data on applicants against the required job criteria, and allow employers to compare and contrast multiple applicants, while *applicants' resumes* (embroidered by them) may provide useful additional information or suggest areas for subsequent enquiries. *Background investigations*, such as police, credit or reference checks, may be legally required or may simply provide relevant information on prior criminal charges, financial improprieties and actual previous work experience. As examples, previous embezzlement convictions may preclude employment as a bank teller, cashier or financial consultant, while child-care attendant or primary schoolteacher applicants should obviously have no former child abuse or Internet child pornography criminal charges. Work references can be useful, but they need to be treated with some caution, as applicants will naturally choose supportive referees. In addition, all these investigations need to conform to the regulatory requirements of the relevant duty of care and privacy legislation, and these investigations should ideally be agreed by applicants.

Selection tests provide a variety of data on the applicants' present skills and competencies, their likely future potential, and their usual work behaviours and attitudes. The aim of these test is to provide '. . . an objective and standardised measure of a sample of behaviour that is used to measure a person's abilities, aptitudes, interests, or personality in relation to other individuals. The basic assumption behind such testing is that differences between individuals can be measured and related to future job success' (Nankervis et al., 2005, p. 241). However, it is important to choose tests that most appropriately reflect job requirements, and which are demonstrably reliable and valid (for a more comprehensive discussion of these issues, see Nankervis et al., 2005, pp. 239–51), and to use them as only one element in the selection process. As examples, applicants for insurance adviser positions may usefully be tested for their numeracy and interpersonal communication competencies, trainers for their communication and presentation skills, and translators and interpreters for their linguistic abilities. As discussed earlier, given the associations of the 'emotional labour' component of service occupations with employee attitudes and behaviours, the value of 'personality profiling' is apparent. It should, however, be noted that such tests should be used with some caution as their reliability and validity are questionable (Nankervis et al., 2005). Moreover, they are regarded with suspicion by some applicants and can be relatively costly to employ.

As examples, it may be useful to include personality tests in selection processes for jobs such as real estate agents, used car salespersons, retail salespersons, public relations specialists or front-line service personnel, especially where 'extroversion–introversion' (that is, whether they are 'outgoing' or 'withdrawn') behavioural characteristics are regarded as being important. Alternatively, there are arguments that different cultures demand different work behaviours, and hence, the required behaviour characteristics that are associated with service quality in diverse cultural environments will need to be customised. For instance, the direct 'hard sell' approach of some Western used car dealers and retailers may not be effective in cultures that rigorously avoid conflict and confrontation (for example, Thailand, Indonesia and

Malaysia). The use of formal modes of address and titles may be obligatory for interactions with colleagues, supervisors, and customers in some countries, with more informal and equitable styles of interaction required in other contexts. Similarly, employee appearance, grooming, and personal hygiene requirements will vary according to cultural context, occupation and services sector.

Equal employment opportunity legislation in Western countries means that employers have limited prescriptive opportunities associated with employee choices based on broad-based social demographics, such as age, gender, ethnicity or religion. Similarly, the ability of employers to impose strict criteria on employee appearance, grooming and personal hygiene has been severely limited by equal employment opportunity legislation in developed countries, although developing countries continue to specify age, gender, height, weight and general appearance requirements in their selection criteria.

Personality profiling has been recently criticised (Stone, 2002) for its Western cultural assumptions, and its potential discriminatory ramifications (Nankervis et al., 2005). Therefore, care should be taken to ensure that such tests are proven to be valid and relevant to the chosen positions; that they have been adapted to fit particular cultures; that they are used only as a part of overall selection processes; and that they are administered and analysed by registered psychologists. The case of an experienced senior manager in the Australian Broadcasting Corporation who resigned from his job in objection to a requested psychological profile, and recent union opposition to such tests because of their potential for discrimination, should urge caution in their use for selection purposes (Nankervis et al., 2005).

Medical examinations may also be useful selection tools, in association with other assessment devices, as they can provide particular job-related information on service work applicants for positions that require physical and emotional labour, and strict compliance with high levels of health and safety. Kitchen staff in restaurants, police, nurses, doctors and cleaners are often exposed to risks (for example, accidents, chemicals, diseases or physical violence), and medical examinations may reveal pre-existing medical conditions, physical incapacities or psychosocial factors that might be exacerbated by the job. However, as with other selection techniques, medical examinations need to be used with caution in order to avoid allegations of discrimination, or invasion of applicants' privacy.

Worksite tours are usually non-controversial, merely involving applicants being shown around their potential workplaces in order to ensure a 'fit' with their working conditions, and sometimes with their work teams. Thus, applicants expecting 'five-star' quarters in five-star hotels (or, indeed, the Sydney Opera House) may be horrified to find narrow, cramped, dusty staff rooms with time clocks, rusty lockers or limited toilet facilities. Alternatively, doctors employed at modern hospitals may be even more attracted to employers by state-of-the-art technology, pristine operating rooms and plush staff quarters.

Perhaps the most common, and most problematic, selection tools are *selection interviews*. These are used by most organisations as a central part of their selection processes (Compton et al., 2003). They involve meeting the applicants for jobs (once or several times) with a range of people, including the HR specialist, the immediate supervisors, colleagues, union representatives and/or independent interviewers. In general, *sequential* interviews – that is, several one-on-one interviews with different people – are favoured by private-sector employers, while *panel* interviews – one interviewee and several interviewers – are preferred by the public sector.

Both types of interview may be valuable, as they allow several people to evaluate applicants against specific job criteria. However, all interviews are liable to subjectivity, bias and potential discrimination. Perhaps these aspects are more evident in services organisations' selection processes than in their manufacturing counterparts, as assessments often favour intangible qualities such as interpersonal and non-verbal communication. For a more detailed discussion of interviewing problems and techniques, consult Compton et al. (2003) or Nankervis et al. (2005).

This section has focused on the recruitment and selection components of staffing processes, exploring the difficulties involved in choosing appropriate employees, and suggesting the particular problems faced in services. In conclusion, all available tools have both benefits and advantages, and a customised strategy should incorporate the most suitable series of techniques within an integrated staffing process. The next section examines the importance of HR development and career development to motivate and retain competent and productive service employees.

Human resource development and career development

The functions of HR selection and recruitment are only the initial stages in building an effective workforce. Managers, supervisors and employees also require training and continual development (*human resource development* – HRD) if their potential is to be effectively utilised. The development of human resources begins with induction and continues throughout their employment with the organisation (Nankervis et al., 2005). Hence, ideally HRD is an integrated and personalised process that involves considerable consultation between individual employees, their supervisors and mentors, and may include on-the-job training, off-the-job training, e-learning, seminars, conferences, symposia, formal education programs, 'action learning' (that is, through job rotation, temporary assignments, project or team work), assessment centres, and internal or external mentoring systems. In reality, few service organisations actually adopt such comprehensive approaches to skill or competency development, and many deliberately avoid providing any training and development for their staff for fear that money spent on training only makes their employees more attractive to their competitors.

At the lower skills level in services (for example, retail checkout assistants, hotel housekeepers) with readily available semi-skilled labour pools, many employers accept exceptionally high employee turnover rates, preferring to constantly recruit new staff, despite the often unrecognised costs and adverse effects on morale, rather than to provide up-skilling programs or career plans for committed employees. Even at this level, however, there are exceptions, including McDonald's extensive HRD system (including its own internal 'university') and the JW Marriott hotel chain, as illustrated in Figure 8.9.

The importance of the Marriott HRD program is that it is:

- designed to reflect the needs of both the organisation and its employees based on organisational goals and HR plans;
- a structured series of training *and* development activities, supplemented by organisational and performance development initiatives;

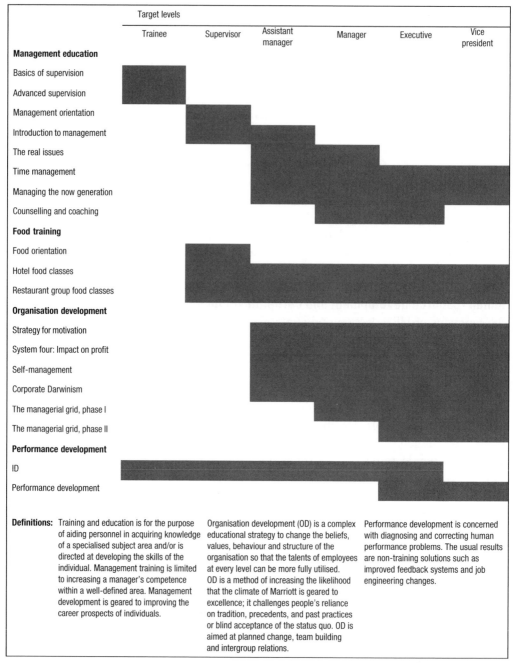

	Target levels					
	Trainee	Supervisor	Assistant manager	Manager	Executive	Vice president
Management education						
Basics of supervision						
Advanced supervision						
Management orientation						
Introduction to management						
The real issues						
Time management						
Managing the now generation						
Counselling and coaching						
Food training						
Food orientation						
Hotel food classes						
Restaurant group food classes						
Organisation development						
Strategy for motivation						
System four: Impact on profit						
Self-management						
Corporate Darwinism						
The managerial grid, phase I						
The managerial grid, phase II						
Performance development						
ID						
Performance development						

Definitions: Training and education is for the purpose of aiding personnel in acquiring knowledge of a specialised subject area and/or is directed at developing the skills of the individual. Management training is limited to increasing a manager's competence within a well-defined area. Management development is geared to improving the career prospects of individuals.

Organisation development (OD) is a complex educational strategy to change the beliefs, values, behaviour and structure of the organisation so that the talents of employees at every level can be more fully utilised. OD is a method of increasing the likelihood that the climate of Marriott is geared to excellence; it challenges people's reliance on tradition, precedents, and past practices or blind acceptance of the status quo. OD is aimed at planned change, team building and intergroup relations.

Performance development is concerned with diagnosing and correcting human performance problems. The usual results are non-training solutions such as improved feedback systems and job engineering changes.

Figure 8.9 Programs for employees at the Marriott

Source: G. Hostage, 1975, 'Quality control in a service business', *Harvard Business Review*, July–August 1975, p. 101

- evaluated through the observation of employee on-the-job performance by 'flying squads' (Hostage, 1975, p. 103) of inspectors (similar to 'mystery shoppers' used in other service organisations); and
- links HRD with subsequent career development plans.

Therefore, it is perhaps not surprising that the Marriott hotel chain's employee turnover rates are considerably lower than those of many of its international competitors. Some studies have found that employee development programs that incorporate 'learning through service failure' reflective processes (for example, group discussions, 'mystery shopper' feedback systems) can '. . . have a significant positive effect on perceived service quality' (Hays and Hill, 2001, p. 347), as can the resultant improvements in employee motivation.

At middle and senior management, and professional levels of services, HRD programs are usually more common, due to their higher expectations, the need for constant knowledge and competency upgrading, and the inclusion of training and career development as a component of their employment 'package'. Prior to the collapse of many of the dot.com companies during the 1990s, and early in the 21st century, many IT service organisations falsely assumed that high salaries were the prime motivator of systems analysts and designers, and that high employee turnover levels were to be expected. Accordingly, many Australian banks spent enormous amounts of time and money recruiting IT specialists from overseas, only to experience massive turnover levels due partly to their lack of proper attention to retention strategies such as the provision of ongoing hardware and software training, and access to managed career development programs.

The lessons to be learned from these examples are that HRD is a means to achieve the satisfaction of employer (employee retention, increased commitment and productivity), and employee (motivation, career development) needs, and an effective link between HR plans and organisational goals. However, to achieve these multifaceted outcomes, a structured HRD process must involve organisational and individual employee needs analysis; an integrated training, education, learning and development program; a comprehensive assessment of the transfer of learning back to workplace performance; and clear and agreed linkages between HRD programs and subsequent career development systems (Nankervis et al., 2005).

Remuneration issues

This chapter will not discuss the remuneration issues of service workers in detail, because of the complexity and differentiations across sectors. However, it is sufficient to indicate the significant diversity between lower- and higher-level positions, and the different capacities of service workers to negotiate their salary packages. In the latter case, the relative power of service workers to negotiate wage and salary levels is heavily dependent on their perceived social importance (for example, doctors and lawyers versus retail sales staff and hospital cleaners), labour scarcity or over-supply factors (for example, nurses and schoolteachers), their bargaining skills, and the strength of their union support.

Motivation theory (for example, Maslow, 1954; Herzberg, 1974) suggests that employee motivation is a combination of 'hygiene' (salary, job security) and 'motivational' (job satisfaction, self-actualisation) factors, and hence that management attention needs to be paid to both factors in order to ensure employee retention and commitment. Motivational factors amenable to support employer control include opportunities for interesting and challenging jobs (job design), attractive recruitment and selection strategies, HRD plans linked to career development plans, and careful attention to the trends and causes of employee absence and turnover (Nankervis et al., 2005).

Employee absence and turnover management

Some services sectors are especially prone to high levels of employee absence and 'turnover', due to their comparatively lower salaries, high stress levels associated with customer service ('emotional labour'), the relative insecurity of many jobs based on casual and part-time contracts, and a lack of career development opportunities. Hotels, hospitals, call centres, fast-food and retail outlets, medical centres, management consultancies and e-commerce companies all depend on casual and on-call staff, and all are characterised by the above employment conditions. *Absenteeism* is defined as '... any failure of an employee to report for, or to remain at work as scheduled, regardless of the reason' (Cascio, 1999, p. 596), and may include authorised (for example, sickness, accidents) as well as unauthorised leave (for example, long lunches, long weekends, 'mental health' days). Employee absenteeism (either authorised or unauthorised) is up to 20 per cent higher in services than in other industries, due primarily to its 'emotional labour' component, the associated stress, and lack of adequate management attention either to its causes or effects (Mills and Dalton, 1994).

There is general agreement, based on considerable research in the United States, Europe, Australia and New Zealand (for example, Lewin and Mitchell, 1995; Hom and Griffeth, 1995; Cascio, 1999; Howes, 2000), that absenteeism trends reflect the levels of employee satisfaction with and commitment to their organisations. Moreover, the proper management of absenteeism costs and consequences demands serious attention to the analysis and remediation of their causes. This view further suggests that analyses of absenteeism rates may enable services managers to improve their employment conditions, employee retention rates, and ultimately the customer service, productivity and competitiveness of their organisations (Nankervis et al., 2005). Undoubtedly, some of this absenteeism can be attributed to the stress involved in particular service occupations, including role ambiguity (unclear job descriptions, inadequate direction from supervisors, lack of training), role conflict (for example, between customer service and organisational efficiency expectations) and role overload (insufficient staff numbers, continual increases in responsibilities).

The findings of most research studies suggest that absenteeism is costly, lowers morale, and often signals employees' intentions to eventually leave their organisations (*turnover* or *wastage*). Employee turnover/wastage refers to the rate (or ratio) of employees who leave their organisations, through resignation, retirement or death, and its analysis involves separating 'uncontrollable' (for example, relocation, death) from 'controllable' factors (for example, job dissatisfaction, lack of job challenges, inadequate remuneration or training, lack of career opportunities). Its management requires measurement of both absenteeism and turnover rates; recognition of the links between absenteeism and turnover trends; diagnoses of the causes of both; and concerted HRM action to address unhealthy levels.

Some services organisations (for example, hotels, retail stores, restaurants) appear to be unaware of, or unconcerned about, extraordinarily high levels of employee turnover and simply accept it to be a feature of their particular business type. This approach may work in areas of high unemployment and semi-skilled occupations, but it is essentially a highly ineffective and costly avoidance of management responsibilities, and will inevitably result in poorly trained and motivated service staff and deteriorating customer service levels.

HRM actions to address unhealthy or unproductive employee absence or turnover levels may include:

- data collection and ongoing analyses;
- attention to current job design, and recruitment and selection systems;
- the provision of realistic training and development, and career, plans;
- the review of remuneration and rewards strategies;
- good supervision and performance management schemes;
- employee consultation and communication forums;
- team- and morale-building activities;
- employee satisfaction surveys or focus groups; and
- exit interviews with departing employees.

In other words, the use of a wide range of HRM activities not only helps to create and maintain employee morale, satisfaction and performance, and to stem worrying levels of absenteeism and turnover, but can also lead to higher levels of customer service quality, and hence, significantly contribute to the overall competitiveness and profitability of services.

Conclusion

This chapter builds on earlier discussions of the management of services by exploring the myriad HRM issues associated with the delivery of service. It should be seen to add another piece to the jigsaw of managing this problematic sector, based upon the application of an integrated services management model approach. The chapter examines the twin concepts of human resource management and industrial relations, and considers their applications to the unique context and features of services. In addition, it explores the relationships between HRM functions, service cultures and service delivery systems. The key notion of 'strategic choice' is used as an evaluative management tool to assist in decisions about the most appropriate HRM techniques for particular service sectors and contexts.

The second half of the chapter discusses the broad services issues of emotional labour, employee empowerment and work teams associated with specific HRM functions; including HR planning, job design, recruitment and selection, human resource and career development, remuneration, employee absence and turnover management. Managing services demands serious attention to its HRM requirements, given its heavy dependence on employees for the creation and delivery of its services, but these aspects must also be balanced with similar attention to the management of its operations, financial and marketing components.

Exercises

Key questions

1 How can 'emotional labour' be factored into the job descriptions and performance management systems of services? Use a particular sector or service organisation to inform your discussions.

2 Discuss the most appropriate recruitment and selection techniques for the following service organisations:
- a ski resort;
- a government employment agency;
- a funeral parlour;
- an e-commerce retailing company;
- a regional community medical centre; and
- an international shipping company.

3 Construct an HRD and career development plan for front-line customer service staff in retailing or the government immigration service.

4 Discuss the issues associated with employee absence and turnover management in a service sector or organisation of your choice. How should these issues be addressed by management?

Web exercises

8.1 Access the websites of two or three service organisations (for example, Telstra, Westpac, the Australian Taxation Office, Starbucks, Virgin Airlines, Deutsche Bank), and go to their employment opportunities/job vacancies link. Examine the job descriptions for current job vacancies, and consider the following:
  (a) Do the job descriptions accurately reflect the job requirements?
  (b) Do they focus on the correct labour markets? Why/why not?

8.2 Choose several multinational companies (for example, Citibank, Singapore Airlines, IBM, Shangri-La Hotels) and go to their websites. Peruse their mission and vision statements, and analyse their relative attractiveness to potential applicants. What do these statements tell you about their approach to HRM? How might they be improved?

Case study 8.1 Revolution through devolution: The case of ElecGen

By their nature, many jobs in services require substantial autonomy on the part of the employee. Examples of this autonomy include the comparative freedom given to room attendants to service hotel rooms allocated to them without the need for close supervision and their customer service decisions when staff are effectively trained. Without this devolvement of the decision-making role, the number of organisations requiring multiple layers of management increases substantially. This is obviously an untenable position, with increased competition having an escalating impact on costs. To ensure competitiveness, employees must be willing and able to undertake more complete roles within service organisations.

This case study examines an organisation in the electricity generation sector, briefly outlining the industrial relations, human resources infrastructure, and other issues that were needed to ensure its ongoing success. The organisation is a public utility responsible for providing a cheap and reliable 'product' to multiple users within Australia. Due to the deregulation and fragmentation of the sector, what was once a unified organisation now finds it competing against its former partners. To make the situation more difficult, what was once a state monopoly has now opened out to allow interstate supply of the service. The industry is highly unionised.

The Australian government, under the banner of award restructuring, initiated the first aspect of the reform program. It encompassed the collapsing of industrial agreements, allowing employees to undertake multiple tasks and training (multiskilling), and providing career paths to individual staff prepared to undertake skill development.

The second aspect of the transformation of the sector occurred when a decision was made by the government to fragment and 'corporatise' it, introducing increased competition and opening it to external providers. What was once a monopoly would become a government business enterprise, paying dividends to the state. It was to operate as a competitive business by becoming more efficient and reducing costs to the customer with no reliance on government subsidy. This directly flowed on from award restructuring, because it allowed organisations to internally restructure, using the benefits of the industrial relations changes to reduce redundant staffing levels through increasing the variety of staff skills and allowing them to undertake a broader role within the utility. For example, the maintenance staff within the utility were provided with skills enabling them to monitor their own quality procedures, as well as being trained in basic competencies of other trades. This enabled them to perform a wider range of maintenance skills such as both mechanical and electrical tasks, reducing the need to wait for an appropriate technician of another trade. Maintenance time was thus reduced as a result, with quality checks automatically done by the staff.

This then led to the third aspect of the transformation, to consolidate the changes. In this respect the HR departments were directly responsible for subsequent staff efficiency improvements. This was undertaken by adopting a continuous improvement focus, directing that all staff had to engage in at least eight days of training each year, ensuring their familiarity with new technologies, procedures and management techniques. On the downside, staff reductions occurred, but to ease the personal pain within the organisation, and to allay any industrial unrest, it was to be on a voluntary basis only. This ensured that no (or minimal) disruption to service provision occurred. Staff numbers were effectively reduced to acceptable levels, and remaining staff members were provided with training to incorporate the skills that were found to be still needed. Performance systems were introduced to ensure that the standard of service was maintained, and new industrial agreements were introduced to remunerate the staff on an equitable basis.

The result of the restructuring, incorporating both HR and IR reforms within the organisation, allowed it to compete with other utilities successfully, and from being the utility that many thought would not survive, it has become the most efficient of the service providers within the state, competing against both private and other publicly owned companies. However, there was a potentially negative side to the changes occurring that will provide new challenges to the HR department in its service provision. Many of those staff who accepted the redundancies were young, often under 40 years of age. This has left the organisation with an ageing workforce, the average age of employees being 47 years. Due to the 'no recruitment' policy imposed on the organisation by senior management and the government, a shortage of qualified and experienced staff to perform many of the functions resulted. This led to the second problem: the cost of training escalated as a result.

The third issue, performance assessment, demonstrated a reduction in staff skills and a lack of ability to take over the effective maintenance and management of the organisation, as they lacked the prior long-term experience. The final issue was a combination of industrial and remuneration issues. With a shortage of suitable staff, the union (in this highly unionised environment) was able to apply leverage to the organisation to obtain much higher salaries for staff with reduced skill levels.

The outcome of these issues has resulted in increased costs and reduced efficiency levels. Instead of the high service component desired for customers, a strong reduction in service occurred. This then resulted in the utility losing both customers and its former leadership position within the industry. A decline in income resulted in lower standards, and the utility was looking at the possibility of closure with subsequent loss of all jobs.

(*Source*: Contributed by Doug Davies, University of Canberra)

Student projects

1 What strategies are needed to remedy this situation?
2 What measures might have been implemented earlier by management to ensure continued competitiveness and success?
3 What industrial relations issues need to be tackled to ensure that the union is supportive of the changes needed?

References and further reading

Albrecht, K. 1988, *At America's Service*, Dow Jones Irwin, Homewood, IL.

Ashkanasy, N., Hartel, C. and Zerbe, W. 2000, *Emotions in the Workplace: Research, theory and practice*, Quorum Books, Westport, CT.

Bagwell, S. 1997, 'Wave goodbye to the golden handshake', *Australian Financial Review*, 6 August, p. 1.

Baum, T. 1996, 'Unskilled work and the hospitality industry: Myth or reality?', *International Journal of Hospitality Management*, vol. 15, no. 3, pp. 207–9.

Bowen, D. E. and Lawler, E. E. 1992, 'The empowerment of service workers: What, why, how and when?', *Sloan Management Review*, spring, pp. 31–39.

Brown, T., Mouren J., Donavan, D. and Licata, J. 2002, 'The customer orientation of service workers: Personality trait effects of self and supervisor performance ratings', *Journal of Marketing Research*, vol. 39, February, pp. 110–19.

Burke, R. 2001, 'Supervision and service quality', *Measuring Business Executives*, vol. 5, no. 4, pp. 28–31.

Carlzon, J. 1987, *Moments of Truth*, Harper and Row, New York.

Cascio, W. 1999, *Costing Human Resources: The financial impact of behavior in organizations*, 4th ed., South-Western, Cincinnati, OH.

Chebat, J. C. and Kollias, P. 2000, 'The impact of empowerment on customer contact employees' roles in service organizations', *Journal of Services Research*, vol. 3, no. 1, pp. 66–81.

Compton, R., Morrissey, W. and Nankervis, A. 2003, *Effective Recruitment and Selection Techniques*, 3rd ed., CCH Australia, Sydney.

De Cieri, H. and Kramar, R. 2003, *Human Resource Management in Australia: Strategy, people, performance*, McGraw-Hill, Sydney.

Farrell, K. 2001, 'Human resource issues as barriers to staff retention and development in the tourism industry', *Irish Journal of Management*, vol. 22, no. 2, pp. 121–42.

Finstall, T. 1989, 'My employees are my service guarantee', *Harvard Business Review*, July–August, pp. 28–32.

Foreshew, J. 2004, 'The reality IT show: Offshoring Survivor', *The Australian* (IT Business), 30 March, p. 1.

Hart, C. W. 1995, 'The power of internal service guarantees', *Harvard Business Review*, January–February, pp. 64–73.

Hays, J. and Hill, A. 2001, 'A preliminary investigation of the relationships between employee motivation/vision, service learning and perceived service quality', *Journal of Operations Management*, vol. 19, pp. 335–49.

Herzberg, F. 1974, *Work and the Nature of Man*, World Publishing Company, Chicago.

Hochschild, A. 1983a, *The Management and Marketing of Services*, 2nd ed., University of California Press, Berkeley, CA.

Hochschild, A. 1983b, *The Managed Heart: Commercialization of human feeling*, University of California Press, Berkeley, CA.

Hom, P. and Griffeth, R. 1995, *Employee Turnover*, South-Western, Cincinnati, OH.

Hostage, G. 1975, 'Quality control in a service business', *Harvard Business Review*, July–August, pp. 98–105.

Howes, P. 2000, 'Measuring human resources', *HR Monthly*, April, pp. 48–49.

Hsieh, Y.-M. and Hsieh, A.-T. 2001, 'Enhancement of service quality with job standardization', *Service Industries Journal*, vol. 21, no. 3, pp. 147–66.

Katzenbach, J. and Santamaria, J. 1999, 'Firing up the front line', *Harvard Business Review*, May–June, pp. 107–17.

Keenoy, T. and Kelly, D. 1998, *The Employment Relationship in Australia*, 2nd ed., Harcourt Australia, Sydney.

Korcynsky, M. 2002, *Human Resource Management in Service Work*, Palgrave, Basingstoke, UK.

Legge, K. 1995, *Human Resource Management: Rhetorics and realities*, Macmillan, London.

Lewin, D. and Mitchell, D. 1995, *Human Resource Management: An economic approach*, 2nd ed., South-Western, Cincinnati, OH.

Lewis, B. and Gabrielsen, G. 1998, 'Intra-organizational aspects of service quality management: The employee's perspective', *Service Industries Journal*, vol. 18, no. 2, pp. 64–89.

Littler, C., Dunford, R., Bramble, T. and Hede, A. 1997, 'The dynamics of downsizing in Australia and New Zealand', *Asia Pacific Journal of Human Resources*, vol. 35, no. 1, pp. 65–79.

McShulkis, E. 1998, 'Why do employees leave?', *HR Magazine*, March.

Mafi, S. L. 2000, 'Managing the HRD function and service quality: A call for a new approach', *HRD Quarterly*, vol. 11, no. 1, pp. 81–86.

Maslow, A. 1954, *Motivation and Personality,* Harper and Row, New York.

Mills, P. K. and Dalton, D. R. 1994, 'Arbitration outcomes in the service sector: An empirical assessment', *International Journal of Service Industry Management*, vol. 5, no. 2, pp. 57–71.

Morris, J. and Feldman, D. C. 1997, 'Managing emotions in the workplace', *Journal of Management Issues*, vol. ix, no. 3, pp. 257–74.

Mudie, P. and Cottam, A. 1999, *The Management and Marketing of Services*, 2nd ed., Butterworth and Heinemann, Oxford.

Nankervis, A., Compton, R. and Baird, M. 2003, *Strategic Human Resource Management*, 4th ed., Thomson Learning, Melbourne.

Nankervis, A., Compton, R. and Baird, M. 2005, *Human Resource Management: Strategies and processes*, 5th ed., Thomson Learning, Melbourne.

Nankervis, A. and Wan, D. 1999, 'Vulnerability and sustainability in tourism: The Singapore and Phuket hotel sectors', 14th Annual Conference on Employment Relations, August, Cardiff.

Piso, A. 1999, 'Hotel and catering workers: Class and unionization', *Employee Relations*, vol. 21, no. 2.

Porter, L. and Lawler, E. 1968, *Managerial Attitudes and Performance,* Irwin, Chicago.

Price, L. 1994, 'Poor personnel practices in the hotel and catering industry: Does it matter?', *Human Resource Management Journal*, vol. 4, no. 4, summer, pp. 44–62.

Raghunathan, V. 2003, 'They have to speak the lingo', *The Straits Times*, 6 December, p. 6.

Sasser, E. 1976, 'Matching supply and demand in service industries', *Harvard Business Review*, September–October, pp. 82–91.

Schmenner, R. 1986, 'How can service business survive and prosper?', *Sloan Management Review*, vol. 21, no. 3, pp. 21–32.

Schneider, B. 1999, 'Human resource management: A service perspective', *International Journal of Service Industry Management*, vol. 5, no. 1, pp. 64–76.

Schneider, B. and Bowen, D. E. 1999, 'The service organization: HRM is crucial', *Harvard Business Review*, pp. 39–52.

Spreitzer, G., Cohen, S. and Ledford, G. 1999, 'Developing effective self-managing work teams in service organizations', *Group and Organization Management*, vol. 24, no. 3, pp. 340–66.

Stone, R. 2002, *Human Resource Management*, John Wiley & Sons, Brisbane.

Timo, N. 1994, 'The organisation of service work – A tourism perspective', unpublished paper, Griffith University (Gold Coast campus), Australia.

Weiss, T. 1997, 'Show me more than money', *HR Focus*, vol. 74, no. 11, p. 2.

Wright, P. and McMahan, G. 1992, 'Theoretical perspectives for strategic human resource management', *Journal of Management*, vol. 18, pp. 295–320.

From managing 'service' to integrated services management

A wave of change

Services have emerged as the most important sector in many economies in recent times. The critical economic importance of services was highlighted by the political 'storm' over the export of service jobs from the United States and Australia to locations such as India and Sri Lanka, and this trend is set to escalate to other developed countries.

Overall, the shift of employment away from manufacturing to services requires managerial principles and practices to be reconsidered in terms of new conceptual frameworks. That is, the historical manufacturing paradigm has traditionally focused on goods, technology and marketing, whereas the services paradigm is rooted in the ideas of partnership, communication and value creation. These contrasting paradigms emphasise very different managerial priorities, although it is becoming clear that there is a considerable and increasing influence of both paradigms in both industry sectors. It is clear that 21st-century management thinking needs to be redefined in terms of the value creation and relationship-oriented services paradigm, since in an interconnected global context most contemporary businesses today have a very strong services component.

The holistic perspective

The preceding chapters explain, explore and argue a strong case for the application of the integrated services management model. The historical transition of economic activities from primary industries such as agriculture and mining, to secondary industries such as manufacturing and construction, has seen a revolutionary change in the development and application of late 19th-century managerial frameworks. However, service-based industries have yet to benefit from a dramatic reformulation of traditional managerial models. Chapter 1 of this book characterised services as being a combination of intangibility and dynamic management, created by customer perceptions and having variable rather than uniform outcomes, and demonstrated the shift from manufacturing-dominated to service-dominated industries over the past century (see Figure 9.1).

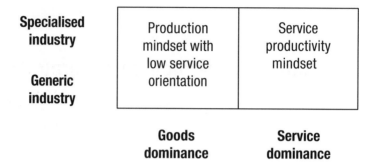

Figure 9.1 Mindset orientations for services

The tools and techniques of Frederick Taylor's formulations of classical management obviously are demonstrably inadequate for the economies of the 21st century service and knowledge-dominated industries. However, many services organisations, including McDonald's, hotels, restaurants and telephone call centres are firmly imbued with such mechanistic managerial approaches.

The ISM model in this book significantly improves on earlier management models by focusing on the marketing, operations, finance and human resources functions relevant to the strategic business management of any services enterprise. Instead of viewing service excellence as a cascading series of sequences, the model presented in this book emphasises the symbiotic and interdependent relationship of the critical functional areas in a dynamic, but homeostatic balance.

The complex influences of local, national and global environments on services functions are dynamic and context-dependent, and, therefore the managerial 'mindset' in strategic thinking needs to be framed in terms of establishing a total organisational approach. Thus, the complex issues of stakeholders and the multiple management challenges need to be incorporated within a strategic perspective. Increasingly, wider stakeholder issues are forcing organisations to account for the environmental, social and economic contexts in which they are embedded. The strategic management perspective of linking internal and external notions of 'service quality' is driven by a holistic managerial view, and encapsulates a range of forces beyond traditional market and customer perspectives, and the attendant managerial challenges. Furthermore, the nature of quality and customer relationships in services are perceived in ways often very different from the managerial models derived from the era of manufacturing. For example, the contemporary debates over the generation and delivery of web-based services through outsourcing from non-traditional countries indicates new competitive frontiers in this area.

Market structures and customer perceptions of quality are not only dependent on cultural, social or other forces, but also may be considered differently according to demographic factors such as age, gender, urban–rural locations, and educational levels. For example, quality expectations may be much higher for financial or professional services, while at the same time moderate for recreational or hospitality services. The assessment of quality will always be more difficult for services than for goods, not only because of their intangibility and non-standard nature, but also because of dynamic 'experiential qualities' in diverse segments of the market. The 'search quality' feature in goods, where a customer may be able to evaluate and establish quality in advance, may be contrasted with the 'experience qualities' of service, where it is essential to experience the service before quality can be determined. Organisations such as IKEA, for example, have been uniquely successful in bridging the 'search' and 'experience' qualities to build their continuing success. It has been argued in earlier chapters that the convergence of quality perceptions occurs as an organisation moves up the global-integration chain, while divergences may persist where an organisation is dominated by its location.

Service competitiveness parameters

Competition in services is increasingly being underpinned by capability development, as opposed to technological advances and capital outlay. As has been pointed out earlier, competitive advantage in services is dependent on the sophistication of its strategic management (Chapter 4) and human resource capability (Chapter 8). The critical elements of knowledge and learning in building a stakeholder management orientation (Chapter 3) are derived through these capabilities.

The integration of knowledge and learning in services cultures can only be optimised through a complex and integrated network of coordinated and responsive HRM activities. For example, Motorola spends over US$100 million on training and development each year in the United States and evaluates that the return on this investment is adequate, with US$300 million in sales revenue. While knowledge can be broadly considered to be the building block of services capability, it is much more than best practices or benchmarks. The creation and management of knowledge is enabled through the synergistic mindset inherent in the ISM model. The new model links the vision and values of a service organisation to specific business models, structures and value propositions.

The installation of an information system can provide the coherence that a service organisation strives for, by clarifying performance data and outlining the roles and responsibilities of functions and people. This 'value-adding' network approach assists an organisation to build a service culture, and provides depth to its capability and culture, and the unique 'value proposition' elements that characterise services. These elements may include functionality, reliability, performance and, perhaps, customisation. Chapter 4 of this book elucidates this concept in the light of Porter's 'generic' values attributes of differentiation and cost leadership. It may be interesting to note a recent counterpoint argument to this:

> The primary change driver behind the service revolution is technology. Forget about the information highway, Moore's law, and the wonders of the wireless. Rather, think of technology as creating an information assembly line – information today can be standardized, built to order, assembled from components, picked, packed, stored, and shipped, all using processes resembling manufacturing's. Industrialized information becomes steadily more efficient, less expensive, and more highly automated. The costs of logistics and storage are minimal; only labour and intellectual property matter. (Karmarkar, 2004, p. 102)

Table 9.1 Sources of competitive advantage of global service organisations

Access to a globally relevant knowledge base
- Financial resources such as banking and insurance
- Specialised value-adding services such as design, entertainment, HR
- Information and knowledge services

Leveraging local and global competencies
- Airline and transport services
- Courier services
- Credit cards

Administrative service competency
- Accounting and tax returns
- Data management
- Billing and customer service

Information-intensive service
- Engineering service
- Publishing

Building commercial competency niches
- Brokerage and travel agency services
- Procurement services
- Shipping agencies
- News agencies
- Hotel chains

Combining knowledge, learning and human services
- Medical and hospital services
- Legal and educational services
- Consulting and training
- IT services

Brand- and reputation-based services
- Hotels
- Fast food

NGO services
- International aid agencies
- Green services management
- Non-profit organisations

Source: Modified and extended from P. Lasserre, *Global Strategic Management*, Palgrave Macmillan, New York, 2003, p. 50.

Engaging with this view on the key role of information technology, Chapters 4 and 5 emphasise the crucial issue of integrating the enormous knowledge management capacity of the new information technology with strategic management.

At the *macro level*, service competitiveness has always been linked to societal infrastructure. Over the past century, the role of key infrastructures has changed dramatically. The essential logistical support of roads, railways and ports is still of significant relevance in a post-industrial economy, but the emphasis has shifted to new areas of society, as service competitiveness becomes a central concern. The infrastructures of traditional economies have been supportive services such as logistics, civic facilities, finance and workforce. Today, education and training are perhaps the key infrastructure strengths needed to build a successful IT sector in a country.

Although service infrastructures are often not associated with the sophistication of the manufacturing infrastructure in a society, it is difficult to establish a bipolar categorisation. The reality is that the strength of railways in the UK or of roads in the US does, in an indirect way, contribute to the service economy. The spectacular rise of Singapore as the world's number one service provider in shipping had its roots in the pre-existing infrastructure of the earlier decades. This dichotomisation is hard to substantiate, either in developed or developing countries, as there is a broad and generic overlap across these industries. Infrastructural services such as roads, railways, security, housing, airlines, education and legal support are equally relevant in services, as well as other industries. This is evident in the case of former command economies such as China and Russia, where infrastructural 'decay' is a significant inhibiting factor for the regeneration of the services sectors.

Many levels of government infrastructural services are being privatised around the world, with mixed outcomes. Legal custody management, waste collection, and airport management and maintenance are but a few examples. Chapter 3 highlights the emerging challenges in a services society arising from environmental concerns. Recycling and the disposal of wastes and scrap signal an extension to the operations management paradigm in services.

Table 9.1 lists a range of sources of competitive advantage for global services organisations. The table also indicates sectoral diversity, highlighting the various sources of competitive advantages for specific services sectors.

Conclusion

As has been argued throughout this text, the competitiveness of service organisations is dependent on strategic management approaches to their effectiveness, as the primary management challenge. The transformation of traditional business models inevitably requires new internal competencies and new design parameters for organisational functionality. Value is added to internal processes by emphasising both front-office interfaces and back-room process effectiveness. In addition, the 'partnership' of a myriad of stakeholders needs a very high priority in this paradigm shift. As Vandermerwe (1993, p. 224) cogently argued, '[T]he inroads made by services will continue . . . bringing success to those corporations which have made the transition from . . . an industrial to service ethos. . . . But whereas the service ethos is now the competitive differentiator, it will become the condition for corporate survival in future.'

The ability to stretch internal and external boundaries is the key feature of the service ethos. The possibility of growing, combining or dismantling areas of internal competence, coupled with a dynamic texture of partnerships and stakeholder alliances, create the life-giving 'hearts' and 'lungs' of service-dominated enterprises. Further, the conditions required to achieve global and regional service competitiveness are being altered, with the regulatory requirements of the WTO, EU and ASEAN being extended from 'goods' to 'service'. The diffusion of service effectiveness from one societal context to the other through franchise chains is another example of the new paradigm in operation. On another dimension, the exporting of one global service often can create a series of corresponding 'import' services, as is evident in tourism.

Another important area of attention is the growth of the non-profit and NGO sectors. These are still the largest employers in many countries, and include social, welfare and medical services, charities, and environmental or consumer groups. This trend has been amplified since there has been a spectacular move towards strengthening the public sector in OECD countries over the past decade. Scandinavian countries, such as Denmark and Sweden, have also expanded their reliance on public services. This has been achieved essentially because of low military expenditures and a high level of social involvement in educational, health and welfare services.

Overall, the concept and practice of strategic services management have undergone a revolutionary transformation around the developed and developing worlds in recent years. This wave of change has witnessed the clear emergence of what might be termed the 'industrialisation' of service. Many developed countries have lost, or are losing, the competition with the developing world in a number of 'sunrise service sectors'. Moreover, even in the traditional manufacturing sector, the 'service' content is what distinguishes one product from another. This fundamental shift in priorities in the non-service sector, where the 'service content' provides the competitive edge of one enterprise over another, or one nation over another, has yet to be fully inculcated into the dominant managerial paradigms. A passion for customer orientation, quality, human resource pro-activity and technology utilisation is only one part of the ongoing processes of sectoral transformation. This passion must be combined with recognition of the imperative to integrate these factors into competitive and interrelated strategic and functional management approaches. This can only be fulfilled through a rethinking of the basic paradigms of services management.

References and further reading

Ferdows, K. and De Meyer, A. 1990, 'Lasting improvements in manufacturing performance: In search of a new theory', *Journal of Operations Management*, vol. 9, no. 2, pp. 168–84.

Fitzsimmons, J. A. and Fitzsimmons, M. J. 2004, *Service Management: Operation, strategy and information technology*, 4th edn, McGraw-Hill Irwin, New York.

Karmarkar, U. 2004, 'Will you survive the service revolution?', *Harvard Business Review*, June, pp. 101–7.

Lasserre, P. 2003, *Global Strategic Management*, Palgrave Macmillan, New York.

Vandermerwe, S. 1993, *From Tin Soldiers to Russian Dolls: Creating added value through service*, Butterworth-Heinemann, Oxford.

Voss, C. A. 2003, 'Rethink paradigms of service: Service in a virtual environment', *International Journal of Operations and Production Management*, vol. 23 no. 1, pp. 88–104.

7- Eleven Japan, 268–272, 291–294

11 September 2001, impact of, 93

ABC (activity-based costing), 268–272, 291–294

absenteeism, 340–341

accrual cash basis, 268

action-reflection-trigger system, 195

activity-based costing, 268–272, 291–294

adoption of mechanisms, 92

advertising, exposure to, 124

agency relationships, 261

Air Asia, 9–11

AIRC, 311

airline industry

    Air Asia, 9–11

    Boeing, 320

    British Airways, 52

    customer focus of, 120

    DIY check-ins, 219

    Qantas, 228

    Scandinavian Airlines, 189

    servicing a jet during layover, 237

    simplifying business, 240–241

    Singapore Airlines, 133–134, 165

    Virgin Airlines, 134–137

Albrecht, Karl, 113

allocation of funds, 254

AMP, 90

'angel' finance, 282–289

anti-globalism, 44

application forms, 335

arbitrage, 260

Arthur Andersen, 296

Asia

    financial crisis, 80

    game software piracy, 65

    impact of financial crisis, 52

    service trade in, 37

asset pricing, 260

aura of a brand, 121

Australia

    conservation policies, 246

    industrial relations in, 310–311

    service industries in, 3–5

    Singaporean-Australian Free Trade Area, 50–51

Australian Bureau of Statistics, industry types, 1

Australian Industrial Relations Commission, 311

Australian Workplace Agreements, 311

aviation, *see* airline industry

back-office operations, trade in, 38–39

background investigations of applicants, 335

balance sheet, 264

bandwidth of industry groups, 179

Bangalore, services provided in, 38

bank drafts, 279

banking industry, *see also* deposit-taking institutions

    Customer First Bank case study, 147–148

    failures in service by, 138–139

    senior customers, 179

    Standard Chartered, 131–132

    US retreats from Europe, 42–43

banks, financing from, 273, 279, 281, *see also* financial services

Barings Futures, 288

Behavioural School, 23

belongings, services acting on, 16

benchmarking best practices, 81

bills of exchange, 279

bodies, services acting on, 16

Boeing, downturn for, 320

branding

    as long-term strategic objective, 125

    brand aura, 121

    power of, 115, 146

    strategic management of, 117–125

Branson, Sir Richard, 134–137

breakthrough projects, 239

British Airways, 52

brokers, finance from, 257

Brookdale waste management plant, 88

bushfire case study, 102–103

business 'angels', 282–289
business ecosystems, 115
business ethics, *see* ethical issues
business model innovation, 119–121 b
business process reengineering, 186
business risks, 282–283
business services, trade in, 36

California insurance industry, 295
call centres
    government agency, 175
    outsourcing to, 129
    training for, 319
capacity management, 230–234
capital asset pricing model, 260
capital gains, 280–281
CAPM, 260
car dealers, 133
car manufacturing, 177
car registration transfer case study, 152–153
career development, 337–339
case studies
    car registration transfer, 152–153
    customer database use, 197
    Customer First Bank, 147–148
    ElecGen, 342–344
    firestorm, 102–103
    IT in India, 62–64
    La Montagne Guesthouse and Restaurant, 28–32
    Lifestyle Wealth Management, 150–152
    Paradise Tours, 148–149
    Rottnest Island, 243–249
    Sun Life Insurance, 291–294
cash flow, 264, 268
casual employment, 311–313, 334
CEIBS, 124
Centrelink, 142, 305
CEOs
    as public face of company, 134–137
    severance payments, 90, 262
chief marketing officers, 119
China-Europe International Business School, 124
China, privatisation in, 60
chipping of Xbox, 64–67
cinema industry, 86–87
classical management theory, 23
classification of services, 15–20
Cleaning Company, The, 173
climates for service, 323
CMOs, 119
co-productive services, 11–12

Coalition of Services Industries, Singapore, 3
Coca-Cola, marketing strategies, 128
commercial presence, 40
commercial services, 36
commodity price risk, 286
communication technologies, *see* technology
competencies of service providers, 318
competitiveness
    environment for, 57–58
    factors in, 217
    globalism and, 46
    parameters of, 349–350
    rivalry, 57
    strategies for, 111
    transformation of, 99
concept of services, 6–8
concurrency of innovation, 238
Consider It Done Personal Concierge Service, 14
consumers, *see* customers
consumption abroad, 40
context of services, 316–318
contingency theory, 24
contractual relationships, 21, 88
contradistinctiveness between shareholders and
    stakeholders, 79
control, financial, 256, 263–275
control self-assessment framework, 288
control systems, 213
convergence between marketing theories and
    practice, 192
coordination, financial, 256
core business philosophies, 162
corporatisation, *see* privatisation
cost drivers of globalism, 46
cost visibility, 272
costs of poor quality, 83
country risk, 58
credit risk, 283–285
CRM, *see* customer relationship marketing
cross-border supply, 40
cross-function management, 168–169
currency risk, 285
Customer First Bank case study, 147–148
customer relationship marketing, 118, 176–178
    resentment of, 130
    technology for, 182
customers
    access zones for, 226
    approach focused on, 126, 188
    as consumers, 140–141, 164
    creation of, 160

databases of, 180, 181, 197, 349
decision making by, 99
extent of contact with, 16, 18–20
in transformation systems, 212
intimacy with, 118
loyalty valued, 125–126
power of, 57
satisfaction of, 90
senior customers, 179
service a basis for planning, 77
customisation, 183
cyclical approach to development, 218

Dawson River dam proposal, 75–76
DBM Consultants
dealers, finance from, 257
debentures, 281
debt
fundraising via, 281
markets for, 257–259
value of, 258
decision making, 91
definition of services, 6–8
delivery systems, 299
failures by, 139–140
HRM and, 318–320
democratic business design, 137
department store boutiques, 126
deposit-taking institutions, 257
derivative projects, 239
descriptive approaches, 70, 89
stakeholder theory, 93–94
Trans Territory Pipeline, 96
design of products and services, 217–219
developing countries, service trade in, 38–39
Dialogue With The City, 98
direct financing, 257–259
direct marketing, 180, 181
direct stakeholder influence, 78
disasters, see environmental issues
disintermediation, 257–259
Disney, treatment of weather risk, 287
dividends, 280–281
DIY check-ins, 219
drivers of globalisation, 45–47
Drucker, Peter, 160–161
dyadic relationship between stakeholders, 85
dynamic processes, 42

e-recruitment, 333
economic drivers of globalism, 46

economic environments, 54–55
economic rationalism, 77
elderly customers, 179
ElecGen case study, 342–344
emotional dissonance, 328
emotional labour, 327–328
employees, see also recruitment and selection
casual, 311–313, 334
culture of fear in, 122
flexible work arrangements, 313
human resources management, 228, 299–346
in service industries, 2
motivation of, 329
paid to wander around, 194
performance required of, 299
remuneration for, 327, 339–340
satisfaction levels, 340
staffing, 30, 333–341
systemic strategic thinking, 170
their understanding of costs, 270
workforce scheduling, 234
Employment Relations Act 1995:, 310–311
empowerment, 329–331
English, as language of business, 49
entrepreneurial approach, 73
environmental issues, see also service
environment
corporate policies, 83
environmental disasters, 97
Industrial Revolution, 97
Rottnest Island case study, 248
sustainability, 84
United Nations Conference on the
Environment and Development, 82
waste management, 84
equal employment opportunity legislation,
336
equity, 258, 280
ergonomics, 227
ethical issues
ethics of stakeholders, 76–78, 88–94
nature of changes, 49
normative approach, 79
unethical business practices, 82
Europe, 42–43, 51–52
excellence theory, 24
exchange rate risk, 285
experience economy, 183–209
external factors in HRM, 304
external recruitment, 333
extroversion-introversion, 335

facilities management, 222
FAI insurance, 295
failures in service industries, 138–140, 197
fast-food industry in Singapore, 320
fast nature of changes, 47
Fayol, Henri, 23
features of services, 8–14
financial analysis, 263–265, 275
financial management, 31, 252–298
financial services, *see also* banking industry;
    banks
  deposit-taking institutions, 257
  lack of comparison in, 140–141
  Lifestyle Wealth Management case study,
    150–152
firestorm case study, 102–103
fiscal policy, 262
flexible work arrangements, 313
Focused Management Information, 291
Follett, Mary Parker, 23
forecasting, financial, 256, 265–272
foreign exchange contracts, 85, 286
franchising, 14, 195
Freeman, RE, 71
front-line service culture, 121–123, 128,
    138
front-of-mind reputation, 132
FSM, *see* functional services management
full-time marketers, 192
functional marketing era, 163–164
functional services management, 27, 157
  domain of, 203
  human resources in, 300
  in operations management, 212
fundraising, 254, 275–281
funds statement, 264
FUTURE, 47–50
future trends in globalisation, 47–50

General Agreement on Tariffs and Trade (GATT),
    40
Ghana, political issues, 53
globalisation, 2–6, 35–40, 41–50, 350
  approach to, 43
  financial management and, 253
  interpretations of, 43–45
  strategy for, 214–217
golden handshakes, 262
goods-services continuum, 6, 145
  as value chain, 126–129
  blurring of boundaries, 121, 131
  operations management, 208

governance issues, 82
governments, *see also* public sector
  drivers of globalisation, 46
  local, stakeholders in, 85
  market involvement by, 55

hard technologies, 20
health care, 273–275
hedging principle, 276–278
Heritage Building Society, 13–14
Herzberg, Frederick, 23
heterogeneity of services, 12
high-contact systems, 226
HIH, 56, 297, 344
holistic perspective, 156, 186, 347–349
Home and Away pet care, 14–17
home maintenance services, 139–140
Hong Kong, X-box modifications in, 64–67
horizontal integration of HRM, 303
hotel industry
  crises in, 321
  job description in, 326
  JW Marriott hotel chain, 337
  quality of, 20
  value in India, 259
Hughes, John, 133
human resources management (HRM), 228,
    299–346
hybrid technologies, 20

ICT (information and communications
    technology), *see* technology
identification of stakeholders, 72–78
IKEA, 137–138, 144
India
  Bangalore, 38
  call centre training, 319
  information technology in, 62–64
  value of hotels in, 259
indirect financing, 257–259
indirect stakeholder influence, 78
industrial relations, 307–311
industrialisation of services, 20, 352
industry types, 1
  financial ratios and, 265
  job growth by, 5
  systems approach in, 214
information and communication technologies, *see*
    technology
information asymmetry, 261
information, services acting on, 16
Infosys Technologies, 62, 123

innovation
    business model innovation, 119–121 b
    management of, 238–240
    service quality and, 144
    short lifespan of, 164
    value innovation, 112, 186–187
inputs, 210
inseparability of services, 11–12
instrumental approaches, 70, 89, 92–93, 96
insurance industry
    HIH failure, 56, 297, 344
    in California, 295
    in Europe, 51
    Sun Life Insurance, 291–294
intangibility of services, 9–11
integrated marketing era, 166–168
integrated services management model, 25,
    347–352
Integrated Solution Management, 174
integrated strategic management, 41, 110, 114–116,
        157, see also strategic management
    external factors in, 71
    in financial management, 254
    in operations management, 203
    service design in, 218
intellectual capital, see human resources
        management
interactive operational model, 157
interactive TV, 59
interest rate risk, 285
intermediation, 257–259
internal marketing, 171
internal recruitment, 333
intrinsic value and moral principles, 91
introversion-extroversion, 335
inventory management, 230–234
investment decisions, 256
investment funds, 140–141, see also financial
        services
involuntary risk, 79
ISM model, see integrated strategic management
ISO 9000+ series, 81, 220
ISO 14001 series, 82
ISO 18001 series, 83

Japan
    7-Eleven stores in, 195
    marketing in, 172
    threat to US industry from, 165
    total quality management, 81
    vehicle manufacturing, 177
    weddings in, 185

Jim's Mowing, 14
job analysis and design, 323–327
job autonomy, 327
job descriptions, 324
job growth by industry sector, 5
just-in-time delivery, 81
JW Marriott hotel chain, 337

Kaizen, 220
key areas in operations management, 214–241
key performance indicators, 127–128
knowledge as input, 210
knowledge work, 71

La Montagne Guesthouse and Restaurant, 28–32
labour characteristics of services, 311–313
labour intensity, 317
labour supply and demand, 322
layout planning, 228
leadership
    by example, 136
    challenges for, 113, 119–125 b
    no substitute for, 123
learning organisations, 123–125, 137
Leeson, Nick, 288, 330
legal issues, 55, 289
legitimacy of stakeholders, 79, 80, 85
leverage ratios, 265
Lifestyle Wealth Management case study,
        150–152
liquidity ratios, 265
liquidity risk, 286–287
loan capital, 281
local government, stakeholders in, 85
location planning, 221–225
locomotive, causes industrial action, 308–310
Long-Term Capital Management, 287
long-term finance, 279–281
loss categorisation framework, 288
low-contact systems, 226
loyalty of customers, 125–126
Lyon, reputation survey in, 129–141

macro level competitiveness, 350
macro level HRM, 306
maintenance activities, 237
makers of meaning, 99
Malaysia, political environment, 54
management, 1–34, 205, see also strategic
        management
    concepts and theories, 23–25
    definition of, 171

management (*cont.*)
  La Montagne case study, 31
  managerial approaches, 89, 94
  of new service industry, 116–117
  of service marketing, 155–202
  of services, 99–101
  of stakeholders, 72–78
  operations management, 203–251
  stakeholder theory and, 71
  strategic template for, 142
  top-down approach, 121
  vs. strategic management, 109–110
managers, 101
  as people developers, 123
  financial, 255–256
  in human resources, 318
  operations management for, 205–207
  quality control by, 21
Manila, interactive TV in, 59
manufacturing industry, 116
market drivers of globalism, 46
'market in' concept, 171
market risk, 260, 285–286
market 'space', 114
market value, 256
marketing, 159–160
  management of, 155–202
  orientation towards, 189
  research in, 163
  theory-practice convergence, 192
markets, financial, 256, 260, 261
Maslow, Abraham, 23
mass marketing, 182
maturity matching
Mayo, Elton, 23
McDonaldisation, 23, 100, 328
medical examinations for applicants,
  336
medical treatment, outsourcing of, 39
Medicare, 273–275
merchant banks, 257
micro level HRM, 307
Microsoft, Xbox games pirated, 64–67
Milton-Smith reputation survey, 129–141
minds, services acting on, 16
mindset orientations for services, 348
mod chipping of Xbox, 64–67
models for classifying services, 17
monetary policy, 262
monitoring, 213
moral hazard, 262

mortgages, 281
most favoured nation principles, 40
motivation theory, 339
multidisciplinary approach to service, 128
Munsterberg, Hugo, 23

Nathan Dam development proposal, 75–76
National Australia Bank, 85
national environments, 53–61
natural gas pipeline, 95–97
natural persons, presence of, 40
nature of services, 6–22
negative aspects of service quality, 21
negative emotional displays, 328
net working capital, 276
new consumerism, 121
New Economy, competition in, 111
new entrants, threat of, 57
New Zealand, industrial relations, 310–311
Nike Town, 10
no-frills airlines, 120
no-shows, 233
Nokia, downturn for, 56
non-government pressure groups, 49
non-profit sectors, 352
normative approaches, 70, 89–92
  to ethics, 79
  Trans Territory Pipeline, 96
Northern Territory gas pipeline, 95–97

offshoring, *see* outsourcing
older customers, 179
on-the-job training, 194
one-to-one marketing, 182
operant resources, 191
operational ratios, 265
operational risk, 287–289
operations management, *see* management
opportunity environments, 115
organic business ecosystems, 115
organisations
  market value of, 256
  organisational environment, 75
  primary function of, 89
  service culture in, 121–123
  structural modifications, 306
  theory of, 23
organised chaos, 175
origins of stakeholders, 76–78
outputs, 212, 271
outside-in design, 118, 127

outsourcing
    for competitiveness, 229
    of personal services, 14–15
    of service functions, 128
    to India, 38, 63

panel interviews, 336
Paradise Tours case study, 148–149
people risk, 287
performance analysis framework, 288
perishability of services, 13, 231
person specifications, 324
personality profiling, 335–336
personnel administration, 302
personnel management, 302
Perth, *see* Western Australia
Philippines, interactive TV in, 59
piracy of Xbox games, 64–67
planning
    financial, 256, 263–272, 275
    for human resources, 321–323
platform projects, 239
point-of-sale systems, 194
politics in national environment, 53–54
politics of change, 49
polyethylene paint, 309
Porter, Michael, 111
positive aspects of service quality, 21
power
    of customers, 57
    of suppliers, 57
    possession of, 79, 85
preference shares, 280
presence of natural persons, 40
price risk, 285
pricing, control via, 213, 232
primary function of organisation, 89
primary stakeholders, 75, 79, 85, 88
privatisation
    ElecGen case study, 343
    in China, 60
    in West Australia, 89
    of water supply, 44
process approach, 156, 239, 288
process risk, 287
process teams
procurement, 230
product design, 217–219
production and sales era, 161–163
production system management, 203, 210–214
professional occupations, 116, 140

professional service approach, 180, 181
profit and loss, 264, 267
profitability ratios, 265
project management, 236–237
promissory notes, 278
prospective payment system, 273–275
Protocol House, 316
prototyping, 218
public participation, 73, 84, 98
public sector, 352, *see also* governments
    call centres, 175
    ElecGen case study, 342–344
    moral hazard in, 262
    Protocol House, 316
    recruitment and selection, 334
purchasing, 230

Qantas, 228
QC, *see* total quality management
quality management 20–22, 219–221; *see also* total
    quality management
    business process reengineering, 186
    in Japan, 166
    quality circles, 220
    quality-embracing ideas, 113
quaternary sector, 183–209
Queensland Department of Transport, 152–153

radical nature of changes, 49
railway locomotive, causes industrial action,
    308–310
rate of return, 260
recruitment and selection, 333–341
    selection interviews, 336
    selection tests, 335–336
references from work, 335
regional organisations, 173
regionalism, 50–53
regulated displays of emotion, 327
regulation of trade, 39–40
relationship marketing, *see* customer relationship
    marketing
remuneration for employees, 327, 339–340
response time issues, 206
resumes, 335
retained earnings, 280
risk management
    capital asset pricing model, 260
    financial, 282–289
    voluntary and involuntary risk, 79
role ambiguity, 314

role conflict, 314
room attendant job description, 326
Rottnest Island case study, 243–249
Ryanair, 120

Saatchi and Saatchi, 124
SAFTA, 50–51
sales era, 161–163
Scandinavian Airlines, 189
scepticist approach to globalism, 43
schedule management, 234–236
Schmenner's service process matrix, 317
Schultz, Howard, 144
scientific management, 23
SCM, 205, 228–230
seasonality of tourism, 248
secondary stakeholders, 79, 85, 88
sector-average ratios, 265
secured credit arrangements, 279
selection, see recruitment and selection
self-managing work teams, 331–333
senior customers, 179
sequential interviews, 336
service business strategy, 214–217
service centres, 166
service contracts, 21
service culture, 306, 323–333
service departments, 98
service design, 217–219
service domain, 100
service encounters, 318–320
service environment, 35
    scanning of, 321
    turbulence in, 58
service factory approach, 180, 227
service gap, 100
service industries
    financial management, 263–289
    operations management, 207–209
    stakeholders in, 84–88
service management, see management
service process, 18, 317
servicescapes, 227
servitisation of business, 155
SERVQUAL, 221
share capital, 279
shareholders, 73, 280–281
Shell, 116
short-term finance, 276, 278
significant events in operations management,
    209–210

simplifying business, 240–241
simultaneity of services, 232
Singapore
    Coalition of Services Industries, 3
    fast-food industry, 320
    reputation survey, 129–141
    Singaporean-Australian Free Trade Area, 50–51
    Temasek, 59
Singapore Airlines, 133–134, 165
single-leader work groups, 331
site planning, 221–225
Six Sigma techniques, 64, 220
Skippers Group, 133, 144
SMWTs, 331–333
social responsibility, 89
social science approach, 79
societal environment, 58
sociology, theories from, 23
soft technologies, 20
solvency ratios, 265
Sony, game software piracy, 66
specific liquidity risk, 286
spot foreign exchange contract, 286
spy flights, 165
staffing, 30, 333–341, see also employees
stakeholders
    influence of, 69–107
    perspectives on operations management, 206
    Rottnest Island case study, 246–247
    stakeholder frameworks, 89–94
    theory of, 78–80
Standard Chartered, 131–132
standardisation of service delivery
    (McDonaldisation), 23, 100, 328
Starbucks, 119, 144
strategic architecture, 112
strategic choice in services, 320–321
strategic management, see also integrated strategic
        management; management
    decision making, 91
    of human resources, 303, 333–341
    of services, 8, 108–154
    strategy formulation, 216
    systemic thinking, 156
    theoretical basis, 25–27
    vs. management, 109–110
structure of services, 6–22
substitute products, 57
Sun Life Insurance, 291–294
superannuation services, 131
suppliers, power of, 57

supply chain management, 205, 228–230
surveys of service reputation, 129–141
sustainability, 84
    of an organisation, 156
    Rottnest Island case study, 247
Swiss Bankers Association, 49
system selling approach, 177
systematic liquidity risk, 286
systemic business management, 176
systemic strategic thinking, 170
systems theory, 24

Taroom, Nathan Dam at, 75–76
Taylor, Frederick, 23
technology
    customer databases, 349
    customer interactions based on, 81, 230
    efficiency improvements from, 240
    for customer relationship marketing, 182
    IT in India, 62–64
    point-of-sale systems, 194
    technoglobalism, 45–47
    technological environment, 56
Telstra, 78, 304
Temasek, 59
terrorism, impact of, 52, 93
tertiary education sector, 139, 223
tertiary industries, *see* services
The Cleaning Company, 173
theories of marketing, 192
theories of strategic management, 111–117
thought leadership groups, 123
time, effect on value, 260
top-down management approach, 121
total quality management, 166–170
    development, 117
    failures, 175
    history, 24
    stakeholders in, 84
tourism, *see also* hotel industry
    impact of terrorism on, 52
    marketing campaigns, 29
    Paradise Tours case study, 148–149
    Rottnest Island, 243–249
TQM, *see* total quality management
trade credit, 278
trade drafts, 279
trade, share of services in, 35–37
training
    for call centres, 319
    for career development, 337

for Qantas pilots, 228
on the job, 194
Trans Territory Pipeline, 95–97
transformation network models, 74
transformation systems, 211
transformationalist approach to globalisation, 43
transience of services, 13, 231
transient employees, 312
tribal nature of changes, 48
triple bottom line approach, 50–53, 73, 220
turnover management, 340–341
typology of stakeholders, 74

uncertainty, effect on value, 260
unethical practices, *see* ethical issues
unions, 308
    demarcation disputes, 309
    ElecGen case study, 343
    in service industries, 313–323
unit cost formula, 271
United Nations Conference on the Environment
    and Development, 82
United States
    marketing theory, 160–165
    response to Japanese competition, 173
    service workforce, 2
    spending on wellness, 121
    US banks retreat from Europe, 42–43
universal nature of changes, 48
universities, failures in service by, 139, 223
unoccupied time, 232
unsystematic risk, 260
urban, nature of changes, 47
urgency of stakeholders, 79, 85
Urwick, Lyndall, 23

value chains, 113
    customisation in, 183
    goods-services continuum as, 126–129
value innovation, 112, 186–187
value of an organisation, 258
variability of services, 12
vehicle manufacturing, 177
venture capital, 281
video cameras for customer observation, 188
Virgin Airlines, 134–137
voluntary risk, 79

waiting, psychology of, 231
Wal-Mart, 143
walking-around employees, 194

wastage (turnover), 340–341
waste management, 84, 88
water supply, 44, 75–76
weddings in Japan, 185
Western Australia
    Department of Transport, 152–153
    Dialogue With The City, 98
    Protocol House, 316
    reputation survey, 129–141
    Skippers Group, 133, 144

Willie the doorman, 330
work teams, 331–333
workforce, *see* employees
Workplace Relations Act 1996, 310–311
worksite tours for applicants, 336

Xbox games pirated, 64–67

yield, concept of, 233
Yolgnu Matha language, 96